IN THE NAME
OF
EXCELLENCE

IN THE NAME OF EXCELLENCE

*The Struggle to Reform the Nation's Schools,
Why It's Failing, and What Should Be Done*

THOMAS TOCH

New York   Oxford
OXFORD UNIVERSITY PRESS
1991

Oxford University Press

Oxford   New York   Toronto
Delhi   Bombay   Calcutta   Madras   Karachi
Petaling Jaya   Singapore   Hong Kong   Tokyo
Nairobi   Dar es Salaam   Cape Town
Melbourne   Auckland

and associated companies in
Berlin   Ibadan

Copyright © 1991 by Thomas Toch

Published by Oxford University Press, Inc.,
200 Madison Avenue, New York, New York 10016

Oxford is a registered trademark of Oxford University Press

Library of Congress Cataloging-in-Publication Data
Toch, Thomas.
In the name of excellence : the struggle to reform the nation's schools,
why it's failing, and what should be done / Thomas Toch.
p.   cm.
Includes bibliographical references and index.
ISBN 0-19-505761-9
1. Public schools—United States—History—20th century.
2. Education—United States—Aims and objectives.   3. Education
and state—United States.   I. Title.
LA217.T63   1991
370′.973—dc20   90-41546   CIP

2 4 6 8 9 7 5 3 1

Printed in the United States of America
on acid-free paper

To my mother and father

Acknowledgments

This book is in large measure a report from the trenches of American public education. Throughout, I draw heavily on the lessons I learned from visiting some sixty schools nationwide in recent years. I am grateful to the many educators who welcomed me into their schools and classrooms and, in some instances, their homes, during my travels. I'm also grateful to the many others I met across the country, from students to state legislators, who spoke to me candidly and frequently at great length about public education and its problems. Their insights were invaluable.

My extensive travel as well as much additional research was made possible by generous funding from the Carnegie Foundation for the Advancement of Teaching. I am particularly indebted to Carnegie's president, Ernest L. Boyer, for the encouragement, patience, and wise counsel that he extended to me. Bob Hochstein, assistant to the president at Carnegie, was unstinting in his advice and support during the two years that I shared an office with him in Washington, and he has been no less generous since.

The first writing I did about the reform of public education was as a staff writer for *Education Week* in the early 1980s, when today's reform movement was in its infancy. It was there that I became interested in chronicling what was clearly going to be an important moment in American education. I'm grateful to Ron Wolk, *Education Week*'s founder and editor, for the many opportunities that he gave me while I was at the paper.

The late Lawrence Cremin, winner of the Pulitzer Prize for his writing on education, graciously read my manuscript before his untimely death in 1990. His observations helped focus my thinking on a number of important topics. Walter Haney, Gwen Newman, and Matt Cooper, my colleague at *U.S. News and World Report*, also are responsible for improvements to several sections of the book.

It was a pleasure having Valerie Aubry as my editor at Oxford. Her suggestions enhanced my manuscript immeasurably and I drew confidence from her steady encouragement. Assistant Editor Niko Pfund was also helpful at every turn, and Ruth Sandweiss did a super job of overseeing the copyediting of the book.

Thanks also to Rick Newman and Ric Manhart of the fact-checking department at *U.S. News* for bringing their tenacity to bear on my manuscript.

Lastly, I owe a huge debt of gratitude to my wife, Ann. She helped and sacrificed endlessly so that I could write this book.

Contents

IN THE NAME
OF
EXCELLENCE

Introduction

Since the early 1980s the nation has struggled mightily to improve public education. From town halls to the White House, the schools have been a huge priority. Indeed, not since the Soviet Union sent Sputnik into orbit has an educational movement gripped the nation with such intensity.

The reformers' rallying cry has been "excellence in education." It has been invoked in numerous ways, in support of initiatives ranging from public schooling of four-year-olds to federal funding of private schools. But in representing the reform movement as a whole, the theme reflects two basic beliefs. First, virtually all students should receive an education emphasizing "book learning" through high school, regardless of their future plans. Second, standards in academic subjects should be raised significantly. Though they don't appear so, the reform movement's twin principles of educational excellence are radical, for since their inception the nation's public schools have afforded a rigorous academic education to only a fraction of their students. Until relatively recently, many students received no secondary schooling at all; as late as 1950 only 25 percent of black students and 50 percent of white students remained in high school long enough to earn a diploma. And since the turn of the century the majority of the students attending public high schools have been taught primarily vocational and "life" skills, rather than the rigorous use of their minds. Thus in pressing the nation's high schools to extend to all students the serious intellectual training traditionally reserved for the gifted and the privileged, school reformers have sought not only to improve public education's performance, but to radically redefine its mission as well.

The reformers' challenge to the schools is crucially important to the nation's economic and social well-being. As the nation makes its much-heralded move into a post-industrial information age, more and more well-educated workers are required. At the same time, the demographics of the nation's population are changing, increasing the proportion of future workers who must be drawn from the ranks of students that the public schools have traditionally educated least well: minorities and other disadvantaged groups. Thus if the reform movement's goals are ambitious, they are necessarily so.

To be sure, there have been improvements in public education since

3

the onset of the reform movement. In particular, the nation's high schools have created many additional academic opportunities for high-achieving students. And significant strides have been made toward re-shaping public school teaching into a profession capable of attracting the best and the brightest. But on balance, the reform movement is failing. Despite a plethora of significant reforms in public education, national and international assessments suggest that attainment of advanced academic skills continues to elude the vast majority of students. After nearly a decade of reform, educational excellence remains a scarce commodity in the public schools.

High schools have failed to translate new curriculum mandates into more demanding academic courses for average and below-average students. Indeed, there has been a broad backlash among public educators against the excellence movement's goal of teaching serious academics to a broader range of students. Union opposition threatens the movement to professionalize teaching. A massive increase in standardized testing, designed to improve the schools by imposing greater accountability on them, ironically has had the opposite effect. Rather than promoting the teaching of high-level skills, it has driven down the level of instruction in many classrooms. Above all, the reform movement has failed to address adequately perhaps the single greatest obstacle to educational excellence: the extraordinary degree of alienation and apathy among secondary school students and teachers, and the schools' contribution to the problem. There is a tremendously important human element of the crisis in education that the reformers have largely neglected.

This book is about the crusade for educational excellence during the past decade. It is about the reformers' struggle to redefine the priorities of the nation's high schools, to replace a largely utilitarian vision of public education with an academic vision. Part I examines the evolution of the reform movement—the people and the developments that shaped it. Part II examines in detail why the excellence movement is foundering. Part III examines the devastating consequences of the apathy and alienation that pervade so many of the nation's public secondary schools, and in so doing proposes a further agenda for reform.

Though the story of the excellence movement begins in the early 1980s, it's necessary to know the lay of the educational landscape in the previous decade to grasp fully the movement's importance to the nation, and the magnitude of its challenge to the nation's public school system. To be blunt, the 1970s left public education in a shambles.

With the passing of the postwar Baby Boom era, enrollment in elementary and secondary schools plummeted from 46 million in 1971 to 39 million in 1982, idling over a thousand high schools and tens of thousands of teachers. Hardest hit were the Northeast and Midwest: in a decade, the student population declined by 20 percent in Illinois; 21 percent in Wisconsin and Minnesota; 23 percent in New Jersey, South Dakota, Iowa, Ohio, Massachusetts, and New York; 25 percent in Pennsylvania and Connecticut; 28 percent in Rhode Island; and no less than 31 percent in Delaware.[1]

The property-tax revolt of the late 1970s devastated many school systems. Absent a discussion in the Constitution of a federal role in education, responsibility for public schooling devolved to the states. And as public education began to spread in the mid-nineteenth century, the states in turn ceded educational authority to local school boards, including the power to levy property taxes. By the 1970s, local taxes produced half of public education's revenues. And as a result, Proposition 13 in California (1978), Proposition 2 1/2 in Massachusetts (1980), and many lesser-known tax-limitation measures adopted by state and local governments sharply curtailed the flow of funding to public schools in many parts of the country, a problem exacerbated by the onset of a recession in the national economy in the early 1980s. The revenue crunch resulted in salary freezes, more layoffs, program cuts, and, in a few extreme cases, bankrupt school districts. In Saco, Maine, 2,400 students were without classrooms for two weeks when their school system shut its doors in 1980 following passage of a local property-tax cap.[2]

The onset of collective bargaining and teacher unionism in public education in the early 1960s led to scores of divisive and often protracted strikes in the 1970s. Between 1960 and 1965, public school teachers struck twenty-five times; between 1975 and 1980, there were over a thousand strikes involving over a million teachers, according to the Bureau of Labor Statistics. "By 1980, teacher strikes were as much a part of autumn as the opening of the football season," observed the authors of a 1982 education textbook.[3] Indeed, when Philadelphia's 22,000 teachers manned picket lines for fifty days in 1981–82, it was the eighth time they had shut down the city's schools in thirteen years.

Public education, moreover, was a major civil rights battleground in the 1970s. The advocates of the handicapped, women, the non-English-speaking, and others targeted education as an area of national life in which they sought to strengthen such groups' rights and opportunities. In passing the Education Amendments of 1972, Congress prohibited schools and colleges from discriminating in their policies and programs against female students and faculty. The following year it approved the Rehabilitation Act of 1973. Together with the Education of All Handicapped Children Act of 1975, section 504 of the Rehabilitation Act opened school doors to thousands of students whose disabilities in the past had limited their educational opportunities. In 1974 the U.S. Supreme Court handed down a decision of equal importance to non-English-speaking students, when in *Lau v. Nichols* it ruled that the San Francisco school system was violating the civil rights of many of its Chinese-speaking students by not helping them overcome their language barriers. The Court said that such barriers deprived students of equal educational opportunities. A year later the U.S. Department of Health, Education, and Welfare issued controversial guidelines—known as the *"Lau* remedies"—detailing services that many school systems must offer such students.

Meanwhile, a series of Supreme Court rulings in the late 1960s and 1970s extended to schoolchildren a range of constitutional "due-process" and "equal-protection" rights. Students facing disciplinary actions won the right to receive written notice of the charges against them, the right to a lawyer, the right to cross-examine witnesses, the right to refuse to answer incriminating questions, and the right of appeal in the event of suspension or expulsion. In the 1975 case of *Wood v. Strickland,* the Court granted students the standing to sue school authorities for damages on constitutional grounds.[4]

By far the greatest civil rights struggle in education, however, was the desegregation of the nation's schools. It began, of course, with the Supreme Court's 1954 decree in *Brown v. Board of Education* that school systems abandon policies of educating blacks and whites separately. Much of the rural South was legally desegregated by the end of the 1960s, but the school-desegregation battle raged on. In 1971 the Supreme Court upheld a controversial order by a federal judge to integrate North Carolina's sprawling Charlotte-Mecklenburg school system through the mandatory busing of students across attendance zones, the first of many such orders in southern jurisdictions. At the same time the federal courts commenced the desegregation of the populous urban school systems of the North. San Francisco and Detroit were ordered to desegregate their schools in 1971, Denver in 1973, Cleveland, Boston, Columbus, and Dayton in 1974, Buffalo, Milwaukee, and Indianapolis in 1975, St. Louis in 1978, and Seattle in 1979. The courts eventually imposed busing plans on half of the nation's fifty largest districts.

The widespread use of busing and the onset of desegregation in the North caused tremendous turmoil in public education. White students abandoned the public schools in droves, unwilling to be educated with blacks or in search of a more stable educational environment. The proportion of whites in Boston's schools, for instance, dropped from 65 percent in 1974, the year Boston was ordered to bus students to reduce "racial isolation" in its schools, to 28 percent a decade later. Boston's total public school enrollment plummeted from 93,000 to 57,000 during the same period.

Enrollments fell just as sharply in other desegregating urban school systems. Between 1970 and 1982 the number of students in the Minneapolis school system dropped by 43 percent, in Pittsburgh by 41 percent, in San Francisco, Columbus, and Buffalo by 36 percent, in St. Louis by 50 percent, and in Norfolk by 30 percent.[5] Busing, in particular, became intensely unpopular. In 1979, in fact, the U.S. House of Representatives approved a constitutional amendment banning the use of busing to achieve racial balance in schools, though the measure died in the Senate.

The actions taken by Congress and the courts on behalf of blacks, the non-English-speaking, women, the handicapped, and others made schools much more responsive to many students. But the actions also produced an avalanche of rules and regulations that made public schools more bureaucratic; they shifted a substantial amount of policy-making power from local educators to the distant state and federal authorities who promulgated the regulations; they increased the litigiousness of public education to the point where many educators became more concerned with dodging lawsuits than with the quality of instruction in their schools; and they made the broadening of educational opportunities rather than the quality of education the priority in much of public schooling.

In many instances, most notably in Boston, desegregation resulted in racial violence as well as white flight. And even in school systems in which desegregation was less explosive, the atmosphere made it difficult to focus attention on academics. "Teaching and learning took a back seat because we were so concerned with how to live with each other, with how to get along," recalled a black North Carolina school board member. "We were, after all, going through a social revolution." Indeed, it was frequently a wrenching process. A black teacher in Charlotte-Mecklenburg recounted how in 1969 she was transferred with a few of her black colleagues to all-white East Mecklenburg High School under a lottery system that put teachers of one race in schools with students of the other. "I'd stand at the front of the room," she said, "and everyone would stare at me, icily. They ignored every word I said." It was perhaps symbolic of the preeminence of civil rights issues in education in the 1970s that in wake of the creation of the U.S. Department of Education in 1979, the first secretary of education, Shirley M. Hufstedler, was not an educator but a federal judge who had participated in the *Lau* case.[6]

Finally, public education in the 1970s bore the burden of two devastating indictments made against it in the 1960s. On the one hand, critics such as A. S. Neill (*Summerhill*, 1960), John Holt (*How Children Fail*, 1964), Paul Goodman (*Compulsory Mis-Education*, 1964), and George Dennison (*The Lives of Children*, 1969) charged that public schools were profoundly undemocratic institutions requiring radical reform. The schools, they argued, quashed individualism, ignored students' emotional needs, and perpetuated an inegalitarian social order. Their attacks led, in part, to a diminishment of the traditional authority of the teacher, to a deemphasis of traditional academic subjects, and to the elimination of many graduation requirements.

In a widely publicized 1966 study entitled *Equality of Educational Opportunity*, meanwhile, sociologist James S. Coleman concluded on the basis of a survey of the verbal ability of 645,000 students in 4,000 schools that there was little correlation between the quality of a school and student achievement but an overwhelming link between student achievement and the socioeconomic background of students. Schools "bring little influence to bear on a child's achievement that is independent of his background and social context," he wrote.[7] Moreover, the highly deterministic view of academic achievement in the Coleman Report, as it came to be called, was reinforced by a second leading sociologist, Christopher Jencks. In his 1972 book, *Inequality,* also widely publicized, Jencks argued that "the character of a school's output depends largely on a single input, namely the characteristics of the entering children. Everything else—the school budget, its policies, the characteristics of the teachers—is either secondary or completely irrelevant."[8] Such assertions eroded the nation's confidence in public education and the confidence of educators in themselves, and by the 1970s the assertions had achieved a widespread orthodoxy.

The tumult of the 1970s took a heavy toll on the performance of the public schools. As early as 1975 the nation was shaken by newspaper reports of a previously unpublicized twelve-year decline in average scores on the Scholastic Aptitude Test, the nation's largest college-admission exam. By 1981 the National Assessment of Educational Progress was reporting that the ability of the nation's students to write and think had declined dramatically during the previous decade. Established by Congress in 1968, the assessment measured large samples of the nation's students in a range of subjects, and as a federally sponsored organization, its reports attracted wide attention.

There was evidence of a decline in academic standards. The National Science Foundation reported in 1981 that graduation requirements in academic subjects had decreased to the point where a third of the nation's school systems required only one year of mathematics and one year of science. Between 1970 and 1980 the proportion of the nation's high school students enrolled in foreign-language courses dropped from 23 percent to 15 percent. And while just 12 percent of high-school students took a less-rigorous "general" course of study in the mid-1960s, 42 percent of all students were doing so by the end of the 1970s. These dismal statistics were contrasted with increasing alarm to the rigorous academic requirements and impressive levels of achievement in the schools of the Soviet Union, Japan, Germany, and the nation's other economic and political competitors.

As the decade wore on, the "consumers" of high school graduates began to voice strong dissatisfaction with the "product" they were receiving. The nation's employers complained of new workers too ill-educated to train. The military complained of recruits unable to understand safety manuals written for ninth-graders. And the federal government reported that by 1983, 16 percent of all college freshmen were enrolled in remedial reading courses, 21 percent were studying remedial writing, and no less than 25 percent were taking remedial math classes.[9]

Public education, meanwhile, was hemorrhaging students to private education. In 1976 private schools educated 7.6 percent of the nation's elementary and secondary students; by 1983, they claimed 12.6 percent of the student population, and pressure was mounting for federal tax credits for parents who paid private school tuition.

The educational upheavals of the 1970s lost public education much of its popular and political support, as the property-tax revolt and the exodus of students to private schools made clear. The declining performance of the schools, in particular, aroused the public's resentment, for the nation's public schooling tab had skyrocketed to $90 billion annually by decade's end, quadrupling the rate of inflation over the previous twenty years.

Polls reflected the depth of the public's disenchantment. A 1981 *Newsweek* survey revealed that 47 percent of the public believed the schools were doing a "poor" or "fair" job, up from 34 percent in a similar poll conducted for the magazine seven years earlier. A 1983 Harris poll reported that only 29 percent of the public had "a great deal of confidence" in the nation's educators, less than half the number that expressed strong confidence in educators in a similar 1966 survey. To make matters worse, the proportion of American families with children of school age declined by nearly 40 percent between 1969 and 1983. To elected officials, education was a political graveyard.

By the onset of the 1980s it was increasingly the view that public education was failing. Among academics and lay persons alike, it was becoming all too clear that it was an institution nearing the point of collapse. As *Time* magazine wrote in a 1980 cover story, "Like some vast jury gradually and reluctantly arriving at a verdict, politicians, educators and especially millions of parents have come to believe that the U.S. public schools are in parlous trouble."

PART I

ORIGINS

CHAPTER 1

The Nation Responds

One sign of a growing national resolve in the early 1980s to address the crisis in education was the election of Louis (Bill) Honig III as superintendent of public instruction in California. Unlike most candidates to head state education agencies, Honig was not a career educationist. A scion of a wealthy San Francisco family that had made its fortune in advertising, he was educated at Stanford, earned a law degree from Berkeley's Boalt Hall in 1963, and then went on to clerk at the California Supreme Court. But Honig then gave up a corporate law practice to join the federal Teacher Corps, a relic of a more public-spirited era, and work with students in San Francisco's housing projects. His successes there earned him an appointment to the California State Board of Education in 1975 by Governor Jerry Brown, who had clerked with Honig in Sacramento. By the time he defeated seven challengers in a nonpartisan primary for the state superintendent's job in mid-1982, Honig was an outsider on the inside; articulate and liberally educated, he also understood the workings of the state's huge public education enterprise. He ran in the general election on a platform of more homework, tougher discipline, required academic courses, and higher standards. It was his experience teaching disadvantaged students in San Francisco, he said, that had made him a believer in "traditional" education. And his convincing 56-44 defeat of twelve-year-incumbent Wilson Riles implied a new era in California's bellwether educational system.

In the previous two years a spate of influential organizations, including several major foundations, had launched studies of American public education. In 1980 the Carnegie Foundation for the Advancement of Teaching initiated a three-year investigation of the nation's high schools; the John D. And Catherine T. MacArthur Foundation sponsored a study of curriculum and instruction in elementary and secondary education by a task force of scholars known as the Paideia Group; the Twentieth Century Fund convened a task force to recommend new directions in federal education policy; and the College Board, a nonprofit consortium of 2,000 schools and colleges, began a study of the academic preparation necessary for college as a first step in a ten-year, $30 million school-improvement effort known as Project EQuality. In 1981 U.S. Secretary of Education Terrel H. Bell appointed a national commission to investigate the public schools, and a former dean of the Harvard Graduate School of Education, Theodore R. Sizer, initiated another national study of high schools, under the sponsorship of the Carnegie Corporation of New York, the Esther A. and Joseph Klingenstein Fund, and two education associations.

Another harbinger of reform was a frank and unflattering report on the status of schooling in the South published in 1981 by the Southern Regional Education Board, a highly regarded interstate compact under the chairmanship that year of Governor Bob Graham of Florida. Written by a panel of leading educators and lawmakers from the fifteen SREB states, *The Need for Quality* made a compelling case for upgrading the region's educational system, and its call for extensive reforms in public education— including higher standards in teacher education, a core curriculum in the schools, a deemphasis of vocational education, incentives for teachers in shortage fields, greater opportunities for liberal-arts graduates to enter teaching, and improved training for school administrators—struck a responsive chord among southern policymakers.[1]

In a few jurisdictions, meanwhile, school-improvement efforts were already under way. Beginning in the mid-1970s, a number of states had reacted to the signs of declining academic achievement by adding passage of basic skills tests to their requirements for a high school diploma, in an effort to pressure educators into ensuring that all students possessed at least a minimum level of academic competence. But the "basic-skills movement" set its academic sights low, and by the early 1980s some states and school systems began to embrace new policies. Common among them were grants or loans for college graduates willing to teach shortage fields such as math and science, licensing examinations for teachers, and increased graduation requirements in academic subjects.

The most ambitious of the initiatives was Mississippi's. In late 1982 the legislature there shocked the education world when in special session it enacted the largest tax increase in the state's history to pay for a comprehensive package of school reforms that included, among other things, higher teacher salaries and mandatory kindergarten. The $106 million legislation was the product of two years of intense lobbying by Governor William F. Winter, a Democrat, who was helped by a crusading Mississippi press, including two reporters from the *Jackson Clarion-Ledger* who won the 1983 Pulitzer Prize for Public Service Reporting for thirty stories leading up to the special session. Winter's triumph in a traditionally antieducation state such as Mississippi earned wide national notice.

But such stirrings were merely a prelude to a series of developments in 1983 that thrust public education into the national limelight.

Nothing did more to galvanize the emerging excellence movement that year than the release on April 26 of *A Nation at Risk: The Imperative for Educational Reform,* the report of Secretary Bell's National Commission on Excellence in Education. A harsh indictment of the nation's schools, it warned in bold prose that "the educational foundations of our society are presently being eroded by a rising tide of mediocrity that threatens our very future as a Nation and a people." "If an unfriendly foreign power had attempted to impose on America the mediocre educational performance that exists today, we might well have viewed it as an act of war," the commission charged. "As it stands, we have allowed this to happen to ourselves. . . . We have, in effect, been committing an act of unthinking, unilateral educational disarmament."[2]

There were eighteen members of the commission, the largest number of whom represented public education, but it was Harvard physicist Gerald Holton and Nobel laureate Glenn T. Seaborg of Stanford, whom Bell had sought for their academic backgrounds and the prestige that they would bring to his commission, who played the largest role in shaping the commission's message. The public educators on the commission argued for a report that was less critical of the nation's schools but were blocked by a coalition led by Seaborg and Holton. Seaborg and Holton held out for the tough stand on academic requirements that the commission eventually made. And it was largely at their urging that the commission eschewed a long, academic report that had been drafted by its staff, and published instead a hard-hitting "open letter to the American people" of only thirty-six pages that was free of footnotes and educational jargon. Much of it was written by Holton himself. Ironically, Bell had had a tough time recruiting Holton and Seaborg. Only after the secretary promised a major effort to disseminate the commission's finding—and after the commission's chairman, then-University of Utah President David P. Gardner intervened on Bell's behalf—did they become commission members.[3]

The powerful language of *A Nation at Risk,* its brevity, its alarming message, as well as the prestige of a number of its authors and the fact that they wrote with the imprimatur of the federal government, focused national attention on public education like no other single event since the Soviet Union's launching of Sputnik in 1957. The response to the report was so great that within ten months of its release 150,000 copies had been distributed by the U.S. Department of Education, another 70,000 had been purchased through the Government Printing Office, and several million additional copies and extended excerpts were estimated to be in circulation through reprints in the general and professional press.[4]

The impact of *A Nation at Risk* was further heightened by the release in rapid succession of several other national reports on education that shared the Bell commission's bleak assessment of the public schools. A week after publication of *A Nation at Risk,* a blue-ribbon task force of the Education Commission of the States (ECS), an education consortium, released a report entitled *Action for Excellence.* Established in 1982 to examine the relationship between the nation's educational system and its economy, the Task Force on Education for Economic Growth charged that the public schools were undermining the economic strength of the United States by failing to produce a competent work force—a sentiment also expressed by the Bell commission, which had warned that "our once unchallenged preeminence in commerce, industry, science, and technological innovation is being overtaken by competitors throughout the world." The membership of the ECS task force—it was chaired by Governor James B. Hunt, Jr., of North Carolina, and its forty-one members included no fewer than eleven governors and the chief executives of thirteen major corporations—gained its report wide publicity.

The following day, May 5, the Twentieth Century Fund's education task force published its report, *Making the Grade*. It recommended a number of major federal education initiatives, including a multi-billion-dollar program to foster merit-based personnel plans in the nation's school systems. Only six days later, the College Board released *Academic Preparation for College*, the product of its three-year effort to define the academic knowledge and skills needed by all high school graduates with college aspirations. Finally, in September the Commission on Precollege Education in Mathematics, Science, and Technology established by the National Science Board in 1982 issued a $6.5 billion blueprint for upgrading the caliber of math and science instruction in the schools, entitled *Educating Americans for the 21st Century*. "Alarming numbers of young Americans are ill-equipped to work in, contribute to, profit from, and enjoy our increasingly technological society," the commission charged.

The alarming warnings of these task forces and commissions were reinforced, moreover, by the findings and recommendations of three trenchant scholarly studies of public education—each based on extensive study of school life—that were released soon afterward. In September 1983 Ernest L. Boyer, president of the Carnegie Foundation for the Advancement of Teaching, published *High School: A Report on Secondary Education in America*, a 355-page critique that was the culmination of the study launched by the foundation three years earlier. A second study of secondary education, *Horace's Compromise: The Dilemma of the American High School*, by Theodore R. Sizer, appeared in March 1984 and was based on the national study of high schools begun under Sizer's leadership in 1981. Then in April 1984 John I. Goodlad, a former dean of the UCLA Graduate School of Education, published *A Place Called School*, a detailed account of conditions in public school classrooms. Drawing on evidence gathered by a team of investigators from over a thousand classrooms in thirty-eight schools, Goodlad concluded pessimistically that the problems of the public schools were of "crippling proportions." Despite their scholarly focus, all three reports were widely read; Goodlad's book, for example, sold 35,000 copies within six months. There were so many reform statements circulating at the time that Boyer recalled a woman phoning his office in Princeton "wanting a copy of the latest study entitled *A Nation at Risk* that had been written by Governor Hunt of Tennessee and published by the Carnegie Foundation."

Yet it was not the flurry of reform reports alone that led to education's emergence as a major national issue in 1983. Most important, the tremendous national response to the reports has to be understood in the context of the severe recession that gripped the economy in the early 1980s. The plant closings and widespread unemployment that the recession produced, especially in the industrial and manufacturing sectors of the economy, awakened the nation to the reality of increasing international economic competition, and sparked demands for improved productivity at home. "Competitiveness" became the rallying cry of a broad campaign to put the nation back on its economic feet, to retool the economy for the post-industrial future. The outcry led to establishment of a presidential commission on competitiveness, the creation of a 200-member Competitiveness Caucus in Congress, and scores of councils, commissions, and consortia formed by academia, business, and labor to grapple with the issue.[5]

A key piece of the competitiveness equation was improvement of the work force; a major investment in "human capital," it was argued, was essential to increased domestic productivity. Thus school reform—as a means to a more highly skilled work force—was seen by many as crucial to the nation's quest for renewed economic competitiveness. This was the argument of *A Nation at Risk* and *Action for Excellence*. And it was the principal reason that the nation supported the push for excellence in education so strongly; more than anything else, it was the competitiveness theme that defined the education crisis in the nation's eyes.

The linkage of school reform to the nation's renewed economic well-being was crucial to expansion of the education reform movement because it gained the movement influential allies that it might not have had otherwise. One such source of support was the nation's governors. Traditionally, governors scrutinized public school appropriations levels (in many states, education receives the largest single share of the budget) and left the drafting of new education policies and programs to legislative committees and state education bureaucracies. But that changed with the recession of the early 1980s, which forced thirty-seven states to adopt austerity budgets in fiscal 1982. Governors of both political parties from Mississippi to Maine began to champion school reform as part of an effort to bolster their states' failing economies. "Education is the keystone to economic prosperity," Texas Governor Mark White told the National Conference of State Legislators in 1983, and Governor Rudy Perpich of Minnesota warned his state that year that "knowledge will be the steel of this post-industrial society."

The states' chief executives fanned out across the nation and around the world in search of new markets and new investors. Some went so far as to establish permanent trade missions in foreign countries. Invariably, a commitment to an improved education system was among their major selling points. The competition for economic development was so intense that no fewer than thirty-six states campaigned for one particularly prized investment: a $3.5 billion assembly plant for General Motors' new Saturn automobile. Tennessee won the contest in mid-1985, partly, GM officials said at the time, on the strength of a school-reform package proposed by Governor Lamar Alexander in 1983.

In the South, a new generation of bright, progressive governors— including Charles S. Robb of Virginia, William J. Clinton of Arkansas, James B. Hunt, Jr., of North Carolina, Richard W. Riley of South Carolina, Winter of Mississippi, and Alexander of Tennessee—embraced school reform as a means of weaning the region's economy from its dependence on agriculture and manufacturing.

Also contributing to the governors' prominent role in the reform movement was a strong desire by the Reagan administration to relinquish much of its policymaking authority in education to the states as part of a broad "new federalism" initiative that sought to reduce the role of the federal government across the board in domestic affairs. As early as February 1981, in an address to a joint session of the Congress, the president complained that "the Federal government has insisted on a tremendously disproportionate share of control over our schools." "Balancing up the divisions of government," he told the governors themselves at the White House a few days later, was "a longtime dream." While the federal government had played an active role in education policymaking in the 1960s and 1970s, the Reagan administration and Congress sponsored few intiatives in response to the many calls for reform in the early 1980s, leaving the governors and other state leaders to act largely on their own.

Many governors, moreover, were drawn to school reform by their political instincts. A backwater issue just a few years earlier, the plethora of reform reports, the wide publicity they received, and the linking of education to economic renewal transformed education into a hot political topic. Polls revealed that school reform was a "winning" issue, one that politicians would do well to be associated with. In early 1983, two months before the release of *A Nation at Risk*, for example, 81 percent of those responding to a *New York Times* poll said they were prepared to pay higher taxes for better public schools. The following year, 86 percent of the Massachusetts residents responding to a *Boston Globe* poll said that improving the public schools was more important than lowering taxes; in 1980, of course, the voters of Massachusetts had approved property-tax-cutting Proposition 2 1/2 by a landslide margin. The proeducation sentiment was no less strong in other regions. A 1983 survey of Oklahomans, for instance, found 62 percent in favor of increased state spending on education and 59 percent in favor of a property-tax hike to support educational improvements, and 51 percent said education reform was one of the two top issues facing the state that year.

With compelling reasons to do so, the governors joined the front ranks of the school reform movement. Many established reform commissions in their states. There was the Governor's Commission on Excellence in Education in Nebraska, the Governor's Commission on Education for Economic Growth in Delaware, the Governor's Educational Summit Task Force in Michigan, and the Governor's Special Advisory Committee for Quality Education in Virginia, among others. Education also became a priority in the public pronouncements of the states' chief executives. The governors of states as diverse as West Virginia, Utah, Kansas, New Jersey, and Georgia made education reform the centerpiece of their 1984 state-of-the-state messages. "There come times when certain issues become so vital to the quality of our society and to its very survival that we ignore them at our peril. Today, education is such an issue," said Thomas H. Kean of New Jersey. A year later, Joe Frank Harris of Georgia made an unprecedented gubernatorial address on education to a special joint session of his state legislature, as did William A. Jankalow in South Dakota.

In addition, many governors sponsored their own comprehensive reform packages. In January 1983, three months before the release of *A Nation at Risk*, Republican Governor Lamar Alexander of Tennessee, in an address before the Tennessee Press Association, proposed a $210-million "Better Schools Program" that included a radical plan to reorganize the state's teaching profession. In September of that year, Governor Kean (in an address to the New Jersey legislature) outlined an ambitious "blueprint for reform" for his state's public schools. A month later, Governor Richard L. Thornburgh of Pennsylvania proposed a wide-ranging reform package entitled "Turning the Tide: An Agenda for Excellence."

Nor were governors reluctant to fight for their proposals. Martha Layne Collins of Kentucky in 1985 went so far as to appoint herself state secretary of education to help push school-reform legislation through the Kentucky legislature.[6] The intensity of their commitment earned Kean, Alexander, Hunt, Robb, Clinton, Thornburgh, Winter, Riley, and others the collective epithet of "education governors." What made them so valuable to the school reform movement was, first, their ability as chief executives to set the political agenda in their states and to exert tremendous influence in state legislative and regulatory matters, and, second, their ability as prominent political newsmakers to focus public attention on the education issue.

By 1986 the National Governors' Association (NGA) itself, then under the chairmanship of Lamar Alexander of Tennessee, issued a detailed and widely publicized call for improvements in public education, entitled *Time for Results: The Governors' 1991 Report on Education*. Based largely on a series of hearings held around the nation that saw seven gubernatorial task forces delve into such exacting educational issues as teacher certification and classroom technology, the report pledged the governors' organization to a five-year school reform effort. The report dominated NGA's annual meeting in 1986. The following year the organization released *Jobs, Growth, and Competitiveness,* a report reiterating the theme that a strong educational system was the foundation of American competitiveness in the world economy. "The twenty first century worker will not be able to compete using twentieth century skills," NGA said. The report was released at NGA's 1987 annual meeting, at which, once again, education reform and the broader theme of economic competitiveness were leading topics on the governors' agenda.

The competitiveness issue also won the excellence movement many allies within the nation's business community. In the decades of the 1960s and 1970s, those whose interests were represented by chambers of commerce did not have much to do with public education. They were largely disinterested in school affairs. Nor, in an era when the bearers of the capitalist standard were much disparaged, was their participation in public education generally sought.

Intensifying foreign competition, a more intellectually demanding domestic workplace, and the devastating effects of the 1981–82 recession, however, changed the business community's attitude toward the nation's schools dramatically. By mid-1983, according to the Business Poll, a quarterly survey of corporate executives, the leaders of 82 percent of the nation's largest companies believed that business should be more involved in education than it had been in the past, and 63 percent said corporate funding should be used to improve public education.[7] It was with a sense of urgency that the nation's business community enlisted in the reform movement. And in a Reagan-inspired conservative political milieu, where the intrepreneurial spirit enjoyed a new legitimacy, its participation was received with open arms.

One way the business community bolstered the reform movement was to amplify the calls for stronger schools. As early as 1982, the U.S. Chamber of Commerce sent a report to its members entitled *American Education: An Economic Issue,* in which it warned that the nation's educational system lagged behind those of Japan and the Soviet Union, and that it was unprepared to train workers for emerging "knowledge occupations." "The time is ripe for change" in public education, said the chamber, in urging its local affiliates to join the reform crusade. The same year the New York Stock Exchange argued in *People and Productivity: A Challenge to Corporate America* that "there must be an effort to raise businesses' awareness of their stake in the problems the schools face."[8]

Over a dozen of the nation's leading corporate executives—ranging from Frank T. Cary, chairman of International Business Machines Corporation, to Philip Caldwell, chairman of Ford Motor Company, Robert W. Lundeen, chairman of Dow Chemical Company, and J. Richard Munro, president of Time, Inc.—were among the signatories of the ECS's *Action for Excellence*. And just days after release of that strongly worded report in May 1983, sixteen corporate executives and college presidents under the aegis of the Business-Higher Education Forum called in a presidentially commissioned report for a coordinated national effort to "rebuild the nation's economy and strengthen our educational system." They argued that "the central objective of domestic policy" for the next decade should be to improve the nation's ability to compete with other industrialized countries.[9]

Then in 1985 the influential Committee for Economic Development (CED), a nonpartisan organization of some 200 leading business executives and a number of college presidents, published *Investing in Our Children: Business and the Public Schools*, which was both a blueprint for educational reform and an argument for a major business role in the reform campaign. The report was written under the sponsorship of the CED's Subcommittee on Business and the Schools, a new panel chaired by Owen B. Butler, chairman of the board of the Procter and Gamble Company. The CED weighed into the education debate again in 1987, when it published *Children in Need*, a compendium of reform strategies focused on the nation's economically disadvantaged students.

The business community also brought its tremendous political influence to bear on behalf of the reform movement. At both the state and local levels, business's backing of the national education agenda was especially important in winning the reform movement the support of fiscal conservatives among the nation's elected officials, many of whom were harshly critical of public education's performance and were reluctant to increase its funding, even to pay for reforms. When chambers of commerce and leading corporate executives came out in favor of increased appropriations and tax hikes for education, the opposition of their budget-minded allies on city councils and in the state legislatures began to dissipate.

In California the heads of forty-seven major corporations headquartered in the state—including Wells Fargo Bank, Macy's, Lockheed, and Kaiser Aluminum—played a key role in the 1983 passage of a major increase in state education spending by endorsing the increase in letters to Republican Governor George Deukmajian, who initially had opposed it. The money was used to pay for a comprehensive package of school reforms proposed by state education superintendent Honig, and enacted by the state legislature that year. The California Business Roundtable, an organization representing some eighty-eight of the state's principal businesses, also played an active role in persuading both the governor and Republican members of the California legislature to buy into education reform in the state. In late 1982 the organization had issued an educational reform report entitled *Improving Student Performance in California*.

Florida's business community in 1983 organized the Citizens' Council on Education to lobby for wide-ranging reform legislation that year. Governor Bob Graham recruited his own team of twenty-seven prominent business and political leaders—known as Education Means Business—to help him pass the school legislation and a tax increase to fund it.

Individual corporations backed the reform movement in other, less conventional ways. Ashland Oil paid for the distribution of 500,000 fliers at Kentucky gas stations and food markets in an effort to encourage citizens to participate in a series of town meetings on education held across the state in November 1984. South Carolina businesses in late 1983 raised over $100,000 for radio, television, and newspaper advertisements in support of Governor Riley's education reform agenda.

In addition, many businesses launched reform projects themselves. Under a project called the Boston Compact, some 300 Boston-area businesses pledged in 1982 to give the city's high school graduates priority among job applicants in return for a pledge from Boston school officials to make improvements in the performance of the city's school system, including higher attendance and lower dropout rates. Businesses in Baltimore, Oakland, New Haven, Dallas, and other cities subsequently established similar programs. The Metropolitan Life Insurance Company, through an affiliated foundation, in 1985 established a "teacher and education division" to conduct national surveys on the teaching profession. Chevron U.S.A. and the BankAmerica Foundation in 1983 created the California Educational Initiatives Fund, one of many corporate-sponsored foundations established in support of public education. Further, scores of businesses established "partnership" and "adopt-a-school" relationships with individual schools, supplying them with resources ranging from tutors to lab equipment.[10]

The corporate community's commitment to reform has not slackened since the onset of the reform movement. In 1989 eight leading national business organizations, including the Business Roundtable, the U.S. Chamber of Commerce, and the National Association of Manufacturers, established the Business Coalition for Education Reform to lobby for national achievement standards, improvements in the teaching profession, fairness in educational funding, and other reforms. The same year, David Kearns, the chairman and chief executive officer of the Xerox Corporation, coauthored *Winning the Brain Race,* a blueprint for radical school reforms.

There was a third major ingredient in the rapid expansion of public education reform in 1983: presidential politics. Ronald Reagan was up for reelection in 1984, and he sought to identify himself with the education movement as a way of strengthening his bid for a second term. As it happened, the president's political needs also served the cause of school reform, for his involvement in the national education movement gave the excellence movement a huge lift.

The president had been anything but concerned with the condition of public education in the early years of his first term. His administration proposed deep cuts in federal education budgets and sought to eliminate many major programs. In one instance, despite warnings about the poor condition of math and science education in the nation, it terminated a federal program aimed at improving precollege instruction in those subjects. The president called for the abolition of the U.S. Department of Education, proposing in 1982 that the cabinet department be downgraded to a "foundation for education assistance." He sought federal tax credits for parents who pay tuition at private schools, and he called for the distribution of billions of dollars in federal aid to disadvantaged students through a system of vouchers that parents would be permitted to redeem at private schools as well as public schools—in both cases, his intention was to foster an alternative to public education, which the president repeatedly denigrated for promoting "uniform mediocrity." In early 1982 his administration proposed an end to the federal policy of denying tax-exempt status to private schools that discriminate on the basis of race. In addition to calling for cuts in instructional aid to disadvantaged students, the Reagan administration proposed lowering the nutritional standards of the free and low-cost lunches supplied through federal subsidies to such children, the vast majority of whom attend public schools. It urged, for example, that ketchup be counted as a vegetable. Reagan also lobbied strenuously for a constitutional amendment allowing organized prayer in public schools. He repeatedly included the prayer amendment—an initiative that had little to do with the caliber of teaching and learning in schools— among his top domestic priorities.[11]

Moreover, the president in early 1981 rejected a suggestion by Secretary of Education Terrel Bell that he appoint a presidential commission to study public education. Bell believed that mounting criticism of public education called for a comprehensive investigation of the nation's schools under the auspices of the federal government, and he wanted to have the influence of the White House behind it. But Reagan, largely on the advice of his longtime adviser and then-Counselor to the President Edwin J. Meese III, turned Bell down. He told the secretary of education that it would be counterproductive to establish a presidential commission on public education when the administration's policy was to diminish the federal role in education. Reagan's aides also warned that a presidential education commission would be a potential embarrassment at a time when the administration was proposing deep cuts in federal education budgets, and that it would antagonize the president's conservative supporters, many of whom were opponents of public education. It was only after being rebuffed by the president that Bell established his own, department-level education task force: the National Commission on Excellence in Education.[12]

By 1983 even leading conservative educators such as Chester E. Finn, Jr., who became a senior Department of Education official in Reagan's second term, were condemning the Reagan administration's "lack of evident interest in public education" as "a failure of leadership."[13] Yet many of the president's top advisers continued to campaign against public education right up to the release of the national commission's report. Bell had won a place for *A Nation at Risk* on the White House calendar in March 1983. But the date had to be broken when David Gardner, the commission's chairman, told Bell that he needed another month to win unanimous consent within the eighteen-member commission on a number of issues, including the report's strong language and its recommendation for a rigorous academic core curriculum. In the interim, Meese and his staff sought to keep the report from being returned to the president's schedule. It was only after Bell pleaded his case long and hard with the president's other senior aides that the release date of *A Nation at Risk* was rescheduled for April 26.[14]

On that day the president was to introduce the commission and its report to an assembly of educators in the East Wing, but Meese and his staff were determined to use the occasion to promote the president's existing education agenda. A speech to that end was drafted for the president. And while Bell fought for and temporarily won revisions that gave greater attention to the commission's reform recommendations, they were removed at the eleventh hour and on the twenty-sixth Reagan called for "passage of tuition tax credits, vouchers, educational savings accounts, voluntary school prayer, and abolishing the Department of Education." He also asserted—erroneously—that the commission had called for "an end to federal intrusion" in education. In fact, the commission had said that "the Federal Government has *the primary responsibility* to identify the national interest in education" (emphasis in original).

Reagan's speech was denounced by members of the national commission. "We've been had," said Gerald Holton in a postceremony interview with the *New York Times*. Later in the day, the president admitted to a *USA Today* reporter that he hadn't read the commission's report.[15]

When an overwhelming public response to *A Nation at Risk* made it clear that the national commission had struck a responsive chord with the American people, however, the White House rapidly changed its stance on education. In a move specifically calculated to aid the president's bid for reelection eighteen months later, Reagan's advisers quickly sought to portray him as a champion of school reform.

The strategy had its origin in polls conducted in late 1982 and early 1983 by Reagan pollster Richard Wirthlin, who was also director of planning for the president's 1984 campaign. According to Wirthlin, the polls revealed that many voters believed that the Reagan administration was "uncaring" and that "it wasn't focused on the nation's future."[16] The White House, as a result, set out to reduce the president's vulnerability on those issues. The intention, in the words of Deputy Chief of Staff Michael K. Deaver, who played an active role in the process, was to "clear them out of the way before we got into the heat of the campaign."[17]

When *A Nation at Risk,* with its warning that education reform was crucial to the nation's economic future, received wide attention, Deaver realized it was a development that could help solve the president's political problems. He moved quickly. Immediately after the report's release, he asked Wirthlin to test the public reaction to the report's major recommendations: among these a core curriculum, higher academic standards, greater accountability within public education, and performance-based pay for teachers. The polling results were unequivocal—the public strongly supported the National Commission on Excellence in Education's reform agenda. So informed, Deaver, together with Cabinet Secretary Craig Fuller, put together a plan to turn Ronald Reagan into a school reformer. "Wirthlin found terrific numbers," Deaver recalled. "So I got the scheduling people in and told them I wanted six weeks scheduled where we go all over the country talking about excellence in education. I told them to find me every kind of venue they could. . . . We just took the commission report and ran with it."[18]

Following the Deaver script, the president participated in no fewer than eighteen education events in the eleven weeks after release of *A Nation at Risk.* He addressed a vocational association in Louisville, Kentucky, and a national student group in Shawnee Mission, Kansas. He visited classrooms and participated in an education panel discussion in Knoxville, Tennessee. He delivered the commencement address at Seton Hall University in New Jersey. He attended forums sponsored by the National Commission on Excellence in Education in Hopkins, Minnesota, and Whittier, California. And he addressed the American Federation of Teachers in Los Angeles and the National PTA in Albuquerque (where he warned that education "must never become a political football").[19] Twice the president made education the subject of his weekly radio address to the nation. And he frequently used the White House as a backdrop: he held a luncheon for state Teachers of the Year; he awarded medals to Presidential Scholars; and twice representatives of national education organizations were brought in for publicized consultations with the president. (After his initial push on education, Reagan continued to use White House ceremonies to identify himself with the education issue. At one in late September 1983, for instance, he gave awards—including a four-by-six-foot "flag of excellence"—to 152 winners of the new federal Secondary School Recognition Program. At another in October, he proclaimed 1983–84 the National Year of Partnerships in Education and announced his intention to sign a memorandum directing all federal agencies to "adopt" a school. At a ceremony in August 1984, just three months before the 1984 election, he announced that a teacher would be the first private citizen to fly on a space-shuttle mission.)

Reagan made so many public statements on education that he complained to Deaver that he was giving "the same speech every day" and that it was "ridiculous" to do so.[20] Publicly, and in sharp contrast to Reagan's assertion on April 26 that the excellence commission had urged "an end to federal intrusion" in education, the White House said the president's many pronouncements on education were a response to the commission's call for the federal government to "identify the national interest in education."

Reagan used his repeated speeches on education in the late spring and early summer of 1983 to claim credit for forming the national commission. He told a White House audience that "when Secretary Bell and I first discussed a plan of action to deal with the declining quality of education in America, we agreed that it was imperative to assemble a panel of America's leading educators." And in an April 30 radio address to the nation he said, "You may have heard the disturbing report this week by the National Commission on Excellence in Education that I created shortly after taking office."[21] The president also discussed the national commission's widely supported recommendations, not in terms of appropriations levels or new federal initiatives but by tying them to broad values and beliefs held by many Americans. He called for high standards, strong discipline, the teaching of "the basics," freedom of choice, and the rewarding of merit. The latter theme, in particular, complemented Reagan's reelection effort, for in amplifying the national commission's call for "performance-based" pay for teachers—so-called merit pay—the president was able to turn public opinion against a powerful organization closely identified with the Democratic party: the National Education Association, with 1.5 million active members, the nation's largest teachers union, and an organization adamantly opposed to merit pay. In contrast to Reagan's "thematic" approach to education reform, his eventual Democratic opponent in the 1984 election, Walter F. Mondale, announced an education agenda shortly after release of *A Nation at Risk* that proposed $11 billion for new federal education programs.

The Deaver strategy worked. The president's education crusade greatly improved his image as a caring, future-oriented leader, and it won the Republican party control of the education issue for the duration of the 1984 campaign, an issue that had traditionally won votes for the Democrats. Said Wirthlin: "It was one of our most successful uses of the President [in the 1984 campaign]."

But more important for the reform movement, because the president has an extraordinary power to set the public agenda nationally, as the governors do at the state level, Reagan's sudden enthusiasm for education expanded the national dialogue on school reform dramatically. Voters surveyed for *Newsweek* in August 1983 ranked "the quality of public education" second only to "economic conditions in the country" among the most pressing issues facing the nation. Ironic though it was, the president played no small role in education's achievement of that status.

The president's participation was such an important catalyst to the reform movement largely because it gained the movement tremendous media coverage. As the country's preeminent newsmaker, the president had the ability to make an issue instantly "newsworthy." When Reagan took up the mantle of education reform, the subject also became a priority for the nation's major news organizations. Suddenly, with the president in the picture, not just the education press but a broad spectrum of the news media, including the influential White House and political press corps, was covering the education story.

A Nation at Risk itself received an extraordinary amount of media attention when it was released by the president at the White House that it probably would not have received had Education Secretary Bell not succeeded in getting the report back onto the president's calendar. It was to a significant extent the White House's involvement in the report's release—the president's participation, an elaborate East Room ceremony, a full briefing on the report for the White House press corps by the president's communications staff—that won *A Nation at Risk* prominent coverage on the evening news programs of the national television networks on April 26 and in the front pages of the nation's major newspapers the following morning.[22]

Moreover, the president's cross-country education crusade helped to keep the national media focused on school reform well after release of *A Nation at Risk*. "Education Emerges as Major Issue in 84 Presidential Campaign" was the headline of a page-one story in the *New York Times* on June 9. A week later, a *Washington Post* White House correspondent reported that education "suddenly has become a hot political issue." Many of the nation's syndicated columnists were sending the same message to their readers.

The staff of the national commission supplied one measure of the extent of the press coverage that education received at the time. In a survey of forty-five daily newspapers, some large, some small, it found no fewer than 700 stories with a reference to the commission written within four months of *A Nation at Risk*'s release. It turned up nearly fifty such stories in the *New York Times* alone. The nation's leading magazines and journals of politics and opinion also weighed in. *Newsweek*, the *National Journal*, *Fortune*, and the *New Republic* all ran cover stories on school reform in 1983, and the topic was the subject of articles in publications ranging from *Esquire* to the *New York Review of Books*, the *Atlantic*, and the *Harvard Business Review*.[23] So much attention was given to school reform that even obscure publications with readerships likely to be little interested in education issues felt compelled to find an angle on the reform

debate. *Camping Magazine,* for example, ran an article in its September/
October 1983 issue on the implications for summer camps of the national
commission's recommendation for a longer school year.

The president's involvement, together with *A Nation at Risk*'s compelling rhetoric and its swift reinforcement by a succession of other national
reports, made the education movement of the 1980s the first to be exposed to the full force of the nation's vast mass communications network.
In the 1950s, when the nation last sought to raise academic standards in
the public schools in the face of an educational crisis, the mass media as
we know them today were just emerging. Television reached fewer
homes. Cable programming didn't exist. And there were fewer mass-
circulation publications. In the 1980s, however, satellite printing technology permitted leading newspapers such as the *New York Times* and the
Wall Street Journal to be home delivered in many parts of the nation. New
publications such as *USA Today* and *People* reached mass audiences. The
Cable News Network, offering programming twenty-four hours a day,
had established itself alongside ABC News, CBS News, and NBC News as
a fourth major television news organization, and C-SPAN, another cable
operation, was beaming live coverage of major press conferences, congressional debates, and other public-affairs events to millions of subscribers. The three major television networks, meanwhile, had expanded
their own news and information programming. To their long-standing
dinner-hour news programs, all three had added late-night broadcasts
(ABC's "Nightline," CBS's "Nightwatch"), morning news ("The CBS
Morning News"), morning variety shows with a news component (NBC's
"The Today Show," ABC's "Good Morning, America") and weekend
news broadcasts (NBC's "Meet the Press," ABC's "This Week with David
Brinkley"). Syndicated television talk shows ("Donahue," "The Oprah
Winfrey Show") had huge midday viewerships. And public television,
through broadcasts such as "The MacNeil/Lehrer NewsHour," had also
become a significant national source of news.

Augmenting the national media was a new independent national
newspaper on elementary and secondary education—*Education Week.*
Launched in 1981, the paper supplied regular coverage of educational
news nationwide, a resource that hadn't existed previously. Many of the
nation's major news organizations were among *Education Week*'s readers.

The coverage generated by this new media juggernaut gave the education reform movement a tremendous boost, both by conveying a legitimacy to the movement and by spreading its message far faster and much
more widely than had been possible in the past. It also spurred the
reform effort by inspiring a wave of local reporting on conditions in the
schools. Scores of local and regional newspapers ran reform-related series on public education in the months following release of *A Nation at
Risk,* the *Wichita Eagle-Beacon* ("Kansas Education: Failing Our Kids"),
the *Louisville Courier-Journal* ("Crisis in the Classroom"), and the *Fort*

Worth Star-Telegram ("Texas Education: Passing or Failing?") among them. Moreover, by conveying the message of the school crisis far beyond academic conferences and professional journals, the mass media played a key role in the making the reform movement essentially a public rather than a professional effort.

Meanwhile, Bell, Boyer, Sizer, Goodlad, and other prominent reformers themselves contributed to the wide dissemination of the reform message by actively promoting their recommendations to educators and policymakers. Like modern-day circuit riders, they barnstormed the nation, exhorting, scolding, challenging—in effect, selling reform. Secretary of Education Bell alone made 140 speeches in the twelve months following publication of *A Nation at Risk*. To help communicate its reform recommendations, the Carnegie Foundation for the Advancement of Teaching produced a documentary film version of its report, *High School*. Not only were hundreds of copies sold, the film was nominated for an Academy Award.

The reform movement received scant support, however, from the powerful professional organizations that represent the managers of the nation's schools and school systems. By and large, organizations such as the National Association of Secondary School Principals, the National Association of State Boards of Education, the American Association of School Administrators, and the Council of Chief State School Officers were cool, and in some cases openly hostile, to the calls for education reform. They charged that the indictments of public education in *A Nation at Risk* and the other reform reports were overstated. And they argued that the critics' recommendations for reform were in many cases ill-conceived and unlikely to bring about improvements in the schools. The executive director of the National School Boards Association, writing in a July 1983 column, condemned the "stridently negative view of public education" and the "near-hysterical narrative" of *A Nation at Risk*. In a May editorial the executive director of the National Association of Secondary School Principals wrote condescendingly of the national reform reports: "The *intent* of all this fuss is to help education" (emphasis in original).[24]

The solution to the crisis in the schools, the organizations argued (even as they denied that a crisis existed), lay not in a spate of reforms but in increased spending on education. Lack of funding became the education establishment's standard rationalization for the parlous condition of the public schools. When the national commission warned in *A Nation at Risk* that the American public school system was performing poorly in comparison with those of other industrialized nations, and in particular Japan's, the executive director of the secondary school principals association told the press: "The simple fact is that [the Japanese] contribute [more money] to their schools." Apart from reducing the public schools' vast problems to a mere matter of money, the assertion contradicted the

statistics that were available at the time, which indicated that the United
States was spending about 5.5 percent of its gross national product on
education, compared with Japan's 5.1 percent.[25]

It was primarily to the task of securing more money for education, in
the form of larger and larger federal education appropriations, that the
major public education organizations had dedicated themselves since the
1970s. As the national commitment to equal educational opportunity
expanded during that decade, and with it the number of federal aid
programs for local school systems, Washington increasingly became the
focus of the professional education associations, which built elaborate
grass-roots membership networks, hired lobbyists, and in some cases
established political action committees in an effort to win support for
greater education funding in the federal halls of power. No fewer than
six major education organizations built multi-million-dollar national
headquarters in and around the nation's capital in the mid-1980s as self-
congratulatory testaments to their political influence in Washington.[26]

Moreover, even when the school-reform movement wheeled around
the education establishment's Maginot Line on the Potomac and into the
state capitals, the establishment persisted in its preoccupation with appropriations levels. When in 1985, for example, the National School Boards
Association reassigned a longtime federal lobbyist to head the new Center for State Legislation and School Law, the rationale for the move had
little to do with school reform. According to one official of the organization, the new center was established because "if there's going to be new
money [for public education], it's going to be at the state level."[27]

Nor did the organizations representing the nation's school authorities
do much to promote a discussion among their memberships of the issues
raised by the school reformers. A number of them did reprint *A Nation at
Risk* and excerpts from others of the major reform reports in their publications. And the report authors and other leading reformers were invited
to address many of the organizations. But by two significant measures—
the content of their professional publications and the agendas of their
national conventions—such organizations largely failed to engage their
memberships in a serious examination of the issues raised by the reform
movement.

The response of the National School Boards Association (NSBA) to the
reform movement was typical. Founded in 1940, it is now one of the most
influential education associations in the nation, with a 120-member staff
and 97,000 constituents who set policy for virtually all of the nation's
local public school systems.

NSBA in 1983 reprinted *A Nation at Risk* and portions of other reports
in its membership newspaper, *School Board News*. And its executive director's criticisms of *A Nation at Risk* notwithstanding, the organization's
leadership passed resolutions that year calling for NSBA members to
"study" the national reform reports and "review" their local policies with

an eye to raising standards and improving teacher quality. It also sponsored the modest Excellence Through School Board Policies project, funded by the U.S. Department of Education.

Yet in the months leading up to and following the release of *A Nation at Risk* in April 1983, the *American School Board Journal*, NSBA's primary publication and the leading professional journal for the nation's school board members, made virtually no mention of the debate on public education that was then raging throughout the nation. In March it ran major articles calling for caution in the use of trained dogs to sniff for drugs in schools, on how to devise a crowd-control policy for extracurricular activities, and on "how to get the most out of a convention." The lead story in the April issue was on the pros and cons of hiring auditors to keep tabs on school administrators. There were also such articles as "Tips on Care and Feeding of Legislators" and "Superspots in San Francisco" (the site of the 1983 NSBA convention), but there was no mention in the issue of the National Commission on Excellence in Education or its report. In July, as President Reagan barnstormed the nation on behalf of school reform, the cover story in the *American School Board Journal* described ways to "pep up flagging spirits" among school board members. Three other articles discussed ways to keep down the cost of new buildings. In August the lead story was "The Secret Ingredients in School Food Service," and five others were about school food service as well. On the cover of the issue was a pizza with a dollar sign cut out of it.[28]

Nor did the NSBA conventions (in drawing upward of 15,000 participants, the annual NSBA convention is perhaps the single largest yearly forum of grass-roots educational leaders) that followed the emergence of school reform as a national issue foster a debate of any significance on reform issues among the NSBA membership. For example, the NSBA declared in its promotional materials for its 1985 convention, held in Anaheim, California, that the "heart" of the convention was a series of 100 ninety-minute issue "clinics." Some of the sessions dealt with teacher compensation and other reform-related topics, but there were many more on such subjects as "The Do's and Don'ts of Due Process," "How to Live Peacefully with Your Local News Media," "How to Unite a Divided Board," "How to Close Schools without (Too Much) Rancor," "A Slew of Hints for Cutting Costs," and "The Best School District Public Relations Program Money Can't Buy." Another series of seminars at the convention, billed as an opportunity to "meet the experts," included such sessions as "Better Schools Through Better Communications: Mini-workshops on Ways to Improve Public Relations in Your School System," "Sport Torts, or How to Prevent Liability for Athletic Injuries," and "Herpes—Advice on the Policy, Legal Issues, and Practical Applications of Dealing with This Sensitive Issue." It was virtually impossible, on the other hand, to find a seminar at the convention on the purpose of public education, the organization of schools, the nature of instruction, or the content of the public school curriculum—all issues crucial to the school reformers.

Despite the fact that the reform movement was sweeping across the nation at the time, the featured speakers at the 1985 convention had little expertise in education and had almost nothing to say about the subject in their remarks in Anaheim. One of them, the columnist Ben Wattenberg, took the opportunity of his address to plug a new book he had written on the media. As do most of the major education associations, the NSBA had recruited Wattenberg and the convention's other marquee speakers— former President Gerald R. Ford; Pearl Bailey, the entertainer; and Alexander M. Haig, Jr., who had been secretary of state early in the Reagan administration—at high prices (ranging up to a reported $18,000 for Ford) from national speakers bureaus, not on the basis of their knowledge of education issues but in the hopes that their names would draw participants to the convention. Such was the pressure for large convention turnouts (convention profits constituted 31 percent of the NSBA's $10.4 million budget in 1985, compared with 8 percent from membership dues) that the NSBA that year ran an article in *School Board News* hyping a scheduled performance at the Anaheim convention by singer Crystal Gayle. The article ran under the headline "NSBA Convention Nabs Nashville's Crystal Gayle for Anaheim Show," together with a vampish photograph of the comely entertainer.

The most widely attended portion of the convention, however, did not have to do with school issues or entertainment. What attracted the largest number of NSBA convention-goers was a huge exhibit hall, where scores of companies displayed a mind-boggling assortment of products, products that had little to do with learning: rugs, bleachers, pianos, whirlpool baths, school buses, blocking sleds, scoreboards, lockers, jungle gyms, vacuums, lathes, computers, sewing machines, floor waxers, lawn mowers, and more. A few textbook publishers had booths in the hall. The NSBA in its convention program described the collective contents of the exhibit hall as "essential to the public schools." The organization's primary purpose, of course, was to make money with the exhibition hall. And by charging $750 for ten square feet of display space, it did—some $400,000.

Nor are the NSBA and the other large public education associations unaware that their conventions are something less than intellectual hothouses. "The bottom line," said a former senior NSBA official, "is to generate revenue, to meet next year's budget. If the membership wanted it, NSBA would put on a circus every year, as long as it made the organization money." In a December 1982 article in the *American School Board Journal*, the president of the NSBA, Rayma C. Page, went so far as to offer school board members tips on "how to head off potential criticism" for using public monies to pay the costs of attending NSBA conventions.[29]

For many of the national education organizations, the imperative as the reform movement unfolded in 1983 and 1984 was not the improvement of schools but public posturing. They sought to blunt criticism of the schools' performance, while also avoiding the appearance of standing in the way of a reform campaign that had broad popular backing. Once again the school boards association led the way. In addition to its convention schedule's being filled with workshops on public relations, a recommendation that local school boards make public relations a priority was included by the organization's leadership in its post-*A Nation at Risk* resolutions. And the same message was conveyed repeatedly in the organization's publications. In a July 1984 *American School Board Journal* column, the NSBA executive director urged his membership to create a public-relations-oriented "action plan" in face of the pressure for reform. "Your local school board needs a plan of action," he wrote. "And in view of our media-oriented world, where perceptions are almost as important as reality, an important component of this plan is public relations."[30]

Despite the untoward response of much of the public education establishment, the forces that coalesced behind the reform movement in 1983 spurred a myriad of state and local initiatives designed to improve the public schools. A plethora of state reform task forces were assembled. In addition to those appointed by governors, there were many established by state boards of education (including the Utah Commission on Excellence in Education and a Blue Ribbon Commission for Excellence in Education in Wyoming), state legislatures (including Iowa's Task Force on Excellence in Education, Illinois's Commission on the Improvement of Elementary and Secondary Education, and Kansas's Special Committee on Education), and state commissioners of education (including Wisconsin's Task Force on Teaching and Teacher Education). A sizable number of reform commissions were appointed by independent organizations. In Illinois a coalition of business, farm, taxpayer, foundation and citizens groups established the Illinois Project for School Reform to study the state's schools and make reform recommendations. Citizens in Missouri formed the Conference on Education to do the same. And in Kentucky, the privately sponsored Kentuckians for Excellence in Education Task Force was a prominent voice in the reform debate. As many as four or five commissions were at work simultaneously in some states. Nationwide, no fewer than fifty-four state-level education reform commissions were established in 1983; and by January 1985 there were well over one hundred.

The reform commissions, which typically included prominent public officials, academics, and business persons but not many public educators, issued a myriad of reports outlining recommendations for reform in the schools. They ranged from short, rhetorical, and essentially political responses to the national reform drive, such as the January 1984 booklet published under the auspices of the governor's office in Kansas, entitled

Toward Excellence in Education: Gov. John Carlin's Commitment to Education in Kansas, to lengthy, detailed documents like the forty-one-point plan, *Move to Quality,* submitted to Governor Riley of South Carolina by two state reform task forces in November 1983.

Drawing heavily on the rhetoric and recommendations of the national studies of public education—in Utah, a gubernatorial "steering committee" on education reform went so far in its late 1983 report as to use typefaces and layout designs identical to those of *A Nation at Risk*—the state reform commissions argued that it was a changing domestic workplace and international economic competitiveness that made education reform essential. "High technology, foreign competition, new patterns of organization, and export of jobs will change the way Americans work, produce, and earn," wrote the Iowa Task Force on Excellence in Education in its 1984 report. "Young people leaving our high schools must be equipped to adapt to these changes." As in the national studies, the overarching theme of the state commissions' reform recommendations was "excellence." The Iowa task force put it this way: "More student and faculty time must be devoted to the schools' primary task. . . . Iowa schools must give top priority to providing *all* students a rigorous, general academic education that stresses the development of intellectual skills and competencies."[31] It was the rare state reform report that didn't have the word "excellence" somewhere in its title. The majority of the state commissions, it seemed, were either "striving for," "investing in," or "moving toward" excellence, or they were offering a "blueprint," an "opportunity," or an "agenda" for achieving it.

Task forces, studies, and recommendations for reform also emerged at the local level as many communities sought to respond to the national calls for improvements in public education. In Houston corporate leaders established the Houston Task Force for Educational Excellence to study conditions in the city's schools and propose reforms; its membership included representatives of the city's Chamber of Commerce and such major corporations as Hughes Tool, IBM, Conoco, Shell, and Tenneco. In Minneapolis the superintendent of schools formed the Blue Ribbon Committee on Educational Standards. In Arlington, Virginia, the school board established a task force of parents, teachers, and school administrators to prepare a report comparing the city's school policies and practices to the recommendations made in *A Nation at Risk.* The fifty-three-page "Educational Excellence Checklist" was submitted in early 1984. In Salem, Oregon, the school superintendent appointed a fifteen-member citizens task force to review both national- and state-level reform reports and recommend reforms. And in Westfield, New Jersey, the school system in the fall of 1983 organized a "convocation for excellence" for the entire Westfield community.

Increasing numbers of state and local lawmakers were attracted to the reform movement. Hundreds of state legislators and members of their

staffs crowded into sessions at the annual meeting of the National Conference of State Legislatures in San Antonio in August 1983 to hear the
authors of the national education reports. Also that summer Secretary of
Education Terrel Bell, who said he previously had had little contact with
the nation's governors, was a prominent participant at the annual meeting of the National Governors' Association, held in Portland, Maine.
Then in December 1983 Secretary Bell drew 2,500 policymakers (among
them governors, members of Congress, and state legislators) and leading
educators, as well as President Reagan, to the National Town Hall Meeting on education in Indianapolis sponsored by the U.S. Department of
Education. The three-day event featured dozens of panel discussions and
addresses designed to "showcase" emerging state and local reform efforts. Scheduled one month before the opening of the 1984 legislative
sessions in the states, the national meeting was also intended to build
support for passage of reform legislation.[32]

The Indianapolis symposium was the culmination of twelve regional
forums held by the National Commission on Excellence in Education
between May and October of 1983 to publicize the findings and recommendations of *A Nation at Risk*. According to the U.S. Department of
Education, as many as 10,000 people attended the forums. Such numbers were an indication of what was an extraordinary level of public
participation in the early stages of the reform movement. Frustrated by
the performance of the public schools and emboldened by the national
calls for reform, private citizens joined the education reform movement
in unprecedented numbers.

Private citizens were an especially strong force in California. In June
1983 some 7,500 people crowded into the football stadium at Orange
Coast College south of Los Angeles to rally support in the state legislature for appropriations needed to fund a reform package proposed by
California Superintendent of Public Instruction Honig.[33] There were
scores of similar rallies across the state, and they sparked thousands of
letters and phone calls in support of increased education funding. In
addition, Honig organized hundreds of local citizens committees to help
lobby the California legislature. One such committee, the Kern County
Alliance for Quality Schools in Bakersfield, had a seventy-two-member
advisory board that included the mayor of the city, the publisher of the
local newspaper, major local landholders, bankers, lawyers, and petro-
leum-industry representatives.

The public was also actively involved in reform campaigns in other
states: Governor Alexander enlisted 40,000 Tennesseans into a coalition
known as Citizens for Better Schools; Governor Winter built a citizens
lobby of 30,000 to buttress his reform legislation; over 7,500 lay persons
participated in a series of "open hearings" on education held by a gubernatorially appointed commission throughout Arkansas in 1983; and
13,000 people participated in seven similar meetings on education re-

form in South Carolina that year. In Kentucky, a nonprofit citizens group, using $200,000 in private donations and 2,000 volunteers, in 1984 sponsored town meetings in nearly all of the state's 120 counties to promote the education reform agenda of Governor Martha Layne Collins. The state's media helped to publicize the meetings by providing free advertising space and airtime. Meanwhile, the membership of the National PTA grew by nearly 200,000 in the year following release of *A Nation at Risk*, the organization's first major membership increase in two decades—an achievement amplified by a steady decline during the same period in the percentage of households with school-age children.

The national debate on public education produced scores of reforms. Many of them were locally sponsored, as the intense scrutiny of the schools led school boards and administrators to refocus their priorities and rewrite their policies. But the overwhelming majority of the reform initiatives emanated from state governments, especially state legislatures. Through 1984, 1985, 1986, and beyond, education was a dominant issue in state capitols nationwide. Many lawmakers were called into special session over school reform legislation, including those in Arkansas (1983), Florida (1983), Tennessee (1984; the first special legislative session called in the state since 1966), Maine (1984), Utah (1984), Kentucky (1985), Alabama (1985), and West Virginia (1988). The result was a plethora of reform laws, including sweeping legislative packages passed in some fifteen states. Florida's 275-page Raise Achievement in Secondary Education Act, and California's Hart-Hughes Education Reform Act, a measure that enacted over eighty reforms, were the first omnibus packages signed into law—in June and July of 1983, respectively. They were followed by no-less-ambitious legislation that included Tennessee's Comprehensive Reform Act of 1984; South Carolina's Education Improvement Act of 1984; a second Florida law, the Omnibus Education Act of 1984; Indiana's Education Board Reorganization Act of 1984; Maine's Educational Act of 1984; Idaho's School Improvement Act of 1984; Georgia's Quality Basic Education Act of 1984; the Missouri Excellence in Education Act of 1985; Massachusetts's School Improvement Act of 1985; Illinois's Better Schools Accountability Act of 1985; and Connecticut's Education Enhancement Act of 1986. In all, there were an estimated 3,000 separate school-reform measures enacted in the states during the mid-1980s.

As part of the reform drive, state legislators pumped vast amounts of new revenue into public education, both to bolster existing programs and to pay for reforms. Their willingness to do so represented a sea change in attitude from only several years earlier.[34] Many states raised taxes. Lawmakers in South Carolina, where bumper stickers read "A Penny for Their Thoughts," increased the state's sales tax from four cents to five cents, a move that won public education an additional $240 million annually. Mississippi hiked its sales tax by .5 percent and most personal and corporate income tax by 1 percent, the largest onetime tax increase in the state's history. Iowa, Arkansas, Idaho, and Tennessee also raised their sales taxes by 1 percent in support of public education. Tennessee's new tax raised $1 billion for the state's schools in three years. The increase in Arkansas was the state's first sales-tax hike in twenty-six years. Governor Robert Orr pushed $750 million in new personal and corporate income taxes through the Indiana legislature in 1987 to fund his A+ Program for Education Excellence, also passed that year. In Oklahoma voters approved higher ceilings on local tax levies, and stipulated that at least 50 percent of the proceeds be spent on elementary and secondary education. And in California voters approved a statewide lottery in 1984 and earmarked a percentage of the proceeds for education, one of several states to do so. In 1985–86, the lottery raised $556 million for California's schools.

Meanwhile, many of the major reform packages included sharply increased education appropriations from existing revenue sources. California's Hart-Hughes Act earmarked nearly $2.6 billion in additional spending for the state's elementary and secondary schools between 1983 and 1985 alone. It was the state's first inflation-adjusted budget increase in education since enactment of Proposition 13 in 1978. Georgia's Quality Basic Education Act of 1984, which was approved without a dissenting vote by the state legislature, called for some $700 million in increased spending on education over four years.

In all, state spending on public education rose dramatically following the onset of the reform movement: by 46 percent in Tennessee between 1983 and 1987, by 69 percent in Minnesota, by 46 percent in New Jersey, by 65 percent in California, by 48 percent in Indiana, by 54 percent in Arkansas, and by 56 percent in South Carolina. In comparison, inflation increased by 14 percent during the same period. The nation's total spending on elementary and secondary education rose from $128 billion to $184 billion between 1982 and 1987, an increase of 44 percent, or approximately 25 percent after inflation. The states' share of the total was 50 percent, the Federal share was 6 percent, and the local share was 44 percent.[35]

The reform movement was lucky. Had the nation's economy not rebounded as dramatically as it did from the 1981–82 recession, leaving thirty-seven states with budget surpluses by the end of 1984 and only three with deficits, there would have been much less money available to pay for education reforms, and lawmakers no doubt would have been far less willing to earmark funds to that end.

Despite the nation's sharply varying political, socioeconomic, and educational conditions, reform agendas were strikingly similar from region to region and community to community. They were drawn primarily from the largely overlapping recommendations of the major national education reports published in 1983.

Virtually all of the states raised their graduation requirements in academic subjects, many created "honors" diplomas with high standards, and many increased the number of academic courses needed for admission to public colleges and universities. Many implemented mandatory homework policies. States and school systems lengthened the school day and school year, and many limited extracurricular activities to emphasize academics. Teacher salaries, especially starting salaries, were raised nationwide, and many states established loan programs for education majors as part of a broad campaign to recruit more talented teachers. Education-school admission standards were raised and the requirements for a teaching license changed, usually to require the passing of a "competency test" and often to require a college degree in an academic subject as opposed to an education degree. Many states and school systems also sought to link teacher pay to performance, and to provide teachers with career ladders to make teaching a more attractive occupation. Many introduced new student standardized testing programs or expanded programs already in place. Frequently, the passing of the new tests was made a requirement for promotion between grades or for high school graduation, or both, in an attempt to abolish "social promotion." Tests were also linked to new financial-incentive programs for schools and school systems in many states. Many states and school systems also sought to standardize their curricula. States introduced a range of preschool programs, and many states reduced class sizes in elementary grades and expanded kindergarten programs to provide students with a sounder academic footing early in their school careers. Though additional reform strategies have emerged more recently, it is primarily with these measures embraced in the first half of the 1980s that the reform movement has sought to broaden the academic mission of the public schools, to promote excellence in education.

Consisting primarily as it does of laws, licensing requirements, rules, and mandates, it is an agenda overwhelmingly regulatory in nature. By and large it imposes reform on public education rather than cultivates it from within. Regulatory reforms became the hallmark of the excellence movement for several reasons. The first is because the impetus for reform in the 1980s came primarily from outside the education community, from a broad alliance of reformers, business leaders, lawmakers, and the public at large. The tools most readily available to that coalition in its attempt to improve the schools from the outside in were regulatory measures. In marked contrast the education reform movement of the Sputnik era was to a significant extent a professional enterprise, led by university scholars who sought to reshape and strengthen the academic curriculum in the nation's public schools, and to retrain teachers in science, math, and foreign languages through federally funded workshops and summer institutes.

There was also a political imperative to the heavy emphasis on regulations and mandates in the national school reform agenda. Having invested a great deal of political capital in their commitment to education reform, lawmakers in the states sought reforms that were easily understood by their constituents and quick to implement. They thus supported new testing programs, higher salaries, class-size reductions and other regulatory reforms, many of which were easily quantifiable. Further, legislative and regulatory fiats lent themselves to the sort of wholesale reform that the reformers and state policymakers sought: they provided the leverage needed to introduce changes quickly and broadly.

Finally, the regulatory approach was a way for a deeply distrustful public to pressure educators into improving the schools. The myriad mandates spawned by the reform movement have reduced the authority of teachers, principals, and local administrators in many areas of school life, from length of classes to content of courses. Most dramatically, a dozen states have granted themselves authority to remove the administrators and school boards of underachieving school systems. Public educators lost the nation's confidence, and they paid the price.

CHAPTER 2

In the Name of Excellence

What tied the nascent school reform movement so closely to the nation's quest for greater economic competitiveness was a revolution underway in the American workplace. With the nation passing rapidly out of the industrial age, lunch-bucket jobs were being replaced by work that stressed brains over brawn. No longer was the assembly line or the steel mill a way into the middle class for the ill-educated. The new jobs demanded more than mastery of basic reading, writing, and arithmetic. They called for workers with "thinking skills," with the ability to master new knowledge on the job. In the future, said Theodore Sizer in *Horace's Compromise*, the 1984 study of public education, "The best vocational education will be one in general education in the use of one's mind." Employers agreed. A task force of business executives and labor experts convened by the National Academy of Sciences concluded in a widely publicized 1984 report entitled *High Schools and the Changing Workplace: The Employers' View* that "technical education, vocational training, and curricula providing specific job skills can enhance a student's employability, but cannot substitute for education in the core [academic] competencies. . . . Those who enter the work force after earning a high school diploma need virtually the same competencies as those going on to college." Such skills were "the new raw materials of international commerce," argued the National Commission on Excellence in Education in *A Nation at Risk*.[1]

The revolution in the nature of work, it was widely argued, meant that the nation would no longer be able to tolerate a badly educated work force. It needed to ratchet up standards dramatically. "The skills that were once possessed by only a few must now be held by the many if the United States is to remain competitive in an advancing technological world," wrote the Twentieth Century Fund's education task force in *Making the Grade*. In much the same language, the national commission warned in *A Nation at Risk* that, "America's position in the world may once have been reasonably secure with only a few exceptionally well-trained men and women. It is no longer."[2]

Meanwhile, the nation was learning from its demographers that the work force the schools would have to educate to high standards would itself be very different in the near future. An increasing proportion of the nation's workers would be minorities and other economically disadvantaged peoples—as students, frequently the products of homes where books and newspapers are scarce, where the level of spoken language is low or where English is not spoken at all, and where the value of education is not stressed by parents who are themselves more often than not ill-educated.

Lacking the language skills, the cultural tools, and the nurturing homes that are the foundation stones of successful schooling, disadvantaged students are invariably difficult to educate. Disproportionately, they are black and Hispanic. Nearly 50 percent of black and Hispanic students are born into poverty. Such students are also the fastest-growing segment of the public school population. At the outset of the excellence movement in the early 1980s, blacks and Hispanics made up roughly 25 percent of the nation's 40,000,000 students; by the year 2000, they are expected to constitute 40 percent of the school population.

There are already overwhelming numbers of disadvantaged minority students in the nation's major cities, where the middles classes (white and minority) have largely vanished over the past three decades. The forty-five member school systems of the Council of the Great City Schools educate 13 percent of the nation's students, but 33 percent of those in families receiving public assistance. Seventy percent of the students in the organization's school systems are black, Hispanic, or Asian. Further, it is in the nation's city school systems where the devastation of drugs, teenage pregnancy, and other social problems has been the greatest.[3]

As a consequence of the nation's changing demographics, public education's future success or failure will be tied directly to its ability to educate disadvantaged students well, to surmount poverty's many barriers to success in the classroom. And to the extent that the nation's drive to recover its economic competitiveness is tied to a higher level of learning throughout the work force, it too will depend on the ability of the schools to educate disadvantaged students.

Yet the argument that public schools must treat intellectual training as a priority for all students if the nation is to win in the world marketplace was a bold, even radical, proposition, for it challenged what had been a basic assumption within public schooling since the beginning of the century: the education best suited to a majority of the nation's students after they acquired basic literacy skills in the early grades was one that emphasized not intellectual training but the acquisition of skills that had immediate practical applications. For decades, public educators had embraced an intensely utilitarian vision of secondary schooling; overwhelmingly, they believed that a rigorous academic education should be reserved for the gifted and privileged.

The influence of utilitarianism in public education dates back to the years before World War I, a time of dramatic expansion in secondary schooling. Since the inception of a national system of free public secondary education in the late 1870s (in wake of a 1874 Michigan Supreme Court ruling that taxes could be levied to support public high schools as well as elementary schools), admission to secondary education had been largely limited to the academic and social elite, what a leading educational statement of the period described as "that small proportion of all the children in the country . . . who show themselves able to profit by an education prolonged to the eighteenth year, and whose parents are able to support them while they remain so long at school."[4] At the turn of the century, less than 9 percent of all those of high school age were enrolled in school, and fewer still—6 percent—actually graduated.[5]

The dominant educational philosophy of the era was expressed in an influential 1893 report by a committee of prominent educators empaneled by the National Education Association to study the relationship between schools and colleges and recommend revisions to the high school curriculum. Chaired by Charles W. Eliot, the president of Harvard, the so-called Committee of Ten argued that the primary task of secondary education should be to develop and discipline students' minds through the teaching of academic subject matter.[6] To achieve their goal of "training the powers of observation, memory, expression, and reasoning," the committee proposed four alternative courses of study—a classical course, a Latin-scientific course, a modern language course, and an English course—all of which called for students to take at least four years of English, four years of a foreign language, three years of history, three years of mathematics, and three years of science. The commission acknowledged that only a small percentage of high school students were bound for college, but it nonetheless urged that "every subject which is taught at all in a secondary school should be taught in the same way and to the same extent to every pupil so long as he pursues it, no matter what the probable destination of the pupil may be or at what point his education is to cease."[7]

Yet within a decade of the release of the Committee of Ten's report, conditions combined to create a new educational outlook, one that increasingly viewed the role of public secondary schools in nonacademic terms. At the turn of the century students with a far broader range of backgrounds and talents began to pour into secondary schools. Spurred by a wave of immigrants from eastern and southern Europe, many of them poor, ill-educated, and unskilled, and by a successful campaign by trade unions and social reformers for laws banning children from the nation's workplaces (in response to the huge number of "unemployed" youths produced by the child-labor laws, states passed compulsory-school-attendance statutes; Mississippi was the last to do so, in 1918), public secondary school enrollment burgeoned and educators were suddenly faced with the task of educating students very different from those that they had been accustomed to. The population of the nation's high schools more than quadrupled between 1910 and 1930, from 1.1 million to 4.8 million. And by 1920 some 60 percent of the nation's fourteen- to seventeen-year-olds were enrolled in school, nearly seven times as many as two decades earlier. Very rapidly, the American secondary school was transformed from an exclusive enclave of the best and brightest into an institution of the masses.

It was widely assumed among public educators that the majority of the "new" students surging into the schools were incapable of mastering academic subject matter. Certainly, since the proportion of children of school age who were attending school was rising, not all of those enrolled could be expected to perform at the level of the academic elite that the schools had catered to previously. But it was increasingly the belief within public education that academic studies per se were beyond the reach of most of the nation's students.

In reaching that conclusion, educators were strongly influenced by the results of the first American experiments in intelligence testing, which were being conducted at the time. Building on the work of French psychologists Alfred Binet and Theodore Simon (who by 1908 had invented the first intelligence "scale," consisting of a series of problems of increasing difficulty, each one representing the "norm" of a different mental level), American testing pioneers set about developing what they saw as scientific methods of measuring mental aptitude.[8] Two of the most prominent were Stanford psychologist Lewis M. Terman and Harvard psychologist Robert M. Yerkes. In 1917, at the onset of the nation's entrance into World War I, Yerkes volunteered as president of the American Psychological Association to help the United States Army write intelligence tests for its recruits. Two types of Army Mental Tests were created under Yerkes's direction: the Alpha series, written examinations; and the Beta series, pictorial tests for illiterates. Yerkes and his colleagues were confident enough about the accuracy of their examinations to compute a mental age for each score on the Alpha tests. Their calculations suggested that the average mental age of Americans was fourteen. Both Yerkes's extrapolations and the tests themselves were badly flawed (Alpha Test 8 included culturally biased multiple-choice questions such as these: "The Pierce Arrow car is made in a) Buffalo b) Detroit c) Toledo d) Flint," and "The Brooklyn Nationals are called the a) Giants b) Orioles c) Superbas d) Indians.")[9] But because the tests were administered to hundreds of thousands of recruits under the auspices of the federal government, Yerkes's pessimistic conclusions about the intelligence of most Americans was widely embraced. As historian Richard Hofstadter wrote in his 1963 Pulitzer Prize-winning study, *Anti-intellectualism in American Life,* "It was very quickly and very widely believed that the Army Alpha tests had actually measured intelligence; that they made it possible to assign mental ages; that mental ages, or intelligence as reported by tests, are fixed; that vast numbers of Americans had a mental age of only fourteen; and that therefore the educational system must be coping with hordes of more or less backward children."[10]

Lewis Terman was best known for his development of the Stanford-Binet Intelligence Scale, a refinement of the original French version, that remains a fixture in American education today. As did Binet and Simon, Terman used his numerical scale to express intelligence as the ratio of mental age (as measured by tests) to chronological age: what is now known as the intelligence quotient, or IQ. Terman sent educators much the same message as Yerkes did. He reported in *Intelligence Tests and School Reorganization,* for example, that no less than 80 percent of the immigrants that he had tested were feeble-minded and "should be segregated in special classes." "Their dullness seems to be racial, or at least in the family stocks from which they come," Terman wrote. He asserted that IQ examinations were able to predict a student's place in the work force, and were thus valuable tools for educators. Terman concluded that: "At every step in the child's progress the school should take account of his vocational possibilities. Preliminary investigations indicate that an IQ below 70 rarely permits anything better than unskilled labor; that the range from 70 to 80 is pre-eminently that of semi-skilled labor; from 80 to 100 that of the skilled or ordinary clerical labor; from 100 to 110 or 115 that of the semi-professional pursuits; and that above all these are the grades of intelligence which permit one to enter the professions or the larger fields of business. . . . This information will be a great value in planning the education of a particular child." He called in the study for a "differentiated curriculum" in the public schools based on students' IQs.[11]

What the new intelligence tests offered secondary school educators—and what they sought desperately—was an efficient and "scientific" way to manage the mass of new students pouring into the public schools. "There was a heightening sense after 1908 that educational measurement had ushered in a new era in which the promise of efficiency could at last be scientifically fulfilled," said historian Lawrence A. Cremin in *The Transformation of the School,* his classic study of Progressivism in American education. With the advent of educational measurement, schools gained a putatively objective means of sorting their students. More significantly, however, the new tests armed educators with a justification for avoiding the difficult task of teaching traditional academic subjects to nonelite students. It was thus convenient for educators to turn a blind eye to the glaring weaknesses in both the tests and the conclusions drawn from them.[12]

There were other developments that were also important to the emergence of utilitarianism in public education in the early decades of the century. Many of them were linked to the larger movement of Progressivism, which Cremin has described as "a vast humanitarian effort to apply the promise of American life" to a "puzzling new urban-industrial civilization," a many-faceted movement that in part sought "to cast the school as a fundamental lever of social and political regeneration."[13]

One element of the Progressive crusade worked to alleviate the wretched conditions in the urban slums that had grown up in wake of industrialization and mass immigration. Lessons in hygiene, nutrition, and child care became a major part of the work of newly established "settlement houses" in the cities. And it wasn't long before settlement workers had persuaded the schools to offer such instruction as well. Similarly, there were widespread calls for schools to help in the process of "Americanizing" the influx of immigrants by broadening their programs to include various social services.[14]

Leaders in the rural United States, meanwhile, sought to insulate their life-style against the quickening pace of urbanization and industrialization by expanding agricultural and other vocational studies in the schools. "Rotation of crops is as inspiring as the position of the preposition; the fertilization of apples and corn as interesting as the location of cities and the course of rivers; the economy of the horse and cow and sheep as close to life as the duties of the President and the causes of the Revolutionary War," said a speaker at the Wisconsin Farmers' Institute in 1901, in capturing the sentiment of the so-called country-life movement.[15]

The increasing industrialization of the nation's economy itself spurred the expansion of vocational studies, as businesses and unions urged public education to play a significant role in meeting "the voracious manpower demands" of the new economic juggernaut. In time the "rural phase" of vocationalism allied itself with this larger industrial-education movement, a development that helped to bring about federal funding for vocational instruction in secondary schools under the Smith-Hughes of Act of 1917.

Central to Progressive doctrine in education was a new school of psychological thought that drew heavily from Darwin's concept of evolution. Of the leading proponents of the new psychology, G. Stanley Hall had perhaps the greatest influence on education. Hall, who earned Harvard's first doctorate of psychology in 1878, argued in books such as *Adolescence* (1904) and *Educational Problems* (1911) that the mind developed naturally through a series of evolutionary stages. As a result, schools needed to tailor themselves to the unique characteristics of each student. The school, Hall said, should be fitted to the child, not the child to the school.[16]

Cremin observes in *The Transformation of the School* that Hall's child-centered vision of schooling "paved the way for . . . fundamental changes in American pedagogical opinion." It "helped shift the focus of teaching to the student, asserting that no education could be worthy, much less efficient, that persisted in ignoring his nature, his needs, and his development." In the past "the burden of proof was on the student: he was told to perform up to standard or get out. Educational opportunity was the right of all who might profit from school to enjoy its benefits. Now, the *given* of the equation was no longer the school with its well-defined content and purposes, but the children with their particular backgrounds and needs. And educational opportunity had become the right of all who attended school to receive something of meaning and value."[17]

Widely embraced by educators (Cremin called its effects "legion"), the new child-centered philosophy of education greatly diminished the primacy of the academic disciplines in public education. Indeed, one of the most influential educational philosophers of the era, William Heard Kilpatrick, spent a career at Teachers College, Columbia University (where he's said to have taught as many as 35,000 students during a time when Teachers College was training "a substantial percentage of the articulate leaders of American education"), attacking the organized subjects—what he called subject matter "fixed-in-advanced"—in favor of a pedagogy that emphasized the use of projects drawn from students' immediate environments and interests.[18]

Another aspect of Progressivism, the movement's commitment to the "democratization" of American life, also contributed significantly to the rise of utilitarian thought and practice in public education. Progressive educators sought to involve the schools in the democratization effort, and none more so than John Dewey, whose countless articles, lectures, and monographs, together with his 1916 masterwork *Democracy and Education*, made him perhaps the most influential education thinker of his day.

As Cremin relates in *The Transformation of the School*, Dewey saw universal secondary education as a crucial first step in the larger process of democratization. But he further believed that there had to be changes in the nature of schooling itself if universal education was to make its fullest contribution to the campaign for greater democracy in American life. "Dewey believed that democracy would be achieved only as schooling was popularized in character as well as in clientele."[19]

The public education curriculum, Dewey argued, had to be rewritten to mesh more closely with the day-to-day experiences of the new students entering the schools and to reflect more fully the diversity of contemporary life in general. As Cremin explains, "For centuries, culture had meant the possession of certain kinds of knowledge marking the knower as a member of a superior social group. From the time of the Greeks it had been associated with wealth as opposed to poverty, with leisure as opposed to labor, with theory as opposed to practice. And in the school curriculum it had come to imply an emphasis on certain literary and historical studies, the knowledge of particular classical works, and the mastery of particular foreign languages. For Dewey, this notion of culture inevitably emphasized the differences among classes rather than their commonalities, exclusiveness rather than association. Moreover, while it was thoroughly utilitarian for some social groups—statesmen, professionals, intellectuals—it was equally irrelevant for others. On two accounts, then—that of exclusiveness and that of inequity—the historic view of culture was blatantly aristocratic."[20]

Dewey called for "a new view of culture extending beyond traditional preoccupation with language and literature to an inclusive concern with the whole vast panorama of human affairs." No disciplines, he argued, were "intrinsically endowed with liberating or cultural powers." If properly taught, a wide range of subjects were capable of producing "intellectual results." In particular, he urged educators to devote more attention to vocational subjects, on the grounds that they were valuable for exploring the characteristics and meaning of an emerging industrial society. Dewey believed "that democracy necessitated a reconstitution of culture, and with it the curriculum, that would conceive of scientific and industrial studies as instruments for making the great body of the people more aware of the life about them." It was his conviction, and that of Progressivism generally, "that culture could be democratized without being vulgarized."[21]

Public educators were quick to embrace Dewey's views on democracy and the curriculum. They found in his commentary what they took to be a rationale for teaching a new, nonacademic curriculum to the students flooding into their classrooms, students whom they strongly believed to be intellectually inferior. Not only were secondary school educators absolved of the daunting responsibility of demanding serious academic work from students they thought incapable of it, they could also in good conscience assert they were serving the purposes of democracy by broadening the curriculum and giving it a utilitarian focus. As the educational historian David K. Cohen has written, "There was ebullient enthusiasm for the good work that schools would do with the new students. High schools would serve democracy by offering usable studies to everyone, rather than dwelling on academic abstractions that would interest only a few."[22] Stanley Hall expressed the new vision of democratic schooling in a 1901 address to New England educators: "When the public high school really becomes, as it surely will, the people's college, permeated with the ideal of fitting for life, which is a very different thing indeed than fitting for college, then secondary education will have become truly democratic."[23]

The growth of utilitarianism in public education culminated in the 1918 publication of one of the most influential educational statements in the nation's history: *The Cardinal Principles of Secondary Education*. Written by the National Commission on the Reorganization of Secondary Education empaneled by the National Education Association, the thirty-two-page report flatly rejected the contention made twenty-five years earlier by the Committee of Ten that the purpose of secondary education should be to develop students' intellectual powers through instruction in academic subjects. "The character of the secondary-school population has been modified by the entrance of large numbers of pupils of widely varying capacities, aptitudes, social heredity, and destinies in life. . . . The needs of these pupils cannot be neglected," said the commission. It hence proclaimed that subject matter and teaching methods "must be tested in terms of the laws of learning and the application of knowledge to the activities of life, rather than primarily in terms of the demands of any subject as a logically organized science." The value of education, in the commission's view, corresponded directly to the extent to which students could put their education immediately to use in the conduct of their daily lives. It was in that way that schools could best meet the "needs" of most students. Civics, for example, "should concern itself less with constitutional questions and remote governmental functions, and should direct attention to social agencies close at hand and [to] the informal activities of daily life that regard and seek the common good."[24]

The "main objectives" of secondary education, the commission declared, should be "1. Health. 2. Command of fundamental processes. 3. Worthy home-membership. 4. Vocation. 5. Citizenship. 6. Worthy use of leisure. 7. Ethical character."[25] The historian Diane Ravitch points out in *The Troubled Crusade,* a study of American education in the twentieth century, that "command of fundamental processes," the only reference to intellectual training in the commission's list of educational objectives, was omitted from the original draft of *Cardinal Principles.*[26] In its final report, the commission implied that "fundamental processes" were nothing more than rudimentary skills in the three Rs, and it argued that mastery of them was "not an end in itself." The commission further stated that the main divisions of the curriculum "should be, in the broad sense of the term, vocational, thus justifying the names commonly given, such as agricultural, business, clerical, industrial, fine-arts, and house-hold arts curriculums."[27] Almost as an afterthought, the commission added that "provisions should be made also for those having distinctively academic interests and needs." The intellectual side of the high school was treated as largely incidental to its other, more practical, purposes.

Cardinal Principles reached a huge audience (the U.S. Bureau of Education itself printed and distributed an edition of 130,000 copies) and it quickly became the pedagogical *corpus juris* of school systems nationwide. The result was a rapid expansion of the public secondary school curriculum beyond its traditional academic boundaries. The Committee of Ten had identified just 40 secondary-school subjects, but within two decades of publication of *Cardinal Principles* there were no fewer than 274 subjects being taught in the nation's secondary schools, only 59 of which dealt with academic topics.[28] Moreover, the ratio of academic to nonacademic courses taught in secondary school reversed itself between the decade before and the decade after publication of *Cardinal Principles.* Nearly two-thirds of all secondary school curricula had involved academic subjects, and one-third had involved nonacademic subjects between 1906 and 1911. But by 1930 two-thirds of all secondary-level curricula involved commercial, general, or trade subjects, and only one-third involved academic subjects.[29] During the same period, the average number of nonacademic courses (primarily household arts, industrial arts, and commerce) offered in high schools rose from eight to thirty-eight.[30] Meanwhile, educators established many new academic courses (such as social studies) that surveyed subjects rather than investigated them in depth, and that were less demanding of students.

The academic curriculum in secondary schools, however, did not disappear. In fact, the average number of academic courses offered in high schools rose slightly between 1910 and 1930, from twenty-four to twenty-eight.[31] As David Cohen has written, the tremendous change that took place in secondary school studies "consisted not in an absolute decline of enrollment in the academic curriculum, but in the much more spectacular growth of a much less demanding curriculum for everyone else."[32] Expansion of the secondary-school curriculum led to establishment.of what became more or less distinct curriculum paths into which educators placed students, based on their individual "needs," a practice later known as tracking. Between the first and third decades of the century alone, the proportion of high schools offering an industrial arts course of study rose from one in six to five in six. The proportion of schools offering a "general" curriculum increased by the same amount. And while half of the nation's high schools provided a commercial course of study in the first decade, all did so by the third.[33]

In addition to placing students on different curriculum paths, educators in that era began advancing students from one grade to the next on the basis of age and attendance, rather than academic performance, a practice that came to be called social promotion. It was, as Cohen has written, "the final, crucial stone in the foundation of mass secondary education, for it meant that progress in school was detached from progress in learning. By the early 1930s high school students could succeed in school without succeeding in their courses." And "the schools could thus succeed in enrolling, holding, and graduating students without success in educating them."[34]

Social promotion, tracking, and the rapid spread of educational measurement reflected the powerful influence of the theory of "scientific management" at the time of the expansion of public secondary education early in the century. Mass production was the cornerstone of the theory, which was fueling the successes of the nation's industrial economy. And educators sought to apply the tenets of industrial production to the task of providing secondary schooling on a mass scale. Schools were organized as educational factories. Teachers were seen as workers manning the production line, principals as foremen, superintendents as CEOs. School boards were likened to corporate boards of trustees and citizens to shareholders.[35] Students, the raw materials of the process, were sorted onto different educational assembly lines according to the type of product they were to become. And then they were moved briskly through the production process. All in an effort to maximize the "efficiency" and "productivity" of the educational system. What became far less important as educators sought to "manage" the influx of students entering secondary schools was academic achievement.

In the period following publication of *Cardinal Principles,* attacks on academic education only intensified. Three widely publicized documents typified the commentary of the time. One was a 1938 report by the NEA's influential Educational Policies Commission, entitled *The Purposes of Education in American Democracy.* It argued that "self-realization," "human relationships," "economic efficiency," and "civic responsibility" should be the primary objectives of education. The commission urged schools to reduce the number of students studying literature, advanced mathematics and science, and foreign languages, and to place greater emphasis on the practical applications of such subjects. "Whatever may be the merits of such exercises as a preparation for a career as an author," it wrote of instruction in grammar and literature in English classes, "the great majority of American boys and girls will profit more by a wide-ranging program of reading for enjoyment and fact-gathering." The following year, B. L. Dodds, a professor of education at Purdue University, argued in *That All May Learn* that it was futile for schools to embrace an academic curriculum that was inappropriate for "the new fifty percent," the less-able students who had swelled the enrollments of the high schools. The academic curriculum, he charged, "fostered and definitely encouraged" unreasonable ambitions among those "unselected" youths. Dodds's book was published by the National Association of Secondary School Principals, reflecting what was broad support among the major professional organizations in public education for the anti-academic sentiment of the time. That sentiment was expressed once again in 1944 in a report by the NEA's Education Policies Commission entitled *Education for ALL American Youth.* "There is no aristocracy of 'subjects,' the commission argued. "Mathematics and mechanics, art and agriculture, history and homemaking are all peers."[36]

The opposition within public education to intellectual training and academic subjects drew a sharp rebuke from Dewey. In an address to the 1928 convention of the Progressive Education Association, he rejected the notion "that orderly organization of subject-matter is hostile to the needs of students in their individual character."[37] And in his 1938 book *Experience and Education,* Dewey castigated educators who believed organized subject matter should be abandoned, who acted "as if any form of direction and guidance by adults [was] an invasion of individual freedom," and who emphasized the present and the future in the curriculum at the expense of knowledge of the past.[38] Dewey had maintained a strong commitment to the academic disciplines and to intellectual training as the goal of education, even as he had championed both the expansion of the public school curriculum and child-centered pedagogy. As

Lawrence Cremin has written, his goal had been to develop a curriculum "that would begin with the experience of the learners" but "culminate with the organized subjects that represented the cumulative experience of the race."[39] "The problem of the educator," Dewey wrote in 1916 of the new vocational studies that he was proposing, "is to engage pupils in these activities in such ways that while manual skill and technical efficiency are gained and immediate satisfaction found in the work together with preparation for later usefulness, these things shall be subordinated to *education*—that is, to intellectual results and the forming of a socialized disposition."[40] But Dewey's message was lost on many of those who thought themselves his disciples.

His warnings did little to slow the spread of anti-intellectual sentiment within public education. And by the founding in 1945 of the "life-adjustment movement," the utilitarian vision of secondary schooling was widely embraced by education professionals. The life-adjustment movement was both a product of that vision and an influential vehicle for its expression for over a decade.

It originated in the work of the U.S. Office of Education. In June 1945 the agency assembled vocational educators in Washington, D.C., to deliberate the plight of students who were not being well served by either college preparatory or vocational programs. It was there that Charles A. Prosser, a prominent vocationalist, introduced a resolution stating that 60 percent of the nation's secondary school students were not suited to training for college or for skilled occupations and that they should be provided instead with "life-adjustment training," consisting largely of what a later document described as "functional experiences in the areas of practical arts, home and family life, health and physical fitness, and civic competence."[41] Those in need of life-adjustment education, said its advocates, were primarily children from unskilled and semiskilled families that had low incomes and provided a poor cultural environment.[42] The source of the 60 percent figure seems to have been Lewis Terman, the testing pioneer, who in 1940 estimated that an IQ of 110 was needed to master an academic curriculum in high school, and that 60 percent of American youth had IQs lower than that.[43] In any case, by declaring "the 60 percent" unfit for academic or vocational work, the proponents of life-adjustment education were, as Richard Hofstadter has written, "with breathtaking certainty, writing off the majority of the nation's children as being more or less uneducable."[44]

The "Prosser Resolution" was adopted unanimously by the conference, and in 1945 the U.S. Office of Education organized five regional meetings to consider further "the 60 percent." It convened a national conference on the subject the following May. In 1948 Commissioner of Education John W. Studebaker established the three-year Commission on Life Adjustment Education for Youth to promote the purposes of life-adjustment education at the state and local levels. He established a sec-

ond commission in 1951, and it, too, had a three-year life span. Both
commissions sponsored a steady stream of reports that were widely distributed by the U.S. Government Printing Office, they organized state
and national conferences, and they launched collaborative projects with
organizations such as the American Association of Colleges for Teacher
Education, the National School Boards Association, and the National
Association of Secondary School Principals. Largely as a result of the
commissions' work—and the solid support for it within the public education establishment—the life-adjustment movement "made substantial
headway in school systems throughout the nation."[45]

At the heart of the movement was the by then familiar utilitarian
doctrine that supplying students with information and skills having direct applicability in their daily lives was inherently more valuable than
expanding their intellectual powers. In the words of the authors of *Life
Adjustment Education for Every Youth,* a publication issued by the federal
Office of Education, life-adjustment was "a philosophy of education
which places life values above acquisition of knowledge."[46] In a lecture at
Harvard in 1939, Prosser himself went so far in defense of that view as to
argue that intellectual skills could not be transferred from one task to
another. "Nothing could be more certain," he told his audience, "than
that science has proven false the doctrine of general education and its
fundamental theory that memory or imagination or the reason or the will
can be trained as a power." Learning was ungeneralizable, he argued,
and therefore education had to focus on the teaching of discrete skills.
Thus, "business arithmetic is superior to plane or solid geometry, simple
science of everyday life to geology; simple business English to Elizabe-
than Classics."[47]

The life-adjustment movement, as Hofstadter has written, stated, in
the extreme, "the proposition toward which professional education had
been moving for well over four decades: that in a system of mass education, an academically serious training is an impossibility for more than a
modest fraction of the student population."[48] The movement illustrated
a deep paradox in American education: its strong belief that the purposes of democracy could be served by extending secondary schooling to
all students on the one hand, and its adherence to anti-intellectual doctrine that severely limited most students' access to intellectual training on
the other. Despite their assertions regarding democracy, public educators, faced with the responsibility of supplying mass education, did not
try in a serious way to break what was essentially a link between social
class and educational achievement. Instead, they reorganized the high
school and its curriculum to accommodate substantially lower expectations for most students. As Mortimer Smith said of educational utilitarianism in *And Madly Teach,* a 1947 critique of the Progressive era in
education: "Here was a doctrine that released the teacher from his
responsibility for handing on the traditional knowledge of the race, a

doctrine that firmly implied that one need not adhere to any standards of knowledge but simply cater to individual interests. . . . With the acceptance of this doctrine American public school education took the easy way to meet its problems."[49]

The life-adjustment campaign, and with it the larger Progressive movement in education, came to a close in the mid-1950s, amidst calls for higher academic standards in the face of the mounting brain race with the Soviet Union. But despite changing national priorities, utilitarianism remained deeply ingrained within the fabric of public education and continued to have a powerful influence on education policy.

It played a key role in shaping public education's response to desegregation. Charles Prosser and his life-adjustment allies had excluded one significant group of students from their "60-percent" solution—minorities. Until the U.S. Supreme Court struck down segregated school systems in 1954, black students had largely been excluded from the nation's secondary-school equation. But in the wake of the *Brown* decision and the civil-rights campaigns of the 1960s, there was an increased effort to graduate black (and Hispanic) students from high school. The proportion of black students earning a diploma more than doubled between 1950 and 1967, to 56 percent. And by 1984 it reached 75 percent. The dismantling of the legal framework of segregation thus helped to complete the transformation of the public secondary school into an institution serving all students of all backgrounds.[50]

Yet educators responded to the influx of minority students (and to an increasing number of disadvantaged white students who were also staying in school longer—the graduation rate for whites rose from 50 percent in 1950 to 80 percent in 1984) in much the same way that their Progressive predecessors had responded to the surge in enrollments early in the century: by deemphasizing academics for the new students. "The emphasis on making a high school education available for every youth . . . has continued, with added attention given to the lower ability groups," wrote the U.S. Office of Education in a report on developments within public education between 1961 and 1972. "This has resulted in considerable experimentation with course offerings, and the introduction of many new courses. . . . Courses of a practical nature in everyday living proliferated."[51]

There was a tremendous increase in remedial courses during the same period. The number of students taking remedial English (which students took as a substitute for academic English courses), for example, grew six times faster than did the total enrollment of the nation's secondary schools between 1960 and 1972. There was also a dramatic increase in the number of courses taught in the high schools: from 1,100 to 2,100.[52] Believing that academic courses didn't best meet the utilitarian "needs" of the increasing numbers of minority and disadvantaged students that they were serving, educators routed the majority of the students into courses with minimal academic requirements. As Cremin writes in *Popular Education and Its Discontents,* "It proved infinitely easier to juggle the substance of the curriculum than to develop pedagogies for conveying the more intellectually demanding materials to most or all of the students."[53] The civil rights movement may have won a place for minority and disadvantaged students in the nation's high schools; it didn't win them a good education.

As it had during the life-adjustment era, the federal government played a significant role in the latest expansion of the nonacademic high school curriculum. Under Commissioner Sidney Marland, Jr., the U.S. Office of Education in 1971 began funding the establishment of courses in "career education" in the nation's secondary schools. Within four years, career-education studies, which focused on rudimentary job skills and often were linked to part-time jobs for students, were being offered in 9,300 of the nation's school systems.

Ironically, the inclination of educators to steer minority and disadvantaged students away from academic studies was reinforced by pressure from civil rights advocates, many of whom argued that to force such students to do demanding academic work would discriminate against children already suffering the consequences of discrimination in other aspects of their lives. To do so, they charged, would "only hasten the disenfranchisement of the inarticulate." Instead, many spokespersons for minority and disadvantaged students argued, the schools should seek to build on the particular "cultural" characteristics of such students. Typical of the commentary of the time was that of Frank Riessman, who wrote in 1962 in *The Culturally Deprived Child,* "It would be easy to say, as many have said, that we must give these children what middle-class parents give their children—we must stimulate them in the use of language through reading, discussion and the like. However, it is probable that this would not work nor would it make the best use of the deprived child's particular mode of functioning." He urged that such children instead be taught through techniques that "stress the visual, the physical, the active."[54] Riessman and others did not say that ways needed to be found to hold minority and disadvantaged students to high academic standards; rather, they argued that a demanding academic secondary education was inappropriate and even discriminatory toward such students.

The utilitarianism of the nation's professional public educators was further strengthened by the intense criticism of public education by the neo-Progressive critics of the 1960s and 1970s. One response to Neill, Holt, Dennison and others, who espoused both the child-centered teaching theories of turn-of-the-century Progressivism and the antiestablishmentism of their era, was a movement to make the high school curriculum more "relevant" and more "democratic." In many school systems, graduation requirements were eliminated, courses covering traditional academic subject matter were deemphasized, student-designed and student-taught courses were introduced, and academic credit was granted for off-campus programs, community involvement, and other nontraditional work.[55] By diminishing the influence of the organized academic disciplines in their pursuit of a more humane and democratic school system, however, the neo-Progressives reinforced the bias against universal academic education within public education by providing educators with an additional rationale for not teaching solid academic subject matter to all students.

In face of the long legacy of utilitarian thought and practice in public education, the school reformers of the 1980s advanced an unswervingly academic vision of secondary schooling. In an extensive body of articles, books, reports, essays, and other writings that formed the philosophical blueprint for the excellence movement, the intellectual leaders of the movement attacked educational utilitarianism and its underlying premises, and advocated in its place a new philosophical foundation for public secondary education, with educational excellence—a high level of *intellectual* training for *all* students—as its cornerstone.

Leading the campaign was a group of conservative and neoconservative academics, who laid much of the intellectual groundwork for the reform movement in the late 1970s and early 1980s. They included Joseph Adelson, professor of psychology at the University of Michigan; Nathan Glazer, professor of education and sociology at Harvard University and coeditor of the *Public Interest;* Denis P. Doyle, director of education studies at the American Enterprise Institute and later a Washington-based fellow in education at the Hudson Institute, a conservative policy organization; William J. Bennett, director of the National Humanities Center in the late 1970s, then chairman of the National Endowment for the Humanities during the Reagan administration's first term, and U.S. Secretary of Education during the second; Edward A. Wynne, professor of education at the University of Illinois–Chicago Circle; Gerald Grant, professor of education and sociology at Syracuse University; and Chester E. Finn, Jr., professor of education and public policy at Vanderbilt University in the early 1980s and later assistant U.S. Secretary of Education under Bennett. Through prolific writing in education journals and such conservative publications as *Commentary, American Scholar, Public Interest,* and *American Spectator;* as contributors to many of the major studies of public education in the early 1980s; as consultants to governors and state legislators; and by virtue of their roles within the Reagan administration or the visibility their work received from the federal government under Reagan, these critics of public education played a key part in shaping the reform movement.

Many of them backed a wide range of conservative education policies, from public funding of private schools to the abolition of sex education and other programs that were said to encourage "social permissiveness," an end to mandatory school-desegregation measures, and the easing of federal regulatory and judicial requirements in a host of areas, including bilingual education, student rights, and services for the handicapped. The conservative education agenda—which also was championed in the late 1970s by think tanks such as the Heritage Foundation and the Ethics and Public Policy Center, by Republican members of Congress such as Congressman Robert Bauman of Maryland, and editorially by *Fortune* magazine and the *Wall Street Journal*—was in turn part of the wide-ranging conservative intellectual and political assault on the liberal values and social policies of the 1960s and 1970s that landed Ronald Reagan in the White House. Conservative education critics saw public schools as a key battleground in the fight against liberalism. "Far more than any other institution in American society, the schools have become an arena for the struggle between the values of traditionalism and of modernity," Adelson wrote in a 1981 essay in *Commentary* entitled "What Happened to the Schools?"[56] One measure of education's importance to the conservative movement was the appointment early in the first Reagan administration of officials of the Moral Majority, the Conservative Caucus, the *National Review,* and other organizations of the ultraconservative New Right to senior positions in the U.S. Department of Education.[57] The school reform movement rejected the bulk of the larger conservative education agenda, but in their advocacy of an academic vision of public education, the conservatives gained allies from across the ideological spectrum.

In addition to defending their academic vision of public schooling on economic grounds, using the new-skills-for-a-new-workplace argument, the conservative critics attacked the educational liberalism of the 1960s and 1970s that discouraged the teaching of rigorous academic subjects to many students. They were harshly critical of public education's response to the civil rights and antipoverty movements of the 1960s, arguing that education policymakers, in their zeal to encourage the fullest possible participation of all students in the nation's educational system, had over-emphasized issues of educational access at the expense of the quality of academic programs.

No one made that charge more emphatically than Chester E. Finn, Jr., who, through the force of his provocative and extraordinarily prolific writings and his involvement in many early reform initiatives, was perhaps the single most powerful intellectual voice within the excellence movement in the early 1980s.[58] In a stinging indictment in a 1980 issue of *Change* magazine of what he called the prevailing "liberal consensus" in American education, Finn, who had worked in the Nixon White House and then as legislative director to Senator Daniel Patrick Moynihan before joining the faculty of Vanderbilt University in 1981, condemned the coalition of individuals and organizations that he argued had dominated education policymaking during the previous fifteen years for "a preoccupation with questions of educational equity and equality and a pronounced lack of interest in the issues of quality." The membership of the liberal consensus, according to Finn, included the Ford and Carnegie foundations; the elite graduate schools of education, such as those at Harvard, Stanford, and Columbia; the two major teachers unions and other national education associations; civil rights organizations; think tanks such as the Brookings Institution and the Aspen Institute; a small number of key congressmen; and the political appointees in the education agencies of the federal executive branch. It possessed "a near-boundless confidence in the ability of the national government to deploy its resources in ways that reduce the educational consequences of individual differences" but it displayed an "abhorrence" of "measures of educational achievement." Their zealous devotion to the achievement of educational equity—primarily through the federally enforced elimination of racial, sexual, cultural, language, physical, and economic barriers to equal educational opportunity—Finn charged, led the liberal consensus to define the success of schools in terms of the opportunities and resources provided to students rather than in terms of their academic achievement.[59] "Education's 'equity agenda' has much to do with participation and completion rates—the outward manifestations of educational successes—but it has very little to do with how much people actually learn," he argued in a later essay.[60]

Finn and other conservatives who were challenging public education's "preoccupation" with equal educational opportunity gained an important ally with the ascendancy of the Reagan administration in 1981. Within weeks of taking office, Secretary of Education Terrel Bell was calling for a reordering of national educational priorities. The result of the nation's "obsession" with equality of educational opportunity was a "neglect of quality," he charged in a speech to the annual convention of the American Association of School Administrators in February. Educators, he said, had "shrugged aside" their commitment to academic achievement. Bell, a lifelong public educator who had been U.S. commissioner of education during the Nixon and Ford administrations, dutifully supported the Reagan education agenda, endorsing tuition tax credits, the elimination of many federal education programs, budget cuts, and even the dismantling of the U.S. Department of Education, but it was especially in the effort to shift the focus of national educational policy from equity to excellence that Bell sought to take the lead within the Reagan administration. It was largely to that end that he created the National Commission on Excellence in Education in August 1981. And he returned to the theme repeatedly in his public statements. Bell's "excellence" campaign was overshadowed by other educational issues early in the first Reagan term, including the administration's proposals for dramatic cuts in federal education funding and elimination of the U.S. Department of Education, and Bell, who had been the thirteenth and last cabinet secretary appointed by the president, lacked the status to attract a sizable audience for his views. But with release of *A Nation at Risk* in April 1983 both Bell and his message were catapulted into the national spotlight.[61]

In addition, the conservatives' criticisms of the nation's pursuit of educational equity were echoed in several of the major reform reports published that year. The Twentieth Century Fund's education task force charged, in *Making the Grade*—a study for which Finn was a major writer—that federal efforts since the 1960s to desegregate the schools and to assist poor and handicapped students through the force of compulsory regulations and mandatory programs had "swelled school bureaucracies, imposed dubious and expensive procedures, and forced state and local governments to reallocate substantial portions of their scarce resources." The federal government's emphasis on promoting equality of opportunity in the public schools, the task force concluded, resulted in "a slighting of its commitment to educational quality." More delicately, the Bell commission said in *A Nation at Risk* that educational equity and academic excellence need to be pursued simultaneously. "We cannot permit one to yield to the other either in principle or in practice," the commission wrote. "To do so would deny young people their chance to learn and live according to their aspirations and abilities. It also would lead to a generalized accommodation to mediocrity in our society on the one hand or to the creation of an undemocratic elitism on the other." Even Ernest Boyer, president of the Carnegie Foundation for the Advancement of Teaching, who as chancellor of the state university system in New York and then as U.S. commissioner of education during the Carter administration had been a prominent player in the fight for educational equity (Finn included him among the leading lights of the "liberal consensus"), stated explicitly in *High School* that "academic quality" was the central theme of the foundation's report. Educational equity continued to be an important goal, he wrote in the report's preface, but it was best served by upgrading the quality of schooling.[62]

The conservative critics charged that the equity movement's emphasis on expanding students' educational opportunities (through, for instance, "open-enrollment" policies adopted by many public colleges and universities) encouraged educators to slacken their academic standards as a way of ensuring the "success" of the greatest possible number of students. They charged that within the equity movement the traditional measures of scholastic success (high school graduation and college admission) came to be seen not as rewards to be earned through achievement but as compensation that all students were entitled to, regardless of their performance. To the equity movement, they charged, high standards were a *barrier* to opportunities in education. It was the "conventional establishment-liberal" belief, Adelson wrote in a 1984 essay in *Commentary*, that "there is an implacable trade-off between excellence" and "equity" in education. Equity, to its proponents, "means leveling, which in turn means intellectual mediocrity; [and] mediocrity is the price we pay for universal education," he argued.[63]

Such logic, the conservative critics charged, led proponents of educational equity to take a "radically egalitarian" position: schools should secure for students not just equality of opportunity but equality of results as well; it led them to argue that policies and programs designed to help talented students were inherently discriminatory. Finn, especially, savaged such reasoning. "There is, and always will be, a fundamental difference between equality of opportunity and equality of result," he argued in a 1983 *Education Week* essay. "To deny people the former is undemocratic and evil. Even I have the right to train for the Olympics. But I'm not going to make it, let alone win a gold medal, and anyone who denounces as unjust a system that doesn't confer a gold medal on me is himself oblivious to the meaning of excellence."[64] Said then-Counselor to the President Edwin Meese III in a 1981 speech to California school administrators: "If equality of opportunity means a clear chance to grow as tall as you can intellectually, then we must not destroy the rights of our students who have been endowed with bright minds. They must have the right to become educationally unequal, in that they should be stimulated to rise to achievements of which they are capable."[65] In *A Nation at Risk*, the National Commission on Excellence in Education itself defined educational excellence primarily in terms of students "performing on the boundary of individual ability" and schools setting "high expectations."

The intellectual leaders of the reform movement also rejected the argument that it was discriminatory to expose a majority of students to demanding academic subject matter. "The important question is whether the regular public schools attended by the vast majority of American youngsters are going to allow the humanities to be scorned and dismissed on the absurd ground that they are elitist, thereby ensuring that they again become the property only of those already most aware of their value and their power," Finn and Ravitch wrote in *Against Mediocrity*, a 1984 collection of essays. "The fact is that opportunities to acquire a serious education in literature, history, and languages have largely been confined to the children of the very classes of society that most valued them as guarantors of their own secure positions."[66] The historian Christopher Lasch had made much the same argument in his 1978 book, *The Culture of Narcissism* (subtitled "American Life in an Age of Diminishing Expectations"). To exempt disadvantaged students from challenging academic work and high standards, Lasch argued, was to "condemn the lower class to a second-rate education and thus help to perpetuate the inequalities [social reformers] seek to abolish. In the name of egalitarianism, [those who advocate lower standards for lower-class students] preserve the most insidious form of elitism, which in one guise or another holds the masses incapable of intellectual exertion. . . . This attitude not only guarantees the monopolization of educational advantages by the few; it lowers the quality of elite education itself and threatens to bring about a reign of universal ignorance."[67]

Many less conservative voices within the reform movement also rejected the notions that universal academic education was undemocratic and academic subject matter beyond the reach of many students. In a 1984 essay in *Daedalus*, Patricia Albjerg Graham, dean of the Harvard Graduate School of Education, condemned the practice of lowering academic standards for "children for whom academic learning does not come easily." The pedagogy used to teach academic subject matter "will vary greatly among children, but the variance needs to be with the pedagogy, not with the rigor or content of the curriculum," she argued, adding that in diminishing the significance of mastery of traditional subject matter, educators eliminate "the prime educational means by which children could achieve a future, if they choose, different from the circumstances into which they had been born." In a 1985 tract entitled *Last Chance for Our Children*, Bill Honig, the California school superintendent, dismissed the arguments that high academic standards were elitist and discriminatory as "well-intentioned but absolutely poisonous sentiments in nominal defense of minority rights." "In too many instances," he argued the same year before a California legislative committee, "we have betrayed the democratic dream by operating our schools as if only the more advanced student could understand and appreciate our cultural, political, and ethical ideals." Honig's purpose in *Last Chance*, he stated in a prefatory note, was "to build the case for traditional education." Honig described himself as an "essentialist," after a group of educators who in the 1930s formed the Essentialist Committee for the Advancement of American Education to defend traditional academic subject matter against the spreading influence of utilitarianism in American education. Honig, however, emphatically rejected conservative education goals such as school prayer and tuition tax credits.[68]

In rejecting the equity movement's arguments against high academic standards, the reformers in effect redefined what "equal educational opportunity" was. Simply ensuring that all students had access to the nation's educational mainstream was no longer enough to fulfill the requirements of "equal opportunity" in education; rather, an "equal" education was one that challenged all students to the limits of their intellectual abilities and held high academic expectations of them. "Real educational opportunity means equal intellectual challenge for all students," said Bennett in a report he authored as U.S. secretary of education.[69]

However, while Honig, Graham, and other moderate reformers accompanied their calls for a traditional language-based curriculum and high standards with warnings that many students would need substantial academic reinforcement to meet such standards, the conservative reformers typically sought to emphasize the link between high standards and academic competition. There was a strand of educational Darwinism woven into the conservative critique of the equity movement. "The function of standards is to distinguish those who achieve them from those who do not," Finn argued in his 1983 *Education Week* essay, in which he endorsed a "strategy of setting standards and letting those affected decide how hard to push themselves to attain those standards." "[P]latoons of educators and child developers . . . would shield youngsters from awareness that the race is to the swift, insulate them from competitiveness, protect them from anxiety . . . ," he charged in an essay in the *American Spectator.* Competition, conservatives argued, was at the heart of a successful educational system. "Without competition, there can be no champions, no records broken, no increasing degrees of excellence," Meese told his audience of California school administrators in 1981. "Excellence in education demands competition—competition among students and competition among schools." Though quick to attack the "devastation" they said was wrought by the equity movement on the nation's educational system, many conservative critics were reluctant to acknowledge the widespread inequality of opportunity in the system that spawned the educational equity movement.[70]

The excellence movement was also fueled by another aspect of the conservative backlash to the educational liberalism of the 1960s and 1970s: in building their case for excellence, the reformers attacked the resurgence during the era of the Progressive doctrine of "child-centeredness." They decried attempts by educators in the 1960s and 1970s to tailor course content and teaching to the individual "needs" and supposed interest of students. In practice, the conservative critics charged, neo-Progressivism led to a deemphasis of academic subject matter and to an excessive emphasis on students' affective, or emotional, well-being at the expense of their intellectual development. The "open-education" movement of the era, in particular, with its stress on an unstructured curriculum, students as "agents" of their own learning, and a less prominent role for teachers in the classroom, dulled the academic edge of the nation's schools, they charged.

Prominent among the critical commentary on child-centeredness, and on educational Progressivism generally, was that of the historian Diane Ravitch. During the early stages of the excellence movement, Ravitch, an adjunct professor at Teachers College, Columbia University, was among the vocal advocates of a traditional, academic-oriented education. And in 1983 she published *The Troubled Crusade,* which included an unflattering portrait of both the evolution of educational Progressivism during the first half of the century and its resurgence in the 1960s and 1970s. Appearing as it did, just as the reform movement was spreading across the nation (the timing was largely coincidental, for the book was seven years in the making), Ravitch's book was a boon to the conservative campaign against the liberal educational doctrine of the previous two decades.

Though she said that there was "much in the progressive program that promised to improve education"—including its calls for less rote instruction, a more engaging curriculum, and an awareness of individual differences among children—Ravitch charged that in the end, the Progressive era in education was marked not only by "extremes of permissiveness in the child-centered movement" but also by "hostility toward books and subject matter," "excessive vocationalism," "rampant utilitarianism," and "the notion that the school was uniquely qualified to meet all needs without establishing priorities among them." The same charges applied to the neo-Progressive period of the 1960s and 1970s.[71]

Conservatives echoed Ravitch's critique. Andrew Oldenquist, an Ohio State University philosophy professor, charged in a 1983 issue of *American Education* that during the previous two decades "self-esteem became the chief good to be achieved by schooling." Instruction focused on "emotions and feelings" became "a booming industry through the 70's," he wrote, while cognitive education became "an embarrassment." "At almost every moment during the last two decades, the schools and the young have been held hostage to our fantasies," Joseph Adelson argued in a 1984 essay in *Commentary.* "[W]hy is it that a James Joyce could be delivered out of the most rigid Jesuitical circumstances, whereas a hundred Summerhills have yet to deliver a James Joyce?" he wrote in reference to the English boarding school founded by a strict adherent to child-centered principles, A. S. Neill, whose 1960 book by the same name played a central role in the revival of educational Progressivism in the 1960s. "Parents are slow in realizing how unimportant the learning side of school is," Neill had written. "Children, like adults, learn what they want to learn. All prize-giving and marks and exams sidetrack proper personality development."[72]

Yet it was not only conservatives who decried the influence of Progressive pedagogical doctrine on public education. Harvard education dean Graham, an education historian, threw the influence of her prominent position within the American education establishment behind the criticism of what she called the "disastrous" consequences of educational Progressivism "partially achieved." In her 1984 *Daedalus* essay, Graham charged that under the guise of ministering to the individual needs and interests of students, educators too often "reinforced expectations associated not with the individual child but with the child's individual circumstances." In many instances, she argued, the schools merely "galvanized the iron cloak of race, class, ethnicity, and sex as the determinants of the child's future," and concern for the individual student thus often "led not to increased learning, but to acceptance of expected poor performance." Graham charged that "being child-centered in the school was absolutely consistent with being opposed to being subject-centered," and she decried the hostility of Progressive educators to academic subject matter as "an abdication of professional responsibility." "We must reject the tired vestiges of progressive education that still dominate much of the educational practice of the schools," she wrote in urging "the primacy of mind and intellect" in public education.[73]

The school reformers also defended their academic vision of secondary schooling on cultural grounds. They argued that literature, history, civics, and other academic subjects were the repositories of the nation's cultural heritage, and that by failing to teach the academic disciplines seriously to many students, the public schools were shirking their responsibility to perpetuate the nation's cultural institutions and values.

Lacking a common curriculum in its schools, American society was drifting dangerously close to losing "its coherence as a culture," argued E. D. Hirsch, Jr., a professor of English at the University of Virginia, in a widely publicized 1983 essay in the *American Scholar* entitled "Cultural Literacy." "We need to connect more of our students to our history, our culture, and those ideas which hold us together as a society," argued Honig in a speech to the American Association of School Administrators in 1985. "Schools are a key institution for transmitting . . . knowledge of and allegiance to our national experience and beliefs." "We're not even getting the most elementary facts about who we are across to students," he argued in *Last Chance for Our Children*.[74]

The same arguments resonated in many of the major reform reports of the early 1980s. Repeatedly, the reports pointed to a need for greater "cultural literacy" in endorsing a common academic curriculum for all students. "For mutual understanding and responsible debate among the citizens of a democratic community, and for differences of opinion to be aired and resolved, citizens must be able to communicate with one another in a common language," said the authors of *The Paideia Proposal.* "*Language* in this sense involves a common vocabulary of ideas." In *High School*, Ernest Boyer of the Carnegie Foundation argued that "the basic curriculum for all students . . . is a study of those consequential ideas, experiences, and traditions common to all of us by virtue of our membership in the human family at a particular moment in history." Similarly, the national commission warned in *A Nation at Risk*, "A high level of shared education is essential to a free, democratic society and to the fostering of a common culture, especially in a country that prides itself on pluralism and individual freedom." Education, the commission said, must be the "common bond of a pluralistic society."[75]

There were many negative consequences of public education's failure to teach cultural literacy, the reformers argued. E. D. Hirsch, Jr., maintained in his much-publicized 1983 essay in the *American Scholar,* and in a 1987 book by the same name, that cultural literacy was crucial to the learning process itself. The development of reading and writing skills, he argued, was far more dependent than had been thought previously on students' understanding of the cultural context of language. "Literacy involves more than just phonics, spelling, vocabulary, and well-grooved reading habits," he wrote. "We have discovered that true literacy also requires specific background knowledge about the human and natural worlds. Literacy is not just a skill, but also a system of background knowledge shared between writer and reader. . . . To grasp the words on a page we have to know a lot of information that isn't set down on the page." "Given our newly gained understanding of literacy, we must be traditionalists about content. For we have learned the paradox that traditional education, which alone yields the flexible skill of mature literacy, outperforms utilitarian education even by utilitarian standards."[76]

The importance Hirsch and others placed on cultural literacy contrasted sharply with the priorities of the so-called minimum-basic-skills movement that swept through the nation's school systems in the late 1970s. Though viewed by many as a precursor to the excellence movement, the basic-skills campaign sought only to ensure that high school graduates possessed the reading, writing, and mathematical skills they needed to function as literate members of society. It paid scant attention to the cultural content of the curriculum. Indeed, many within the excellence movement repudiated the basic-skills movement, on the grounds that it did little to promote cultural literacy, but also because it focused instruction on low-level skills that were believed to be inadequate for the workplace of the future. The basic-skills movement "meant a classroom emphasis on drill, rote learning, and the mastery of fundamentals through repetition. Traditional education, as I understand it, implies a much more expansive, ennobling, and—in the best sense—ambitious program," said Honig in *Last Chance for Our Children*. The phrase "back to basics" referred in the 1970s to instruction in literacy skills; to the reformers of the 1980s, it meant a renewed emphasis on traditional academic subjects.[77]

Meanwhile, Bennett and others argued that cultural literacy was crucial to the maintenance of Western political and intellectual traditions. In an address to the Columbia College Club of Washington in 1987, one of the many times he returned to the theme, Bennett called for "the systematic study of Western civilization and traditions" in the nation's schools and colleges because, he said, "the West is under attack—aggressively from without, and less obviously but no less seriously from within." "For some 15 to 20 years now, there has been a serious degree of embarrassment, of distancing, even of repudiation of [the ideals of Western civilization] on the part of many of the people whose responsibility, one would think, is to transmit it," he charged in a 1985 newspaper interview. The year before, in a report he authored as chairman of the National Endowment for the Humanities, he had written, "The West is ours. . . . The West is good." Students "are now being deprived of the very culture that created the past, sustains the present, and should continue to shape the future," he said in calling for "a core of common study" for all students in "the history, litera-ture, art and philosophical foundations of our civilization."[78]

Bennett and his conservative allies saw the defense of Western culture in the schools at least partly in terms of a struggle against communism, and their discussions of cultural literacy included much anticommunist rhetoric. The nation's schools must "make the case for our political sys-tem," Bennett said in 1985. "If students have never heard of the Cuban missile crisis, they cannot comprehend the Sandinista head of secret police when he states that 'Cuba's friends are Nicaragua's friends, and Cuba's enemies are Nicaragua's enemies.' " The schools, he said, should transmit "a particular heritage, a distinct set of social and political val-ues," and, in particular, it was their responsibility to teach students that "the United States is morally superior to the Soviet Union."[79]

The conservative defense of "the West" culminated in 1988 in a pitched battle in the nation's magazines and op-ed pages between Ben-nett and his critics over a decision by the faculty of Stanford University to replace a required freshman course, "Western Culture," with a course entitled "Cultures, Ideas and Values," which placed somewhat less em-phasis on fifteen "classic texts" and required inclusion of writings by "women, minorities, and persons of color." Bennett charged in a speech at Stanford that the faculty's action would "trivialize" the university's academic enterprise.

Liberals and conservatives alike took the stance that the public schools should strengthen the moral education of the nation's students by teach-ing the Western cultural canon universally. The schools, they charged, were failing to bring a moral dimension to learning. "We are woefully short on teaching ethics and morality," said Secretary of Education Bell in 1981.

Literature, history, and other academic disciplines were valuable vehi-cles for teaching secular values such as honesty, integrity, tolerance, dili-gence, respect for law, fidelity, fairness, magnanimity, and self-discipline, the reformers argued. "Exposure to the cultural heritage carries with it a powerful message," wrote Honig in *Last Chance,* in which he included examples of "the great stories in our tradition"—Icarus flying toward the sun on wings of wax; Oliver Twist asking for a second bowl of gruel; Nathan Hale's dying words; Penelope at the loom. Those stories, he said, "speak to us with the force of parable about the perils of pride and greed and honor of patriotism and fidelity." "In the end," he wrote, "the moral sensibility and social conscience of a civilization can only be learned by reading and discussing the classic works of its literature and history and the biographies of its exemplars."[80]

Schools, Honig argued, should have an "explicitly moral tenor"; they should consciously cultivate "common cultural values." He rejected the position that public schools, because they are public, "must wear the

institutional poker-face of moral neutrality." "People have to feel con-
nected to a shared moral community." He and others made frequent
references to the Judeo-Christian roots of American "secular" values.
"The most acceptable American secular ethic is a direct extension of
Judeo-Christian teaching and cannot be detached from it, however hard
the constitutional lawyers may labor," wrote Theodore Sizer in *Horace's
Compromise.* Nonetheless, "traditionalists" like Honig and Sizer were
quick to disassociate themselves from calls by conservatives to use religious practices in the schools as a means of teaching morality. There is "a
difference between those who want group prayer in the public schools (a
practice of religion) and those who want moral content in the curriculum
(a fundamental purpose of the schools)," Honig declared. He advocated
a middle position, "between the equally unacceptable poles of religious
dogmatism and institutionalized public amorality."[81]

Finally, the reformers argued that the low level of cultural literacy
among public school students, and in particular their poor knowledge of
civics, rendered many students incapable of effectively fulfilling their
responsibilities as citizens. The reformers pointed to a plethora of evidence suggesting that Jefferson's warning on the need to "inform the
discretion" of citizens in a democracy was going unheeded. One frequently cited survey of seventeen-year-olds, for example, revealed that
two-thirds of the students tested were unable to locate the Civil War
within the correct half century and nearly one in three did not know that
Columbus reached the New World before 1750.[82]

Conservatives within the reform movement blamed the public schools'
failure to teach cultural literacy primarily on what they said was a preoccupation with pluralism and an adherence to "radical individualism"
among educators and within contemporary thought generally. Their attacks on pluralism and individualism represented another aspect of the
conservative backlash in the late 1970s and 1980s against the legacy of
the antiestablishmentism and civil rights movements of the previous two
decades.

In the 1960s and 1970s, argued Oldenquist in his essay in *American
Education,* education professors and social scientists "preached the equal
rights of individuals to respect, to reward, even to truth itself; they taught
the supremacy of self-interest over the common good, of the emotions
over knowledge and intellect, of children's autonomy over society's need
for their socialization. . . . For educational policy, it followed that academic standards had to be subjectified, made a matter of self-expression,
sincerity, and good will."[83]

In a 1984 essay in *Education Week,* Allan C. Carlson of the Rockford
Institute, a conservative, Illinois-based research center, spoke of an "in-
ner contradiction" within public education. "On one hand," he wrote,
"public educators still claim that the work that clearly sets them apart

from the private schools is the binding together, or integration, of a pluralistic society through the inculcation of 'public values.' For example, the National Education Association declared in 1982 that 'Free public schools are the cornerstone of our social, economic, and political structures and are of utmost significance in development of our moral, ethical, spiritual, and cultural values.' " Yet, "the educational hierarchy has come to deny that there is or should be any single national identity. In its vast array of 1982 policy statements, the NEA never once referred positively to matters such as patriotism, sexual modesty, family stability, religious belief, the free market, or traditional American ideals." Rather, Carlson charged, the teachers union "forcefully encouraged" such causes as "educational self-determination" for Hispanics and endorsed "multicultural/global education" as "a way of helping every student perceive the cultural diversity of U.S. citizenry so that children of many races may develop pride in their own cultural legacy." The public schools, Carlson concluded, were "actively engaged in the negation of national identity through support for an absolute pluralism."[84]

The intellectual leaders of the reform movement rejected what they said was the contemporary argument that in a nation as culturally pluralistic as the United States, a "national culture" was impossible. When participants at a 1984 conference on the California history curriculum argued with Nathan I. Huggins, professor of history and Afro-American studies at the Du Bois Institute at Harvard, that "to talk about a common culture in a nation with as much diversity as this one requires such a level of abstraction as to make it meaningless," Bennett, who was then chairman of the National Endowment for the Humanities, countered that "the public school is not principally an international food fair for the mind. We cannot do justice in depth for all and to all that is diverse about us. . . . The thing I reject is the notion that there is no story that applies to all of us."[85]

The reformers similarly rejected the charge that teaching all students a core of cultural knowledge drawn from traditional academic studies smacked of "cultural imperialism." "Objectors have said that traditional [academic] materials are class-bound, white, Anglo-Saxon, and Protestant, not to mention racist, sexist, and excessively Western," wrote Hirsch in *Cultural Literacy: What Every American Needs to Know,* his 1987 book. But "the claim that universal cultural literacy would have the effect of preserving the political and social status quo is paradoxical because in fact the traditional forms of literate culture are precisely the most effective instruments for political and social change." As evidence, Hirsch pointed to *The Black Panther,* which he said was "a radical and revolutionary newspaper if ever this country had one," but a paper "highly conservative in its language and cultural assumptions." Teaching students "traditional information by no means indoctrinates them in a conservative point of view," said Hirsch. Honig made the same argument in *Last Chance for Our Chil-*

dren. "Steeping students in the ideas, personalities and stories of our civilization is not an indoctrination that warps," he wrote. "Ultimately, all the traditional curriculum makes absolutely certain is that students will be confronted with the important questions in life. How they answer them is, and must remain, up to them." As evidence of the extremes to which they argued the commitment to cultural pluralism was pursued during the 1960s and 1970s, Honig and others pointed to a 1977 ruling by a federal judge requiring reading teachers in Ann Arbor, Michigan, to undergo training in "black English" on the grounds that black students there were being denied equal educational opportunity because their teachers were insensitive to the fact that they spoke "an identifiable dialect of the English language."[86]

Educators' unrestrained devotion to pluralism and individualism encouraged the spread of moral and cultural "relativism" within the nation's educational system, the conservative intellectual leaders of the reform movement charged. Bennett argued in his Columbia College Club address that Western culture was under attack from educators "so blinded by subjectivism and relativism that they cannot discern the qualities and importance their own intellectual legacy represents." For nearly two decades, he declared in a 1985 speech, "the teaching of social studies in our schools has been dominated by cultural relativism," the belief that "all cultures and traditions are equally valid, that there are no real criteria for good and bad, right and wrong, noble and base."[87]

One of the most outspoken critics of "relativism" in the schools was Syracuse University sociologist Gerald Grant. In a widely publicized 1981 essay in *Daedalus* entitled "The Character of Education and the Education of Character," Grant attacked the public schools for "prematurely declaring that children are adults capable of choosing their own morality as long as they don't commit crimes." In many schools, he said, "all behavior is regarded as tolerable unless it is specifically declared illegal." Grant argued that in a "democratic pluralistic society" there must be "salient or core beliefs to which all subscribe"; without them, "one does not have a public but a kind of radical relativism, not pluralism but mere coexistence." But, said Grant, there was a "crisis of authority" in the American school; "in many places, we no longer have any agreement on what that provisional morality ought to be, or we feel that any attempt to provide it is a form of indoctrination." "We need to reinvent a modern equivalent for the McGuffey's Reader, a provisional morality that expresses some of the common beliefs of a democratic pluralist society."[88]

To Grant and other intellectuals within the reform movement, nothing epitomized the ethical relativism of the schools as did "values clarification," an instructional program introduced in the early 1970s to provide teachers with techniques to help students identify feelings, ideas, and beliefs without imposing external values on them. The basic assumption of values clarification, said Sidney B. Simon, a University of Massachusetts education professor who became the concept's leading advocate, was that "none of us has the 'right' set of values to pass on to other people's children." The reformers attacked that stance. In a 1978 essay in *Public Interest,* Bennett blasted values clarification for treating "moral life as though it consisted essentially of dilemmas and highly problematic choices, ignoring the important, unproblematic affairs of morality." In an interview with the *Claremont Review of Books* in 1982, he charged that "the mistake in the values clarification movement is the unwillingness to argue for certain reasonable standards of right and wrong. The relativism or subjectivism that one finds either implicit or explicit in much of the so-called values movement of our time is both offensive and pernicious." Honig was no less harsh on values clarification: "While pretending to Olympian detachment in its neutrality on moral issues, values clarification actually affirms the shallowest kind of ethical relativism. It tells students that on matters of profound moral significance, their opinion— no matter how ill-informed, far-fetched, or speciously reasoned—is all that counts. Ethics and morals are reduced to matters of personal taste." It was, he said, a "blithe invitation to moral anarchy."[89]

In addition to encouraging a relativistic morality within public schools, the strong devotion within public education to pluralism and individualism had led to an instructional emphasis in the nation's classrooms on skills rather than on subject matter, to a "formalistic" approach to learning, the reformers stated. The unwillingness of educators to define the cultural content of the curriculum caused them to embrace the mistaken belief "that we can teach our children *how* to think without troubling them to learn anything worth thinking about, the belief that we can teach them *how* to understand the world in which they live without conveying to them the events and ideas that have brought it into existence," argued Lynn V. Cheney, Bennett's successor as chairperson of the National Endowment for the Humanities, in a report to Congress on the status of the humanities in the nation's public schools. Cheney acknowledged in her report the significance of both the "how" and the "what" of learning. "Both are important, extremely important in the teaching of history and literature," but so much emphasis has been placed on "process" in learning, she declared, "that content has been seriously neglected." "One can see the imbalance in the opening pages of a teacher's guide to a widely used textbook series," she wrote. "Scores of skills to be taught are set forth, everything from drawing conclusions and predicting outcomes to filling in forms and following recipes. The cultural content of learning, on the other hand, is given only brief mention." "Long relied on to transmit knowledge of the past to upcoming generations, our schools today appear to be about a different task. Instead of preserving the past, they more often disregard it."[90]

Bennett, too, attacked what he called "curricular relativism," the belief that "it doesn't matter what a person is taught, but only how a person is taught." "This theory is wrong and misleading and conspires with an equally dangerous theory that content is not really important because American culture has become too fragmented and pluralistic to justify a belief in common learning," he stated in a 1985 speech to school administrators.[91]

The assault on relativism in American education culminated in publication in 1987 of two best-selling books on the subject. One was Hirsch's *Cultural Literacy*. Like Bennett and Cheney, Hirsch blamed curricular "formalism" for the failure of the schools to promote cultural literacy. "The whole conceptual basis of the curriculum as inculcating skills independently of specific content has been wrong—fundamentally so."[92] The public schools "have been attracted irresistibly to a quantitative and formal approach to curriculum making, rather than one based on sound judgments about what should be taught." The reason, Hirsch stated, is that the formalistic notion that "any suitable content will inculcate reading, writing, and thinking skills" held "political advantages for school administrators"—it allowed them "to stay scrupulously neutral with regard to content," to "regard the indiscriminate variety of school offerings as a positive virtue, on the grounds that such variety can accommodate the different interests and abilities of different students."[93]

Helped by the inclusion of a provocative list of 5,000 pieces of cultural knowledge—ranging from black holes to Humpty Dumpty—that Hirsch said all truly literate Americans should have at least a passing familiarity with, *Cultural Literacy* was a publishing sensation, the subject of cover stories in newsmagazines and a best-seller in both hard-cover and paperback editions. By early 1990 there were over half a million copies of the book in print.

The Closing of the American Mind reached a huge audience as well. Written by Allan Bloom, a professor of social thought at the University of Chicago, it, too, warned of the diminishing knowledge among recent generations of students of the nation's cultural and intellectual traditions. "We are like ignorant shepherds living on a site where great civilizations once flourished," said Bloom. "The shepherds play with the fragments that pop up to the surface, having no notion of the beautiful structures of which they were once a part." In the most widely publicized and undoubtedly the harshest of the indictments of "modernism" in the 1980s, Bloom too blamed the decline of cultural literacy on the moral and cultural relativisms that he said were the guiding principles of the nation's academic institutions. "Openness" was the distinguishing characteristic of contemporary American intellectual life. Not an openness "that invites us to the quest for knowledge and certitude, for which history and the various cultures provide a brilliant array of examples for examination," but an openness of "indifference." "There is no hierarchy of good and bad" in American education, he charged; students are taught "the relativity of truth," the result being a decline of intellectual standards, an increasing irrelevance within academia of the traditional "great books" and the Western culture that they represent, and a weakening of the "social contract." Bloom, suggesting as he did in *Closing of the American Mind* that there was room in the curriculum only for classical works traditionally taught, was on the ultraconservative fringe of the reform movement. But with over 900,000 copies of the book in print, his was nonetheless an influential voice in the intellectual climate from which the movement emerged.[94]

There have been strong advocates of an academic vision of public secondary education in the past, of course—most notably the Committee of Ten at the turn of the century and the Sputnik-era critics of educational Progressivism. The historian Arthur Bestor, one of the leading commentators of the Sputnik period, wrote in his influential 1953 book, *Educational Wastelands*, that the *raison d'être* of all education was "the deliberate cultivation of the ability to think" through training in the academic disciplines. Bestor and such contemporaries as Robert Maynard Hutchins, Mortimer Smith, and Paul Woodring argued, as did the traditionalists of the 1980s after them, that a truly democratic education was one that made available to all students the caliber of intellectual training that traditionally had been reserved for the privileged few.[95]

But the intellectual leaders of the excellence movement fundamentally redefined the academic vision of the Committee of Ten and the Sputnik-era critics. In practical terms, the earlier calls for educational excellence did not pertain to all students in the nation. The Committee of Ten focused its attention on only "that small proportion of all the children in the country . . . who show themselves able to profit by an education prolonged to the eighteenth year, and whose parents are able to support them while they remain so long at school." And in the Sputnik era the nation still lived largely in official innocence of race and poverty; the reformers of that period concentrated on preparing the academic elite among the nation's students to meet the challenges of Soviet technological advances.[96]

Only after the conscience of the nation had been transformed by the crucible of civil rights were the full implications of universal academic secondary education able to be considered. Its shortcomings notwithstanding, the equity movement permanently altered the moral landscape in American education, establishing the widest possible participation in the educational mainstream as a national priority. In this changed environment, the school reformers' calls for educational excellence in the 1980s implied much more than did similar exhortations in earlier eras: for the first time, the full range of students served by the nation's public secondary schools were included in the excellence equation.

Texas: The Reform Battle in the States, Writ Large

With the nation's governors in the vanguard of the reform movement, the particulars of the excellence campaign were hammered out largely in state capitals. As a result, the school reformers had to carry their message to the state legislatures. And because the excellence movement sought major funding increases for public education, as well as controversial changes in educational policy, winning legislative backing for the excellence agenda was no simple task. Desite a fertile national climate for reform and strong intellectual backing for new priorities in public education, it took an enormous amount of political will to transform the reformers' blueprints for educational excellence into new policies and programs in the states.

Nowhere was the legislative battle more intense or the political drama greater than in Texas. True to the state's sense of scale, Texas lawmakers debated and eventually enacted one of the most sweeping packages of educational reforms in the nation. The passage of the omnibus Texas Educational Opportunity Act of 1984 is the story of the legislative phase of the excellence movement writ large. It is the story of the powerful public commitment to new educational goals in the 1980s; of the many forces that influenced the reform agenda in the states; and, perhaps above all, of the immense political resistance to reform that must be surmounted if rigorous academic instruction is to be a universal priority in the nation's schools.

In January 1983 Mark White was a newly elected governor with a political promise to keep. Needing a boost in his campaign to unseat the Republican incumbent, William P. Clements, Jr., in the elections of the previous November, White had sought the help of the state's campaign-savvy teachers unions by pledging higher pay in public education. The state affiliates of the National Education Association and the American Federation of Teachers, representing some 65 percent of Texas's huge 170,000-member teaching force, liked what they heard and in 1982 mobilized thousands of members in White's name to register voters, staff phone banks, walk precincts, write letters, raise money, and get out the vote. To those in Austin who followed the race, the unions had made the difference in White's 233,000-vote victory. So it did not come as a surprise when on January 27, White, in his first speech to the Texas legislature, called for an "emergency" increase in teachers' pay of "at least" 24 percent, a proposal with a $1.5 billion price tag.

In fact, it had been easy for White, a former Texas attorney general with a law degree from Baylor University, to make such a pledge during the campaign. Texas's oil-based economy had temporarily spared the state from the recession that ravaged the nation in 1981–82, and as late as September 1982 it enjoyed a budget surplus of $5.1 billion. The reserves were so great that White also was able to promise during the campaign that if elected he would not raise taxes.

But the surplus didn't hold. The state's economy began to soften under the pressure of the national recession, the February 1982 devaluation of the peso, and a drop in oil revenues after the OPEC countries cut their oil prices in March 1983, a move that drove down the price of Texas crude. Nine weeks after White's address to the legislature, the surplus was only 45 percent of what it was in September and still shrinking.

Just after taking office, then, White was in the awkward position of having to break one campaign promise or another; with the surplus drying up, a substantial pay hike for teachers would require new taxes. The governor decided to keep his promise to the teachers. On March 8 he called for higher taxes on "luxuries which people choose to consume and not on necessities which people need to survive." On May 13 he provided the specifics: a doubling of the taxes on beer, liquor, and video machines, and a nickel increase on a pack of cigarettes and on a gallon of gas. But two key legislators, Stanley Schlueter, who as chairman of the House Ways and Means Committee was the gatekeeper of Texas revenue bills, and Gibson Lewis, the newly elected speaker of the House, balked. Both viewed a huge, across-the-board pay raise as a dubious investment. Many teachers, they argued, didn't deserve the increase.

In the midst of the debate—just eighteen days before the governor announced the details of his tax plan—the National Commission on Excellence in Education released its wide-ranging indictment of American public schools at the White House. The commission urged in *A Nation at Risk* that good teachers be paid more than poor ones.

While the teachers unions led protax marches on the capitol, White pushed his tax plan on statewide television, calling on citizens to write their legislators in support of the plan. He even flew into Lewis's district to protest the speaker's opposition to it. Finally, with only days left in the 1983 legislative session, he offered to alter his tax package, to substitute tax "reforms" for new taxes. The legislature didn't budge.

Stymied, but anxious to save face with the unions, White, at the urging of Lewis and others in the House, called for the legislature to create a gubernatorially appointed panel to "study" the teacher-salary issue. (White, the son and husband of former teachers, was so popular with the unions at that time that in July the NEA invited him to address its convention in Philadelphia.) Exuding public confidence that the findings of such a panel would justify his tax plan, the governor vowed to call the legislature into special session "as soon as [the panel] can come up with a report on the salary needs of the teachers."[1] He suggested an August deadline.

In reality, the strategy was as vulnerable as it was expedient. If White packed the panel with teacher representatives and others from the education establishment, its recommendations would have little credibility. If he appointed "outsiders," those whose judgment on taxes was likely to be accepted by the state's powerful business leaders and their fiscally conservative allies in the legislature, he might not get the recommendations he was looking for. But there was really no choice to make. Without the support of big business, there was little chance of talking the legislature into raising taxes. So, on June 16 White called a press conference at his office in the capitol in Austin and told the state that he had appointed as chairman of the newly created Select Committee on Public Education (SCOPE) H. Ross Perot, a self-made Dallas billionaire, staunch antiunionist, and active supporter of White's Republican opponent in the 1982 gubernatorial campaign.

SCOPE indeed was not the panel White wanted it to be. Established under House Concurrent Resolution 275 late on May 30 (the last day of the 1983 legislative session), both its membership and mission had been transformed by the leaders of the legislature, Speaker Lewis and his Senate counterpart, Lieutenant Governor William Hobby. The resolution gave the governor only five appointments, including the chairmanship, to the twenty-two-member committee, the same number allotted to Lewis and to Hobby. It reserved places on the panel for the governor, the chairmen of the House and Senate education committees, and for the chairman and two other members of the State Board of Education. But it also included Hobby and Lewis, Ways and Means Committee Chairman Schlueter, his Senate counterpart (Finance Committee Chairman Grant Jones), and Robert Bullock, the state's elected comptroller. They were five extraordinarily influential foxes in the Governor's tax-hike henhouse. Just to be safe, Hobby assigned two of his top aides to staff the committee. No teachers were appointed to SCOPE.

Moreover, instead of focusing on "the salary needs of teachers," Resolution 275 instructed SCOPE "to study the issues and continuing concerns related to public education in Texas,"[2] a far more open-ended mandate than that envisioned by the governor. Before it started talking taxes, the legislature wanted to know what it was going to get for its money. It wanted an investigation of Texas public education, an $8 billion-a-year industry that educated nearly 8 percent of the nation's public school students.

When he agreed to head SCOPE, Ross Perot knew practically nothing about the education enterprise in Texas, other than what he remembered of the Texarkana public schools he had attended during the depression and World War II. But he believed in public service. And it was his conviction that without decent public schools the talents of many—especially the underprivileged—would remain uncultivated.[3] As a businessman, he saw a key role for education in weaning the Texas economy from its overdependence on oil and gas. The public posturing by the governor and the unions on the salary issue notwithstanding, Perot intended to take Resolution 275's call for a report card on Texas education seriously. "We will not be sunshine soldiers," he warned on the eve of the first SCOPE hearing.

The truth was, Perot had thrived on challenges all his life. As a young computer salesman in the early 1960s, he had proposed to his superiors at the International Business Machines Corporation that the company sell data-processing services as well as computers. Told there was no market for such a "product," he quit the company, took $1,000 out of the bank, founded Electronic Data Systems Corporation in 1962, and built it into a billion-dollar enterprise in seven years. He became known throughout Texas as a modern-day Horatio Alger, and the label appeared to fit. Crew-cut, given to hard work and straight talk, loyal to family and country, Perot was "squeaky clean" in the eyes of friends and foes alike. His taste in art—Norman Rockwell originals, the Wild West bronzes of Frederick Remington, a Gilbert Stewart portrait of George Washington—suggested as much.

But as a corporate chairman, Perot was something less than orthodox. In the early 1970s, for example, the shah of Iran awarded EDS a $45 million contract to set up and operate an Iranian social security system. In December of 1978, with the shah in exile and his country in the throes of revolution, the two top EDS executives in Iran were abducted and held for ransom in Tehran's Gasr Prison. When high-level diplomatic negotiations failed to win their release, Perot sent in his own commando team of volunteer EDS employees, under the leadership of a former Green Beret colonel. After six weeks in captivity, the two executives were freed in February, when revolutionaries of the Ayatollah Khomeini, led by an Iranian working for the EDS team, stormed the prison. They escaped overland to Turkey, where Perot, who had turned the operation of EDS over to others while he spent millions of dollars and hundreds of hours orchestrating "Operation Hotfoot," was waiting for them. In mid-January, just days before the ayatollah had returned from exile in France, Perot himself had gone to Gasr to visit his imprisoned employees, after entering Iran aboard a rented Learjet from Aman, Jordan, disguised as a film courier for NBC News.[4]

Perot's flamboyance—and his intense patriotism—had surfaced a decade earlier, when he volunteered to carry out a campaign contrived by the Nixon White House to publicize the plight of American prisoners of war in Vietnam, who the White House charged were being held by Hanoi outside the strictures of the Geneva Convention. Unsatisfied with the timetable for a media campaign proposed by J. Walter Thompson, the giant advertising agency, he assembled a team of EDS employees who called editors and wrote the campaign's advertising copy themselves. The effort unleashed a torrent of mail on Hanoi. Perot also met with North Vietnamese officials in Laos and helped raise money to send people to Paris to press North Vietnamese diplomats there. Just before Christmas of that year, Perot tried to land in Hanoi (he was aboard one of two planes he had chartered) with dinners and presents for the American captives. Though his planes were turned away by the North Vietnamese, the stunt gained worldwide attention and helped prod Hanoi to release the names of many American prisoners.[5]

But in the summer of 1983, Perot's attention was focused on education.

In retrospect, SCOPE's strategy was in place by the time of the committee's initial meeting, on July 13 in Austin. On one hand, it needed, naturally, to educate itself about the issues it faced before it could recommend reforms. As a first step, its members received copies of and testimony on the national education reports that had been released in the spring and were receiving widespread attention. In fact, the emergence of education as a national issue (emphasized for Texans in August, when the National Conference of State Legislators gathered in San Antonio for its annual meeting and hundreds of participants packed sessions on education reform) lent an air of immediacy to the committee's work. To the Texas media, it gave the SCOPE investigation an important context, thereby making it more newsworthy.

The national debate complemented the second part of SCOPE's strategy, which was to bring the issues of education to life for the people of Texas, to broaden the school debate beyond the corridors of the state capitol. To that end, SCOPE enlisted at its first metting the aid of a young Vietnamese-American student from Dallas, who was invited to give a computer demonstration. She sat before her terminal and typed "The tree kicks the cat." And as the computer obediently produced a graphic display of a tree booting an electronic feline, the hearing room roared its approval.[6] Captured by television cameras, the two vivid symbols of the changing educational landscape in Texas—the young immigrant girl and the computer—were hours later broadcast across the state on the evening news programs.

Yet, despite the stature and the independent-mindedness of the SCOPE membership (apart from the Texas political leadership, a number of the state's prominent citizens—such as Charles W. Duncan, Jr., the former president of Coca-Cola—also held seats on the committee), it was clear from the outset that Ross Perot was going to dictate the terms of the committee's work. He gave committee members agendas only the day before meetings were to be held. He often convened the committee not in state buildings but in splashy Dallas hotels, complete with catered meals. He commissioned a high-priced Dallas consulting firm to outline a career ladder for teachers and a New York firm to survey the state's teachers. And he flew in for consultation experts from around the country who were shaping the national debate, including Mortimer Adler, John Goodlad, Michael Kirst, and John Augenblinck. He engaged Thomas W. Luce, his personal lawyer and founder of Hughes and Luce, perhaps the largest law firm in Texas, to coordinate SCOPE's staff work. In November, Luce took what was to be a seven-month formal leave of absence from his law practice to work for the committee. Sally Walters, Perot's secretary at EDS, took over the logistical responsibilities of the committee; she had played a key administrative role in the Iranian mission. And when SCOPE was in need of something—transportation, a sound system, editorial work—EDS provided it.

All, from Luce's leave of absence to the catered lunches, was paid for out of Perot's pocket. Kirst, who described his work for Perot as that of a "personal consultant," recalled being paid with checks that had Perot's *and* his wife's names on them.[7] In fact, between mid-1983 and mid-1984, Perot spent an estimated $2 million on behalf of SCOPE. The state gave the committee a budget of $68,500.

But above all, it was Perot who took the SCOPE investigation to the public. He was in a good position to do so. Under journalistic convention, his wealth and international exploits guaranteed attention to virtually whatever he said or did. He enjoyed an ability to "make news." So did the other prominent SCOPE members. But when Perot began to erase the distinction between the committee and his role as chairman, the prestige of his SCOPE colleagues shifted to Perot. Moreover, Perot knew how to use his platform. His campaign for the Vietnam POWs demonstrated his mastery of the art of publicity. He also performed artfully as a public speaker, combining a gift for simplifying ideas into powerful images ("Texans looked smart in the past because God put so much oil and gas here," was the way he began remarks about education and the new Texas economy) with the stage presence of an actor and a disarming East Texas twang.

As Governor White correctly had anticipated when he installed Perot as SCOPE chairman, Perot's commentary on public schools gained added currency because he spoke as an outsider, independent of the state's education and political establishments. And by using his own resources to support SCOPE, Perot distinguished the committee from the many governmental "paper commissions" on education that had preceded it. By coincidence, William Morrow and Company published *On Wings of Eagles,* an account of the EDS mission in Iran, just as SCOPE was gearing up. Soon a best-seller, the book portrayed Perot as a no-nonsense, never-say-no leader who would "move heaven and earth" to accomplish a goal.

He was ready just two weeks after the opening SCOPE hearing to tell Texas that its schools were failing. In a speech on July 29, 1983, given not at a SCOPE meeting but to a convention of one of the state's teachers unions, Perot blasted Texas schools as "places dedicated to play" rather than to academics. He charged that extracurricular activities and their proponents left little time in the school day for learning. "I don't know if we should call the public school system of Texas a public school system or a department of human resources," he said.[8] In a state where the Friday night game, the band, the pep squad, the drill team, and agricultural clubs are sacrosanct, Perot's indictment amounted to heresy. But it was only the beginning.

In mid-August, Perot led the SCOPE committee on a two-week "fact-finding" tour of the state's schools. The SCOPE entourage, at times approaching fifty in number, moved around Texas with much fanfare, holding a hearing in a school cafeteria or in a gymnasium, sometimes talking to local educators informally, drawing attention to a community's schools wherever they went. The committee mostly listened, primarily to teachers and administrators, whose themes in a number of cases became the focus of SCOPE's work: the need to reach many children educationally at an earlier age, the absence of professional opportunities for teachers, and the inability of poor schools to make ends meet under the current state finance system. The testimony from the "trenches" also reinforced Perot's conclusion that the school day was being held hostage to extracurricular activities.[9]

Convinced that any changes in the state's school system would need the public's support and that the public would endorse change only if it was satisfied that serious problems existed, Perot resumed the offensive in a series of SCOPE hearings that he scheduled between September and November in Austin and at the Registry Hotel in Dallas. Readied with evidence drawn from what was by then two and a half months of intensive study by him and his staff, Perot opened fire.

He called the standards of the University Interscholastic League (UIL), a powerful body headed by school superintendents that sponsors state-wide competitions in everything from football to forensics, "a bad joke on the children of Texas." In fact, Perot so pummeled the UIL that Bailey Marshall, its director, soon proposed sweeping changes in the organization's regulations, including a ban on the common practice of "red shirting" seventh-graders (whereby students repeat a grade in order to "beef up" for athletic competition), a reduction in the amount of practice time for teams, and a rewriting of a standard that required only that students earn a "D" average and pass three of six courses to be eligible for competition.

Perot railed against Astroturfed stadiums, electric cleat cleaners, towel warmers, twelve-coach football teams, and indoor field houses as symbols of misplaced priorities. He ridiculed courses in poultry broiler production, feedlot employment, and hardware sales. He wondered aloud why 600 of the state's 1,071 school systems spent all of their local revenues on extracurricular activities. "If your reading skills allow you to finish this article, please pause to reflect that many of our Texas high school graduates do not have the vocabulary, reading skills or concentration to read such material," he said at the end of a September op-ed piece in the *Dallas Morning News*.

He didn't pull any punches. Suburban students, he suggested, were "more concerned about what kind of polo shirt they are wearing than about academic achievement." Over and over he told the story of an agricultural student who missed thirty-five days of school in 1982–83 taking a pet chicken to livestock shows around the state. When a Houston newspaper sent reporters to the Houston Fat Stock Show to check on the accuracy of the story, Perot came out the winner: no students interviewed had missed fewer than twenty days of school and, in Perot's words, "a new world champion at forty-two days with a sheep" had been discovered.

He invited every education association in the state to "testify" at the fall hearings. But more often than not, he took advantage of the appearance to give the organization or the field it represented a bashing. At a hearing on teacher education in September, he pointed out that the education school at the University of Texas at Austin, the state's flagship institution, employed a 231-member staff but produced only 500 new teachers a year. "If they were paving roads instead of educating teachers," he commented, "they would be arrested for fraud and sent to prison."[10] When an education-school dean at the hearing rejected Perot's assertion that "teachers hate their schools of education," Perot shot back that he'd be happy to pay for a poll on the subject. He wasn't afraid to throw his weight around.

The businessman in Perot focused on Texas education's bottom line. Spending for public schools had risen astronomically, from $1.75 billion in 1973 to $8.3 billion a decade later, but there was no evidence of improved student achievement during that period. In fact, the state's education "establishment" was unable to tell SCOPE with any accuracy how funds were being spent. Rising costs, stagnating productivity, faulty accounting—to Perot, it was "a recipe for bankruptcy" and a classic case of "bad management." One of his most frequently asked questions became, "Who's in charge here?"

True to form, he had his own answers. The only accountability in Texas education, he often said, cynically, was for coaches. "A losing coach is either going to get fired or be made principal."

School administrators were "a good-old-boy network of old coaches standing around holding hands humming the status quo. . . . They're a great bunch of guys, but their priorities are in letting kids play, not in making them learn. Half of them still have whistles around their necks."[11] Perot's discovery of the secret Order of the Red Red Rose, a male-only Texas school administrators club, added still more bite to his rhetoric.

But Perot waged his harshest campaign on the issue of leadership against the twenty-seven-member Texas State Board of Education. The immense size of the budget it administered and the autonomy it enjoyed as an elected body gave the board tremendous power over the state's public schools. It had the power to interpret the legislature's intentions in education (in practical terms, that meant it enforced or didn't enforce education laws as it saw fit), as well as its own rule-making authority (in the 1970s, the board gained national notoriety when it decreed that textbooks used in the state had to treat evolution as one of a number of theories of human development). It exerted its strength over the vast Texas school network through the nearly one thousand well-heeled employees of the Texas Education Agency. It was to the state board that those groups with vested interests in the policies and programs of education—the school boards and administrators associations, the teachers unions, the education schools, the array of vocational associations—turned for support. Rarely were they disappointed. To those in Austin who followed education, the state board was "more or less a political tool for the education establishment."

To Perot, the board was the single largest obstacle in the way of change. Not only was it powerful, it was consistently and openly hostile toward SCOPE and the committee's findings. Joe Kelly Butler, the board chairman and a member of SCOPE, on September 17 told the Texas School Boards Association that the committee's investigation wasn't likely to amount to "anything at all." But Perot wasn't about to be intimidated. Instead, he launched a campaign to eliminate the elected board and replace it with a new, gubernatorially appointed body. "It was simple as hell," recalled Tom Luce. "If the board stayed, there wouldn't be any change."[12]

Board-bashing became a standard part of Perot's speeches. "Go to Austin and sit in on a meeting," he would say. "It costs you $5 to see a movie that funny." "They've got people who think the world is flat," was another standard line, as was "The good old boys tell us we're moving too fast, but anything looks fast when you're standing still." The board, Perot charged, was responsible for mismanaging the huge, decade-long increase in state education aid.

The confrontation evolved quickly into a personal battle—played out in public—between Perot and Butler, a Houston oil-drilling contractor who had ruled the board with an iron hand since 1974. In October Perot suggested that Butler, who entered education politics in 1963 as a member of the Houston school board, had led the board "since the Ark docked." Butler called Perot a "dictator" and voted against many SCOPE recommendations. He eventually stopped attending the committee's meetings. Perot ridiculed Butler for outfitting the board's Austin meeting room with an electronic voting device. He said the life-sized oil portrait of Butler that hangs in the meeting room "probably glows in the dark." The conflict between Mr. Outsider and Mr. Establishment raged through the winter, but by the following spring it was over. Overwhelmed by Perot, Butler lost a reelection bid in a Republican primary to a former social studies teacher.

The image of the wiry, 5'7" Perot laying siege to public education from a speaker's podium or a hearing-room dais dominated the Texas media throughout the fall, as Perot and Luce had hoped. Day in and day out the state's newspapers and television stations, treated to irresistible television footage and newspaper copy, stayed with the SCOPE story. (Perot shrewdly interspersed his rhetorical blasts with a series of attention-grabbing ideas, such as requiring all new teachers to attend a sixty-day "boot camp" or abolishing interscholastic sports in the state's junior high schools.) In the words of an aid to the governor, Perot's campaign "moved education from the sports page to the front page." Even the national media took note. In October Perot earned an appearance on ABC Television's "Nightline" news program.

But the Texas press was more than a megaphone for Perot. As early as August 4, 1983, the *Dallas Times-Herald* used its editorial page to urge "every citizen" to support Perot's "tenacious and thorough approach" to education reform. It was among the first of a chorus of endorsements in the opinion pages of the state's major newspapers. Perot's "refreshing candor" and "good sense" were praised repeatedly. Columnists began writing approvingly of Perot's "crusade" for better schools. Moreover, many of the major Texas newspapers ran series of stories on the condition of Texas education that tended to confirm Perot's bleak assessment of the state's schools. The *Fort Worth Star-Telegram*'s "Texas Education: Passing or Failing?," the *Waco Tribune-Herald*'s "Texas Dilemma: Public Education," and the *Austin American Statesman*'s "Education: The Texas Challenge" all ran in October 1983. In December the *Times-Herald* ran an eleven-part series titled "American Education: The ABC's of Failure," It took three reporters six months to complete.

By December, Tom Luce, who had sued Iran for Perot in an international court over the EDS contract dispute in 1978–79, had become SCOPE's full-time staff director (like Perot, he had had no prior experience with the Texas education system) and the committee had broken into subcommittees to begin writing recommendations. Charles Duncan headed a group focused on "organization and management." Comptroller Bullock directed a discussion of school finance issues. Carl Parker, chairman of the Senate Education Committee, headed a panel on "legislative action." William Haley, Parker's counterpart in the House, chaired a subcommittee on the teaching profession. And Jon H. Fleming, president of Texas Wesleyan University, led a panel on "educating the child." Some of the subcommittees held hearings during the winter, but private drafting sessions and then votes on recommendations by the reassembled full committee were the focus of SCOPE's work through mid-March of 1984.

By then, seven months past the governor's deadline, SCOPE was ready to go public with a preliminary report. Compared to Perot's autumn war of words, it was a piece of rhetorical deadpan. It made no mention of the alarming findings of the SCOPE investigation. Nor was there any reference to the governor's call for a report on teacher pay. In fact, there were only eight paragraphs of narrative in the first forty-two pages of the forty-four-page document. The report was not really a report. It was a laundry list of some 140 recommendations, presented in outline form. Its prose was clear but expressionless. And it was written in the future tense ("The Board *will* develop and publish a four-year plan"), which only accentuated its pedestrian tone.

But the recommendations themselves were explosive, and they reverberated throughout Texas education. A passing grade was to be 70 instead of 60, and students with any grade below 70 were to be barred from extracurricular activities. No credit was to be given to those who missed more than five meetings of a course in a semester, and no students were to be exempted from final examinations. No interscholastic competition was to take place among junior high schools. Local school systems were to provide annual performance reports to the public and to the state board. All principals were to be given eleven- or twelve-month contracts and a role in the selection of the teachers in their schools. Textbooks were to be adopted on six-year rather than eight-year cycles. Accreditation standards were to be toughened, and state aid shut off to school systems that didn't measure up.

The state funding formula was to be written to give poor systems more money. Judges were to be given authority to award attorney's fees to teachers and other school employees in "frivolous" lawsuits against them involving student discipline. An investigation of "the spoils system" in Texas public education was to be conducted. Prekindergarten programs were to be provided for all four-year-olds and full-day kindergarten for all five-year-olds. Class sizes in grades one through four were to be limited to fifteen. Predictably, the state board was to be replaced by a nine-member panel appointed by the governor for staggered six-year terms.

Ten days were to be added to the state's 175-day school year. Two hours were to be added to the school day, and all school buildings were to be open from 7:00 A.M. to 6:00 P.M. Standardized tests were to be given to all students annually. Scholarships and loans were to be offered to top college students who agreed to teach, and a "career ladder" was to be created in every school system. "Peer review" was to be used in deciding placement on the ladder. The committee didn't discuss graduation requirements because the legislature had established new requirements in 1981.

The state was to raise the salary for new teachers from $11,110 to $15,200, but there was to be no across-the-board pay raise for Texas teachers. On the contrary, the career ladder was to be used as a way of tying teacher pay to performance, and all of the state's teachers were to pass a literacy test or be expelled from the profession.

The unions and the governor didn't get exactly what they had asked for.

Perot called the preliminary SCOPE package a "wish list." With good reason. Its estimated five-year cost was $19.1 billion, a figure far beyond the state's reach. Nonetheless, Perot continued to draft recommendations. A newly completed study by the highly respected Texas Research League revealed that only forty-five cents of every instructional dollar was being spent on core academic subjects, while nineteen cents of each dollar was going to support vocational programs—programs Perot didn't think much of.[13] As a result, the final SCOPE report, released on April 19, 1984, called for elimination of the state subsidy for vocational classes (which had grown from $80 million in 1974 to $240 million in 1984) and insisted that any vocational class with fewer than twenty students be dismantled.

By paring down some of the most expensive SCOPE proposals, Perot was able to cut the overall costs of the committee's package substantially—without reducing the number of recommendations in it. Instead of lowering class size to fifteen in grades one through four in 1985, the committee proposed a twenty-student limit, covering grades one and two in 1985 and grades three and four in 1988, at a savings of $785 million in 1985. The introduction of all-day kindergarten and an extended school day was also pushed back till 1988, saving another $550 million in 1985. And preschool programs were required for impoverished and non-English-speaking four-year-olds only, at a savings of $350 million. Overall, the first-year price of recommendations was cut from $2.4 billion to $987 million.

The cuts were deep enough. When Perot presented the package to Texas at a Dallas news conference on the nineteenth, the state's entire elected leadership stood by his side, symbolizing their endorsement of the most radical education reforms the state had ever seen. The goal, according to SCOPE, was no less than the creation of "a new school system," one that would "make academic achievement in Texas first in the nation" and allows Texas children "to be competitive throughout the industrialized world." Even Governor White signed on enthusiastically, though the widespread endorsement of the SCOPE recommendations suggested the political price he probably would have paid in opposing the SCOPE agenda.[14] White's staff quickly put together a new tax package to fund the SCOPE recommendations. Made public on May 11, it called for $4.89 billion in new revenue over three years.

Meanwhile, Perot, anticipating White's announcement of the long-promised special legislative session on education, set out across Texas in his private Learjet to sell the SCOPE reform package. He spent little time talking to the education establishment. Instead, he sought out the state's political power brokers, the civic and business leaders who, in his words, "get legislators elected." Nonstop for over a month, Perot worked his rhetorical magic before the Texas and Southwest Cattle Raisers Association, the Mid-Continent Oil and Gas Association, the Texas Association of Businesses, the Texas Association of Taxpayers, and other pillars of the state's economy. Audiences doubled over in laughter at his homely but telling portraits of life in Texas schools. They sat in silence through his lectern-pounding homilies on education and the state's economic well-being. Time and again they greeted his calls to action with standing ovations. "The big shots in Dallas and the good 'ol boys from West Texas—he mesmerized them all," recalled a SCOPE staffer who traveled with Perot. To extend his reach, Perot videotaped his presentation and sent it to cities he was unable to get to.

Perot's preaching gained public education powerful new allies within organizations that in the past had been disinterested in, if not hostile toward, the state's schools. But he won converts on his own terms. He urged his influential audiences to press for new taxes to support education. But he asked them not to do so until the SCOPE recommendations were enacted. "Millions for reform, not another penny for the status quo" became his theme. He was asking the state's civic and business leadership to help him hold White's tax package hostage to the SCOPE recommendations, and he wasn't afraid to say so. "People all over this room have chits with legislators," he told the North Dallas Chamber of Commerce in April, "now is the time to call them in."

Chamber members across the state soon had an opportunity to act. On May 25, 1984, White ordered a special, thirty-day session of the sixty-eighth Texas legislature to convene on June 4.

Education was never a popular issue among Texas lawmakers. Champions of free enterprise and the entrepreneurial spirit, they tended to view schools, public institutions, as "a low priority." None were able to ignore the subject completely: state aid to schools had been a major source of revenue in many Texas communities since the late 1940s. In fiscal 1984 education funding accounted for 51 percent of the state's budget. But if they kept an eye on funding formulas, legislators typically avoided the

arcane task of shaping education policy. That job was left to their colleagues on the education committees, who, as a result, held enormous
sway over schooling issues. Bills reported by those panels were routinely
approved on the floors of the House and Senate, according to veterans of
Austin politics, often with little or no debate.

Neither House Public Education Committee Chairman Haley, who had
taught high school history before becoming a state legislator, nor his
counterpart in the Senate, Carl Parker, a longtime "labor man" in the
legislature, cared much for major portions of Perot's reform agenda, as
their voting records on the SCOPE committee suggested. Now, with the
education debate shifting to the capital in Austin, where the agenda
would be cleared of all items save the SCOPE recommendations and
White's tax package, Haley and Parker were going to meet the SCOPE
package on their own turf. Or so they thought.

By the time the session opened, Gib Lewis and Bill Hobby knew the
SCOPE agenda in detail and were firmly committed to its success in the
legislature, for in the year since they had created SCOPE, they had
become actively involved in its work. Instead of playing cameo roles on
the committee, as might have been expected of prominent public officials, they attended meetings, visited schools, and talked with Perot regularly. It was Gwen Newman and Camilla Bordie, the staffers Hobby had
lent to SCOPE, who with the help of the legislature's legal office translated the SCOPE recommendatons into legislation in the weeks prior to
the special session. Hobby and Lewis had the power to challenge the
hegemony of the education committees.

If his trademarks—white oxford-cloth shirts, pipes, and bow ties—
suggested Philadelphia instead of Austin, Hobby's authority in the Texas
capitol was firmly established. The scion of one of the state's leading
families, he owns a string of television stations and, until 1983, he owned
the *Houston Post*. The Houston airport is named for his father, who served
as governor from 1917 to 1921. As lieutenant governor, a post he had
held since 1970, Hobby's contitutional powers gave him broad authority
over the state Senate. It was he, for example, who made committee
appointments and dictated the order of the Senate's daily business.

Hobby's strategy for countering Carl Parker's resistance to key SCOPE
recommendations was simple: he limited Parker's access to the SCOPE
bill. As soon as the bill was introduced on June 4, he transformed the
thirty-one-member Senate into an education committee of the whole.
Each senator was assigned to one of four subcommittees. Parker was
given the chairmanship of a subcommittee on the teaching profession;
that left him with a fourth of the jurisdiction over the SCOPE bill he
would have had otherwise.

Next, Hobby worked at selling the SCOPE bill to the remaining Senate
membership. He took the rare step of testifying personally on behalf of
the SCOPE recommendations at hearings held by the newly created

subcommittees. He promoted the SCOPE bill with Speaker Lewis in television commercials, aired during the special session as part of a $300,000 pro-SCOPE media campaign paid for by Governor White, who worked hard for the SCOPE bill during the session. Day in and day out Hobby summoned senators to private meetings in his office behind the Senate chamber. Though others denied it, Parker asserted that Hobby won votes for SCOPE recommendations the old-fashioned way, with promises of politicial favors.[15]

On June 23 the Senate passed the SCOPE bill, with some amendments, by a vote of 22 to 9.

Meanwhile, the SCOPE package had stalled in the House Public Education Committee, its first hurdle on the House side. The membership of Haley's nine-member panel favored the interests of affluent suburban school systems and teachers. Ernestine Glossbrenner, the committee's vice-chairman and a member of the Texas State Teachers Association (TSTA), the NEA's Texas affiliate, was among the three or four committee members the TSTA declares it "put in office." Like its chairman, the committee objected to many SCOPE recommendations.

Hearings dragged on for almost two weeks. SCOPE supporters grew impatient. "If . . . the legislature fails to come up with the reforms the people of Texas have clearly indicated they want, the blame can be laid squarely at the feet of the House Public Education Committee," scolded the *Fort Worth Star-Telegram*. Finally, with the midpoint of the special session approaching, the committee met on Sunday, June 17, Father's Day, to mark up House Bill 72, the SCOPE legislation. The meeting began at 10:30 in the morning. By the time it ended, fifteen hours later, key SCOPE proposals had disappeared from the bill. The mandatory preschool program for disadvantaged four-year-olds was deleted, the career-ladder plan was watered down and the teacher test eliminated, the Perot committee's state-aid formula was rewritten, and the plan to abolish the elected state board was dropped. The Texas newspapers dubbed the event the "Father's Day Massacre."

Gib Lewis, who had been present at the meeting as a spectator, was outraged. On the morning of the eighteenth, just hours after the education committee's final vote, he summoned Haley, a fellow Democrat, to his office and threatened to strip him of his committee chairmanship if he refused to introduce a substitute for H.B. 72 on the floor of the House the same day. Said Lewis: "I'm asking you to offer a substitute. If you can't handle it, I'll find someone who can."[16] Haley cooperated. After compromises were worked out on the state board and state aid issues, the contents of the SCOPE bill passed by the Senate were put into the shell of H.B. 72 and introduced on the House floor that Monday afternoon. It was approved by a vote of 119 to 29 on June 23.

In a poem about the special session titled "The Ballad of the Second

Called Session," Hobby wrote, ". . . promise and plead as he might, / Gib had to break several arms and a leg / To be sure that Chicken Haley really laid an egg." Politically, Lewis's performance was one of the best investments of his career. An undistinguished freshman speaker in 1983, he won widespread praise for his tough stand on school reform.

Texas acknowledged as far back as 1949 that many of its students were being shortchanged because they lived in communities that couldn't afford decent schools. The Gilmer-Aikin Act of that year established a minimum level of state funding for each student, but the disparities between rich and poor school systems persisted. In 1971 a U.S. district court in San Antonio declared the Texas system of school finance unconstitutional. Its excessive reliance on the local property tax, the court ruled in *Rodriguez v. San Antonio I.S.D.,* violated the equal-protection clause of the Fourteenth Amendment. The U.S. Supreme Court reversed the *Rodriguez* decision on appeal two years later, on the grounds that education is not a constitutionally protected right. It nonetheless urged Texas to develop a fairer system of school funding.

According to a study commissioned by SCOPE, the system hadn't improved much by 1982–83. That year, the state's 107 poorest school districts (those with less than $100,000 per student of taxable property within their borders) spent an average of $2,184 per student—with state aid making up 88 percent of the total. The state's 156 richest districts (those with in excess of $600,000 per student of taxable property), spent an average of $4,042 per student—with state aid representing only 35 percent of the total. The spending disparity existed even though the poor districts taxed their residents more heavily than the wealthy districts taxed theirs: 5.5 cents versus 5.0 cents on a $100 of property at its market value. What's more, because Texas law prohibits districts from using state aid to pay capital expenses (which range from library books to buildings), the 107 poorest districts were able to budget only $202 per student for such expenditures, compared to $835 per student in the 156 richest districts.[17]

Hoping to amplify the grim message in such statistics, fifty of the state's property-poor school systems in March of 1982 created the Equity Center, a lobby. Its first major task was to press its members' case before the SCOPE committee at the hearings in the fall of 1983. And the centerpiece of its testimony was a call for a new formula that distributed a greater proportion of state monies to poor school systems.

The Equity Center's recommendation wasn't new. There had been proposals in the past to direct a large share of state aid to communities with few resources, but they had been blocked in the legislature by affluent school systems (concentrated in suburban areas and in a few large cities) that stood to lose money if funds were redistributed. Although

SCOPE was persuaded of the need for a new funding formula, the stalemate between the center and the state's wealthy school systems continued into the winter.

Then, in early 1984, the state's most affluent urban school systems—Dallas, Houston, Fort Worth, and Austin in particular—changed their strategy. It was a development that would mean as much to the fortunes of the SCOPE bill during the special session as the support of Hobby and Lewis did.

The wealthy urban systems had concluded that the state's existing aid formula wouldn't withstand a constitutional challenge once a new, statewide system of property appraisal took effect later in 1984. (Despite its obvious inequities, the existing formula was difficult to challenge because a multitude of local appraisal practices made it hard to prove the relative wealth of school systems). And they feared huge losses in state aid should the formula be overturned.

At the urging of Linus Wright, superintendent of the Dallas system and later U.S. undersecretary of education in the second Reagan administration, the urban districts went to the Equity Center with a compromise. They would endorse a new funding formula that favored poor school systems—if the formula were weighted to reflect the large numbers of students in urban areas needing costly bilingual, special education, and remedial programs, and if the formula recognized the higher cost of educating all students in cities. The affluent urban school systems would lose state aid under the compromise, but not nearly as much as they might before the courts.

The Equity Center, its goal a step closer to realization, quickly endorsed the plan and the new allies took it to the SCOPE subcommittee on finance. By March it was part of the SCOPE recommendations. Suddenly, the two organizations had a reason to fight for the SCOPE bill. And they had powerful allies in the legislature.

With a predominantly rural membership that had tripled in the two years since its founding, the Equity Center was a natural constituent of House Ways and Means Committee Chairman Schlueter and Senate Finance Committee Chairman Jones, influential lawmakers with strong ties to rural Texas. Both men represented the Central Texas region where the leaders of the Equity Center work as school superintendents. The political clout of the Dallas, Houston, Fort Worth, and Austin school systems came from the size of the legislative delegations that the four cities sent to Austin and from their membership in a political coalition of Texas's eight largest school systems, known as the Urban Council. The Urban Council endorsed the compromise funding formula, gaining Dallas, Houston, Fort Worth, and Austin additional support among legislators representing the several nonaffluent school systems in the council. Together, the council's eight members educate 21 percent of Texas's students.

Twelve days before the opening of the special session, Linus Wright's predicition came true. On May 23 the Mexican American Legal Defense and Educational Fund, the plaintiff in the *Rodriguez* case, filed suit against the Texas school finance system in the state court in Travis County.

The Equity Center and the Urban Council fought hard for their new formula during the special session, but their value to the SCOPE campaign can be measured in terms of what they didn't do as well as in terms of the lobbying that they did. Throughout the session, the organizations' members complained about other parts of the SCOPE bill—such as the career ladder for teachers—but, fearful of jeopardizing the new funding formula, they never expressed their dissatisfaction publicly. Hobby and Lewis, in fact, warned the organizations that if they didn't remain at least neutral toward the rest of the SCOPE agenda, the new formula might disappear from the bill. Not taking any chances, the organizations' leaders in several instances testified on behalf of other SCOPE recommendations. The finance issue, then, neutralized two imposing potential adversaries of the SCOPE bill.

It also brought another significant ally into the SCOPE camp: a network of activist, mostly Hispanic church congregations that saw passage of a new funding formula as an opportunity to help the children of their often desperately poor communities. Established in the 1970s to fight poverty, the network is wide and tightly knit. Communities Organized for Public Service (COPS) in San Antonio, the largest of its nine associations, boasts a membership of 90,000 families in twenty-eight parishes. It trains each of its members in "community action" by means of organizers assigned to each three-parish "cluster." Hoping to seize the moment presented by the special session, the associations mobilized their forces in the churches. Thousands of people were bused to Austin for rallies, while their leaders lobbied legislators, presented testimony at hearings, and reminded the governor of promises he made in 1982 to seek a fairer funding formula. The network's activities lent a populist air to the SCOPE campaign.

Predictably, Perot wasn't willing to leave the fate of the bill in the hands of others, as influential and committed as they might be. He sent Tom Luce to Austin to lobby for the SCOPE agenda. Luce brought Rick Salwen, Perot's counsel at EDS, with him from Dallas. And he hired, at Perot's expense, three of the most expensive lobbyists in Austin: Jack Gullihorn and Rusty Kelley, former executive assistants to House Speaker Bill Clayton (Gib Lewis's predecessor), and Jack Wheeler, who had once worked the capitol for the University of Texas system. Joe Kelly Butler called them "the $100,000 boys."

They worked on a number of fronts at once. Each morning they gathered at 6:30 A.M. or 7:00 A.M. over breakfast at the Driskill Hotel to select the legislators with whom they would meet during the day, using a computer profile of the voting records of each member of the legislature to target those likely to be unsympathetic to the SCOPE agenda. With names collected from audiences at Perot's pro-SCOPE speeches in the spring, and with mailing lists from a statewide "War on Drugs" campaign that Perot had participated in three years earlier, they organized a letter-writing campaign. They also had a computerized list of each legislator's campaign contributors. They called the largest donors, asking them to urge their candidates to support the SCOPE bill.

Luce's team also wined and dined the predominantly male legislature with the assistance of a group of female EDS employees from Dallas on loan to Luce during the session. "Bright, attractive, articulate women who were at the capitol early till late," is the way one lobbyist not representing Perot during the session recalled them. "What with taxes and all, / Lobbyists were as thick as roaches. / So it took all the Luce women, / To win the war against coaches," said Hobby in his poem.

Luce had a second responsibility during the special session. While his colleagues gathered frequently during the day in the office of the SCOPE ally Senator Ray Farabee, Luce used the phone in the senator's office to help negotiate for Perot the final details of the $2.55 billion sale of EDS to the General Motors Corporation. The merger was announced on June 28.

Perot kept a low profile during the session, traveling to Austin only to address a joint meeting of the House and Senate on June 5. Once again he insisted on the need for change in Texas education, and once again he brought his audience to its feet in applause as he concluded with Winston Churchill's line "Never give in, never give in, NEVER, NEVER, NEVER."[18] He helped Luce from Dallas, though, by persuading former Governor Clements to refrain from public criticism of the SCOPE bill and by urging conservative legislators to support the tax bill that was needed to implement many of the SCOPE reforms.

Nonetheless, Luce and his colleagues faced a formidable task. The size and irreverence of the SCOPE agenda galvanized a huge number of hostile lobbyists, whose influence on legislators was multiplied by their tendency to concentrate their energy on particular parts of the SCOPE bill. The Vocational Agriculture Teachers Association of Texas spent most of its time fighting SCOPE's recommendation to kill the state subsidy for vocational classes, for instance. Unlike the majority of the lobbyists fighting SCOPE on behalf of the education establishment, Luce and his colleagues didn't represent easily identifiable constituents with jobs at stake. Nor did they enjoy the advantage of defending the status quo. Recalled Rusty Kelley: "It was tough, for example, going into an office where the representative really believed in traditional voc ed and try to convince him that it has become a thing of the past."[19] In fact, few of SCOPE's foes in the education establishment had faced a serious lobbying challenge in years.

Joe Kelly Butler and the other twenty-six members of the elected State Board of Education lobbied to save their jobs. The suburban superintendents banded together as Texans for Local Control of Public Education and fought the SCOPE funding formula. They were supported by Butler and Raymon Bynum, the commissioner of education. The Texas High School Coaches Association opposed SCOPE's so-called no-pass, no-play recommendation to ban from extracurricular activities students who didn't have passing grades in all subjects. Disquieted by the potential cost, the Texas Association of School Boards sought to water down the prekindergarten program for four-year-olds and fought the enrollment cap in elementary classrooms.

The discovery that a vocational teacher in the small town of Plano was giving students grades for writing letters to legislators criticizing SCOPE recommendations illustrated what Luce was up against. One letter earned a "C" from the teacher; two earned a "B"; and three an "A."[20]

Nor was the opposition limited to the state's education establishment. Fundamentalist groups such as Traditional Families in Texas, the Texas Eagle Forum, and the Pro-Family Forum led five demonstrations on the capitol in two weeks against the prekindergarten proposal, on the grounds that it would undermine the family as a source of values. They also protested the loss of taxpayer control of schools they said would result from a shift from an elected to an appointed state board of education.[21] Texas's tourist industry trade association lobbied against SCOPE's call for an extended school year.

The major recommendations involving the teaching profession—higher starting salaries but no across-the-board raises, linking pay to performance with a career ladder, and a one-time literacy test of all current teachers—were intended in large measure to mollify the legislators whose antipathy toward the state's teachers had led to SCOPE's creation. That enmity didn't diminish during the session. Many legislators simply refused to endorse other elements of the SCOPE agenda or the tax bill in the absence of steps to ensure that new appropriations would not go to incompetent teachers. "No test, no tax," was Ways and Means Committee Chairman Schlueter's blunt declaration.

To the state's four teachers unions—the 95,000-member TSTA, the NEA affiliate; the 35,000-member Association of Texas Professional Educators (ATPE); the 30,000-member Texas Classroom Teachers Association (TCTA); and the 15,000-member Texas Federation of Teachers (TFT)—most or all of SCOPE's agenda for their profession was nonetheless unacceptable. At their annual meeting in April, TSTA members went as far as reacting to the just-released draft SCOPE report with chants of "We're mad as hell and we're not going to take it anymore."

Once the special session opened, the union's lobbyists pressed legislators to reduce the size of the salary bonuses for teachers on the career ladder, to distribute bonuses to more teachers, and to allow school systems to decide whether teachers' seniority and academic credentials should be more important than their performance in the classroom in their selection to the career ladder. They called for across-the-board salary increases. They urged the abolition of the one-time test. And they fought a recommendation to replace Texas's practice of increasing state aid to school systems with teachers in higher salary brackets. (Poor school systems suffered under the practice. Unlike wealthy systems, they had few teachers in the upper brackets of the longevity-based pay scale because they couldn't afford to add sufficient local money to the state base salary to convince teachers to remain in their communities.)

Yet, after Gib Lewis outflanked the TSTA's Ernestine Glossbrenner and other members of the House Public Education Committee, the unions became conciliatory. On June 21, four days after the "Father's Day Massacre," the four organizations sent a terse letter to Lewis that called for unspecified amendments to be made to Lewis's version of H.B. 72 in conference committee but nonetheless seemed to endorse the bill. "We would like to express our support for your efforts," they wrote.

However, when the ten-member conference committee passed a bill on June 27 that included the teacher test, the career ladder, the revised funding formula, and no across-the-board pay raises, three of the teacher organizations mutinied. Becky Brooks, president-elect of the TSTA, called a press conference to denounce the committee report. "Even a dog knows the difference between being stumbled over and being kicked," she said to the embarrassment of many of her members. "As H.B. 72 stands in its final form, Texas teachers are being kicked." The ATPE and the TCTA also withdrew their endorsement of H.B. 72. Only the TFT continued to back the bill.

When word reached Hobby of the unions' public criticism of the bill, he exploded, for he realized that the union's defection would jeopardize the tax bill, which had yet to be passed. He summoned the unions one at a time to his office for an explanation. He demanded an apology and a retraction from each of them. When he didn't get either, he told the unions' lobbyists to leave his office and not return—ever.

While the three defectors took a pummeling in the press ("School Reform, Despite Teachers," "Teachers Made a Mistake," "Lobbying: F" were the headlines on the editorial pages) and among legislators ("They've caused themselves more damage than they'll ever know," said one senator), the TFT was hailed for its support of H.B. 72. After the Senate (22 to 9) and the House (106 to 42) gave final approval to the bill on June 30 (in spite of the three unions' opposition to it), the president of the TFT was invited to address the legislature, where he received a standing ovation. Much the smallest of the four unions, the American Federation of Teachers affiliate had much to gain from the positive publicity.

The ignominious defeat of the TSTA, one of his major political backers, was awkward for Governor White. "It was not something that we ever wanted to see happen," recalled his education adviser, Larry Yawn, a former TSTA president.[22] But the direction of the political winds was clear: White had to back the SCOPE bill and face the consequences of the TSTA's vow to not support his 1986 reelection bid.

The tax bill was Perot's trump card during the special session. The corporate commitment he had won for the bill in the spring remained strong. On the eve of the session, for example, Admiral Bobby Inman, chairman of a prestigious high-tech corporation established in Austin in 1983 by eighteen corporate giants such as Control Data, Kodak, and Lockheed, warned the legislature not to "squander an opportunity" to help Texas "to become the newest [high-technology] manufacturing center" by improving its public schools.[23]

But when legislators balked at SCOPE recommendations—especially its call for an appointed state board—Perot and Luce threatened to turn their corporate allies against the tax bill, just as Representative Schlueter had threatened to abandon the tax bill without reforms in the teaching profession. "We said we weren't going to support a tax increase until the reform bill was passed, and we didn't," Luce recalled.[24]

The tactic gave them leverage against more than the education establishment. Since Texas law stipulates that a quarter of the revenue from the state's gasoline tax be given to school systems, it made sense for SCOPE's backers to propose an increase in that and other transportation-related taxes as part of its package to fund the SCOPE reforms. Luce and Perot also knew that the inclusion of those taxes would prompt the state's powerful "highway lobby," represented in Austin by the Texas Good Roads and Transportation Association, to work hard on behalf of the tax bill. The bill earmarked no less than $1.4 billion for new highway construction funding. Perot's threat, in turn, inspired paving contractors, trucking executives, and a variety of engineering firms to fight for the SCOPE bill. In spite of Perot's tactics, the appointed board and finance recommendations skidded through the Senate by votes of 16 to 15 and had to be rescued by Lewis in the House.

A tax measure (H.B. 122) was passed on the last day of the special session, July 3. It hiked taxes on everything from car rentals to hotel rooms, malt liquor, snuff, cigarettes, gasoline, license plates, commercial franchises, tractor trailers, and amusement machines, and it established new taxes on computer software, automobile parking and storage, cable television, dry cleaning, escort services, massage parlors, newspaper subscriptions, and nonfarming uses of fertilizer. Expected to produce $4.7 billion in new revenue between 1985 and 1987, it was the first tax increase in Texas in thirteen years.

In the end, H.B. 72 bore a striking resemblance to the report issed by SCOPE in April. Of the $2.8 billion increase in state aid to education engendered by the tax bill, almost $2 billion was to go to the poorest one-third of the state's school systems. Total state spending on education was increased 25 percent over three years—by $963 million in the 1984–85 school year alone.

Virtually all of the SCOPE recommendations intended to "make schools get back in the business of educating students" were approved. Extracurricular activities were banished from the school day. The passing grade was raised to 70. Promotion to the next grade of students with less than 70 average was prohibited. Students were denied credit in each class they failed to attend five times without a valid excuse. And the controversial "no-pass, no-play" proposal was approved. The existing 175-day year was retained, though.

The teacher test passed, and a March 1986 deadline was set for its administration. With an eye to projections of a need for 14,000 new teachers a year in Texas till the year 2000, starting salaries (the state base pay) were raised 36 percent, from $11,110 to $15,200 a year. The state board was directed to provide for the certification of college graduates from out-of-state education schools, and loans were established for prospective teachers of math, science, and other shortage areas. Each education school was required to publicize an annual "performance report" that includes the scores of its graduates on the state's licensing examination. The state board was empowered to place an education school that doesn't meet accreditation standards on "probation" for up to twenty-four months, during which time it must decrease its enrollment "significantly." Implementation of the four-rung career ladder was scheduled for the 1984–85 school year, with a new, statewide program for evaluating teachers scheduled for use in 1986. All teachers were required to teach at least four hours a day.

There were to be no more than twenty-two students in first- and second-grade classes by 1985–86 and in third- and fourth-grade classes by 1988–89. Voluntary after-school tutorials were to be offered for students with failing grades. (SCOPE had recommended a longer school day for such students.) There were to be prekindergarten summer programs in each school system where fifteen or more underprivileged or non-English-speaking four-year-olds were identified, though SCOPE had initially recommended that they be available to all four-year-olds. The state was also directed to give school systems enough money to expand kindergarten from a half day to a full day in 1988–89.

The 226-page bill mandated standardized testing in reading, writing, and math for all students in grades one, three, five, seven, and nine, and testing of language skills and math in grade twelve. It required eleventh-graders to pass a basic-skills test in order to graduate. School systems were required to file regular "performance reports" and a discipline plan with the state board. Legislative leaders were given a greater say on education matters with creation of a "legislative education board" to be chaired by the speaker of the House or the lieutenant governor.

The current state board was to be abolished and replaced for four years by fifteen gubernatorial appointees. One role of the new legislative board was to nominate those appointees. Beginning with the general election in 1988, the new board members would stand for reelection every four years. Despite his lobbying, Perot did not get the permanent, nine-member appointed board he wanted, but he did get the existing twenty-seven-member board removed.

Of all the blows struck at the education establishment, the fewest landed on vocational educators. It was a testament to the power of their lobby. The legislature did call for the setting of minimum enrollments for voc-ed classes. But not only did it reject SCOPE's recommendation to eliminate the state subsidy for vocational classes, it stipulated that school systems be given 45 percent more aid for each student enrolled in a vocational class. It also reaffirmed the practices of giving vocational teachers double the planning time of other teachers (thereby reducing the number of courses voc-ed teachers teach) and giving them eleven- and twelve-month contracts (though it indirectly reduced funding for such contracts). To the legions of Texas voc-ed teachers, H.B. 72 more or less meant business as usual.

But as Governor White's signature on July 13 transformed H.B. 72 into the Educational Opportunity Act of 1984, the atmosphere in Austin was celebratory. An overflow crowd cheered and television cameras rolled during the signing ceremony in the spacious rotunda of the state capitol, as White, seated at a plain, oak teacher's desk and flanked by bushel baskets of apples, penned his name to the most sweeping set of school reforms in Texas history. The newspapers called passage of the SCOPE bill "historic" and "a victory for the future of Texas." An editorial headline in the *Fort Worth Star-Telegram* seemed to capture the triumph of the moment, as well as the magnitude of the campaign just waged: "School Reform: A Mountain Moves." Never had education so dominated public life in Texas. Never had so much change been called for in the Texas school system at once, nor had there been brought to bear on the system so much influence from so many points on the state's political spectrum. Never had the Texas "public" so successfully challenged the power of the state's education establishment.

Yet the final act of the SCOPE drama was not played out until 1986. In a final ironic twist, White was defeated in his bid for reelection after a collapse in world oil prices in early 1986 had left the Texas economy in a shambles—exactly the eventuality White, Perot, and others had hoped to avoid in the future by reforming the state's schools. The new governor of Texas was William P. Clements, Jr.

PART II

REPORT
CARD

CHAPTER 4

The New Basics:
Crisis in the Classroom

The reformers were particularly critical of the nation's high schools for failing to set priorities in the curriculum. In wake of the antiestablishmentism of the 1960s and 1970s, they charged, educators were permitting students to select virtually at random from a vast array of often-superficial courses. "[W]e have a cafeteria-style curriculum in which the appetizers and desserts can easily be mistaken for the main courses," wrote the National Commission on Excellence in Education in *A Nation at Risk*. A 1985 study of public schools, *The Shopping Mall High School*, captured the criticism in its title.

Pressing their twin themes that the traditional academic disciplines were the best vehicle for strengthening students' minds and that they taught students a common "cultural language," the reformers called for an academic core curriculum in the nation's high schools. The national commission urged in *A Nation at Risk* that all students receiving a high school diploma complete a curriculum of "New Basics": four years of English, three years each of mathematics, history, and science, and a half year of computer science. "Whatever the student's educational or work objectives, knowledge of the New Basics is the foundation of success for the after-school years and, therefore, forms the core of the modern curriculum," it declared. Since establishing a core curriculum in the nation's secondary schools has been a cornerstone of the reformers' pursuit of educational excellence, measuring the reformers' progress in achieving that aim is a good place to begin a report card on the reform movement as a whole.[1]

The reformers have persuaded policymakers to take a wide range of steps toward making traditional academic subjects a higher priority in the nation's public high schools. Virtually all the states have increased their graduation requirements in academic subjects. And a number that previously allowed local school systems to set their own graduation requirements—California, Florida, Mississippi, and Wisconsin, for instance—have introduced statewide standards. To put pressure on schools from above, thirty states have raised the quota of academic courses needed for admission to public colleges and universities.[2]

New "advanced" and "honors" diplomas have sprung up across the nation, requiring a full complement of academic courses. Students seeking Virginia's new "advanced studies diploma," for instance, must finish four years of English, three years each of math, science, and social studies, and two years of a foreign language, compared with a combination of five years of math and science and no foreign-language study for recipients of the state's regular diploma.

The reform movement also has spawned a range of radically new specialized programs with an academic bent. At least eight states—North Carolina, Louisiana, South Carolina, Mississippi, Illinois, Texas, Indiana, and Oklahoma—have established public boarding schools, such as the North Carolina School of Science and Mathematics, in order to offer advanced training in academic subjects to their best students. Others have created residential summer schools for high-achieving students, the Governor's School of Global Studies in New Jersey and the Missouri Scholars Academy among them. States such as Virginia, New York, and California have strung together networks of regional "magnet" schools, to which students commute for advanced academic work. Meanwhile, school systems have launched scores of academic magnets themselves.

To spur student interest in academics further, several states have established new college scholarships awarded on the basis of academic achievement rather than need. Under Florida's new Academic Scholars Program, for example, students who earn high marks in a set academic curriculum gain automatic admission to the state's public colleges and universities and become eligible for special "merit" scholarships.[3]

Similarly, Florida, South Carolina, Alabama, Kentucky, and Utah now offer local school officials financial incentives to expand their "advanced-placement" programs. Founded in 1955 by the College Board, AP, as it's known colloquially, supplies high schools with course outlines, curriculum materials, and set examinations for introductory college courses in fifteen academic fields, and nearly 1,500 of the nation's colleges and universities grant incoming freshmen credit for passing AP examinations. Since 1983 Florida has paid its school systems roughly $600 for each AP exam that a student passes. Utah launched a similar program the same year, and by 1988 fully 15 percent of the state's graduating seniors were taking the examinations.

In many instances such reforms have been reinforced by other measures designed to "recapture the school day for academics," as H. Ross Perot put it during the Texas debate. States and school systems have passed laws and regulations requiring students to meet tougher standards in academic courses in order to participate in extracurricular activities. Texas's "no-pass, no-play" law, the most widely publicized measure, prohibits students with less than a "C" average from involvement in extracurricular activities for six weeks. Other states have banned pep rallies, field trips, and other nonacademic activities during the school day.

To be sure, there has been intense resistance to these measures in many local communities. In Texas, "no-pàss, no-play" has been hugely controversial. When the law decimated the state's baseball playoffs upon taking effect in the spring of 1985—in some communities, virtually entire teams were disqualified from competition—there was a tremendous public outcry, and an immediate but unsuccessful challenge to the law's constitutionality in the Texas courts. Similarly, the superintendent of a rural Florida county school system that I visited recounted being besieged by irate parents after he turned down an invitation for one of his high school bands to perform at the 1984 Super Bowl in Tampa on the grounds that four days of classes were too many for the students in the band to miss. The poor rural community, after changing the superintendent's mind, quickly raised $25,000 to outfit the band with new uniforms for the trip. Yet the hard-nosed state regulations exposed a serious drain on academics in many public schools. Within a year of the Florida legislature's 1984 banning of nonacademic meetings during regular school hours, for example, the number of clubs at the high school with the Super Bowl band plummeted from forty to twelve.[4]

Also in the name of raising the priority of academics, Virginia and Florida have decreed that students must take a full complement of courses throughout their senior year. Texas has increased from four to five the number of courses students must take each day for credit. And Idaho has ruled that students must attend 90 percent of the classes in a course to receive credit for it. California and Florida are among the states and school systems that have sought to increase instruction in academic subjects by extending the school day and school year. Under its 1983 Hughes-Hart legislation, California pays millions of dollars in additional aid to school systems willing to extend their academic year to 180 days (the national average) and to those willing to increase the number of "instructional minutes" in their school day. Florida is paying similar bonuses to all but four of its school systems under an incentive program designed to extend the school day in the state from six to seven periods.[5]

As a result of such measures, enrollment in academic subjects has surged since the onset of the reform movement. A study sponsored by the U.S. Department of Education, comparing the transcripts of 15,000 students from the public high school class of 1987 with those of a similar sample of 1982 graduates, revealed increases in course taking in *all* of the academic disciplines, despite the fact that many of the new graduation and college-admission requirements had not been implemented by 1987. Graduates that year studied an average of 4.0 years of English in high school, 1.9 years of history, 2.9 years of math, 2.6 years of science, and 1.4 years of foreign languages. In contrast, their 1982 counterparts had studied 3.8 years of English, 1.7 years of history, 2.5 years of math, 2.2 years of science, and 1.0 years of foreign languages. Twelve percent of 1987 graduates satisfied the requirements of the excellence commission's

New Basics course of study, versus just 2 percent in 1982. And 28 percent of the 1987 graduates satisfied the commission's standard when the computer-science requirement and an optional foreign language standard were set aside, versus 12 percent of their 1982 counterparts.[6]

Some of the increased enrollment in academic subjects has been in the sorts of rigorous courses championed by the school reformers, courses that offer students a solid grounding in the academic disciplines, and that challenge students to use their minds in sophisticated ways. The U.S. Department of Education-sponsored survey revealed higher percentages of 1987 graduates taking such courses as geometry, advanced algebra, trigonometry, biology, chemistry, and physics than had their predecessors five years earlier. And the College Board reported in 1989 that the 456,000 Advanced Placement tests taken by high school students that year was more than double the number administered in 1983, and that the number of high schools participating in the AP program had increased by 52 percent during the same period.[7]

But despite these developments, the reformers' goal of teaching a rigorous academic curriculum to a wider range of students is being undermined in three important ways: by a proliferation of courses that treat academic subject matter with extreme superficiality, by the assignment of large numbers of teachers to academic subjects that they are unprepared to teach, and by the failure of educators to explore ways of teaching academic subjects to the many students who traditionally have not received a serious academic education—students for whom academic subjects frequently do not come easily, and for whom traditional teaching methods are often inadequate. In implementing the curriculum reforms of the 1980s, the nation's educators have failed to take the steps in the classroom necessary to achieving more than a superficial compliance with the reforms. They have largely sidestepped the difficult but essential task of supplying the capable teachers and fresh instructional strategies needed to reach a wide range of students with the type of challenging academic course work traditionally reserved for the academic and social elites. The vast majority of the nation's high school students, as a result, are getting little more exposure to rigorous course work than they did previously. Despite the reformers' successful push for new graduation requirements, they are receiving an academic education in name only.

Even with the increase in advanced academic programs in many states, tremendous numbers of students are being permitted to satisfy new graduation requirements in a host of insipid new courses that are appearing where requirements have been raised. School systems are expanding their course catalogues with offerings such as "consumer economics," "science by investigation," "community science," "introduction to physical science," "fundamentals of general science," "biological science skills," "practical math," "discovery math," "math concepts," "informal geometry," "fundamentals of mathematics," "math skills," "functional math," "applied business math," "applied basic skills math," "mathematics for daily living," "functional communication," "business communication," and "language skills."

Rarely do the watered-down courses cover what is commonly thought to be high-school level subject matter. Rather, they typically teach students only the most rudimentary aspects of the academic disciplines. "We downgraded the usual life-science course to make it an introductory class," explained the chairperson of the science department of a Sacramento-area high school, as he described to me a course introduced by the department in 1985–86 in response to new California graduation requirements in science. Life science was itself a low-level ninth-grade course. A North Carolina science teacher described a new course called "science by investigation" as "a little bit of everything—greenhouse biology." Said the teacher as we chatted in the back of her classroom one afternoon, "It's easy enough so they feel good about themselves." Likewise, a new course in "language skills" is described in the course catalogue of a Southern California high school system I visited as a "review of grammar skills needed in the world of work, personal, and business communication [*sic*]."

In a 1981 law that raised the state's graduation requirements, the Texas legislature went so far as to *require* Texas high schools to offer students high-school-caliber English courses *and* "correlated language arts" courses that Texas educators say rehash fundamental literacy skills mastered by many students in elementary school. The legislation also mandated several new science courses, including "introduction to biology." According to Texas education authorities, the course "surveys the major kinds of living things, examines their features and life processes, and emphasizes consumer, health and nutritional applications" of such knowledge. Its focus, in other words, is essentially that of a home economics course. Texas lawmakers, it seems, both strengthened and weakened the state's graduation standards with the same stroke of the pen. And eager to raise academic requirements but pressured by educators seeking to ease the burden of such requirements on students and on themselves, policymakers in many other parts of the nation have taken similarly contradictory steps.

Because the new low-level courses are frequently sequenced, students are able to spend three or four years in high school studying only the most basic aspects of academic subjects. In one Florida school system I visited, students are able to study four years of science without taking a biology course. They may take a progression of courses that includes "introduction to earth/space science," "earth/space science," "general science," and "physical science." The same is true in mathematics nationwide:

students enroll in "general math I, II, III, and IV" or "math skills 9, 10, 11, 12" and in most cases study nothing but arithmetic for four years. A tenth-grader at a Florida high school said of her general math class: "General math? It's easy. I studied the same stuff last year." Similarly, correlated-language-arts students in Texas are taught essentially the same basic grammar skills for four years.

Nowhere is the proliferation of superficial "academic" courses in wake of new graduation requirements more vividly illustrated than in Florida. Some recent research suggests that enrollment in weak academic courses has declined since the onset of the reform movement. The federally sponsored 1987 transcript study, for instance, suggested that the proportion of public-school graduates taking a remedial English course declined from 16 percent in 1982 to 13 percent in 1987.[8] But Florida's course-taking trends in recent years offer compelling evidence that the opposite is true: enrollment in watered-down courses is burgeoning in the wake of new graduation requirements. Florida is a particularly good state to study because it raised its graduation requirements substantially, and was one of the first states to do so. Legislation passed in 1983 required 1985 Florida graduates to take three years each of mathematics and science; 1987 graduates were also required to take four years of English and three years of social studies (a year of American history, a year of world history, a half year of economics, and a half year of American government). In contrast, the majority of the state graduation requirements didn't take effect until 1988 or 1989; several, including those in Nevada, New Jersey, and New Mexico, are not scheduled to be in place until early in the 1990s. Further, Florida is one of the few states that collects reliable course-enrollment information from all of its school systems, though until now, Florida's statewide totals have never been published.

The state's statistics reveal sharp increases in enrollments in new low-level courses following passage of the legislature's curriculum mandates. Consider biology. The number of students taking a biology course in Florida in 1982–83, the last school year before the legislature raised graduation requirements, was 97,700. Five years later, in 1987–88, after three senior classes had graduated under the new requirements, the number was up by 35 percent, to 132,000. But three-fourths of the increase in biology enrollment was the result of 26,500 students in 1988–89 taking a course known as "fundamentals of biology," which was created by the state in 1984–85. According to the state's science supervisor, it is an intellectually undemanding course that emphasizes "practical applications" of the subject, and it is taught at a "basic level" to students who "don't like or have not done well" in science in earlier grades.[9] The remaining one-fourth of the state's increased biology enrollment is explained by a 9 percent increase in Florida's total high school enrollment during that period. Thus, there was actually no increase in the proportion of Florida's students taking a standard biology course during the five-year period.

The state introduced several other new science courses in 1984–85. All are described by the Florida science adviser as much less demanding than "regular" science offerings. By 1987–88, enrollments in such courses were up sharply: "fundamentals of earth/space science" by 86 percent; "fundamentals of environmental science" by 17 percent; "fundamentals of chemistry" by 48 percent; "fundamentals of general science" by 47 percent; and "fundamentals of physical science" by no less than 370 percent, to 19,700 students. By contrast, 47,600 students took Florida's regular physical science course that year.

The situation is the same in math. In 1984–85 Florida education authorities created a course in "informal geometry," one of a number of math courses they introduced that year in anticipation of increased graduation requirements for 1985 graduates. By 1987–88 enrollment in the course, which does not teach students formal geometric proofs and which the state's mathematics supervisor described as a "weak academic course," more than quintupled, to 5,500. Similarly, enrollment in "fundamentals of math I," another new course described by the Florida official as "remedial," increased by 57 percent, to 12,400, while enrollment in "fundamentals of math II," which essentially repeats the first course, climbed by 62 percent. In addition, enrollment in "basic skills math," a course created for high school students who fail a state literacy examination required for graduation, increased by 13 percent, to 16,800.[10]

Nor are the lowest achievers the only students taking such courses. As did its Texas counterpart, the Florida legislature required school systems to offer different levels of English courses, beginning in the 1984–85 school year. Within three years, the number of freshmen in the lowest-level courses—so-called skills classes, where little more than basic literacy is taught—more than doubled and included nearly one-fifth of Florida's ninth-graders. There were equally large enrollment increases in skills courses in the tenth, eleventh, and twelfth grades. The results have been the same in Texas. Between 1983–84, the year Texas's correlated language arts mandate took effect, and 1986–87, the proportion of Texas ninth-graders enrolled in the state's "English I" course for "average and above average" students dropped from 87 percent to 70 percent, while the proportion of students in "correlated language arts I" increased from 7 percent to 21 percent, and there were similar shifts at other grade levels. The chairperson of the English department at one large Texas high school I visited reported that no less than 40 percent of the school's senior class was enrolled in a "correlated language arts" class. The inference drawn by many commentators on the reform movement that increased graduation requirements are synonymous with higher academic standards is clearly false.

Enrollments in Florida's existing low-level courses also have burgeoned in wake of the state's new graduation requirements. The number of students taking an introductory "business math" course, for instance, nearly quadrupled between 1982–83 and 1987–88, reaching nearly 13,000. Business math, according to Florida's math supervisor, is an arithmetic-based course that teaches such skills as check writing. Enrollment in "consumer math," a course virtually identical to "business math," increased by 28 percent during the same period, and enrollment in "pre-algebra," a heavily subscribed course that is "mostly arithmetic," according to the Florida math supervisor, jumped by 79 percent. Enrollment in second-year "general math," another arithmetic-based course, increased by 25 percent. In all, 91 percent of Florida's 493,000 high school students were enrolled in a mathematics class in 1987–88, but no less than 48 percent of them were in courses where arithmetic was the focus of instruction.[11]

The discouraging message in Florida's enrollment trends was echoed in a 1988 study measuring the results of new graduation requirements in thirteen demographically diverse school systems in Arizona, California, Florida, and Pennsylvania. Based on data gathered in the school systems by the federally funded Center for Policy Research in Education, researchers at the University of Wisconsin–Madison concluded that there has been "a proliferation of lower level courses" in the districts in response to higher state graduation requirements, as well as enrollment increases in existing "basic, general, or remedial" courses.[12]

Like the federally funded transcript study, Florida's enrollment statistics suggest that greater percentages of graduates are taking advanced academic courses.[13] Yet Florida's figures also indicate that new graduation requirements had led many students to take *fewer* rigorous academic courses. Between 1984–85, the year the Florida legislature first required school systems to teach different levels of English courses in every grade, and 1987–88, the number of freshmen in honors English classes dropped by 61 percent, and the number of sophomores, juniors, and seniors in such courses declined only slightly less severely. What's more, many juniors and seniors are fulfilling graduation requirements in academic subjects by taking courses designed for freshmen. In 1987–88, for instance, eleventh- and twelfth-graders made up nearly a quarter of the 47,600 Florida students enrolled in "physical science," a course typically taken by ninth-graders, and nearly half of the Florida students enrolled in geometry, a course also heavily subscribed by ninth-graders, were eleventh- or twelfth-graders.

Another 1988 study by researchers at the University of Wisconsin–Madison also reveals a migration of students toward easier courses in wake of rising graduation requirements. Investigating the consequences of new graduation requirements at sixteen Dade County, Florida, high schools, the report concludes that "although overall enrollment in mathematics showed little overall change between 1982–83 and 1986–87 in

Dade County, a high degree of change took place within the math department. The bulk of this change involved the redistribution of students toward less academically oriented courses." The researchers found the greatest enrollment increases in "basic skills math," "informal geometry," and "general math I," and the greatest declines in "algebra" and "computer applications."[14]

At an affluent suburban high school in Texas that I visited, enrollment in introductory chemistry dropped by half between 1984–85 and 1985–86, and in algebra II by a third, following implementation of the state's "no-pass, no-play" law early in 1985. "They don't want to take the chance of failing the tougher courses and becoming ineligible for extracurriculars," the principal of the school said. Indeed, guidance counselors in many school systems acknowledge urging students to take less-demanding courses to keep up their grades.

Moreover, it's clear that many of the supposedly *advanced* courses that students are taking are really nothing of the sort. Teachers describe Spanish courses that teach students about Spanish culture but not the Spanish language, geometry courses that do not require students to use geometric proofs, and literature courses in which there are no writing assignments. "We're starting up courses like remedial chemistry and remedial algebra II and remedial American literature. Who are we kidding?" said an English teacher at a California high school. A principal at another California high school commented, "A lot of schools will call anything and everything an honors class." At a third California high school, the principal admitted falsifying course code numbers on reports sent to state education authorities in order to make it appear that his students had taken a state-required world-civilization course, when in fact they had not. Meanwhile, guidance counselors say that many students are fulfilling new graduation requirements by taking academic courses in summer school, where they can receive course credit while in many cases spending up to one-third less time in class than they would if they enrolled in the course during the regular academic year. During the regular school year, according to guidance counselors, such students take nonacademic electives.

States and school systems nationwide also are permitting students to meet new graduation requirements in academic subjects with credits earned in courses taken outside academic departments. Usually vocational courses, the majority of these substitutes are intellectually undemanding. In 1986 the Pennsylvania State Board of Education amended its regulations to permit high school students to substitute up to three vocational courses for three of the ten academic courses recently required by Pennsylvania for graduation. Under the new regulations, such courses as "typing" earn students English credits and such courses as "metal shop" earn them math credits. Similarly, a Virginia school system

I visited permits students at its vocational "career center" to fulfill *either* the state's new graduation requirement of two years of science *or* its new requirement of two years of math by taking two years of such courses as "auto-body repair," "television production," "commercial-food preparation," and "cosmetology." In Florida, where the state allows students to earn graduation credits in academic subjects by participating in job-preparation programs, students who work as receptionists are eligible to receive credits in both English and math.

I visited a California high school that permits students to fulfill a new state fine-arts requirement by taking such courses as "beginning auto mechanics," "foods and nutrition," "consumer clothing," and "child development." According to the school's course catalogue, the topics studied in "consumer clothing" include "selecting and buying garments and accessories to fit your body type as well as budget [*sic*]." Such substitutions were sanctioned—on the grounds that some vocational courses cover academic subject matter—in California's 1983 Hughes-Hart Act, legislation that also raised the state's academic graduation requirements. Within a year of its 1985 release, a California vocational advisory council booklet outlining how to use vocational courses to meet the state's new graduation standards was in its third printing. A 1986 survey by the School of Business and Public Administration at California State University–Sacramento revealed that school systems were using the substitution provision in the 1983 legislation to grant English credit for courses such as "shorthand," "typing," and "word processing," math credit for "business machines," "general business," and "marketing/sales," and social studies credit for "business law." A school system south of Los Angeles that I visited was permitting students to earn math credits by enrolling in "Junior ROTC," a cadet-corps extracurricular activity that has become fashionable in public schools nationwide in recent years.

With thousands of jobs and millions of dollars in funding at stake, the nation's vocational educators, one of the most politically powerful constituencies within public education, have pressed hard for policies permitting such substitutions. Indeed, the vocational community has waged an aggressive campaign against the excellence movement's emphasis on academics since publication of *A Nation at Risk* in 1983. It hasn't been totally successful. Vocational enrollments, especially in home economics and traditional "shop" courses, have declined in face of increased academic graduation requirements. Further, a number of states have passed laws setting mandatory job-placement rates for vocational programs. Since 1984–85, for instance, individual secondary-school and post-secondary-school vocational programs in Florida have faced the loss of state funding if for three consecutive years at least 70 percent of their graduates do not use the specific knowledge and skills acquired in the program in a job, the military, or as part of their continuing education.

But the vocational establishment nonetheless has won many battles against the reform movement. In addition to successfully lobbying state legislatures, state boards of education, and local school systems for rulings allowing academic credits to be earned through vocational courses, it has defeated or diluted numerous attempts to reform vocational programs themselves. The most prominent example was the demise in Texas of the SCOPE recommendations to eliminate the special state subsidy for vocational classes and to abolish eleven- and twelve-month contracts for vocational teachers. In a Virginia school system I visited, a regulation requiring all classes to have fifteen or more students was waived, to protect the jobs of vocational teachers. Officials in several Florida school systems said they shifted from a six-period to a seven-period school day primarily to ensure students a continued opportunity to take vocational courses once the state's new academic graduation requirements were in place. Ironically, to avoid increasing the total time students are in school each day, a number of Florida districts that added a seventh period also cut the length of their classes from an hour to fifty minutes. Thus, over the course of four years of high school, instruction in each academic subject will be reduced by the equivalent of over two-thirds of a full-year course—presumably not what the sponsors of the state's new graduation requirements had in mind.

Further, the vocational community, led by the 46,000-member American Vocational Association, has issued a steady stream of commentary attacking the theoretical foundations of the reform movement. The AVA's powerful presence in public education dates back at least to passage of the Smith-Hughes Act in 1917, which established one of the first federally financed education programs—and a power base for the AVA. The AVA has used its influence in Washington to win huge increases in government spending on vocational education in the past two decades. In 1982 it became the first and only national education association besides the American Federation of Teachers and the National Education Association—the nation's two major teachers unions—to create a political action committee to funnel member campaign contributions to congressional candidates. The organization's state and local affiliates are also potent political entities, buttressed by extensive lobbying networks and by the fact that many lawmakers have strong ties to vocational education. An official of the National Conference of State Legislatures declared in a 1984 report that "within each chamber [of the nation's state legislatures] there is a cadre of staunch supporters who look out for the interests of vocational education." It's not by coincidence that vocational students receive preferential treatment in the education funding formulas of virtually every state.[15]

In January 1984, as the excellence movement was spreading across the nation, the federally funded National Center for Research in Vocational Education appointed a "national commission on secondary vocational education" to conduct "a frank assessment of the strengths and weaknesses" of vocational education in secondary schools. Though it was created by Congress in 1976 to be an independent source of information and research on vocational education, the controversial center was for all intents and purposes an auxiliary of the AVA during the twelve years it was located at Ohio State University (management of the center was shifted to the University of California–Berkeley in 1988). Center officials were active AVA members and a number of them held positions in the organization's leadership. After ten months of study paid for by $225,000 in federal monies, the commission, heavily weighted with past and present vocational educators, issued a report that was little more than an extended defense of vocational education. Entitled *The Unfinished Agenda: The Role of Vocational Education in the High School*, it flatly rejected the premise of *A Nation at Risk* and the other leading reform statements of the early 1980s. "The assumption [of the reports] is that more academics, which may be the best preparation for college, is also the best preparation for life. This assumption is wrong." The commission accused school reformers of "educational myopia" and insisted that academic and vocational learning must be of "co-equal importance."[16]

The same message resounded in the AVA's publications, at its conventions, and in its communications with policymakers and the press. A speaker at the organization's 1984 convention called recommendations for new graduation requirements in academic subjects "an unreasoned, hysterical expression of . . . the arrogant, isolated mentality of 'the best and the brightest.' " To a university professor writing in a 1985 issue of *VocEd,* the AVA's monthly magazine, the excellence movement was a "threat" to American education.[17]

The curriculum reforms of the 1980s have been undercut in another important way: school systems are enrolling millions of students in academic courses taught by teachers lacking adequate knowledge of their subjects. The fifty states license teachers and, in theory, require applicants to demonstrate a grasp of the subjects that they want to teach, usually by demanding that they earn a substantial number of college credits in the subject. But for a host of reasons—many of them invisible to the public—education authorities nationwide "misassign" teachers to subjects that they are ill-prepared to teach. Unpublished results from a 1987–88 survey of teachers by the U.S. Department of Education reveal that nearly 17 percent of the nation's one million public high school teachers have less than a college major or minor in the subject they teach most frequently. That means—if they teach two classes per day in their primary field of assignment (a conservative figure, since teachers typically teach four or five classes daily in their primary field), and they have twenty-five students in each class—that over eight million high school students a day attend classes taught by teachers lacking a college degree in the subject being studied.[18]

New graduation requirements and other measures aimed at increasing the amount of instruction in academic subjects have only intensified the pressure on administrators to misassign teachers as they scramble to find additional teachers in the academic disciplines while simultaneously preserving positions for those in subjects where enrollments are declining. In particular, the recent surge in enrollment in academic courses has exacerbated an already severe shortage of math and science teachers. Despite successes in recruiting teachers in those fields, an overwhelming majority of the states responding to a recent survey by the Council of State Science Supervisors reported "shortages" or "critical shortages" of math, chemistry, and physics teachers during the 1987–88 school year. According to Martha J. Miller, who tracks teacher supply and demand for the Florida Department of Education, "The improvement that has been made in the supply of math and science teachers is not good enough. There is still a tremendous gap between what we have and what we need." As a result, teacher misassignment in math and science classes has remained particularly prevalent, and in many school systems has increased during the 1980s. The American Institute of Physics in 1988 reported that nearly *one-third* of the participants in a large-scale survey it conducted of the nation's physics teachers held neither a major nor a minor degree in the subject, and had taught physics for less than five years. A 1987 survey of twenty-five states by the Council of Chief State School Officers revealed significantly higher rates of misassignment among "new hires" than among veteran teachers in those subjects, an indication of the continuing severity of the misassignment problem in math and science.[19]

The academic courses most commonly staffed by misassigned teachers are those enrolling students who arguably need well-trained teachers the most: less academically able students who traditionally have had little serious exposure to the academic disciplines. A science-department chairman at a California high school described four teachers who had been hired in 1984–85 to teach introductory physical science, none of whom had been trained in the subject. "They are learning along with the students," he said. "It's a sad situation." A North Carolina high school I visited had recently assigned an auto mechanics teacher to low-level biology and a graphics teacher to introductory history. The highest rates of teacher misassignment in Florida's high schools are in the low-level courses where enrollments have burgeoned in wake of the state's new graduation requirements—in such courses as "fundamentals of earth/space science," "fundamentals of biology," "general math I," "fundamentals of math I" and "fundamentals of math II," "basic skills math," and "English skills I." No less than 30 percent of the state's heavily subscribed "fundamentals of physical science" classes were taught by misassigned teachers in 1987–88. Similarly, a 1988 report by Rand Corporation researcher Lorraine McDonnell, based on the six-state study of the Center for Policy Research in Education, concluded that "the most common pattern" for schools with teacher shortages was to assign physical-education and home-economics teachers to low-level math and science courses. One California high school in the study reported that only four of its nine math teachers had degrees in the subject, and that all four were teaching advanced courses.[20]

Compounding the misassignment problem is the fact that virtually every state permits teacher misassignment in one form or another. Thousands of teachers are working in public high school classrooms under "general" certificates that permit them to teach *any* subject, regardless of the fields that they've been trained in. Though by 1988 most states had stopped issuing permanent general licenses, it will be another generation before the teachers possessing them retire from the nation's high schools. And many states continue to issue general certificates to the teachers of academic subjects in departmentalized junior high schools, where many high school students spend their freshman year. In fact, the number of junior high school teachers assigned outside their specialty under general certificates has increased in many school systems in wake of new graduation requirements, especially in math and science, as school officials have transferred junior high teachers with expertise in shortage fields into high schools, in an effort to staff the new academic classes there. "Robbing Peter to pay Paul" is how a Texas school administrator described the practice to me.

Many high school teachers are also working outside their field of expertise under "temporary" licenses. According to a 1988 study of teacher-licensing regulations by the National Association of State Directors of Teacher Education and Certification (NASDTEC), at least thirty states issue such licenses, ranging from Oklahoma ("minor teaching assignments"), to Kansas ("provisional endorsements"), Connecticut ("temporary authorizations"), Minnesota ("personnel variances"), and Texas ("temporary classroom permits"). Temporary licenses permit teachers with a license in one field to teach a subject in another field without regard to their background in that field. The licenses are typically issued for a year, but many states will renew them indefinitely, as long as teachers take one course or school-system workshop a semester in the subject to which they are misassigned. Twenty states permit school systems to misassign teachers on a temporary basis without obtaining state approval to do so, meaning that local educators are able to misassign teachers under temporary licenses virtually indefinitely without fear of state intervention. California issued 4,000 temporary "limited authorization" licenses in 1988–89, resulting in at least 100,000 students studying under misassigned teachers.[21]

Many states, according to the NASDTEC survey, also allow the misassignment of teachers during a portion of the school day. Maryland, for instance, permits out-of-field teaching for up to two periods daily. Yet a majority of such states do not classify teachers who are misassigned part time as misassigned at all. In a 1985 report on teacher misassignment, the Council for Basic Education termed this practice "an Alice-in-Wonderland device that simultaneously encourages and disguises the misassignment of teachers."[22]

The assignment of teachers to subjects that they are ill-equipped to teach is further encouraged by the commonplace practice of issuing licenses in broad academic fields. The holder of a secondary school certificate in social studies, for instance, is authorized in many states to teach courses ranging from anthropology to economics, geography, history, political science, psychology, and sociology. The result is that many teachers who are ostensibly working "in-field" are in fact teaching subjects of which they have little or no knowledge. In her 1988 study of new graduation requirements, McDonnell reported that several Arizona school systems assigned teachers with general social studies credentials to teach the state's newly required world history and economics courses. One such teacher told McDonnell: "I am struggling with teaching the required free enterprise course. I only had one semester of economics in college about fifteen years ago, and I didn't find out that I was teaching the course until two days before school started." According to William Aldridge, executive director of the National Science Teachers Association, the same problem is widespread in the sciences. "Certified is not synonymous with qualified," he says.[23]

Virtually every state also issues some form of "emergency" or "long-term substitute" license that permits school systems to employ teachers lacking a license in any subject. The then-superintendent of the Boston public schools, Robert Spillane, several years ago described such licenses as "Labor-day specials." "If principals had vacancies by that day," he said, "we let hundreds of people into the classroom who were neither qualified nor certified."[24] In several states, according to the NASDTEC survey, it's possible to obtain a secondary school emergency license without a bachelor's degree. And of the states that do require a college degree, no fewer than thirty permit emergency license holders to teach any high school subject, regardless of their college majors.

In Chicago in 1987–88, fully one-fourth of the city's 28,700 teachers were classified as "full-time basis substitutes," permitting them to be assigned to subjects regardless of their qualifications to teach them. In California, where standards are higher—to receive an emergency license an individual must have a bachelor's degree, be admitted to an education school, and pass a basic content exam in the subject he or she will teach or have fifteen hours of college credit in the subject—teacher shortages led to the issuance of 11,000 emergency certificates in 1987–88, nearly half the number of *regular* licenses issued by the state that year. It was also three times the number of emergency certificates issued in 1983–84, the year the legislature established statewide graduation requirements, which sug-

gests the pressure new graduation requirements have placed on administrators to misassign teachers.[25]

The misassignment problem is further exacerbated by the lax credentialing standards that most states have for day-to-day substitutes. Only a
handful of states require the same subject-matter background of secondary school substitutes as they do of regular teachers, while many issue
licenses that allow substitutes to teach any high school subject, and many
more set no standards for substitute teachers at all. Of the states that do
issue licenses to daily substitutes, half don't require a bachelor's degree,
according to the NASDTEC survey. Such standards are troublesome because teacher absenteeism is a tremendous problem in the public schools.
It's not uncommon to find high schools with 10 percent, 15 percent, or
even 20 precent of their teachers absent each day. As a result, thousands
of the nation's public high school classrooms are staffed by ill-trained
substitutes daily.[26]

One other element of the misassignment problem warrants mentioning: endorsements. Many teachers earn endorsements to their licenses,
certifying them to teach additional subjects. Unfortunately, states typically
rubber-stamp endorsements, issuing them to virtually any teacher who
has earned a requisite (and usually minimal) number of college credits in
the endorsement subject. In most instances neither the quality of the
college courses not their timeliness is weighed. As a 1983 report by the
New Jersey State Department of Education observes, "Endorsements to
the initial certificate appear to be awarded frequently through a clerical
review of college transcripts, without any assessment of individual competence or mastery." In wake of new graduation requirements, school systems are shifting many veteran teachers into academic subjects that their
endorsements permit them to teach—despite the fact that in many instances they received their endorsements long ago, in subjects they never
taught. But though their knowledge of their new subjects is frequently
weak, and in the case of fast-changing fields such as science, badly out-
dated, on paper they are fully licensed, permitting school systems to proclaim that they are staffing new academic courses with qualified teachers
when, by a reasonable standard, they are not.[27]

Frequently, the endorsement problem is exacerbated by a staffing practice known as bumping. Used throughout the nation's public school systems, it grants senior teachers broad preferences in teaching assignments,
including the opportunity to claim new openings in any subject that they
are licensed or endorsed to teach, the right to take the jobs of colleagues
working under temporary or emergency licenses, and, if their jobs are
eliminated due to falling enrollments or changes in the curriculum, the
right to claim the jobs of fully licensed but less-senior teachers in any
subject in which they are state sanctioned.

Bumping and the seniority system that underlies it encourage teacher
misassignment in public education. In a Florida high school I visited, a

newly hired science teacher with an undergraduate degree in chemistry, an M.D., and twelve years of teaching experience at the college and high school levels was teaching biology because she lacked seniority within the school system to teach chemistry—even though there were chemistry classes in the school being taught by teachers who lacked even an endorsement in the subject.

The curriculum reforms have prompted a surge in bumping, as teachers of art, music, physical education, vocational education, and other subjects in which new graduation requirements have hurt enrollments have used their seniority rights to secure jobs for themselves in academic subjects. A large Arizona school system told McDonnell that under the terms of its collective bargaining contract, it was forced to fill thirty new math and science positions with teachers already on its payroll in subjects in which enrollment was declining. According to the district's curriculum supervisor, the teachers were "barely qualified" for their new roles.[28] Similarly, the only calculus teacher in a California high school I visited had recently been transferred to a junior high school (where his expertise wasn't needed) because a more-senior voc-ed teacher with a math endorsement (but no experience teaching calculus) claimed his position.

Though bumping clearly hurts students, and is demoralizing to the many qualified teachers who lose their jobs because of it, few school administrators express strong opposition to either bumping or other seniority provisions—perhaps because they are bound to them by collective bargaining contracts and tradition, and perhaps because it's simply easier to treat all certified teachers as qualified teachers.

There have been efforts to tighten certification regulations in recent years. Washington State abolished all-subject high school licenses in 1987. Maine did so in 1988. In 1983 New Jersey limited teachers' bumping rights to subjects that they have taught, and the state in 1985 abolished nearly all emergency certificates. In 1988 the California legislative required special training of the holders of emergency licenses by 1990 and elimination of emergency certificates by 1994; in 1989–90, the state began monitoring teacher misassignment. In 1988 Oklahoma required new junior high school teachers to have at least an endorsement in each subject they teach. Michigan made the same requirement of *all* junior high teachers that year. A 1988 Maine law permits the state to suspend or revoke the licenses of superintendents in school systems in which teachers are misassigned. And Vermont approved similar regulation in 1989.

But by and large, states have failed to police their teacher misassignment statutes. In addition to the new initiatives in Vermont and Maine, many states have regulations on their books calling for cuts in state aid or loss of accreditation for schools and school systems that misassign teachers. But despite the magnitude of teacher misassignments in the nation's school systems, the NASDTEC survey reveals that only nine states withheld either state aid or accreditation in 1986–87 because of such misassignments. What's more, half the states reported that they had no recent information on the extent of teacher misassignment within their borders; their regulations call for penalties for teacher misassignment, but they have no idea where teachers are being misassigned. In its 1985 study—aptly titled *Making Do in the Classroom*—the Council for Basic Education concluded that "few or none [of the states] have reliable means for measuring its incidence within their own jurisdictions" and that "rules or sanctions against misassignment are rarely enforced." If the situation is improved today, it is only marginally so.[29]

Finally, the curriculum reforms of the 1980s are being undercut by the failure of educators to make academics rewarding to a wide range of students. Public schools traditionally have taught advanced academic courses in a dry, unimaginative manner, using banal teaching techniques and abstract and frequently lifeless curriculum materials. Because the students enrolled in such courses traditionally have been bright and ambitious, they frequently have done well in academic subjects despite the uninspiring environments they learn in. But the excellence movement has challenged educators to teach serious academics to less-able students who are not as highly motivated, students who often are not strong enough to endure the banality of many academic classrooms. As a result, say many teaching specialists, public secondary schools must adopt new teaching techniques and curriculum materials if the excellence movement's aims are to be achieved. "We haven't been doing a very good job of teaching science to our best students, so we can't expect to do the same old thing with new audiences," says Senta A. Raizen, director of the federally funded National Center for Improving Science Education.[30]

Dull, superficial textbooks, ceaseless teacher lecturing, and an emphasis on the abstract, Raizen and other experts say, must be replaced by more vibrant learning that links instruction more closely to students' own experiences, that makes use of biographies, narratives, speeches, diaries, and other engaging readings, and that involves students more actively in the learning process through the use of debates, speeches, experiments, problem-solving projects, and other techniques. Instruction, they argue, must be reshaped so that students gain knowledge of their own and on their own, instead of merely parroting back what they've learned from teachers' lectures. "We need to give kids a stake in the material that they are studying," said Arthur Appleby, head of the National Center for the Learning and Teaching of Literature at the State University of New York at Albany. "The task is to make it real and important to them."[31]

Revamping the pedagogy in the nation's high schools is a costly, time-consuming task. In Raizen's words, it can't be done "overnight or on the cheap." But to date, few serious attempts have been made to make academic course work more compelling to the many students who are turned off by the tedium of traditional academic instruction. Indeed, in responding to new graduation requirements by placing such students in watereddown courses, school systems have taken an easier, less-expensive route.

California is virtually the only state to have complemented its new curriculum mandates with the technical assistance and funding needed by school systems to design serious academic courses for students who are not easily motivated. Between 1983 and 1988 the state's Department of Public Instruction, working under a legislative mandate, drafted a series of broad "curriculum frameworks" and more-detailed "model curriculum standards" that set forth rigorous subject matter to be taught in academic courses in the state's high schools. Simultaneously, the state launched teacher-retraining programs in academic disciplines aimed at making the new subject matter come alive in the classroom.

The California Literature Project (CLP), for instance, was established in 1985 in response to new model curriculum standards recommending that much more literature be taught in the state's high school English courses. Under the CLP, local teachers attend state-sponsored summer institutes on university campuses, where, with the help of faculty specialists and curriculum experts, they develop instructional strategies and materials designed to use literature less as a vehicle for teaching basic grammar skills and more as a means of stimulating students to develop and express their own ideas and interpretations. "Many teachers have been taught to chop up works of literature into excerpts and ask skills questions about them, on the grounds that if the material is simple enough, less-able students will read it," says Mary A. Barr, the project's director. "But they're wrong. Kids won't read it because they can't connect to it and it's boring. It turns them off. Our goal is to teach real literature in ways that turn students on to it." The project's first summer teacher-training center was established at the University of California at Los Angeles, and by 1989 the project had expanded to four additional campuses. California has also established similar training initiatives in math (1984), history (1989), and science (1989). Unfortunately, only a fraction of the state's teachers have participated in the programs. Neither California nor its local school systems, which are required to pay a fee for each teacher they send to an institute, have appropriated sufficient funds for training teachers on a wide scale.

There have been a handful of curriculum-building projects at the national level. Mathematics educators at the University of Chicago are writing an entirely new kindergarten–twelfth grade curriculum for "average" students. Teaching math "as a tool for life," the new curriculum both introduces students to more advanced courses at an earlier age (the average student would study algebra in eighth grade) and places a stronger emphasis on the practical uses of the mathematics. Launched in 1983, the initiative, known as the University of Chicago School Mathematics Project, is drafting textbooks, teacher's guides, and training materials, and is scheduled to make the materials for the secondary grades available through a commercial publisher by 1991–92.

Similarly, the American Association for the Advancement of Science in 1985 launched an overhaul of the nation's science curriculum. In the first phase of Project 2061, named after the next scheduled return of Halley's Comet, a panel of leading scientists and educators has outlined the types of scientific knowledge that all students should study by graduation. The panel's recommendations are presented in a 1989 report entitled *Science for All Americans*. Rather than cursory coverage of a wide range of scientific subjects, the report's authors envision students studying a dozen or so interdisciplinary themes in depth during their school careers. For instance, a yearlong investigation of the atmosphere and weather would include the physics of molecules, the movement of energy around the Earth, and the geophysics of the Earth, but also the economic and social consequences of climate and weather. During Project 2061's second phase, scheduled to be completed by 1993, teams of teachers, school administrators, and university scholars in eleven school systems spread across six states are drawing up new curriculum blueprints based on the panel's recommendations.

More modestly, the American Chemical Society has been developing a nontraditional high school chemistry course built on the exploration of scientific issues in students' communities and in society. Designed to be as rigorous as traditional courses (though it makes less use of math), Chemistry in the Community, or CHEMCOM, takes a hands-on approach to teaching chemistry. Students spend half their time in the laboratory, and the course makes extensive use of field trips and class projects. In a unit on water pollution, for instance, students learn about the possible causes of a fish-kill problem in an imaginary community, study a purification plant, and, at the conclusion of the chapter, put the chemistry they have learned to use in a mock town meeting where responses to the fish problem are debated. "We're encouraging students to interpret information, synthesize it, apply it," says Sylvia Ware, CHEMCOM's director. "And, importantly, we're trying to make chemistry fun." A textbook for the course was published in 1988.

Yet there have been virtually no national teacher-retraining initiatives of a scale large enough to reach more than a fraction of the nation's students with these and other curriculum innovations. One of the few sizable training initiatives to date is the American Math Project, launched in 1988 with foundation funding and cosponsored by the Mathematical Association of America and the National Council of Teachers of Mathematics. Using the California Math Project as a model, the University of California at Berkeley-based organization has been building a network of teachers and university experts around the nation to teach new instructional strategies to math teachers through summer workshops on university campuses. And like the California program, it has sought to promote a livelier, more experiential pedagogy in math classrooms.

Significantly, not only do today's curriculum rewriting and teacher retraining initiatives fall far short of the level needed to teach rigorous academic subjects to the schools' "new audiences," they also fall short of the national commitment to curriculum building during the 1950s and 1960s, when the nation last sought fundamental changes in the teaching of academic subjects. Arguing that the public school curriculum was uninspiring and insufficiently challenging for top students, leading university scholars of that era led what evolved into a $2 billion, federally funded campaign to redesign the curriculum in virtually every academic discipline.

As early as 1952 mathematicians at the University of Illinois organized a Committee on School Mathematics to draft new high school materials that emphasized "learning through discovery." And in 1956 scientists at the Massachusetts Institute of Technology under the leadership of the physicist Jerrold Zacharias created the Physical Science Study Committee to revise the content and methods of high school physics teaching.[32] Two years later the American Mathematical Society appointed the prestigious School Mathematics Study Group, and during the next four years a sweeping new elementary-secondary math curriculum was written by scholars and classroom teachers under the panel's auspices. Then in the early 1960s a group of scholars that included Harvard anthropologist Douglas Oliver and Harvard psychologist Jerome Bruner developed a new interdisciplinary social studies curriculum. Ironically, though these and other less widely publicized curriculum projects of that era generally focused on high-achieving students, they criticized the lifelessness of many academic courses and sought more exciting alternatives to traditional teacher- and textbook-dominated instruction, just as today's pedagogical critics have.[33]

Through the National Science Foundation (NSF), the federal government was a major force within the curriculum movement of the 1950s and 1960s. The NSF financed many of that era's major pedagogy projects. And following passage of the Sputnik-inspired National Defense Education Act in 1958, thousands of teachers attended NSF-sponsored summer institutes and workshops designed to disseminate the fruits of the curriculum-developers' labors. But, incredibly, the Reagan administration abolished nearly all funding for the agency's precollege mathematics and science education activities in fiscal 1982. And though resuscitated the following year by Congress (over the administration's objections), the programs remained essentially moribund until fiscal 1985 for lack of sufficient staff to read grant proposals. Mounting congressional concern about the nation's "technology gap" raised the agency's precollege education budget to $140 million in fiscal 1990. But NSF's initiatives remain wholly inadequate to the task of revamping instruction in the nation's schools. It has supported initiatives such as the University of Chicago math project, CHEMCOM, and the American Math Project, but it has diluted its effectiveness by funding a wide range of unrelated "model projects" rather than marshaling its resources behind large-scale initiatives. And despite increases in recent years, NSF's total budget for curriculum and teacher-retraining projects is far below its Sputnik-era funding levels. Said NSF's director, Erich Bloch, in 1990 congressional testimony on the agency's educational efforts: "Are we doing enough? Quite frankly, no we're not." Under the Economic Security Act of 1984, Congress established a U.S. Department of Education program to supply school systems with funds for retraining math and science teachers. But funding for the Dwight D. Eisenhower Mathematics and Science Education Program was $136 million in fiscal 1990, a fraction of the resources required. Diane Ravitch, the educational historian, comments that the national commitment to curriculum reform in the 1950s and 1960s "was bought," primarily with federal funds. Clearly, another major federal investment in instructional improvement is needed today.[34]

In the main, the curriculum reforms of the 1980s have resulted not in a broader range of high school students receiving a serious academic education, but in perpetuation of the traditional practice in American education of sorting students into curriculum "tracks," where they receive distinctly different educations.

There are two types of tracking in public schools. Under the first, students of differing abilities study different subjects. In the "college-prep" track, students study primarily academic subjects; in the "general" track, their curriculum is heavily weighted with "personal service" courses such as health and drivers education; and in the "vocational" track, they develop skills for the world of manual work. The second type of tracking sorts students within academic subjects, usually on the basis of their prior performance in the subjects. There are typically three such tracks per subject at each grade level. Their names range from the prosaic ("honors," "regular," "skills") to the abstruse ("challenge," "core," "basic").[35]

The advocates of "ability grouping," as tracking is sometimes called, argue that the practice insulates slower learners from image-damaging comparisons to their brighter peers, allows the best and brightest to work to their fullest potential, and makes teaching a more efficient task by permitting students of varying abilities to progress toward the same academic goals at different speeds or by different routes. The reality is quite different. In the overwhelming majority of American schools, there are marked differences in the kind and quality of students' educational experiences from track to track.

One major difference is in course content. As the content of Florida's plethora of new courses reveals, bottom-track students are exposed only superficially to the academic disciplines. In a 1985 study entitled *Keeping*

Track: How Schools Structure Inequality, an investigation of nearly 300 English and mathematics classes nationwide, social scientist Jeannie Oakes observed, "Not only did [bottom-track English classes] not read works of great literature, but we found no evidence of good literature being read *to* them or even shown to them in the form of films. What literature they did encounter was so-called young-adult fiction—short novels with themes designed to appeal to teenagers (love, growing pains, gang activity) and written at a low level of difficulty." Similarly, the lower-level math classes in Oakes's study "focused grade after grade on basic computational skills and arithmetic facts—multiplication tables and the like."[36]

The quality of teaching in bottom-track courses is typically weaker as well. Students in bottom-track courses spend more time working in silence at their desks, filling out workbooks, copying notes from a blackboard or from a teacher's lecture, or watching filmstrips—the sorts of tedious activities that turn kids off to learning. Little reading, discussion, and writing take place. When teachers ask questions, the sought-after answer is usually yes or no, or a name or a date. Indeed, in a low-level freshman history class in a Texas high school I visited, a test question on World War II asked students to identify "what the C stands for in George C. Marshall." Pedagogy is far from perfect in upper-level courses, but at least there is a modicum of dialogue and debate in many of them, some cultivation of an appreciation for complexity and ambiguity, some demand for independent thought, and some interest in ideas and the ability to express them well.

Oakes captured the differences in teaching techniques between bottom- and top-track courses through a survey of the students in the classes she studied. She asked, "What is the most important thing you have learned or done so far in this class?" The students in top-track classrooms gave such answers as "How to prove things by experiments" and "Learned to analyze famous writings by famous people"; the students in bottom-track classes gave such responses as "To fill out things where you get a job" (English class), "How to do income tax" (math class), and "To be a better listener in class" (English class).[37]

Because students in the bottom tracks are arguably the toughest to teach, the tracking problem is exacerbated by the fact that school systems commonly assign their least-experienced and least-qualified teachers to bottom-track courses. In some cases, they are required to do so by state education authorities. Alabama, for instance, issues emergency math licenses to any teacher with six math credits on his or her transcript, but the holders of the licenses are permitted to teach only bottom-track courses.

Not only is the quality of instruction typically worse in bottom-track classes, there's often less of it. Oakes recorded how much time was spent "on task" and how much was spent on small talk and other diversions in the 300 secondary school classrooms she studied. She found that 82 percent of class time was spent on instruction in high-track English classes and 72 percent in high-track math classes, compared with 71 percent in low-track English classes and only 63 percent in bottom-track math classes. Thus, in a typical school—one with fifty-minute class periods and a 180-day school year—a student in academic-track math and English classes receives a combination of 240 hours of legitimate instruction a year in math and English, compared with only 201 hours for a student in bottom-track classes, a difference of almost 20 percent.[38]

Bottom-track students are also assigned less homework. Those in bottom-track English classes in Oakes's study were assigned an average of thirteen minutes of work a night, compared with forty-two minutes for top-track students. Such disparities are frequently reinforced by official policies. A large Florida school system I visited states in its teachers' manual that students in "advanced" English classes must write an average of 50 percent more often than students in "average" classes, and that students in "average" classes must write 50 percent more often than those in "basic" classes. Several years ago, two Stanford University professors discovered that many California schools prohibit bottom-track students from taking their textbooks home.[39]

Ironically, studies increasingly suggest that less-demanding work loads *encourage* class cutting and truancy among low-achieving students. For example, researcher Edward McDill concluded in a 1986 study entitled "A Population at Risk: Potential Consequences of Tougher School Standards for Student Dropouts" that "students of all ability levels respond positively to more challenging standards when they have a chance to achieve them. . . . Teachers might think that the lack of academic pressure makes the class more pleasant and reduces cutting, but in reality there is little activity going on in the low-demand classroom to merit attendance. Students who feel that they are not missing anything when they cut class are more likely to cut."[40]

As a result of the poor quality of instruction and the shallowness of content in the bottom tracks of many schools, the longer students are enrolled in bottom-track courses, the further they fall behind their peers in the upper tracks, and thus the less likely it is that they will be able to get out of the bottom tracks. They are caught in an educational catch-22: they can't escape the bottom tracks without a curriculum with more content or without better teaching, but they can't get the teaching or the content they need *unless* they escape the bottom tracks.

To make matters worse, tracking also places psychological barriers between students in bottom-level classes and the academic rigor that today's school reformers are urging. Tracking tells bottom-track students in many different ways that they are incapable of doing demanding work and, therefore, that they shouldn't try to do it. It tells them, in effect, that they *belong* at the end of the academic line.

The message is pervasive in many schools. The course catalog of a California high school I visited warned students that "it is difficult to change from the 'skills' level to the 'English' level" in the school's English curriculum. At another California school, an eighth-grade English teacher said to her class in the course of reviewing a test, "Even a lot of people in the other class got this one wrong." The "other" class was a top-track section of the course. In an inner-city New Jersey high school, a chapter on "payroll records" in the textbook of a bottom-track accounting class I observed began: "Many people in the United States are paid an hourly wage for their work. Max King works for Harbison Company. He is paid by the hour. Each morning when Max arrives at work he punches a time card on a time clock." The passage's underlying message to the students in the accounting class was clear: "You, too, are destined for clock-punching work." What's more, the teacher of a bottom-track social studies class in a Pittsburgh-area high school spent a large part of a class period the day I visited dictating welfare-eligibility requirements to his students.

The self-esteem of bottom-track students is also undermined in a subtle way by the passive classroom roles—working silently on assignments at their desks, dictating teachers' lectures, watching a myriad of movies and filmstrips—that teachers typically assign to them. Acted out often enough, such roles engender dependence and self-doubt.[41]

The assault on the self-esteem of bottom-track students isn't always subtle. The course catalog in an urban New Jersey high school that I visited included the following listings under English: "English 284-285: for sophomores who are very slow learners and poor readers." "English 283: for sophomores of below-average ability." "English 292 (regular): a course for underachieving students with college aspirations. . . . The pace of instruction is mindful of the pupil's impairment." "English 297: a course designed for terminal non-academic pupils. . . . Since terminal pupils will probably write only letters, attention is given to personal and business letters." Perhaps the school had in mind good-bye notes to friends and formal correspondence to lawyers and undertakers.

"Children are very quick to pick up other people's expectations about both their academic competence and their behavior," wrote Michael Rutter and his colleagues in a landmark 1979 study of inner-city London secondary schools, *Fifteen Thousand Hours*. "To an important extent, people tend to live up (or down) to what is expected of them." It seems that in many public schools the very act of placing students in bottom-track courses sets in motion a self-fulfilling prophesy of academic failure.[42]

By the measure of its educational rigor, the vocational track is largely an extension of the bottom academic track. The nation's total annual expenditure on vocational education has mushroomed from $1.8 billion to $8 billion over the past two decades, with federal appropriations alone growing from $56 million in 1964 to $918 million in 1989. Vocational instructors are the single largest block of teachers in the nation's public high schools; there are more vocational teachers than English teachers. And despite the recent increases in academic graduation requirements, the nation's vocational programs continue to offer courses ranging from poultry production to typing, cooking, and carpentry—in fields spanning agriculture, marketing, health, industrial arts, consumerism, office occupations, home economics, technical training, and building trades.[43]

Yet the majority of secondary school vocational courses are intellectually undemanding and of little real value to the students who take them. Courses in "retail merchandising" teach students to become cashiers. Courses in "advanced consumer clothing" teach students to "get organized to save time." Students in automotive programs spend class after class washing and waxing cars. Agricultural programs offer courses in "hardware selling," "recreation and tourism," and "vehicle marketing." Nor, astonishingly, is it uncommon to find public high schools with vocational programs that include classes in fast-food-restaurant work held in full-scale working models of the fast-food kitchens used by McDonald's or Burger King. Such kitchens are an example of the vast amount of expensive equipment that public school systems lavish on their vocational programs. Computerized typesetters, memory typewriters, automotive garages complete with sophisticated diagnostic equipment—the list goes on and on. One gets the impression that educators believe spending money on vocational students will compensate for not educating them.

The cynical pretense of many vocational courses only puts their shallowness into sharper focus. The course catalogue at a California high school I visited stated a course in "general business" would "help students better understand our American business system." But the course proposed to accomplish that ambitious task by imparting to students such "competencies" as "women's grooming," "telephones," "job applications," and "making change." At the student-run restaurant of a multi-million-dollar Florida vocational school, I was handed a lunch menu in Italian by a student-waiter enrolled in the school's "commercial foods" program who wasn't able to recognize the language as Italian, much less translate the menu.

Proponents of vocational education argue that the "hands-on" nature of vocational instruction captures the attention of hard-to-educate, dropout-prone students, and in doing so keeps them in school. "The real strength of vocational education lies in its ability to motivate students," in the words of the 1984 National Commission of Secondary Vocational Education. That may be so with some students, though vocational-education advocates rarely acknowledge the difference between keeping students on the attendance rolls and giving them a decent education. But *motivation* or *inspiration* are hardly words I would associate with the vocational classes I visited. More characteristic of what I found was a carpentry teacher in the multi-million-dollar vocational school in Florida who blamed students for what he called "the low productivity" of the school, *as all three students in his class slept at their desks;* a bookkeeping class in another Florida high school, one recognized for "excellence in education" by the U.S. Department of Education, where students spent a class period working crossword puzzles; and an electronics teacher at a third Florida school who insisted over lunch in the faculty cafeteria that without vocational-education classes his students would surely lose interest in school and drop out, only to complain afterward, as a dozen laconic eleventh-graders sat at their work stations in his classroom soldering wires without any apparent purpose, that "a lot of these kids are placed in this course, they come in here with a 'we're-not-going-to-do-anything' attitude." Rather than a place of opportunity for the dropout-prone, the vocational track is frequently a dumping ground for such students, a place where real learning is not a priority.

At best, the majority of vocational courses today train students rather than educate them. They teach them skills, but not the sort of intellectual skills that can be transferred from one subject to another; they don't attempt to lead students beyond information to understanding. The members of an automotive class are taught how to repair the power steering on a car, but they aren't taught the principles of hydraulics that make power steering possible; the students in a drafting class are taught how to draw the blueprints of a passive-solar-heated house, but they aren't taught why such houses are designed with double walls and other unique features.

What's more, the training that students receive in vocational classes is frequently of little help to them once they enter the job market, despite assertions by vocational educators that their programs are unique in their ability to teach students "marketable" job skills. One example: A Pennsylvania Department of Labor and Industry report revealed that only 29 percent of the state's 57,000 vocational-education graduates in the class of 1983 found employment in their fields. And such statistics frequently overstate vocational-placement rates because many school systems define working "in field" exceedingly broadly. A student in the commercial-foods program at the Florida vocational school was listed as "in field" while working as a dishwasher in a local hospital. As the business-oriented Committee for Economic Development concluded in its 1985 report *Investing in Our Children: Business and the Public Schools*: "Too often, [vocational courses] are a cruel hoax on young people looking to acquire marketable skills."[44]

If today's vocational courses are a far cry from the types of courses championed by school reformers, they are also a far cry from those envisioned by John Dewey, a lifelong advocate of vocational education, who in *Democracy and Education* wrote of his Laboratory School in Chicago: "I have woodworking in the school not to teach kids how to be carpenters but to teach them to think in a medium other than words."[45]

In the years since the signing of the Education of All Handicapped Children Act in 1975, "special education" also has become a dumping ground for many bottom-track students. Hailed as the handicapped children's Bill of Rights, P.L. 94-142, as the act came to be called, decreed that school systems identify all students with "educational, developmental, emotional, or physical disabilities" and then take steps to eliminate the disabilities as impediments to the students' education. In conjunction with Section 504 of the Rehabilitation Act of 1973, the law has created new educational opportunities for thousands of students, from the dyslexic to the autistic, who in the past had been sequestered in the nation's educational closets. But it has also created a convenient way for school systems to dodge the difficult job of educating all students.

The majority of the ten categories of handicapped students established under P.L. 94-142—such as "orthopedically impaired," "visually handicapped," or "speech impaired"—are unambiguous. Students in wheelchairs or without sight are not difficult to identify. One category, "learning disabled," however, has proven particularly hard to define. The U.S. Department of Education's definition of the term, "a disorder in one or more basic psychological processes involved in understanding or in using language spoken or written . . . ," is broad. And it is only one of approximately fifty official but often vague and overlapping definitions of the term in use in public education today. As a result, in many school systems "learning disabled" has become a catchall category, and an increasing number of disadvantaged but otherwise "normal" students are being relegated to it, even though P.L. 94-142 prohibits inclusion in the category of students whose learning problems stem from "environmental, cultural or economic disadvantages."

A special-education administrator in New York City went so far as to say in an interview that "the bulk of the youngsters being labeled "learning disabled" aren't handicapped [in any clinical sense]." The majority of them, he said, merely have underdeveloped language skills, which cause them to fall behind in their regular classes. A special-education teacher in a suburban Florida school system commented, "If kids [in the bottom track] aren't achieving up to par, or they are difficult to teach, teachers try to push them into learning-disabled classes." Even Madeleine C. Will, the U.S. Department of Education's official in charge of special education between 1983 and 1989, acknowledged that the "misclassification" of learning-disabled students is now a "great problem."[46]

Educators say they place "slow learners" in classes for the learning disabled so such students can benefit from the smaller class sizes, the presence of aides, and the instruction in literacy skills that such classes afford. Having classes for the learning disabled, however, also allows school systems to lower their expectations for the students they assign to such classes. As Alan Gartner, a former director of special education in the New York City school system, has written, "The students in such programs are not held to common standards of achievement or behavior."[47] Only rudimentary skills and topics are taught in classes for the learning disabled, homework is rarely if ever assigned, and the instructors of the learning disabled typically have little or no background in the academic subjects that they teach. Indeed, "babysitting" is perhaps the best way to describe many classes for the learning disabled. Occasionally a teacher or an aide helped an individual student with some schoolwork in the classes I visited, but more often students were free to do what they wanted, so long as they weren't disruptive. There is a powerful stigma attached to "special education" in the school culture; to be labeled a learning-disabled student in a public school is to suffer the disparagement of peers and teachers alike. And rarely do students who have been labeled learning disabled return to the mainstream of school life. Indeed, since schools receive additional funding for learning-disabled students ($338 per student from the federal government in 1988–89), they have an incentive to continue classifying a student as "LD."

Yet the number of students classified as learning disabled has burgeoned since enactment of P.L. 94-142. The number more than doubled between 1976–77 and 1987–88, according to a 1989 U.S. Department of Education report, to nearly 2,000,000. By 1987–88, learning-disabled students accounted for no less than 60 percent of the secondary school special-education enrollment, and 9 percent of the nation's total public secondary school enrollment. What's more, the Education Department warned in 1988 that the number of placements in learning-disabled programs is accelerating as a result of the curriculum reforms of the 1980s. "Higher standards in the name of educational reform seem to be exaggerating the tendency to refer difficult children to special education," it said in a report.[48]

By far, the nation's economically disadvantaged students pay the highest price for the pervasiveness of tracking in public education. According to a large-scale U.S. Department of Education study, only 21 percent of the nation's students of "low socioeconomic status" (as measured by an index that includes parental income and education, parental occupation, and the presence of consumer goods in a household) are enrolled in the academic track, compared with 62 percent of their affluent peers, students of "high socioeconomic status." Conversely, 35 percent of the nation's disadvantaged students are enrolled in the vocational track, compared with only 11 percent of their affluent peers. In other words, disadvantaged students are three times *less* likely to be in the academic track than affluent students are, but three times *more* likely than affluent students to be in the vocational track.[49]

Supporters of public education say it is a bulwark of our egalitarian ideals. And indeed, the American experiment with what Lawrence Cremin called "popular education" is as noble as it is radical. But the

tendency of tracking to sort students into courses and curricula of different quality on the basis of their social class (and, thus, to a considerable
degree, on the basis of their race) belies the notion of public schools as a
common ground of opportunity. Because affluent students frequently
receive a far better education under tracking than disadvantaged students do, tracking often intensifies rather than eases the social-class differences that students bring with them to school; it broadens rather than
narrows the opportunity gap between the nation's affluent and its poor.
During a trip to a Texas high school, I happened to visit two American
history classes that were going on next door to each other. They captured
the reality of tracking in public education: one was a "scholars" section of
white sophomores wearing expensive Benetton clothes, pearls, and
Gucci bags; the other was a "basic" section, a virtually all-black class clad
in worn T-shirts and sneakers.

Yet, despite the increasing importance of disadvantaged students to public education and the nation, the vast majority of the nation's public
educators—some 2.5 million administrators, principals, and teachers—
remain deeply committed to student tracking and its underlying premise
that only top students, the "college-bound," should study academic subjects in depth. Theirs is essentially the same philosophy that has per-
vaded the professional ranks of public education since the turn of the
century, the strongly utilitarian philosophy that today's reformers have
rejected.

In talking to teachers and administrators in public schools, one learns
quickly that astonishing proportions of them believe that the majority of
their students are lacking in the ability to study academics seriously. "I
don't see any problem with four years of English for some students," a
guidance counselor in a rural Florida high school told me. "But you want
to identify [the aptitude of] your students and require more of some than
of others." Said a math teacher in a suburban California school system:
"Everyone likes to think that everyone is capable of adding fractions and
decimals, [of] doing percents, [of] learning elementary algebra. But it's
not true. I remember when I went to school. In order to take algebra you
had to have an IQ of at least 120." At another Florida high school, the
principal told me, "Instead of more math and English, what we really
need for many kids are courses in how to plant trees and such." To a
striking degree, educators' assumptions about their students' academic
abilities correspond to the students' social class. Nearly all of the principals I interviewed discussed the aims of their schools in terms of percentages of students receiving free or reduced-price lunches, a form of federal aid to the poor. "Remember," cautioned the principal of a Texas high
school at the outset of my visit to his school, "we're in a low socioeconomic community here." Affluent students generally are assumed by

educators to be capable of doing demanding work; disadvantaged students generally are not.

Despite the revolution under way in the nation's workplaces, public educators generally reject the notion that non-college-bound students need to study academic subjects in more than a superficial way. "These kids are 'work-oriented,' " a guidance counselor in a blue-collar Pennsylvania community told me, in explaining his ambivalence toward his state's new graduation requirements in academic subjects. "College isn't important to them." The principal of a Florida high school expressed the same sentiment: "Unless he's going to college, there's no need for a student to take geometry." In a survey several years ago, the Minneapolis school system found that only 65 percent of its teachers believed that all high school graduates needed "critical thinking skills," and only 57 percent believed that graduates should have knowledge of "different cultures and societies." Administrators are no less ambivalent toward academic subjects. A 1985 survey by the American Association of School Administrators found its membership "widely divided" on the question of whether all students should study a core academic curriculum.[50]

Do public educators believe that there is *inherent* value in intellectual skills and cultural knowledge? Many, it seems, do not, much less that it's public education's responsibility to teach such skills and knowledge to all students. When I asked a California math teacher what he thought the value of increased graduation requirements might be for students who otherwise wouldn't take two years of math, he could think of only one answer: "It'll make them better qualified to take the entry-level tests that they give in the department stores." "The new graduation requirements create problems here," said the Pennsylvania guidance counselor I spoke to. "Our cosmetology girls, for example, are in a half-day, off-campus program for three years. It's going to be tough for them to fit the extra [academic] courses in."

Clearly, there's a broad consensus within the educational establishment that public schools should teach a large proportion of their students vocational skills rather than intellectual skills. Floretta McKensie, a prominent educator and then-superintendent of the Washington, D.C., school system, argued in a 1983 issue of the *Harvard Educational Review*, "The best education for the best is not the best education for all." Declaring that "career training" was more valuable than academic subjects to many students, she described *The Paideia Proposal*'s recommendation that non-academic electives be abolished as "educational Oz, . . . as specious as the wizard's magic powers." In a response to *A Nation at Risk* and other reports on school reform, the directors of the National Association of Secondary School Principals in 1983 urged that "the opportunity to develop technical and occupational skills" be a high priority within public education. Two years of math and science during high school "is sufficient" for "job-bound" students, the organization asserted. Also responding to *A Nation at Risk,* a teacher advisory panel in the Arlington, Virginia, school system in 1984 questioned "whether geometric and algebraic concepts are necessary for the non-college-bound students." It recommended development of a "life-skills mathematics course" for such students.[51]

To public educators, the comprehensive high school—offering a full range of courses for students bound for a variety of different futures—is a truly democratic institution. "It is the school's responsibility to provide educative experiences that are meaningful and challenging for all youth, with an almost infinite diversity of interests, capacities and needs," according to the teachers' handbook of a Florida high school. "We need to make sure that we have provided courses or programs that will *put the students in their proper places* [emphasis added]," the school's principal told me. It's hard to imagine a statement more inegalitarian in its implications. Yet it is broadly believed within public education that a curriculum focused on academic subjects is not only undemocratic but punitive as well. A professor of education at the University of Wisconsin–Milwaukee argued in a 1985 issue of the *New York Times Educational Review* that "four years of English and two years of science . . . may not be an appropriate education" for many students. Instead, "an appropriate education may include auto mechanics and how to read bus schedules. Time spent in a science class deprives these youngsters of the chance to learn what *is* appropriate for their needs. . . . By increasing high school graduation requirements, we are doing these students a disservice. We are denying them their right to an appropriate education." On the same grounds, many public educators have attacked the academic recommendations of *A Nation at Risk* as "elitist." Of course, to the education reformers, comprehensive high schools are emphatically undemocratic. They symbolize the failure of public education to teach intellectual skills to a majority of students.[52]

If the perpetuation of tracking in the nation's schools has hurt disadvantaged students, the excellence movement's emphasis on early childhood education has helped. Seeking to ensure that disadvantaged students start their school careers on a more nearly equal level with their affluent peers—on the grounds that disadvantaged students would be better prepared to tackle academic subjects in high school if their educational deficiencies were more fully addressed while they were still young—the reform movement has brought about a resurgence in "compensatory education," a cornerstone of the federal War on Poverty during the 1960s.

The same belief expressed in President Johnson's 1965 declaration that "no American child" should be "condemned to failure by the accident of birth," has prompted some twenty states to launch preschool programs for disadvantaged students since the onset of the reform movement in the early 1980s. South Carolina, for example, has required establishment of half-day sessions in every school system for four-year-olds lacking school "readiness" skills, and Texas's 1984 reform legislation requires prekindergarten summer school programs in every Texas school system with fifteen disadvantaged or non-English-speaking four-year-olds.[53]

The Missouri legislature has put the public schools in its state in the business of educating students at an even younger age. In 1984 it required school systems to provide language, hearing, and other types of screening for one- and two-year-olds and to offer instruction in child development to parents of children up to three years old. The parent program is based on the pilot New Parents as Teachers Project, in which four Missouri school systems between 1981 and 1985 hired child-development experts to work with 380 families in their homes and at group meetings in local schools. Evaluators found that at age three, children whose parents took part in the program scored "significantly" higher on "all measures of intelligence, achievement, auditory comprehension, verbal ability and language ability" than did a control group of children whose parents did not participate.[54]

The new public preschool programs have been reinforced by recent research documenting striking improvements in the educational achievement and social circumstances of disadvantaged students who participate as young children in high-quality preschool activities. In particular, the High/Scope Educational Research Foundation revealed in a widely publicized 1984 report entitled *Changed Lives: The Effects of the Perry Preschool Program on Youths through Age 19* that severely impoverished children enrolled in a Ypsilanti, Michigan, preschool program in the early 1960s and tracked by the foundation into early adulthood graduated from high school at a significantly higher rate than did children with similar backgrounds who had not participated in a preschool program. The study also found a much higher employment rate, fewer arrests, and fewer welfare recipients among the Perry preschool students. Society, *Changed Lives* concluded, received a seven-dollar "return" on each dollar invested in the Perry program.[55]

Those who teach disadvantaged students strongly support the spread of preschool programs. They contend that such programs not only help disadvantaged students acquire important basic academic skills but also afford disadvantaged students a head start in gaining the emotional discipline they need to learn. "Many disadvantaged children come to school hyperactive, very physically oriented," said the principal of an inner-city elementary school in California. "They have little structure in their lives that they can carry over into the tasks of learning. There isn't a time for dinner, a bedtime, a time for homework. So when they come to school, they don't understand that there is a time to learn." Enrolling such students in school at an earlier age, he said, helps develop their emotional "school skills" before it's too late. Educators who work with disadvantaged students also point out that an increasing number of students from middle- and upper-income families attend private preschools, so that public programs are necessary just to keep disadvantaged students from falling further behind their peers.

Another strategy has been to expand kindergarten programs. North Carolina was the first of several states to fund full-day kindergarten programs. The New York City school system began offering full-day kindergarten classes in 1983, and some 62,000 students now participate in the voluntary program. In addition, a number of states and school systems have reduced class sizes in kindergarten and elementary grades in their effort to strengthen the education of disadvantaged students in their early years. Under Project Prime Time, for example, Indiana has spent $316 million since 1984–85 for new teachers in school systems that have limited the size of their kindergarten and first-, second-, and third-grade classes.[56]

Finally, states and school systems have begun systematically to measure students' "readiness" for school. Under a 1985 legislative mandate, Georgia requires its school systems to factor kindergarteners' scores on a statewide "readiness assessment" into decisions on whether to promote them to the first grade. Readiness measures have been controversial. Opponents argue that paper-and-pencil tests of young children, in particular, are imprecise instruments, that students who do poorly on them are unfairly stigmatized, and that it's counterproductive to make students repeat early grades. But readiness testing that includes broader measures such as listening and speaking skills frequently works well. Since 1984 Minneapolis has used a "benchmark" test to gauge kindergarteners' preparedness for first grade. Students who fail the test, which measures such skills as ability to copy a geometric shape and to identify rhyming words, usually attend summer school. If they then fail the test again, they are placed in all-day "transition" kindergarten classes, where they repeat regular kindergarten work in the morning and get intensive basic-skills training in the afternoon. The first-grade teachers I talked to during a visit to Minneapolis were pleased with the program. They reported that many of their students who had been in the transition program had "caught up" educationally to their peers.

The many new state and local initiatives are buttressing the major federal early childhood program, Head Start. Created in 1965, Head Start today supplies some 450,000 disadvantaged preschoolers with medical care (including hearing, speech, vision, and dental examinations), nutrition (a hot meal and a snack each day), and preschool learning activities at 1,200 centers nationwide, though, despite a $1.4 billion fiscal 1990 budget, the program reached less than one-quarter of the nation's 2.4 million poor children that year.

The spread of state and local early childhood programs is an important step toward educational excellence. But the new investment in compensatory programs may be for naught if public educators cannot be disabused of their belief that only the most talented students should receive an "intellectual" education in the nation's public high schools. Decades old, that notion remains a tremendous barrier to disadvantaged students, and to the emergence of public education as a truly democratic institution. Unless many more public educators can be persuaded to embrace the spirit as well as the letter of reform, unless they can be convinced that the majority of the nation's students, the work-bound as well as the college-bound, are best served by a rigorous academic education, many students will continue to be treated as second-class citizens in the nation's secondary schools. They will continue to be victimized by superficial courses, unqualified teachers, and failed instructional strategies.

CHAPTER 5

Blue Collar? Or White? The AFT, the NEA, and Teacher Reform

"Shanker Urges Teachers Move Past Bargaining," read the headline on page one of the *New York Times* on April 28, 1985. A day earlier Albert Shanker, president of the American Federation of Teachers, had warned a teachers convention in Niagara Falls that the fruits of collective bargaining—shorter hours, due-process protections, a guaranteed wage scale, smaller classes—had failed to make teaching an attractive occupation. "[W]e have not been able to achieve all that we had hoped for through the bargaining process," he told his stunned audience, "and it is now time to go beyond it to something additional and quite different. . . . We can continue working away only at collective bargaining. But if that is our decision, I predict that in 10 or 15 years we will find we've been on a treadmill."[1]

Shanker's statements rocked public education. For it was Shanker, one of the nation's most influential and militant teacher unionists, who had led the campaign to unionize public school teaching two decades earlier. As an organizer with the New York City Teachers Guild in the late 1950s, and then with the United Federation of Teachers (UFT) after its founding in 1960, he had spread militancy within the ranks of the nation's largest school system. In 1960 he helped persuade 5,000 teachers to walk off their jobs, a move that pressured New York officials into sponsoring the election of a bargaining agent for teachers a year later, an election the UFT won easily. Shanker and other UFT officials launched a second strike in 1962, winning the city's 40,000 teachers a major salary increase and public education's first collective bargaining contract.

Born of immigrant parents on Manhattan's Lower East Side and speaking only Yiddish when he entered the city's public schools, Shanker became president of the militant UFT in 1964. And before long, teachers from Trenton to Sacramento, influenced by the tough talk emanating from the UFT's New York headquarters, were demanding the right to bargain for wages, hours, and working conditions in the tradition of the nation's industrial labor unions. By the time Shanker was elected president of the American Federation of Teachers (AFT), the UFT's parent organization and itself an affiliate of the AFL-CIO, in 1974, over 60 percent of the nation's 2,000,000 teachers were working under collective bargaining agreements, and within several more years, nearly 90 percent were members of either the AFT or the nation's second major teacher union, the National Education Association (NEA), making public school teaching the most highly unionized occupation in the nation.

But by the onset of the 1980s, teaching was also an ailing occupation. It was attracting only the least talented of the nation's college graduates, having become a vocation of last resort, a refuge for the unaccomplished and the uninspired. School reformers were particularly troubled by teaching's plight, for they viewed high-quality teachers as crucial to their goal of broadening public education's academic mission. As one reform report warned bluntly, if the problems in teaching were not addressed, the education reform movement would grind "to a dead halt."[2] Thus, recruiting a greater share of the best and brightest into public education's classrooms has been a major thrust of the reform movement, an important priority in the pursuit of educational excellence. And because the two major teachers unions achieved such wide influence within teaching and over the operation of the public schools generally during the 1960s and 1970s, understanding their response to the reform movement in teaching is crucial to measuring the movement's progress.

The evidence of teaching's parlous condition in the early 1980s was overwhelming. Teachers' after-inflation purchasing power dropped 12 percent in the decade between 1972–73 and 1982–83. With an average salary of just over $20,000, they were receiving less than middle-class wages in 1982–83—defined by the federal government that year as $25,000 for a family of four. The College Board reported that during the 1970s the Scholastic Aptitude Test scores of high school seniors intending to teach declined at a far faster rate than those of college-bound students generally; by the early 1980s, the average score of future teachers was eighty points below the national average, on a scale of 400 to 1,600.[3]

Meanwhile, several states had made basic literacy tests prerequisites for a teaching license, only to find that many of their college graduates couldn't pass the exams. Nearly one-third of the applicants for licenses failed the California test when it was introduced in 1983. Press reports of ungrammatical letters to parents and of blackboards covered with misspelled words were commonplace. "Help! Teacher Can't Teach!" shouted *Time* magazine on its June 6, 1980, cover.

Two University of North Carolina researchers revealed in a widely publicized 1982 study that attrition within public school teaching was highest among the brightest in the field. And in a measure of the low

morale within teaching, the 1981 edition of a teacher survey conducted
every five years by the NEA revealed that one in three teachers wouldn't
go into teaching again if given the chance, compared with fewer than one
in five in 1976 and fewer than one in ten in 1961.[4]

Teaching had never been a high-status occupation in the United States,
or one able to attract a large proportion of talented people. In his classic
1932 study of teacher status, *The Sociology of Teaching*, Willard Waller
noted that "the teacher in our culture has always been among the persons of little importance." Historian Richard Hofstadter suggested as
much in *Anti-intellectualism in American Life*. He cited a 1776 edition of the
Maryland Journal announcing the arrival in Baltimore of a ship from
Belfast and Cork, listing among its products for sale "various Irish com-
modities," including "school masters, beef, pork, and potatoes." Waller
himself called teaching "a refuge for unsalable men and unmarriageable
women."[5]

Over half the nation's teachers in the early decades of the century
lacked college degrees, and the aptitude of teachers who did study beyond high school was below that of all other students except those majoring in business, art, agriculture, and secretarial services, according to a
1938 survey of Pennsylvania college seniors by the Carnegie Foundation
for the Advancement of Teaching. A similar survey of 10,000 graduates
of forty-one colleges in 1954 put teachers above only home economics,
physical education, and social science majors, many of whom were also
headed for the classroom. Nor were conditions in teaching significantly
different by 1963, when James D. Koerner, the president of the Council
for Basic Education, observed in *The Miseducation of American Teachers*
that "teaching continues to attract the poorer students." In Hofstadter's
blunt words, the public schools were staffed from their founding primarily by the sons and daughters of "culturally constricted lower- or middle-
class homes."[6]

But if there was never a golden era in school teaching, the field for
generations was bolstered by bright women and minorities shut out of
other career opportunities. By the onset of the 1980s, however, teaching's subsidy was evaporating. Increasingly free to enter occupations of
their choice, many talented women and minorities were shunning the
classroom in favor of more prestigious and higher paying fields such
as finance, law, and medicine. And with women constituting two-thirds
of the nation's teachers, such trends took a heavy tool on the public
schools.[7]

A changing job market also was shrinking the pool of talented teaching
prospects. There was a sharp rise in the 1970s and early 1980s in the
number of low-level but relatively well-paid managers needed to train
and supervise the many salespersons, cashiers, and service representatives joining the labor pool via the growing service sector of the economy.
The U.S. Department of Labor reported that in 1980 there were more

openings for managers and administrators (711,793) than for any occupation except salesclerks (757,750). Such jobs usually involved working with people and organizing and communicating ideas—the basics of teaching. It meant that for the first time, virtually the entire labor market was bidding for those whose talents traditionally had led them into the classroom. The ability of the schools' competitors to offer more pleasant working conditions, a greater degree of collegiality, and higher status, as well as higher salaries, created a one-sided competition for talent.[8]

Demographics compounded teaching's woes. The pool of eighteen- to twenty-four-year-olds, the typical age group of teacher recruits, declined by 15 percent between 1980 and 1990, while public education enrollment increased by 6 percent. In addition, the average age of a public school teacher increased from thirty-six in 1976 to forty-two in 1985, contributing to a rising attrition rate within teaching that the U.S. Census Bureau pegged at 9 percent in 1984, or 50 percent higher than it had been during the 1970s.[9]

These developments prompted the U.S. Department of Education to predict that a staggering 1.3 million new teachers would be needed in public education between 1986 and 1992, no less than 60 percent of the nation's 2.2 million teachers. As many as 215,000 new teachers would be needed by 1992, the department estimated, almost double the 115,000 hired in 1981 and nearly one-quarter of all college graduates.[10]

Evidence of a severe teacher shortage mounted. Georgia school systems hired math and science teachers in West Germany. New York City sent recruiters to Spain. Houston began running ads in the English-language *Mexico City News*. Florida officials launched an annual teacher job fair in 1986, complete with a toll-free phone number, 1-800-FL-TEACH, for out-of-state applicants. The same year the California Department of Public Instruction sponsored a multi-million-dollar television and radio ad campaign featuring actor Richard Dreyfus and the theme "A Class Act: Be a Teacher."

In many school systems, "teacher recruitment" took on an entirely new meaning. Florida's Broward County sponsored a Spring Break II "conference" in order to fill 300 vacancies in 1985. Candidates were treated to three days of Fort Lauderdale beachfront accommodations, as well as pitches from local realtors, day-care operators, and utility representatives. Similarly, business leaders in Prince Georges County, Maryland, on the eastern border of Washington, D.C., in 1986 announced a package of incentives to lure teachers into their county's schools that included low-rate loans, credit cards free of annual fees, discounts at local restaurants, apartments with no security deposits, and a month's free rent.

Thus the nation faced the huge task of supplying the public schools with thousands of new teachers of an unprecedented caliber as the odds of doing so grew steadily longer. Yet the national response to the crisis has been impressive: teaching's plight has attracted the attention of more influential institutions and individuals since the early 1980s than at any time in the nation's history.

It was a major priority of the 1983 studies on school reform. In *A Nation at Risk,* the National Commission on Excellence in Education recommended that teacher salaries be made "professionally competitive, market-sensitive, and performance-based"—in contrast to the traditional method of paying teachers strictly on the basis of seniority and academic degrees. It urged that salary, promotion, tenure, and retention decisions "be tied to an effective evaluation system that includes peer review so that superior teachers can be rewarded, average ones encouraged, and poor ones either improved or terminated." School systems, the commission wrote, should develop "career ladders" that distinguish between "the beginning instructor, the experienced teacher, and the master teacher," and they should proffer new roles and responsibilities to master teachers. In *High School,* the Carnegie Foundation for the Advancement of Teaching recommended much higher average teacher salaries and a "career path" for teachers "based on performance." It proposed that teacher candidates "complete a sharply focused major in one academic discipline, not in education," that a fifth year be added to teacher preparation, and that prospective teachers be required to pass a rigorous written examination administered by newly created state boards of examiners, independent bodies with teacher majorities. The foundation further recommended a teacher evaluation system "largely controlled by other teachers who themselves have been judged to be outstanding in the classroom," the transfer of teachers' nonteaching duties to aides and others, and the creation of a national teacher service, a college-scholarship program for high-achieving students who make a three-year commitment to teach in the public schools. The Education Commission of the States' reform task force in *Action for Excellence* endorsed the concept of "career ladders" and the principle that outstanding teachers be rewarded with higher salaries, called for higher standards in teacher education, and urged school systems to toughen their procedures for firing incompetent teachers. The authors of *Making the Grade* also called for teachers to be paid on the basis of performance. And they recommended establishment of a national master teacher program, a federally funded initiative to recognize and reward teaching excellence.

Three years later a second series of national reform reports dealt almost exclusively with teaching's woes. Building on the ideas in the earlier studies, the recommendations in these reports received wide attention and moved the national interest in teacher reform to a still higher level.

In *Tomorrow's Teachers,* released in April 1986, the education deans of forty of the nation's leading universities strongly criticized their own profession in condemning the nation's teacher-training programs as "intellectually weak." The Holmes Group, as the deans called themselves, urged the dismantling of undergraduate education programs and their replacement with a five-year program that required future teachers to earn liberal arts degrees. Founded in 1983 to promote teacher reforms, the Holmes Group also urged school systems to create a hierarchy of "instructors," "professional teachers," and "career professionals" (based on teachers' training, career aspirations, and performance), as a way of enhancing the status and rewards of teaching. To prepare new teachers better, the deans proposed the creation of schools analogous to teaching hospitals in the medical profession, facilities operated jointly by school systems and colleges, in which beginning teachers would serve "internships" and "residencies."[11]

In 1985 the Carnegie Corporation of New York, one of the nation's largest foundations, established the Carnegie Forum on Education and the Economy to explore the link between economic growth and education. As its first initiative, the forum created a $3 million task force on teaching, headed by Lewis M. Branscomb, chief scientist of IBM. A month after release of the Holmes Group report, the Carnegie task force published *A Nation Prepared: Teachers for the 21st Century,* a blueprint for producing what it said were the "pay and conditions of work" essential to attracting the best and brightest into teaching. The prestige of the Carnegie Corporation gained the report a wide national audience, and its recommendations dominated subsequent discussions of teacher reform.[12]

A Nation Prepared's premise was that the need for higher salaries notwithstanding, able and ambitious people wouldn't be drawn to teaching or stay in the field unless schools and teaching were "restructured" to permit teachers a greater degree of judgment in their work and better career opportunities. The report called for teachers to be full participants in the managing of public schools, with the authority to make, or at least to influence strongly, decisions on such matters as organization of the school day, selection of teaching materials and methods, assignment of students and staff, allocation of the school's budget, and even employment decisions; the task force went so far as to suggest that "the teachers might hire the administrators, rather than the other way around." Building on the earlier career-ladder proposals, the Carnegie panel proposed a hierarchy of teaching positions within schools, beginning with "interns," "residents," and "instructors," and continuing through several levels of career teachers to the new category of "lead teacher." Salary, status, and responsibilities were to be differentiated according to rank, with lead teachers assuming many of the managerial responsibilities of their schools. As a basis for ranking teachers within schools, and as a means of enhancing the status and public recognition of teaching, the task force also called for creation of an independent national board for professional teaching standards to set high standards for teachers in each discipline and convey "board certification" on teachers who voluntarily meet them, as similar boards do in accounting, architecture, and other fields. The Carnegie panel again called for abolition of undergraduate education degrees and creation of "clinical schools" where beginning teachers would hone their skills under the supervision of accomplished peers.

The nation's governors threw their weight behind the Carnegie agenda three months later at their annual meeting in Charleston, first in a resolution, and then in a 173-page educational manifesto of their own. The key recommendations on teaching in *Time for Results: The Governors' 1991 Report on Education* all had appeared in *A Nation Prepared*: a realignment of governance in schools to "empower" teachers, an easing of "top-down" state and local regulations for the same purpose, creation of a national teaching standards board, and new "career patterns" for teachers.[13]

Teaching's plight drew the attention of many other influential voices, as well. Two months before release of *A Nation at Risk,* more than forty college presidents and the education commissioners of nearly forty states gathered for two days at Yale University to explore solutions to the teacher crisis. In wake of the report's 1983 release, the chairman of the U.S. House Education and Labor Committee appointed a congressional task force of legislators and educators to investigate the linkage of teacher pay to performance. In its recommendations, the panel urged states to try the concept. Many leading philanthropies joined the Carnegie Corporation in promoting changes in teaching. The William and Flora Hewlett Foundation, for instance, provided a $400,000 grant to establish a commission on teaching in California. The commission's report, *Who Will Teach Our Children?*, released in late 1985, contained many of the recommendations that received wide attention in the Carnegie task force report the following spring, including the concepts of board-certified teachers and greater teacher involvement in school decision making. Education Secretary Bell, as well as President Reagan, pressed for reforms in teaching, calling for career ladders, master teachers, and "performance pay." Bell awarded $1 million in grants in 1984 to school systems and other organizations to draft career-ladder and master-teacher plans. The nation's corporate community also sought solutions to teaching's troubles. The financier David Rockefeller, Jr., and other corporate executives, for instance, contributed to the founding in 1986 of a national nonprofit organization to recruit new teachers.[14]

The overarching goal of the reform movement in teaching has been to make the occupation attractive to the nation's best and brightest by transforming it into a full-fledged profession. The reformers have sought to recast an occupation marked by low pay, low standards, repetitive work, narrow career opportunities, little recognition of achievement, and a poor public image—characteristics of traditional assembly-line work—into an occupation offering tough entrance requirements, respectable salaries, collegiality, a serious intellectual environment, opportunities for leadership, rewards for achievement, a career path, and status—the hallmarks of professions such as law and medicine, and the characteristics of teaching itself in Japan, Germany and other of our educational and economic competitors. "Recruiting the most able college graduates to teaching will require schools to offer pay and conditions of work that are competitive with those to be found in other places where professional work is done," the Carnegie task force wrote.[15] It was to this movement to professionalize teaching—to transform it, in effect, from blue-collar work to white-collar work—that Shanker allied himself in Niagara Falls.

Shanker's theme in Niagara Falls was unambiguous: it wasn't possible to transform teaching into a true profession by bargaining over wages, hours, and working conditions. The unions needed to "go beyond" their emphasis on collective bargaining to something "quite different" because the gains achieved through traditional collective bargaining "fell short" of creating a "professional workplace" within schools. Shanker, who began his career in public education as an elementary school math teacher in New York City in the 1950s after completing the course work for a doctorate in philosophy at Columbia University, acknowledged that the rise of industrial-style unionism within teaching itself contributed to the dim view the nation's best and brightest held of the field. "We tend to be viewed today as though we are acting only in our own self interest. . . . That image is standing in the way of our achieving professional status," he warned.[16]

He also acknowledged that many of the distinguishing characteristics of professions conflicted with fundamental union principles, and that many of the reformers' proposals for "professionalizing" teaching clashed with long-standing union policies. But, he argued, if teacher unions failed to bend their policies to the needs of the reform campaign in teaching, if they used their vast influence to block change, they themselves would suffer the consequences. "Unless we go beyond collective bargaining to teacher professionalism," he warned his Niagara Falls audience, "we will fail in our major objectives: to preserve public education in the United States and to improve the status of teachers economically, socially, and politically."[17]

If teaching was not reshaped into a more attractive occupation, Shanker reasoned, the new labor market would force schools to recruit from lower and lower levels of the talent pool, further eroding teachers' status and undermining the influence of their unions. Shanker also argued that because the welfare of teacher unions was so closely linked to the status of public education generally, unions risked a great deal by not responding to calls for reform at a time when public education was under attack. The deep dissatisfaction with the public schools, he warned, threatened an exodus of students to private schools and raised the specter of tuition tax credits and other policies that would encourage such an exodus; it threatened a dissolution of political and budgetary support for public education. Such developments would be "devastating" to teacher unions, eroding their memberships and greatly diminishing their "voice" in education.

Shanker's Niagara Falls address also echoed the warnings of the AFL-CIO's Committee on the Evolution of Work, of which Shanker, an AFL-CIO vice-president, was a member. The AFL-CIO established the committee in 1982 to "review and evaluate changes . . . taking place in America in the labor force, occupations, industries, and technology." In its two reports, one published in 1983 and the other in 1985, the committee argued that Americans' perceptions of work were changing, and that this held important implications for unions. "Workers, particularly better-educated workers, are becoming more insistent on securing more freedom in the workplace," it said in *The Changing Situation of Workers and Their Unions*, published just three months before Shanker's address. "It is increasingly true that the measure of a good job is high discretion as much as high pay. . . . Americans are less likely to see work as a straight economic transaction providing a means of survival and more likely to see it as a means of self-expression and self-development." Moreover, the committee said, many workers, while supporting the concept of unionism, wanted their interests advanced "in ways other than what they view as the traditional form of union representation—an adversarial collective-bargaining relationship." It was thus important to their continued strength, the committee warned, that unions "experiment with new approaches to representing workers and should address new issues of concern to workers."[18] Shanker made the same argument to his Niagara Falls audience: teachers unions had to be responsive, as he put it, "to all sorts of new ideas," or risk becoming irrelevant to the professional lives of their members.[19]

To Shanker, supporting the movement to professionalize teaching thus was nothing less than a matter of survival for teachers unions. Motivated by that belief, he took bold steps during the 1980s to align the 750,000-member AFT with the teacher-reform movement, overturning many of the organization's hard-line union policies in the process. Shanker's immense power—drawn in varying degrees from his national stature as a spokesperson for teachers, the power of his intellect, the force of his personality, and the length of his tenure as AFT president—permitted him to move the AFT virtually as far and as fast as he wanted to.

As early as 1983 Shanker supported a gubernatorially sponsored career-ladder plan in Tennessee that sought to give outstanding teachers increased status, higher pay, and leadership roles in schools. He backed the initiative by Governor Lamar Alexander even though it violated traditional union policies that teachers should be paid strictly on the basis of seniority and academic credentials, and that no teachers should assume supervisory roles in schools. "We will not attract good teachers if we have the same boss-teacher relationship [in schools] as we have today," he said in discussing the merits of the Tennessee proposal at the AFT's 1983 annual convention in Los Angeles. Shanker also expressed a willingness to review the career-ladder proposals in *A Nation at Risk* and other 1983 national education studies. "We will not have a knee-jerk reaction rejecting these new proposals," he said on the NBC News program "Meet the Press" in late May. Shanker was later to argue that the "differentiated staffing" and "performance pay" of career ladders were needed in public education because the huge number of people required to staff the nation's schools could never be drawn entirely from the ranks of the best and brightest, and therefore school systems needed to make the best use of their most talented teachers by giving them greater authority in schools.[20]

Shanker then endorsed a controversial "peer-assistance" program launched in the Toledo, Ohio, school system in 1981. Designed to strengthen new teachers and struggling veterans, and to sweep bad teachers out of the classroom, the program created a cadre of senior "mentor teachers," selected jointly by the local teachers union (an AFT affiliate) and the school system, to work with new employees and senior teachers recommended for remediation by their principals. Under the program, the mentors assist teachers for a year and then recommend to a special review board of five teachers and four administrators whether the contracts of their charges should be renewed. If two-thirds of its members concur, the board sends mentors' recommendations to the superintendent, who makes a final judgment. Teachers slated for dismissal under the process are permitted to appeal through the union's regular "grievance" system. The mentors' negative evaluations become part of the evidence against teachers filing grievances, however, making success difficult. The Toledo program was attacked by many within the AFT—despite the fact that the Toledo Federation of Teachers proposed it—because it clashed with the traditional union philosophy that workers mustn't participate in the hiring and firing of their colleagues and that a union's first duty is to protect its members' jobs. But in a speech to the 1984 AFT annual convention and regularly after that, Shanker praised the "Toledo plan" as a wave of the future in public education. "We don't have the right to be called professionals—and we will never convince the public that we are—unless we are prepared honestly to decide what constitutes competence in our profession and what constitutes incompetence and apply those definitions to ourselves and our colleagues," he warned in Niagara Falls.[21] Eventually Shanker was to criticize as "excessively long and expensive" the traditional legalistic system used to dismiss teachers, an extraordinary charge because adversarial due process was a pillar upon which the union movement in teaching was built. He endorsed the Toledo system as an alternative that was fairer, "faster and a lot cheaper."[22]

Speaking to the National Press Club in Washington in January 1985, Shanker outlined a plan for a rigorous national entrance examination in teaching modeled on law's bar examination. He called for a test of subject matter and pedagogy administered by an "American Board for Professional Education," to be followed by a mandatory internship of one to three years. Shanker pledged that the AFT would eventually accept as members only those who met these standards. He also urged that a directory be published of school systems employing only teachers with "board certification" as a way of pressuring others to do so. "After all," he told his audience, "the number of Michelin stars that a restaurant has is important." (In 1963 Koerner had urged creation of national entrance examinations and discussed the notion of "board certified teachers" at length in *The Miseducation of American Teachers*. "Stringent and well-recognized qualifying examinations," he wrote, "could perhaps do more than anything else to make teaching truly a profession." Koerner also proposed a series of "advanced certificates," which he said "might be compared to specialty boards in medicine" and "would be awarded to candidates who had demonstrated a much deeper knowledge and understanding of their teaching fields than holders of the basic certificate.")[23]

Three months later, on April 28, 1985, in his Niagara Falls address, Shanker expanded the role of his "professional teacher board." In addition to administering national examinations, it would develop standards and an ethical code for the teaching profession, investigate public complaints against teachers, and act as an independent board of review in local teacher-dismissal proceedings. He also called for wider use of career ladders. He proposed that top-rung teachers who work with new recruits receive appointments as adjunct faculty at local colleges, as well as higher salaries. He again praised the Toledo plan and the principle that outstanding teachers determine who among their colleagues "pass muster." Shanker called, too, for students and their parents to have a greater say in the public schools the children attend—another "huge and revolutionary" departure from past union philosophy because it meant that school faculties (and union members) would be forced to compete with one another for students and ultimately, perhaps, for jobs. To Shanker, expanded "choice" in public education was another step toward professionalizing teaching. "Most clients *choose* the professionals they see—a lawyer, a doctor, an accountant," he said.[24]

To promote change in teaching, the AFT in 1985 began sponsoring a series of QUEST conferences (held in Washington every two years, they attracted several thousand AFT members) that offered reformers a forum for their ideas and showcased reform activities in progress, as well as the districts sponsoring them. At the 1985 conference Shanker again defied union doctrine on job protection when he argued in a speech titled "The Revolution That Is Overdue" that teacher organizations should support periodic testing of tenured teachers as a way of building public confidence in teaching. Shocking many of the dues-paying union members in the audience, he reasoned that teacher testing was necessary because "there are teachers teaching in this country who are illiterate and who shouldn't be in the classroom." Said Shanker: "I'm not so sure that if [administrators] hired an illiterate teacher twenty years ago that we've got to compound the error by subjecting kids to the same illiterate teacher for another ten or fifteen years." Also in his speech, Shanker proposed a level of national teacher certification akin to Koerner's "advanced certificates." Echoing Koerner, he called for "specialty boards" to design examinations in the various subject areas, using classroom observations, videotaped simulations, and written tests. The rigorousness of the examinations would permit only approximately 20 percent of the nation's teachers to pass them, Shanker said, but those who were successful would be rewarded with higher salaries. Thus Shanker challenged in yet another way the all-for-one, one-for-all doctrine of traditional unionism.[25]

A year later Shanker was championing the radical recommendations of the Carnegie Forum's task force on teaching. At his behest, the AFT passed a resolution at its convention in July 1986 praising the task force's report, and it released its own reform blueprint that included much of the Carnegie agenda. Shanker, who was himself a member of the foundation's task force, subsequently attracted national attention to several school systems that sought to "restructure" schools and "empower" teachers in ways the Carnegie panel recommended. One was Dade County, Florida, the nation's fourth-largest school system, with 255,000 students and 280 schools in Miami and its environs.

The Dade plan to "professionalize" teaching—like the others Shanker endorsed—was drafted in cooperation with the AFT's local affiliate. In 1987–88 school officials and the United Teachers of Dade launched a four-year experiment to enhance the rewards in teaching through a combination of "shared decision-making" and "school-based management," as the Carnegie recommendations on teacher empowerment came to be called. In thirty-two Dade schools, authority was transferred to "management teams" of teachers and principals (and, in some instances, other school staff and parents). These teams, in turn, were granted an unprecedented degree of autonomy on budget, staffing, and instructional matters. Rather than the 10 percent discretionary fund traditionally given to Dade's schools, they were permitted to appropriate their schools' entire budgets virtually without restriction, and they were allowed to seek waivers from both school system regulations and Dade's collective bargaining contract.

Restructuring the leadership in the schools and freeing it from external rules and regulations resulted in many schools' taking steps unimaginable to traditional teacher unionists. One management team voted to pay an extra $3,500 a year to each of several "lead teachers" who were made responsible for curriculum development. Another replaced an assistant principal with ten part-time aides. Ten schools decided to train teachers to evaluate their peers. Others scheduled classes on Saturdays (without increasing teachers' salaries). And an elementary school contracted with the Berlitz School of Languages to teach its students Spanish, thereby potentially eliminating jobs for union members.

A new collective bargaining contract expanded the experiment into nearly ninety schools in 1988–89. It also gave teachers in all Dade schools a say in the selection of their principals and assistant principals and in the design, construction, and renovation of schools. Further, it established a "professional-leave bank" to enable teachers to attend meetings and conferences, expanded a program that permits teachers to take "minisabbaticals," and created a pilot career-ladder program.

Shanker also praised the Rochester, New York, school system and a campaign it launched in 1987 to professionalize teaching. Within the AFT and without, in speeches, interviews, articles, and in a weekly column that he runs as a paid advertisement in the *New York Times* and *Education Week,* Shanker lauded Rochester's reform blueprint as a model for the nation. (He didn't note, however, that the quality of teaching and learning was so bad in the 33,000-student school system that administrators and union officials embraced radical change partly out of desperation.)

The Rochester plan was written into the city's 1987 collective bargaining contract with the Rochester Federation of Teachers. It, too, gave teachers a greater role in the running of their schools, through "faculty committees." Significantly, the committees were granted authority to hire the teachers in their schools, a step made possible by a major shift in policy by the RFT. In Rochester and virtually every other school system in the nation where teachers work under a collective bargaining contract, unions have negotiated "teacher-transfer" clauses that require all vacancies to be posted centrally and bid on by teachers districtwide according to seniority. The RFT's willingness to sacrifice that cardinal union policy in the name of reform surprised even teacher unions' staunchest critics.

The Rochester plan also established a career ladder for teachers, with Carnegie "lead teachers" on the top rungs eligible for salaries of $68,500 by 1989–90. They were to spend half their time in the classroom and half in leadership roles, including working as "mentor teachers" in a peer-review program similar to Toledo's that was established in Rochester in 1986. As the Carnegie task force had urged, the Rochester blueprint awarded mentors adjunct professorships in the teacher-education program at the University of Rochester. The Rochester plan also responded to Shanker's call for "choice" in public education in a provision permitting students to attend any of the city's twelve high schools. With the overturning of Rochester's teacher-transfer policy, "open enrollment" in its high schools promised an intense competition for students because teachers would no longer automatically be able to transfer elsewhere if enrollment declined in their schools.

Shanker continued his reform crusade in a 1988 speech at the National Press Club, where, building on the Carnegie recommendation that teachers be decision makers in schools, he proposed that small groups of teachers be permitted to create their own "schools-within-schools." These teachers would organize the instruction of a group of students as largely autonomous teams within regular schools. In addition to expanding the role of teachers in school decision making, Shanker saw "charter schools," as he called them, encouraging teachers to police their own ranks. "Teachers working as a team over long periods of time gives you great accountability," he said in a later interview. "Because if you have someone who is constantly screwing things up or who is lazy, the other members of the team are going to say shape up or get out." Once again, Shanker the labor leader sought to promote "professionalism" in teaching at the expense of solidarity among union members in the workplace.[26]

Finally, in 1989, as a way to "stimulate schools to change internally," Shanker proposed a national "merit school" program. Seeking what he called "the right combination of cooperation within schools and competition among schools," Shanker proposed that bonuses of up to $15,000 per teacher be made available to the 10 percent of the schools in each state that produced the greatest improvement in student achievement over a five-year period. In effect, the plan called for union members to compete with each other for monetary awards—a heresy to traditional teacher unionists but not to Shanker. "You see from [the recent economic upheavals] in Russia and the East Bloc and China that in systems where workers are given a lot of security, they produce garbage," he said in a statement that was a capstone to the tremendous transformation in his rhetoric during the 1980s. "Here you have a market. The market has a lot of victims, a lot of injustice, and everything else. But, dammit, it also lays a lot of golden eggs."[27]

Shanker's campaign to professionalize teaching represents nothing less than a counterrevolution against the militant, industrial-style unionism in teaching that he advocated so strongly for two decades. The AFT since the onset of the excellence movement has downplayed the importance of adversarial collective bargaining to the welfare of its members, and has pledged itself to taking greater responsibility for the performance of its profession, even in instances where doing so conflicted with its members' narrower interests. "We tend to think of unionism in the last forty or fifty years, a period dominated by groups like the United Auto Workers, the steelworkers, as the only model of unionism, but it isn't," Shanker said in a 1989 interview. "Who says a union has to be adversarial? Why can't it be an organization that has the resources and the wherewithal to help in the professional development of its members, to provide them training and collegiality, while at the same time giving them a sense of security and the collective strength in the legislature to get funding? To say that that's not a union anymore is ridiculous. There are different ways of representing the interests of your members."[28] Shanker argued in his *New York Times* column and elsewhere that many of the old-line industrial unions were themselves forging new relationships with employers. As an example, he cited the United Automobile Workers and its collaboration with General Motors to increase the involvement of workers in plant governance and decision making at GM's new Saturn plant in Tennessee. The plant's landmark 1985 labor agreement abolished time clocks, pegged salary bonuses to productivity, cut the number of assembly-line job classifications from seventy to six, organized production around "work groups" of six to fifteen employees, assigned labor a role in setting work standards, and reduced the role of union shop foremen by simplifying grievance procedures. In a 1986 column praising the contract, Shanker called for an "educational Saturn project."

Shanker's support of the reform movement in teaching transformed his public image. Disparaged for two decades as an obstreperous unionist (in the film *Sleeper,* Woody Allen prophesied that civilization would end "when a man named Albert Shanker got hold of a nuclear warhead"), Shanker has won wide public praise in recent years. "He is a legitimate leader of the nation's small corps of educational statesmen," said a 1985 article in *Phi Delta Kappan,* a leading education journal. The *New Republic* titled a flattering 1985 profile of Shanker, "Albert Shanker, Statesman." Over 100 newspapers endorsed his 1985 call for a national teacher examination. Suddenly, Shanker the union president was speaking as a leading school reformer to corporate boards, governors, state legislatures, and a host of other influential bodies. And increasingly his ideas were determining the direction of the reform movement in teaching.[29]

To be sure, Shanker didn't launch his radical transformation of the AFT's policies until *A Nation at Risk* and the other 1983 reports turned the nation's attention to the crisis in public education. In 1981 the AFT was assuring a congressional subcommittee that "our educational system, in general terms, is very healthy." The organization originally attacked many of the reforms that Shanker later endorsed. "We're not encouraging [other AFT locals] to adopt it," a senior AFT official said of Toledo's peer-evaluation program in 1982. When Governor Lamar Alexander first announced his career-ladder plan in February 1983, Shanker responded in a press release that rewarding outstanding performance with higher pay "might work with encyclopedia salesmen, but it won't fly with teachers." He reversed his stance two months later—in wake of the national reform reports.[30]

Indeed, there has been an element of opportunism in Shanker's policy shifts. Immediately after Shanker endorsed Tennessee's career ladder the AFT launched a membership drive in the state. With much fanfare, Shanker opened an AFT office in Nashville and pledged $300,000 to a campaign to organize Tennessee's teachers, the overwhelming majority of whom were members of the Tennessee affiliate of the National Education Association. Yet when career-ladder legislation was introduced in 1985 in New York, where one-quarter of the AFT's entire membership is concentrated, Shanker lobbied against it. Similarly, when President Reagan's rhetoric on education captured headlines in 1983 and won him popularity as a school reformer, Shanker invited him to address the AFT at its convention in Los Angeles, in spite of Reagan's vocal support of tuition tax credits and proposals for deep cuts in federal education funding. To his detractors, Shanker's reformism is merely a ploy to expand the scope of teacher collective bargaining to include "professional" issues, and thereby broaden the power of his union.[31]

Also, Shanker is far out in front of the majority of the AFT's 2,000 local affiliates in his commitment to reform. Many of the union's locals remain committed to the policies and tactics of industrial-style unionism. In 1985, less than a month after Shanker asserted in an interview that "teacher unions' concentration on trade unionism has given way to issues of professionalism," the Seattle Federation of Teachers went on strike for twenty-five days. Two years later the AFT's Chicago affiliate left the city's 400,000 students without teachers for nineteen days; it was the union's ninth strike in nineteen years. Similarly, the president of the Houston Federation of Teachers in 1988 denounced as "scab programs" attempts in Houston and elsewhere to bring talented people without education degrees into teaching. "Alternative certification," she told an interviewer, "creates an artificial surplus of teachers" that permits school systems to keep salaries low.[32] Shanker, on the other hand, endorsed alternative certification as a way of recruiting bright teachers. Moreover, the AFT locals that have shared Shanker's strong commitment to reform are nearly all led by veteran presidents who are Shanker's trusted lieutenants within the AFT hierarchy. Shanker acknowledged in a 1989 interview that he was fighting an uphill battle for reform within his own organization. "It's not easy," he said. "Many of our people have gotten the notion that the only function of the union is collective bargaining, and that everything would be achieved that way. . . . We do have members who don't believe that there should be change. . . . It's very wrenching for people, changing a whole set of habits."[33]

Finally, Shanker's commitment to reform in teaching and to a new model of teacher unionism poses substantial risks to the AFT. If the movement to professionalize teaching is successful—in particular, if teachers gain a significant role in the management of schools—the importance of unions and collective bargaining to teachers may diminish dramatically. Shanker argues that teachers unions must help professionalize teaching or risk the consequences of its becoming an occupational backwater. But in granting teachers the authority to set budgets, hire and fire staff, and organize the work day in schools, shared decision making and other reforms undermine the primary basis for collective bargaining on "wages, hours, and working conditions." An internal 1988 NEA report on "employee-participation programs" of the sort recommended by the Carnegie task force and introduced in Dade County described the dangers of such programs to teachers unions. "The greatest dangers of site-based decisionmaking programs concern the security of the bargaining unit," it said. "There is a possibility that the decision-making program will emerge as a substitute for, rather than a supplement to, the collective-bargaining process. In this instance, the critical decisions affecting the bargaining unit are transferred to the labor-management forum, marginalizing the collective bargaining process. While the [teacher] association will continue to exist as an independent entity, it will no longer have any real authority." In consequence, the report warned, "members will be increasingly likely to identify more strongly with school administrators than with their own organization. . . . To the extent that employee problems are dealt with outside regular association channels, public sector unions will experience difficulty attracting members. In extreme cases, union members themselves will question the necessity for a union."[34]

As a result, Shanker has worked hard to convince both the public and his membership that only through their unions can teachers achieve and maintain the status of true professionals. "Unionism and professionalism are inextricably linked," he says. He declares repeatedly, as he did in a 1988 *New York Times* column entitled "School Change Is Union Made," that radical reforms in Rochester, Miami, Toledo, and other school systems were achieved only through the auspices of local AFT affiliates. The AFT echoed Shanker's self-justifying rhetoric at its 1988 convention in a resolution on school reform: "As the union was the key to attaining even the minimal professional status our members now enjoy, so too is the union now the key to achieving the professionalization of teaching and the improvement of student learning." "Any reform agenda that attempts to separate teachers from their unions is committed neither to true professionalism nor to the betterment of public education." Shanker also has sought to assure his membership that the AFT's commitment to collective bargaining is sacrosanct, despite the union's increased attention to professional issues. "The process works," he wrote in a 1988 column, "collective bargaining is here to stay." His aim, he said earlier, was to "leave traditional bargaining in place, but expand its scope." And if school systems refuse to broaden bargaining beyond "wages, hours, and working conditions," the reforms needed to professionalize teaching could be achieved without relinquishing teachers' bargaining rights. They could be implemented outside collective bargaining contracts, through such voluntary arrangements as "trust agreements" and "side letters."[35]

Nonetheless, AFT affiliates in systems where teachers have assumed managerial responsibilities in schools face the potential loss of their collective bargaining rights. In 1986 the University of Pittsburgh filed an action with the Pennsylvania Public Employee Relations Board to block an

AFT effort to organize the university's 1,600-member faculty. It based its case on a 1980 U.S. Supreme Court decision that denied faculty members of Yeshiva University in New York bargaining rights under the 1935 National Labor Relations Act on the grounds that they "exercise authority which in any other context unquestionably would be managerial." The Yeshiva faculty, the Court wrote, played a prominent role in deciding admissions standards, teaching methods, grading policies, course offerings, and many other matters. Because the NLRA established collective bargaining only in the private sector, the Supreme Court's ruling in *National Labor Relations Board v. Yeshiva University* did not extend to public employees (in the absence of a federal bargaining law in the public sector, they receive bargaining rights under state statutes; thirty-three states permit public school teachers to bargain collectively). But if the University of Pittsburgh (a public institution; Yeshiva is private) wins its case against the AFT, it would extend the *Yeshiva* precedent to the public sector, creating the possibility of similar challenges to public school teachers unions supporting reforms that give teachers a greater role in the running of their schools, as in Miami, Rochester, and Toledo, where teachers now participate in hiring decisions.[36]

Shanker has insisted that AFT affiliates would abandon their reform efforts rather than relinquish their collective bargaining rights. "It will be the end of all the schemes of [teacher] participation [in school management] if Yeshiva gets applied to the public sector," he said in a 1989 interview, "because unions wouldn't allow it." Thus, the University of Pittsburgh case is a threat not only to the AFT and Shanker's reform agenda but also to the teacher-professionalism movement generally. "If these ventures [career ladders, peer-evaluation plans, shared-decisionmaking projects, and so on] were successfully challenged on the basis of the *Yeshiva* decision—that teachers have become managers, and therefore may not bargain—the complex pattern of teacher and union involvement in policymaking that does exist could quickly unravel," wrote Susan Moore Johnson, a Harvard University specialist on teachers unions, in a 1987 issue of *Teachers College Record.* To stop the unraveling, states would have to redraft their labor statutes to protect the bargaining rights of teachers participating in such reforms, as Ohio did in 1983, when legislators wrote a clause into the state's new teacher-bargaining law preserving the bargaining rights of Toledo teachers involved in peer evaluation.[37]

Shanker is walking a fine line between the new policies that he believes the AFT must embrace and the dangers those policies pose to his union. It is as yet unclear whether he will be able to do so successfully. Nonetheless, he has set the AFT on a very different course. And he has been an invaluable ally to the excellence movement in doing so.

The National Education Association's response to the reform movement in teaching, on the other hand, has been far different. With 2,000,000

members and 13,000 local affiliates, the NEA is probably the most powerful organization in public education, and one of the strongest political
forces in the United States. While the AFT's 450,000 teachers (300,000 of
the union's members are nurses, state employees, paraprofessionals, and
college professors) are concentrated in the major cities of the East Coast
and Midwest, the NEA's 1,500,000 working teachers are widely dispersed, making the NEA the dominant teachers union in every state but
New York, Shanker's power base. Overall, the organization represents
two-thirds of the nation's public school teachers; the AFT one-fifth. The
NEA is buttressed by a staff of 550 at its headquarters in Washington and
an annual budget that reached $136 million in 1990, triple the AFT's. Its
vast membership and tremendous resources make the NEA crucial to the
reform of teaching on a national scale, but the NEA has not supported
the professionalization of teaching. To the contrary. While it has sought
to convince the nation otherwise, the organization has fought hard to
preserve public school teaching as an occupation defined by industrial
trade unionism.

Founded in 1857 as the National Teachers' Association (NTA), the
NEA for decades was the leading professional organization in American
public education. Following the NTA's merger with the National Association of School Superintendents and the American Normal School Association in 1870, the organization represented a wide range of the nation's
educators. By the time it celebrated its centennial in 1957, only ten of its
ninety-seven presidents had been teachers. The NEA was long a leading
source of educational research, and it sponsored many of the nation's
major statements on school reform, including those of the Committee of
Ten in the 1890s and the Commission on the Reorganization of Secondary Education in the 1910s and 1920s.

But the United Federation of Teachers' victory in New York City in
1961 marked the beginning of a new era in the NEA. With its history as a
"professional association," and with no ties to the labor movement, it was
briefly skeptical of Shanker's attempt to unionize teaching. But as the
AFT's ranks swelled (from 60,000 in 1961 to 300,000 in 1970) in wake of
collective bargaining, the NEA seized upon its rival's militancy as its own.
It abolished its departments of "superintendence" and "school administration," banned nonteacher members from holding NEA offices, and
eventually forced such members out of the organization. A new department of "negotiations" was formed in 1968. Union organizers were hired
and scholars dropped from the staff, as instructional and professional
matters were downplayed in favor of collective bargaining issues. The
organization's leadership sanctioned the use of strikes, and in the late
1960s the U.S. Department of Labor and the Internal Revenue Service
designated the NEA a union. In its new role the organization doubled its
membership during the 1970s, and by the early 1980s the NEA was
second only to the Teamsters as the nation's largest union.[38]

The dominant influence within the NEA during its evolution into an industrial-style labor union was Terry Herndon, the organization's acid-tongued executive director from 1973 to 1983. Herndon, just thirty-two when he took over the leadership of the NEA, was deeply committed to the unionization of American teachers and to the unionization of the NEA. He was also a strident advocate of the liberal political agenda of his day. He led the NEA against what he charged was a right-wing conspiracy of "chronic tax resisters, congenital reactionaries, dangerous witch hunters, energized superpatriots, wayward dogma peddlers and vitriolic race haters" bent on destroying public education.[39] In 1981 the NEA published a 292-page teacher's guide to counter "attacks on public education" by "the radical Right." In addition, the NEA under Herndon became a standard-bearer for liberal political causes ranging from gun control to a nuclear freeze. Herndon himself was president of Citizens Against Nuclear War, a pro-nuclear-freeze coalition that operated out of the NEA's Washington headquarters. Herndon also sought to promote such causes in the nation's schools. In the early 1980s, for example, the NEA developed a curriculum on nuclear war that urged students to collect signatures on petitions calling for a freeze on the production of nuclear weapons.

To help spread collective bargaining and to promote the NEA's broader political agenda, Herndon and others built the NEA into a powerful political force. A year before Herndon was appointed executive director, the NEA became the first education association to organize a national political action committee, known as NEA-PAC. Endorsements, campaign contributions, and volunteers began flowing to friendly congressional candidates. By 1988 annual contributions to NEA-PAC reached $3.1 million; only the National Association of Realtors, the American Medical Association, and the Teamsters had larger political war chests.[40]

The NEA also influences lawmakers in other ways. In 1989 it spent $7.4 million on such things as a computerized system of mass producing letters to Congress from 300,000 NEA members who "pre-authorize" the use of their names; "Congressional Contact Teams" made up of two NEA members in each congressional district who are specially trained as lobbyists and flown back and forth from Washington to promote the NEA's cause "from the local level"; a computerized file of the political work of the NEA's entire membership; a satellite linkup between a television studio in the NEA's Washington headquarters and its state affiliates; and a full-time lobbying staff of fifteen.

The NEA also has been a major backer of Democratic presidential candidates since 1976, when it played a leading role in the Carter campaign. (Carter signaled the size of the NEA's contribution to his election by pushing through Congress the law that established the U.S. Department of Education—a longtime NEA goal). The organization has developed a national political network of such strength that NEA members have been the single largest block of delegates at every Democratic convention since 1980.

Yet the NEA's clout is, if anything, even greater in the state capitols, where there are usually fewer lobbyists competing for lawmakers' attention, where small numbers of activist voters can more easily sway the outcome of an election, and where education is typically the largest item in the annual budget. In one instance of the NEA's state-level clout, 84 percent of New Jersey legislators responding to a 1987 Associated Press survey identified the New Jersey Education Association as the most powerful lobby in Trenton.[41]

The NEA achieves its influence in the states with a combination of membership power and money. Virtually all of the NEA state organizations and some 3,000 of its local affiliates make campaign contributions through political action committees. Under a special provision of Texas's campaign-finance law, members of the Texas State Teachers Association (TSTA) are able to claim tax credits of 50 percent of their contributions to the TSTA's Texas Educator's Political Action Committee. NEA affiliates regularly outspend other organizations. The Minnesota Education Association and the much smaller Minnesota Federation of Teachers, for example, typically contribute more money to candidates for statewide office than do all other Minnesota political organizations *combined*. Affluence also buys the NEA state affiliates full-time lobbyists. And the NEA state organizations encourage their members to work in the campaigns of favored candidates. "That's really what we're all about," said the executive director of the Minnesota Education Association. "We've got teachers running campaigns all over the state in both parties. In some districts teachers *are* the Democratic party. We encourage teachers to be political because the job is political." The NEA state organizations go so far as to run "campaign schools" to teach their members the ins and outs of the political process.[42]

In many instances NEA affiliates are working to elect their own members to state legislatures. In a recent year four of the ten members of the Minnesota House Education Committee were MEA members on leave from the classroom, as were three of twelve members of the Senate Appropriations Committee. In Alabama no less than 40 percent of the state's 140 legislators were teachers, retired teachers, or spouses of teachers. In 1988 the speaker of the Alabama House of Representatives told an interviewer that Paul Hubbert, the executive secretary of the Alabama Education Association, "controls" matters in the state legislature affecting classroom teachers. In 1990, Hubbert was the Democratic candidate for governor in Alabama.[43]

The NEA also spends $25 million annually on 1,300 political organizers who link the NEA to its 13,000 local affiliates. These "UniServ directors" live and work in the communities they serve, supported by a special fee ($17.90 in 1990) assessed of every NEA member. In addition to tying locals to the NEA's national political network, the UniServ organizers assist affiliates with such matters as organizing strikes and boycotts, securing legal representation, organizing campaigns for or against school board members and lawmakers, writing grievances, and the production of newsletters and other publications. It is this vast national, state, and local political organization that the NEA has marshaled against the reform movement in teaching.

Like much of the education establishment, the union initially denied there was a crisis in public education or in teaching. At the NEA's 1983 convention, Donald Cameron, Herndon's former deputy and the union's new executive director, dismissed *A Nation at Risk* and the other recently published reform reports as "the usual doom and gloom." With Herndon's shrill rhetoric, he denounced teacher competency and performance pay as "tertiary issues" and accused Shanker of dancing "political pirouettes" with "ultra-conservative paramours" in the Reagan administration. In the following months the NEA published a series of documents that sought to discredit the reform reports. One, entitled *Studying the Studies,* charged that *A Nation at Risk* "waffles" on the issue of federal funding of public education.[44]

Next the NEA argued that the cause of public education's troubles was a lack of funding, especially for teachers' salaries. "The nation's students today are threatened only by the failure of policymakers to give education the money it deserves," the NEA's newly elected president, Mary Hatwood Futrell, said in her acceptance speech at the organization's 1983 convention. That fall, as the excellence movement gained momentum, the NEA issued a flood of press releases and spent $1.5 million on television commercials calling for increased education funding. In particular, it demanded that the federal government increase its education budget.[45] The NEA state affiliates also hammered at the money theme. Recalling the role of the Texas State Teachers Association in the battle over House Bill 72, Representative Bill Haley, the chairman of the Texas House education committee, said: "The NEA was for more money. Period." Then he added: "Money, money, money, money, money—that's all they're ever for."[46] There was little disagreement among school reformers that salaries needed to be raised substantially to make teaching more attractive, and between 1982–83 and 1985–86 alone spending on teacher salaries in public education rose from $46 billion nationally to $55 billion. But the NEA ignored the improvement and steadfastly argued that low pay was the single source of teaching's troubles. "I am asking my colleagues on the staff to join with me to make higher salaries this year's top priority," exhorted Cameron at the 1985 NEA convention.

Meanwhile, the NEA and the majority of its affiliates have opposed virtually all of the other major teacher reforms, especially those that would raise standards and reward performance within teaching, steps that the reformers have argued are crucial to improving teaching's status as an occupation.

The NEA and its affiliates have battled the reformers' attempts to draw better-trained recruits into teaching, particularly their attempts to strengthen the preparation of new teachers in academic subjects, a key to bolstering instruction in the nation's schools.

In his critique of teacher education in the early 1960s, Koerner wrote of "remorselessly fragmented, subdivided and inflated" subject matter marked by "intellectual impoverishment" and suffused by a jargon that "masks a lack of thought, supports a specious scientism . . . and repels any educated mind that happens upon it." He indicted teacher education for "puerile, repetitious, dull, and ambiguous" courses and "inferior" faculty. "It is a national scandal that large numbers of [teachers] are inadequately prepared in the subject matter that they teach," he quoted the U.S. Commission of Education, Sterling M. McMurrin, as saying in 1962. Twenty years later, little had changed. Though two-thirds of the nation's 2,000 four-year colleges and universities were training teachers, the vast majority of them were second- and third-rate institutions with low admissions standards and weak students.[47]

Instruction in academic subjects was superficial. In 1985 the Southern Regional Education Board (SREB) published a study of the transcripts of 3,283 education graduates and 2,760 arts and science graduates at seventeen major state universities in the South. It revealed that three-quarters of the teachers from the seventeen universities graduated without having taken any courses in foreign languages, philosophy, economics, physics, and chemistry. Nearly half had taken no political science. Elementary teachers, the study showed, had taken an average of only 6 percent of their college course work in math and 9 percent in English, the two subjects that elementary teachers spend the bulk of their time teaching, while education and physical education courses together had accounted for half of their college studies. The SREB study also revealed that secondary teachers—who, unlike elementary teachers, commonly major in the subject they plan to teach rather than in education—had taken fewer courses in their major than had arts and sciences graduates, in part because at many institutions the requirements for an academic major were lower for prospective teachers than for arts and sciences students. In sharp contrast, in Germany, where teacher education is far more rigorous, most secondary teachers double major in two academic subjects.[48]

What's more, the academic courses that prospective teachers in the SREB study had taken—both as part of their general studies and within their majors—were predominantly lower-level ones. The study revealed that secondary teachers had taken fewer upper-level courses in their academic major than had arts and sciences students in every discipline but foreign languages. Future science teachers, for instance, had taken only one-third of their science courses at the junior or senior level, while arts and sciences students majoring in the sciences generally had earned at least half their credits in their major in upper-level courses. In the SREB study only 22 percent of the math credits earned by teachers not majoring in the subject had been earned in college-level courses (those requiring second-year algebra as a prerequisite), compared with 53 percent for arts and sciences nonmajors. Indeed, many education majors had been enrolled in remedial courses designed specifically for teacher trainees, such as "understanding arithmetic." Likewise, 83 percent of the teachers in the study not majoring in English had taken no upper-level courses in the subject and many received degree credit for remedial courses.[49]

Similarly, a 1984 study of the transcripts of graduates of Arizona State University's college of education revealed that 95 percent of the math, science, and English credits earned by prospective teachers were in introductory courses taken mainly in the freshman year.[50]

The 1984 Arizona State study also revealed that nearly 90 percent of the university's education majors had earned credits at community colleges. In the SREB study, 28 percent of all the teachers' credits had been transferred from community colleges. The vast majority of community colleges (which enroll roughly 40 percent of the nation's 12,500,000 million college students) require only a high school diploma for admissions, and it is estimated that the average community college first-year student reads at an eighth-grade level.[51] Thus, large numbers of future teachers were fulfilling many of their academic requirements in low-level community college courses. In fact, the SREB study found numerous instances of students meeting liberal arts course requirements at community colleges in their junior and senior years after repeatedly failing the courses at their four-year colleges.

There was also little rigor in education courses. Rather than a systematic exploration of the many important and challenging philosophical, psychological, sociological, and historical issues in education, pedagogical training in the overwhelming majority of the nation's education schools was in the early 1980s a profoundly anti-intellectual enterprise. Rather than studying Plato or Piaget, teachers were earning education credits in such courses as "Standard First Aid and Personal Safety" and "Coaching Track and Field," in counseling courses that taught how to write grant proposals, in courses on the "sociological foundations" of education that required the memorization of flow charts of personnel in state education bureaucracies, and in "curriculum-design" courses that taught teachers how to write lesson plans. Much of teachers' pedagogical training was taken up with classroom "methods" courses such as "Lettering, Posters, and Displays in the School Program" and "The Culturally Diverse Classroom," in which teachers were taught to seat white students near black students to foster racial harmony. A prominent activity in methods courses was "role playing," whereby education students learn about the likely behavior of their future charges by acting out such behavior themselves. At one urban education school I visited, a group of doctoral candidates were asked to stand at the front of a classroom while their seated colleagues attempted to recognize which of them was playing the role of a bored student.

The SREB study amply illustrated the shallowness of such courses. In one "case study," it described a math-education major who earned grades of "D," "F," or "W" in 30 percent of the math courses he took, while receiving "A"s or "B"s in no less than 75 percent of his education courses. Moreover, the SREB study revealed that elementary teachers took two-thirds more education courses than state regulations required and secondary teachers nearly one-third more than necessary. In all, according to the study, elementary teachers earned nearly two-fifths of their college credits in education courses (the largest number of which were methods courses) and secondary teachers one-fifth. At a major state university I visited, English-education majors were required to take nearly as many courses in how to teach English as English courses themselves. The result, in the words of Virginia's director of teacher education, is that many teachers "don't have a grasp of what they're teaching."[52]

The low caliber of the instructors in the nation's education schools only made matters worse. Over 90 percent of the nation's roughly 38,000 education professors were not scholars but former elementary and secondary school teachers, the majority of whom earned education degrees from the same mediocre institutions where they were teaching. Though trained primarily as pedagogues themselves, many taught courses in academic disciplines. The dean of education at one of the nation's largest state universities acknowledged to me that his faculty was not as academically able as those in other parts of the university. But he argued that "intellectual capability is not the only criteria for judging professionals in teaching, maybe not even the most important criteria."

There have been attempts since the early 1980s to raise standards in teacher education and to strengthen teachers' subject-matter preparation. Education schools have ratcheted up their admissions requirements, establishing or raising minimum grade point averages for admission. Twenty states have set minimum admissions grade point averages for their public teacher-training programs, usually 2.5 on a 4.0 scale. Others have curtailed the proportion of education courses future teachers are permitted to take. The Texas legislature in 1987 abolished a regulation requiring teacher trainees to take a *minimum* of twenty-four credit hours in education; it enacted a new requirement limiting education majors to a *maximum* of eighteen hours (including student teaching) in pedagogy courses. Similarly, the Florida legislature stipulated in 1985 that prospective secondary teachers earn at least thirty hours of credit in their teaching subject in courses not taught by education professors. Arkansas and Colorado have gone further, requiring prospective teachers to major in an academic subject rather than in education. Similar measures are scheduled to take effect in Massachusetts and in Connecticut in 1993. Education schools within the Holmes Group are expanding their teacher-training programs from four to five years, as a way of increasing teachers' exposure to academic disciplines. To improve their pedagogy departments, others have created compressed programs of "core studies" on teaching and learning and appointed joint committees of teacher educators and arts and sciences faculty to write new courses. But such reforms generally have been achieved only on a small scale. The emphasis on superficial instruction in pedagogy at the expense of demanding course work in academic subjects, in particular, remains pervasive in teacher education. And the majority of the nation's teachers continue to be trained at the weakest colleges and universities. In the main, Koerner's charge that in teacher education "a weak faculty operates a weak program that attracts weak students" still applies.[53]

Early in the reform movement New Jersey pioneered a much more radical approach to recruiting teachers with stronger academic backgrounds, especially graduates of top colleges and universities that traditionally have not trained public school teachers. Overturning a provision that has been at the heart of the fifty states' teacher-licensing laws for decades, New Jersey abandoned its requirement that prospective teachers attend education schools. Governor Thomas H. Kean first proposed encouraging liberal arts graduates to teach in New Jersey's classrooms in a 1983 speech, saying it would "bring a breath of fresh air" into the state's public schools. He signed legislation establishing a system of "alternative certification" two years later. Under the law, liberal arts majors must first pass a state-sponsored test in their teaching field. Then, during their initial teaching year, they participate in a training program that includes a monthlong apprenticeship with a senior teacher, 200 hours of pedagogical training, and regular observations and evaluations from a team of teachers, administrators, and curriculum specialists. The Provisional Teacher Program, as it is called, was revolutionary in breaking the long-standing education-school monopoly on teacher training.

The initiative has been tremendously successful in attracting large numbers of highly talented recruits into New Jersey's schools. In its first four years (1985–86 to 1988–89), the Provisional Teacher Program attracted 6,800 applicants, a greater number than that received by the state's education schools. A total of 830 public school teachers were hired under the program (an additional 254 participants were hired by nonpublic schools), and the 160 provisional teachers employed in 1988–89 represented 29 percent of all the new teachers hired in New Jersey's public schools that year. Moreover, nearly 30 percent of the provisional teachers hired since the program's inception have degrees in the shortage fields of math and science, and 21 percent have been minorities.[54]

According to New Jersey's department of education, 93 percent of alternative-certification candidates meet the state's standards on the National Teacher Examinations (NTE), required of all new teachers in New Jersey, compared with 86 percent of those in traditional teacher-training programs.[55] In a 1988 study of the program, the Council for Basic Education wrote: "The average performance on the [NTE] is significantly higher for provisionally certified candidates than for those who have received standard certification. . . ." Many of the teachers hired under the program have attended the nation's most prestigious private colleges and universities, where the state has recruited heavily since it established its alternative-certification program. Among the provisional teachers hired in 1988–89 were an Amherst College graduate with a double major in math and English, a *summa cum laude* and Phi Beta Kappa graduate in Spanish from Tulane University, and a Princeton political science major who also has a master's degree in international relations from the university.[56]

In addition to their strong subject-matter background, provisional teachers have performed well as pedagogues, according to reports filed with New Jersey education officials by their principals. They also have been more committed to teaching than their regularly certified colleagues. The attrition rate among provisionally certified teachers was 4 percent in 1987–88, one-fourth the rate of first-year teachers who attended education schools. In its 1988 report the Council for Basic Education concluded that the New Jersey alternative-certification system "has thus far been a notable success. It is a truly heartening sign for education in the state. . . ."[57]

Despite New Jersey's success in attracting talented recruits, the NEA and its affiliates have opposed alternative certification. The New Jersey Education Association (NJEA) sought to kill Kean's initiative in the legislature. "[Kean] should not be allowed to ram through his recent proposal that asks no more [of new teachers] than a degree, a test, a five-day cram course, and simply a lot more first-year observation," NJEA President Edith A. Fulton charged in 1983 committee testimony. Together with the state's teacher educators, who perceived the legislation as a threat to their livelihoods, the NJEA attacked the provisional-teacher plan as a "sleight-of-the-hand trick of certification" and an attempt to abolish teachers colleges. Indeed, the faculty senate at Trenton State University, where one-third of the student body majors in education, censured the university's president after he endorsed the Kean plan in 1983. But Kean's influence in the legislature was too great and the climate of reform too strong. Realizing that it was fighting a losing battle against alternative certification, and that its opposition could cost it legislative approval of new funding for teacher salaries that Kean also had proposed, the NJEA dropped its opposition to the provisional-teacher plan in 1985. But the NEA continued to attack the plan from a safer distance. As an NEA official subsequently told me, "The NJEA cooled it on New Jersey's alternative-certification scheme and let the national organization take the heat, because there were other, big-money items in Kean's package."[58]

The NEA harshly criticized the New Jersey program. At a much publicized "back-to-school" press conference in 1985, Futrell likened it to emergency-certification provisions that in some states permitted teachers into classrooms without bachelor's degrees of any type. Hiring teachers without pedagogical training "makes a sham out of efforts to improve the teaching profession" and a "mockery" of education reform, she charged. Futrell ignored the program's academic requirements. She failed to mention its training and supervision provisions. And she neglected to note that New Jersey had recently abolished emergency certificates, the first state to do so. Nor did Futrell, a vocational teacher from Alexandria, Virginia, acknowledge New Jersey's goal of recruiting teachers with stronger subject-matter training.

Five years later, at its 1990 convention, the NEA announced its support for "nontraditional routes" to teacher licensing as a way of opening the doors to teaching more widely. The union dropped its requirement that prospective teachers earn undergraduate degrees in education. But the NEA's new policy focused narrowly on scientists, mathematicians, and other professionals wanting to become teachers in midcareer. And it stipulated that such recruits be paid with special state or private funds rather than out of school system salary budgets, a provision that NEA officials acknowledged would sharply limit the numbers of nontraditional-route teachers. The policy also required that such teachers receive "substantial" pedagogical training before being permitted into the classroom, and it called for the training to be completed under the auspices of education schools. In reality, therefore, there was little substance to the NEA policy shift. The union continued to oppose New Jersey's alternative-certification program.

Indeed, as an organization, the NEA has largely rejected the importance of subject-matter competency in teacher training. As the executive director of one of the union's largest local affiliates said to me, "Content knowledge is not at all correlated to classroom effectiveness, so why should we get up on it?" Though the NEA represents no private-school teachers, it has an official policy stating that private schools "must" employ only teachers with education degrees.[59]

The NEA has defended such policies on the grounds that teachers need extensive training in teaching methods before they are capable of performing well in the classroom, an assumption that the success of New Jersey's alternative-certification teachers undercuts. But the union has also championed education schools and education degrees for reasons that have nothing to do with the quality of teacher training. Though the union doesn't say so publicly, it backs traditional teacher education in large measure because requirements for specialized training reduce the supply of teachers, which in turn helps to drive up salaries. By expanding the pool of potential teachers, alternative certification diminishes teachers unions' ability to press for pay increases. Teacher licensing based on the attainment of education degrees also reinforces the unions' stance that all certified teachers are equally qualified. In the words of one New York City principal, "Ours is a system that treats teachers like interchangeable parts; if three people have the same license they are taken by number, no one cares if one is better than another." The NEA supports such a system. At the same time, education schools steep prospective teachers in the union-dominated values of public school teaching, a process that the NEA encourages by sponsoring chapters on many college campuses. Alternative certification, on the other hand, poses the threat of greater numbers of independent-minded teachers entering the occupation, people less inclined to support a union agenda or become union members.[60]

To preserve requirements that the majority of the nation's teachers earn education degrees, the NEA has sought to gain control of teacher licensing in the states. It has poured millions of dollars into a campaign to persuade states to shift authority for teacher licensing from state boards of education to independent licensing boards with teacher majorities. Such boards "should have the exclusive authority to establish standards regarding licensure," the union has argued. Recently the NEA has backed state licensing boards as an important step toward self-governance (and thus professionalization) in teaching. But its underlying intention was revealed in a 1982 report, in which it called for state boards governed by "members of the majority national teachers organization." To date, Iowa, Nevada, and Minnesota have established licensing boards with teacher majorities, but only Minnesota and Iowa have granted their board final authority over teacher certification.[61]

Yet when jobs are at stake, the qualifications of teachers are of little importance to the NEA. The same year Futrell charged that New Jersey's provisional-teacher plan was permitting improperly certified teachers into the state's classrooms, the NEA's Maryland affiliate was battling, unsuccessfully, to defeat a measure by that state's board of education to reduce the incidence of teachers teaching subjects that they had not been trained in. Two years earlier the NJEA opposed changes in New Jersey's seniority regulations designed to achieve the same goal. Similarly, the Michigan Education Association's lobbying defeated a legislative proposal to ease Michigan's shortage of math and science teachers by hiring mathematicians and scientists without teaching credentials, while pushing through the Michigan legislature a $2 million program to retrain English teachers to teach math and science. Indeed, it is the NEA's policy to "resist any attempts to diminish the quality of learning . . . through *involuntary* assignment [of teachers] out of [their] field [of certification]" (emphasis added)—despite the fact that *voluntary* misassignment of teachers is no less detrimental to students than involuntary misassignment. It is also the union's policy to "negotiate RIF policies that exclude performance evaluation from consideration in the reduction-in-force process."[62]

The NEA also has been a principal opponent of another major reform in teaching: teacher testing. Since the late 1970s scores of states have introduced testing requirements as a way of raising standards in the profession. As of 1988 thirty-five required standardized testing for admission to education schools, nearly forty made tests prerequisites for teaching licenses, and three states—Arkansas, Texas, and Georgia—tested veteran teachers. No other teacher reform has been adopted as widely.[63]

Unfortunately, the tests are keeping only the most grossly incompetent teachers out of the nation's classrooms; they aren't tough enough to do more than that. In contrast to the demanding entrance and licensing exams in law, medicine, and other professions, the majority of the new teacher tests measure only rudimentary academic and professional skills, and many of the tests don't measure teachers' professional or subject-matter knowledge at all. Rather than promoting the cause of teacher professionalism by setting high standards that signal to talented candidates that teaching is both a serious and prestigious profession, the majority of the state teacher tests aspire only to ensure that teachers are literate.

In many instances teachers are tested at a level below that of their students. Forty percent of the math section on the California exam, for example, tests knowledge learned in elementary school: addition, subtraction, percentages, fractions, and geometric shapes. The National Teacher Examinations (NTEs) are the tests most widely used in the licensing of teachers, and their maker, the Princeton-based Educational Testing Service, has asserted that teacher candidates need to be "well-educated" to answer questions on the tests successfully. But the questions themselves suggest otherwise. A sample item, for example, asks the test taker to identify the correct chronological order of these events: the beginning of the Great Depression, the First World War, the New Deal, and the Korean War.[64]

Nor have the tests of veteran teachers been any more rigorous. Arkansas's 1985 examination of its 28,000 teachers attracted wide attention as the nation's first state-sponsored test of tenured teachers. But according to Arkansas officials, the test of reading, math, and writing skills demanded only enough math to compute student grades, only enough reading ability to understand teacher's guides, and only enough writing ability to send a comprehensible note home to parents—tasks a well-educated ninth-grader could manage. What's more, while the intent of the Arkansas testing law was to remove incompetent teachers from the state's classrooms, it permitted teachers to avoid the test by taking six hours of college credit in their fields between 1985 and 1987. It also allowed those who failed the test to retake it an unlimited number of times in that period. Teachers who didn't manage a passing grade by June 1987 were barred from having their licenses renewed. But since the state issues teaching licenses on a six-year cycle, those who were relicensed in 1986 but didn't pass the test by 1987 will not be dismissed until 1992—seven years after they first failed what was essentially a literacy examination. The Texas test was equally undemanding. "People who can read will pass the test," the president of the company that constructed it said in 1986.[65]

Not only are the majority of the state teacher tests absurdly easy, the scores needed to pass them are astonishingly low. One example: to pass the Arkansas licensing test, the NTE, prospective teachers need do only as well as the bottom eighth of those who take the test nationally. Nonetheless, the failure rates on the tests have been extraordinarily high. Texas in 1984 established a basic-skills test as an admissions requirement to the state's education schools, and 40 percent of those who have taken the test since then have failed it at least once. Nearly 20 percent of California's teaching candidates have failed that state's basic-skills test at least once since its inception in 1983. Similarly, one of every ten veteran teachers in Arkansas failed that state's simplistic 1985 exam; an equal percentage of Texas's 170,000 teachers flunked that state's 1986 test; and the failure rate has hovered near 10 percent among Georgia's veteran teachers, who have been required since 1985 to pass basic subject-matter tests to renew their licenses.

In particular, tremendous numbers of minorities have failed the new teacher tests. Fully 72 percent of blacks and 52 percent of Hispanics have failed the Texas education-school admission examination, compared with 27 percent of whites. In New York 64 percent of blacks failed the communications-skills section of that state's teacher-licensing examination in 1987, 65 percent failed the general-knowledge section, and 43 percent failed the professional-knowledge section; the failure rates for whites were 17 percent, 22 percent, and 9 percent, respectively. In Florida 63 percent of blacks, 50 percent of Hispanics, and 12 percent of whites have failed the state's basic-skills teacher-licensing examination since its inception in the early 1980s. Similarly, 64 percent of blacks, 55 percent of Hispanics, and 19 percent of whites have failed the California licensing examination, known as the California Basic Educational Skills Test. In 1989 the Arizona Board of Regents lowered the passing score on its teacher-education entrance examination in order to increase minority participation in its teacher-training programs.[66]

The tests have filtered out of teaching many candidates lacking basic literacy skills. The nearly 20 percent annual failure rate on California's test, for example, represents roughly 8,500 rejected applicants for teacher licenses, whereas in 1982–83, the year before the state added the test to its licensing requirements, California turned down only 72 license applications.[67] And the tests also have aided the reform movement politically. Backing new teacher tests during the struggle for reform legislation in the states helped reformers win the support of skeptical legislators for the tax hikes and appropriations increases that funded reforms. In Arkansas Governor Bill Clinton launched a campaign for a teacher test on statewide television on September 19, 1983, the eve of a special legislative session he called to consider a range of school reforms and a tax increase to pay for them. At one point in the legislative debate, forty members of the Arkansas House signed a letter to Clinton warning that they would not vote for a tax hike without passage of the teacher test. Said Carl Parker, chairman of Texas's Senate education committee, of the Texas teacher test, "It was a small price we asked teachers to pay to enable us to extract more money from their fellow citizens to pay them."

Unfortunately, the political origins of many of the states' teacher tests is perhaps the primary reason for their low standards. More interested in using tests to protect themselves politically from budget-conscious voters than as a serious means by which to raise teaching standards, legislators left the details of the tests to state education officials, who generally turned to the NTEs and other superficial standardized tests already on the market, and who set standards primarily with an eye to ensuring an adequate supply of teachers rather than to ensuring that the nation's teachers are academically able. In the words of one leading testing expert, the majority of the state teacher tests have been "nothing more than a slick public relations ploy."[68]

Yet the tests have made plain the depth of the crisis in teaching: many students selecting teaching as a career lack even the simplest of academic skills. They also have supplied additional evidence of the arid intellectual climate on the nation's education campuses. And, unfortunately, they have revealed just how badly many of the nation's minority students are educated.[69]

Nonetheless, and despite the organization's own policy calling for "rigorous standards for entry into the teaching profession," the NEA and its affiliates steadfastly opposed the spread of teacher testing. Officially, it argued that "no single test can judge whether a teacher can teach." Unofficially, the union attacked the tests because they undermined the notions that graduation from an education school was sufficient qualification to teach and that all teachers with education degrees were equally qualified.[70]

NEA officials waged an intense rhetorical campaign against teacher testing, and the union's affiliates worked to block new testing programs in the states. Two years after the Texas State Teachers Association failed to kill the teacher-testing provision in Texas's 1984 reform package, it was in state court attempting to have the results of the test of basic reading, grammar, and arithmetic skills nullified. (Yet in the period leading up to the 1986 exam, the TSTA touted refresher courses for the test in its membership-recruitment drives.) In Arkansas over 50 percent of the first-year's revenue produced by the sales tax increase that Clinton's teacher test helped pass—$160 million—was earmarked for teacher salaries. Yet the Arkansas Education Association (AEA) battled the Arkansas testing law in state court (unsuccessfully), sent thousands of teacher-lobbyists to Little Rock to work for its repeal (in 1985 the state's largest school system was shut down for a day when the teachers of the Little Rock-area schools marched on the state capitol in opposition to the test), and called in top officials of the NEA in 1984 to "investigate" the test at a series of public "hearings." The union also attacked Clinton, one of many Democratic governors, the union's traditional allies, whom the NEA alienated with its opposition to education reform. AEA members picketed his house and sported "No More Clintons in 1986" bumper stickers on their cars.

Similarly, the Georgia Association of Educators filed suit against the state's 1985 law requiring all veteran teachers who hadn't passed Georgia's teacher test to do so prior to renewing their licenses (since passage of the test had been a requirement for an initial license in the state since 1978, the new law applied to teachers with eight or more years of experience). The suit was settled out of court in 1988 and use of the test was upheld, but not before the state agreed to pay "study grants" of $6,000 to 325 teachers who lost their jobs in 1987 after failing the rudimentary test. The Alabama Education Association, on the other hand, was one of many NEA affiliates that filed legal challenges against teacher tests required for first-time licensing. The organization won a settlement requiring the Alabama State Board of Education to repeal the test and pay damages to 650 prospective teachers who failed the basic-skills examination.

The NEA officially dropped its opposition to teacher testing as a licensing requirement in 1985. It had had enough of the bad publicity heaped on it by policymakers and the press for failing to support the reform. "From a public-relations point of view, [a test] was a small price to pay," said Parker of the NEA's Texas affiliate. "But the TSTA had a million excuses. . . . The teachers' performance in Texas is a perfect case study for freshmen public-relations majors in how not to handle a problem."[71] Also, over half the states had already introduced teacher-licensing tests by 1985, and it was clear that many others were soon to follow suit, so there was little at stake by the time the NEA changed its policy on licensing testing. Its opposition to the use of minimum test scores in education-school admissions and to the testing of veteran teachers remained unchanged, however.

In attacking the New Jersey provisional-teacher program, Futrell urged certified teachers to frame and post their credentials in their classrooms "like doctors, lawyers and other professionals." That, the NEA president said, would "let the public know who is qualified to teach." But the extraordinary failure rates on the states' licensing tests give the lie to the NEA's defense of traditional teacher credentials. If so many education majors fail the states' simplistic tests, is there any reason to be confident in the academic ability of those who pass the tests and are admitted into teaching? The spuriousness of the credentialing system in public education was vividly illustrated in 1985, when the Baltimore school system hired twenty teachers who performed, in the school system's words, "extremely badly" on a basic literacy test required of all teacher applicants. A Baltimore official explained the decision to hire such teachers by saying, "We were concerned about having certified teachers in classrooms, and these folks were all certified."[72]

The NEA has waged its toughest campaign against attempts to pay and promote teachers on the basis of performance. Since the 1920s, the overwhelming majority of the nation's school systems have rewarded teachers strictly according to educational level and seniority. With the enthusiastic support of teachers unions, they have used a "single salary schedule" that does not take into account quality of classroom work. The school reformers have argued that in failing to reward excellence in the classroom the single salary schedule diminishes the value of talent in teaching, and is thus a major barrier to teaching's recruitment of the best and brightest. They have argued that tying pay and other rewards to classroom performance is crucial to transforming teaching into a true profession.

The rewards system in teaching has been criticized in the past. "Every effort must be made to devise ways to reward teachers according to their ability without opening the school door to unfair personnel practices," wrote the Committee for the White House Conference on Education of 1955 in its report to President Eisenhower. "Present salary schedules have the effect of discouraging many able people from entering the profession." Similarly, a 1958 report sponsored by the Rockefeller Brothers Fund warned: "Teachers at the pre-college level tend to be handled as interchangeable units in an educational assembly line. The best teacher and the poorest in a school may teach the same grade and subject, use the same textbook, handle the same number of students, get paid the same salary, and rise in salary at the same speed to the same ceiling. Clearly, if the teaching profession is to be made more attractive, this will have to be changed."[73] But the single-salary schedule was never attacked the way it has been since the onset of the excellence movement. The major reform reports all have urged its end, as have corporate leaders, the nation's governors, a congressional task force, the U.S. secretary of education, and the president.

Past attempts to reward teachers for their classroom performance with "merit pay" hadn't worked very well in public education. Though commonplace prior to the advent of the single salary schedule in the 1920s, merit pay was used in only a small number of school systems afterward, and in virtually all instances it was eventually abandoned as unworkable. It was typically a bonus earned by teachers who—in theory—were considered on the basis of some form of evaluation to be doing superior work. In practice, merit pay was usually imposed on teachers by school boards and doled out arbitrarily by principals who had neither the time nor the ability to judge teacher performance adequately. Frequently, things like punctuality with paperwork rather than good teaching were rewarded, and in most places where it was tried, merit pay amounted to only a few hundred dollars, not enough to mean much to those who got it but just enough to irk those who didn't. Rarely did schools make merit pay a permanent part of salary structure. In contrast, the single salary schedule was far easier to administer.[74]

Believing that more money alone was not enough to keep talented people in teaching (the 1980s reformers argued that teachers were as frustrated by the nature of their work—the prospect of remaining isolated in their classrooms for the duration of their careers—as they were by being paid the same as the incompetent down the hall), the reformers championed a more ambitious solution, one that incorporated the performance-based pay idea into a blueprint for a broader redivision of labor in the public schools that would allow career teachers of demonstrated ability to assume new roles and responsibilities and gain greater status and higher salaries in doing do. This new vision of the organization of teachers was the basis of the reformers' calls for "career ladders," "head teachers," "differentiated staffing," and other reforms, and it emerged as the centerpiece of the campaign to professionalize teaching.

U.S. Secretary of Education Terrel H. Bell urged establishment of career ladders and master-teacher positions in public education as early as 1981. In an August speech to the Education Commission of the States in Boston, he declared: "There is no academic rank for teachers that could in any way parallel the academic rank system enjoyed by college professors. We do not recognize distinguished teachers in schools as we do our most able professors in our colleges. . . . The reward system we have demands that we pay the worst at the level of the best if we want to pay the best what they are worth." But Bell's commentary on teaching attracted scant attention in the early years of the Reagan administration because Bell didn't have much stature in either the administration or the education community at the time, and because in Washington the issue was overshadowed by the larger and more controversial educational matters of school prayer, tuition tax credits, budget cuts, and the fate of the Department of Education.

The notion of restructuring teaching first received national attention in early 1983, when Governor Lamar Alexander of Tennessee included a four-step career ladder in his $210 million Better Schools Program. Alexander's plan proposed a statewide ranking system that allowed Tennessee's best teachers to receive higher salaries, greater status, and new roles. When *A Nation at Risk* and the other major education studies also called for a new rewards system in teaching a short time later, education policymakers nationwide took up the issue. Indeed, soon after release of *A Nation at Risk*, Bell found himself speaking about career ladders and master teachers to the National Governors' Association, the U.S. Chamber of Commerce, and other influential organizations that had been disinterested in his ideas two years earlier.[75]

Ronald Reagan also played a major role in the rise of the performance-pay issue. Seizing an opportunity to associate the president with an idea strongly supported by the public but anathema to the Democratic-aligned NEA, Deaver and Reagan's other handlers decided to make performance pay a major theme of the president's education rhetoric as he barnstormed the nation in the weeks following release of *A Nation at Risk*. Beginning with his May 21, 1983, commencement speech at Seton Hall University, Reagan argued that "teachers should be paid and promoted on the basis of their merit." The NEA played right into the president's hands. When the union's leaders labeled the Seton Hall address "a disgraceful assault on the teaching profession," the White House on May 26 sent an open letter to NEA president Willard H. McGuire charging that the union was blocking "badly needed reforms" in teacher pay and promotions. Reagan's performance-pay rhetoric and his confrontation with the NEA (several weeks later, at the AFT's convention in Los Angeles, he accused the NEA of "frightening and brainwashing American schoolchildren") were front-page news in major newspapers throughout the spring and summer of 1983, transforming a little-known education reform into a major national issue.

Reagan complicated matters for the reformers by repeatedly referring to the whole range of performance-pay-based reforms as "merit pay plans," and Bell was compelled in a July 1983 speech to apologize for Reagan's confounding of merit pay with career ladders, master teachers, and other reforms designed to create a permanent career path for teachers. "We ought to stop using [the term] 'merit pay,' " he said, explaining that it connoted a simplistic system of teacher bonuses and not the broader restructuring of the reward system in teaching that the reformers sought.[76] Nonetheless, the president's merit-pay campaign hurt the NEA badly. The union received a tremendous amount of bad press and its ratings in opinion polls plummeted. The Reagan attacks were a public relations disaster, many within the organization acknowledged. The union was not prepared for either the sudden prominence that the president's commentary gave to performance pay, or for the intensity of the White House campaign against the NEA. Moreover, the union was thrown on the defensive just as the reform movement was gathering momentum (thus tainting the public's view of the NEA's response to the excellence movement as a whole), and just as the union was undergoing a major transition in leadership. Cameron replaced Herndon as executive director on June 1, 1983, ten days after Reagan's opening merit-pay salvo at Seton Hall, and at the NEA's convention in Philadelphia a month later the union elected Futrell to succeed McGuire as president.

The upheavals within the NEA led to the union's issuing a series of conflicting statements on performance pay as it struggled to defend itself against Reagan's attacks. Shortly before the president's Seton Hall speech, Herndon had vowed to defeat the Tennessee career-ladder plan and others like it "anywhere" they were introduced. McGuire called Reagan's speech "a disgraceful assault" on teaching on May 22, and he continued to attack the linking of pay to performance in newspaper, magazine, and television interviews through the end of his term on September 1. But on June 2 Cameron told an interviewer that "superior teachers ought to be given in some way, shape, or fashion additional status or money or something." And in congressional testimony in late June, Futrell (who was then the NEA's secretary-treasurer) outlined circumstances in which the NEA would "seriously consider" plans to "retain and reward excellent teachers."[77]

The NEA's inconsistent stance on an issue within teaching that was suddenly attracting national attention forced the union, after years of concentrating on broader national and international political matters under Herndon's leadership, to shift its attention to professional issues. The development pleased many within the NEA; one senior NEA staff official at the time called Reagan's performance-pay campaign "a blessing in disguise." And as a debate evolved within the organization over what its definitive performance-pay policy should be, there was strong opposition to traditional merit pay but also substantial support for the idea of linking pay to performance within a career path for teachers that offered the best of them greater status and new opportunities, as well as higher salaries. Indeed, in the late 1960s, the NEA's specialists on professional issues had strongly endorsed such staffing plans. In 1968 the union's now-defunct National Commission on Teacher Education and Professional Standards sponsored regional conferences on "differentiated staffing," urging school systems to establish a series of ranks within teaching, each carrying different responsibilities and rewards, in the manner of a career ladder. "We maintain that differentiated staffing deserves a careful trial, that it holds promise for both the improvement of instruction and the emergence of a mature profession of education," the commission wrote in a 1969 report on the conferences. The NEA even passed a resolution on the subject in 1969, describing differentiated staffing as "one of many concepts of school organization and staff development that hold promise for enhancing educational opportunities for children and that may provide a means of better utilization of teacher time and talents."[78]

The enthusiasm for differentiated staffing in wake of Reagan's attacks was such that an influential NEA task force endorsed the idea of hierarchies of teachers within schools in an early-1984 draft report. Established in 1983 to respond to *A Nation at Risk,* the task force included the NEA's vice-president and secretary-treasurer, as well as the presidents of several of the union's state affiliates.

But militant elements within the union attacked the recommendation. Power in the NEA is not concentrated in the president's office, as it is in the AFT. The union's nine-member executive committee and the presidents of the NEA's state affiliates wield great influence within the organization.[79] And the presidents of the union's largest and most combative affiliates—including California, Michigan, New Jersey, and Massachusetts—allied themselves with hardline unionists on the executive committee, particularly John I. Wilson, a North Carolina special-education teacher, against the differentiated-staffing recommendation. And they prevailed. The task force's final report, released at the NEA's 1984 summer convention in Minneapolis, stated defiantly: "There will be no hierarchical staffing systems within the teaching profession, only an exciting mix of equally important educational roles. . . . The NEA is opposed to any alternative compensation plan that acts as a substitute for proportionate, across-the-board salary increases." The militants within the NEA demanded that the organization preserve its commitment to the traditional trade union policy that all union members be treated as absolute equals, a concept known within organized labor as "fair representation."[80]

The debate within the NEA during the first half of 1984 was a watershed. After release of the task force's report, the earlier traces of conciliation by the union on the performance-pay issue all but disappeared. The NEA drafted a policy that summer rejecting "instructional performance pay schedules" and the union's leadership launched a rhetorical attack on the whole range of reforms designed to reward teachers according to their performance. "I contend the single salary schedule is a far cry better than the fly-by-night merit pay schemes we have seen over the last few years," the NEA's vice-president said in a 1985 speech, referring to Tennessee's career ladder. "Others would have us ascend to oblivion on the rickety rungs of ill-conceived career ladders," Executive Director Cameron shouted in an address to the NEA's 1985 convention. "We aren't selling our profession, and we aren't buying that kind of reform. . . . We will never accept the supercilious and self-serving pap currently paraded out as educational reform." Criticism of the single salary schedule, he said, was "unwarranted, self-serving, and usually uninformed." The NEA's national staff, meanwhile, rallied the union's membership against performance pay. In one instance it put on seminars for its state leaders entitled "Merit Pay: AKA Pin the Tail on the Teacher." Again and again the NEA rejected the argument that the single salary schedule deterred talented people from entering teaching.[81]

In the states NEA associations have worked tirelessly to defeat career ladders and other methods of rewarding good teaching with higher pay and promotions. They have done so despite the fact that a majority of their own members in polls favor performance-based pay and reforms such as career ladders.[82]

In New Jersey officials were forced to scuttle a two-year-old pilot master-teacher project in the face of opposition by the NJEA and its local affiliates. At the urging of Governor Kean, the state legislature in 1985 established a program to reward outstanding teachers in five school systems with $5,000 salary increases and new responsibilities in their schools. It was to be a multiyear, multi-million-dollar experiment. But the NJEA persuaded the legislature to grant local teacher unions veto power over a school system's decision to participate in the project. As a result, only nine of New Jersey's 600 school systems submitted applications to the program. Of the five that were selected, three with local NJEA affiliates withdrew under union pressure before their master-teacher programs could be put in place, and a fourth was dropped from the project by the state after its teacher union, an AFT affiliate, was charged with manipulating the selection of master teachers (there was a disproportionate number of shop stewards and other union officials among the 200 teachers awarded master-teacher status). The project was dismantled in 1987.

Intense lobbying by the Tennessee Education Association (TEA) killed Lamar Alexander's career-ladder plan in 1983. "Everyone is a master teacher," the TEA insisted in calling instead for an across-the-board pay increase of 10 percent for tenured teachers and the creation of a teacher-licensing board controlled by TEA members. NEA president Willard McGuire termed the Tennessee legislature's rejection of Alexander's career ladder "a great victory."[83]

Alexander, however, refused to abandon the plan, and in 1984, following what Tennessee political commentators called one of the most intense gubernatorial lobbying campaigns in the state's history, Tennessee's lawmakers reversed themselves and included a career ladder in a broad reform package approved during a special session on education. They created a five-step ladder that was implemented in 1984–85. Under the program, new teachers spend a year on the first, or probationary, rung. If promoted by their school system, they serve a three-year apprenticeship and receive an annual salary supplement of $500. Those who are promoted at the end of their apprenticeships receive full licensure; those who are not promoted face dismissal. Teachers at the next level, "career-level one," receive an annual salary supplement of $1,000 and, in addition to their normal duties, supervise student interns and probationary teachers. Career-level-one licenses are valid for ten years. But after three years, teachers may apply to the state to advance to the next level, "career-level two," where they earn an additional $1,000 annually (they are able to earn $4,000 over their base pay by working under an eleven-month contract; teacher contracts in Tennessee are usually ten months).

In addition to their regular teaching assignments, teachers at career-level two work with remedial and gifted students, develop curriculum materials, and supervise apprentice teachers. Career-level-two licenses are also valid for ten years, but teachers who receive satisfactory evaluations may apply to the top rung of the ladder, "career-level three," after four years. At that level they receive a salary supplement of $3,000 and are eligible for annual bonuses of $5,000 or $7,000 by working under eleven- or twelve-month contracts. As a check against favoritism, the state conducts evaluations of teachers for career-levels two and three, using career-level-three teachers who are not employed in the school system of the teacher being evaluated.

The Tennessee career ladder has created a very different system of rewards in teaching, but the TEA has succeeded in weakening it. Early on the union won a reduction in the top salary supplement (thereby reducing the plan's attractiveness to teachers) from $8,900 to $7,000. It persuaded the legislature to lift limits that the Alexander plan had set on the number of teachers on the top two rungs of the ladder (25 percent and 10 percent of the state's teachers, respectively). And after the education committees of both houses of the Tennessee legislature approved career-ladder provisions during the special session and it was clear that the legislature as a whole would pass teacher-ladder legislation of some sort, the TEA, which represents 36,000 of Tennessee's 46,000 teachers, traded its endorsement of the bill for further amendments (nervous legislators sought the TEA's endorsement of the bill because it made it much easier politically for them to support a costly reform). In negotiations with the career ladder's House sponsors, the TEA won the right of teachers who fail to achieve level one status to reenter the career ladder in another school system. It also won a provision creating a one-year "fast track" onto the career ladder for veteran teachers. There were no fewer than five ways for veteran teachers to move directly onto career-level one, including taking forty hours of workshops, a route that permitted teachers to sidestep the rigorous evaluation process built into the career ladder to ensure that only qualified teachers are promoted onto its top rungs. Seventy-five percent of the veteran teachers on the Tennessee career ladder (29,000 of 40,000) entered through the workshop route.

Nor has the TEA diminished its attempts to hamstring the Tennessee career ladder. Not long after the career ladder was implemented, the TEA brandished a survey of a "scientifically selected sample" of TEA members as evidence that the ladder was destroying teacher morale in the state. In another instance, the union acquired and distributed to its members copies of the state's confidential rating system used by evaluators during interviews with career-ladder candidates. The TEA has attacked and frequently misrepresented the Tennessee career ladder at conventions, in workshops, and especially through its monthly newspaper, *TEA News*.[84] The organization has sought legislation abolishing the career ladder. In 1987 Tennessee lawmakers defeated a TEA-sponsored bill that would have gutted the career ladder by permitting teachers to advance up the ladder by earning additional college credits rather than on the basis of their performance in the classroom. But the union did win legislation that year eliminating the first two rungs of the ladder and making the program voluntary for all teachers. Originally, it was voluntary for veterans and mandatory for all new teachers. The TEA also persuaded the Tennessee legislature in 1987 to increase from five to ten the number of years teachers on the ladder are permitted to receive bonuses under the career ladder without being reevaluated. The following year lawmakers approved a TEA proposal permitting all teachers, not just those who earned the opportunity by meeting the standards of the career ladder's upper rungs, to work under longer contracts and earn higher salaries for doing so, a development that weakened the ladder's linkage of pay to performance. The same year the TEA's president proclaimed that the union "has never taken a position in opposition to the [Tennessee] career ladder."[85]

The scenario was much the same in Texas. In its campaign against the Texas career ladder, the Texas State Teachers Association lobbied unsuccessfully during the special session in 1984 for an amendment to H.B. 72 allowing school systems to weight, according to a formula of their own choosing, the criteria that the legislation required school systems to use in evaluating teachers applying to the five-step career ladder: years of experience, academic credentials, and classroom evaluations. Its goal was to weaken the link between pay and performance in the Texas ladder by diminishing the significance of classroom evaluations in the career-ladder selection process. Texas teachers were already paid on the basis of their experience and credentials under the single-salary schedule; H.B. 72 added an evaluation system. The TSTA also sought to make the career ladder less attractive to teachers by tying the higher salaries under the ladder to longer contracts or other types of additional work, instead of solely to distinguished teaching. "We tend to favor variations of differentiated salary schedules or plans that utilize extended contracts for extra work," the TSTA said in testimony before the Perot committee.[86]

Like its Tennessee counterpart, the TSTA has attempted to weaken the Texas career ladder in the years since its implementation in 1984. H.B. 72 required that applicants for the ladder's third rung have a bachelor's degree and at least nine semester hours of additional college course work. During the 1985 Texas legislative session, the TSTA sought unsuccessfully to overturn a requirement that the courses be in the subjects that the career-ladder candidates teach. The same year, the union filed suit against the Texas career ladder on the grounds that it violated the constitutional rights of unpromoted teachers, but the Texas Supreme Court upheld the program's legality in a 1987 decision.

In Pennsylvania the NEA's state affiliate defeated a legislative proposal by Governor Richard Thornburgh for a $10 million annual "Excellence in Teaching" program. Under the plan, Pennsylvania would have made one-year grants of $2,000 to top teachers selected by local school systems.

The NEA's North Carolina affiliate attempted to block 1983 legislation exempting the state's largest school system, the 72,000-student Charlotte-Mecklenburg School District, from the state's teacher-tenure law. The school system had sought to grant its teachers tenure after six years instead of the traditional three years under an ambitious career-ladder experiment it had been planning. The union's lobbying defeated the bill in its second reading in the North Carolina House, and only the personal intervention of Governor James B. Hunt, Jr., saved the legislation. The North Carolina Association of Educators then unsuccessfully opposed 1984 legislation establishing pilot career ladders in sixteen of North Carolina's school systems, calling it "a cruel hoax to be played on children and the citizens of this state." Five years later, the organization's lobbying killed legislation that would have established career ladders statewide.[87]

When the Florida legislature created a statewide master-teacher program in 1983 over the opposition of the state's teacher unions, the unions vowed to topple the program and did. The Florida Master Teacher Program was designed to reward talented teachers (and thus keep them in the state's classrooms) by awarding $3,000 and $5,000 annual bonuses and the ranks of associate master teacher and master teacher to those who met high academic and teaching standards. The program was voluntary, and teachers were to gain the higher salaries and status for three years on the basis of a superior score on a subject-matter test (or a master's degree), a top rating on classroom evaluations conducted by a team of state-trained local educators, and a minimum number of years of experience. But in early 1985, before a single teacher had been evaluated, the NEA's state affiliate, Florida Teaching Profession (FTP-NEA), challenged the program in court (as did the AFT's state affiliate), seeking to halt its implementation on the grounds that it violated Florida's collective bargaining law. "We're of the view that there is no objective means to establish who is a meritorious teacher, it's a flawed concept," a lawyer for the FTP-NEA said at the time.

The unions' legal maneuvering was unsuccessful, but the FTP-NEA's local affiliates quickly threw up other barriers as implementation of the program proceeded. The Pinellas Classroom Teachers Association persuaded its 4,000 members to boycott the Master Teacher Program. "It didn't last long, because $3,000 bucks is $3,000 bucks," said the union's executive director. "But it was great while it lasted."[88] The NEA affiliate in the rural Santa Rosa County school system was one of many in the state that inundated Florida education officials with procedural appeals on behalf of members who weren't selected as associate master teachers in 1985. "We're going to try to overload the system in Tallahassee; we don't want the program to become successful," the local NEA UniServ director told me as he brandished a thick stack of union-drafted appeals. "There is only one education issue to be resolved in Florida in 1985," said FTP-NEA literature denouncing the program that union officials distributed in Santa Rosa's schools: higher teacher salaries.

Under pressure from the teachers unions and their legislative allies, Governor Bob Graham, who had sought the Master Teacher Program, called on the state legislature in 1986 to replace it with the Career Achievement Program, a five-step career ladder that offered teachers greater opportunities to work as mentors and in other new roles and eliminated a quota system that sharply limited the number of teachers rewarded under the Master Teacher Program. The legislature dismantled the two-year-old master-teacher initiative and reluctantly passed the governor's career-ladder legislation. But two years later the legislature refused to fund the Career Achievement Program, and it died with the career ladder still on the drawing board.

In Delaware career-ladder legislation was dispatched by the lobbying of the powerful Delaware State Education Association.

In Iowa and California, states in which an overwhelming majority of the teachers are NEA members, local teachers unions have used collective bargaining to dilute programs for rewarding outstanding teachers by requiring that the recipients of salary increases and other rewards do extra work, the requirement that the TSTA had sought unsuccessfully to include in the Texas career ladder.

The Iowa legislature passed the Educational Excellence Program in 1987 that earmarked $42 million for the development of local "teacher-incentive" programs. In exchange for the Iowa Education Association's support of pilot projects, Iowa lawmakers stipulated that the projects' designs be subject to collective bargaining. As a result, fully 87 percent of the 427 school systems that participated in the program in 1987–88 drafted "supplemental-pay" plans offering teachers salary bonuses in exchange for more work (participation on curriculum committees, extended contracts, and so on). Twelve percent drafted plans linking pay increases to additional work *and* classroom performance, but only three school systems proposed rewarding teachers strictly on the basis of teaching ability.[89]

In California the legislature established the Mentor Teacher Program to reward outstanding teachers as part of its omnibus 1983 education bill. It funds $4,000 annual grants for approximately 5 percent of the state's teachers, who, according to the program's guidelines, have distinguished themselves in the classroom. But, anticipating the California Teachers Association's opposition to a pure pay-for-performance arrangement, the legislative sponsors of the mentor program mandated that mentor teachers take on additional responsibilities as well as fulfill their regular teaching assignments. They described the program as "extra pay for more work." Moreover, while the 1983 law calls for mentor teachers to be selected on the basis of "exemplary teaching ability," it leaves the definition of that term and many other implementation issues to the local collective bargaining process. As a result, the majority of California's mentor programs do not serve as incentives to top teachers. A 1986 evaluation by the Far West Laboratory for Educational Research and Development, a federally funded institute, found an absence of explicit criteria for selecting mentor teachers in many school systems, and it reported that the "dominant" role of union representatives on many master-teacher selection committees has "skewed the selection toward teachers who are heavily involved in the union or are related to someone who is heavily involved in the union." The study also revealed that many local teachers unions demanded in collective bargaining that mentors be selected for very short terms (one year), thus increasing the number of teachers rotated through mentor positions and diminishing the prestige of being selected as a mentor teacher.[90]

The unions' cynicism toward the California mentor program is reflected in the story of a highly regarded biology teacher in a small school system I visited in the heart of the state's San Joaquin Valley agricultural region. The teacher was unanimously selected as a mentor in 1983–84 by a local panel of teachers and administrators, and he enthusiastically embarked on a project to revamp the school system's science curriculum. But when he applied to have his appointment renewed two years later, he was voted out of the mentor program by the union-appointed teachers, who by law hold a majority of the seats on local mentor-selection committees. His reappointment was rejected because during 1984–85, in addition to teaching five science courses a day and working on his mentor project, he had volunteered to work as a high school counselor one hour a week, a duty that was technically an administrative assignment and thus grounds for disqualification as a mentor in the eyes of the local NEA affiliate. The irony is that in steadfastly rejecting career ladders and master-teacher and mentor programs, the NEA and its affiliates are depriving many of their members of legitimate career opportunities. In effect, they are holding their members hostage in their battle to maintain the principles of industrial-style unionism in teaching, as the example of the California biology teacher illustrates so vividly.

Despite its repeated demands that teachers be permitted to police their own ranks, the NEA has rejected the reformers' recommendation that teachers evaluate the work of their peers. "We are negative about peer review," said Keith Geiger, then NEA vice-president, in a speech at the organization's 1984 convention. "The role of the teacher is to teach—period," argued Executive Director Cameron at the union's 1986 meeting. Two years later the NEA's 8,000 convention delegates approved a resolution stating that "mentor teacher plans and other peer programs must be used *solely* for the development of professional expertise," and not in making employment decisions. NEA affiliates have blocked the passage of peer-review measures in California and Minnesota, and in 1990 the Ohio Education Association sought unsuccessfully to defeat legislation protecting the Toledo peer program under Ohio's labor laws.[91]

Indeed, the NEA and its affiliates have attacked virtually any attempt to strengthen evaluation systems used in the dismissal or promotion of teachers. When the United Teachers of Dade, the AFT-affiliated bargaining agent for the teachers in Miami, endorsed a proposal to replace the school system's cursory evaluation checklist with a more comprehensive plan intended to give teachers "feedback" on their performance and to weed out incompetent instructors from the school system, the NEA's Miami-area affiliate took out full-page ads in the *Miami Herald* charging that the AFT local was undermining teachers' job security. Similarly, the California Teachers Association unsuccessfully sued to overturn provisions of California's 1983 reform law that reduces the bureaucratic red tape necessary to fire incompetent teachers. Teachers unions traditionally have supported superficial teacher evaluations because in the absence of thorough-going evaluations, it is virtually impossible to build a case against an incompetent teacher strong enough to withstand the long series of legal challenges granted teachers by the due-process language in collective bargaining contracts. Weak systems of evaluation are a primary reason that virtually none of the nation's public school teachers is fired for incompetence, the poor performance of many teachers notwithstanding.[92]

Like its responses to other major teacher reforms, from its opposition to performance pay to its defense of seniority provisions, the NEA's stance on peer review and evaluation represents a rejection of higher standards in teaching. Since the inception of the excellence movement, the organization has pursued a traditional industrial-labor-union agenda: preserving the jobs of members at all costs, and fighting for concessions on wages, hours, and working conditions. Indeed, after the 1983 California legislation established the minimum length of a school day in the state, the NEA's Sacramento local negotiated a *reduction* in the city's school day to the state minimum. Yet it is high standards—and the willingness of the profession itself to maintain them—that the reformers have argued repeatedly is crucial to enhancing teaching's status as a profession.

Where the reformers have gained the support of NEA affiliates, invariably it has been because policymakers have made salary concessions to the unions. The NJEA's about-face on alternative certification is a good example. In another, the Fairfax (Virginia) Education Association—with 8,000-plus members, the NEA's second-largest local—in 1986 agreed to a new, tougher evaluation system in the Fairfax County school system with salary increases for the highest-rated teachers, but only after the Fairfax school board agreed to a 30 percent pay hike over three years for every teacher in the school system, and when the school board in 1989 changed the rewards for teachers with the highest ratings from permanent salary increases to one-year bonuses, the union dropped its support of the program. Similarly, the NEA state affiliates in South Carolina, Arizona, and Iowa all predicated their backing of career-ladder pilot projects on substantial across-the-board salary increases. "If the political community reneged [on its commitment to a series of statewide pay hikes], then we would no longer be a part of the [career-ladder] consortium," the president of the South Carolina Education Association told a reporter in 1987.[93]

Though the NEA has fought virtually all of the major teacher reforms, it has poured millions of dollars into a public relations campaign designed to convince the nation that it is committed to the reform of the public schools, and of teaching in particular. Since it was thrown on the defensive by Reagan's skillful attacks in 1983, the NEA has sought to "repackage" its image, using media consultants, Madison Avenue advertising agencies, and its own forty-member "communications" staff to foster a public perception of the union as a leader of the excellence movement. It has fueled the campaign with an annual communications budget that reached $13.2 million in 1990.[94]

Its initial tactic was quickly to appropriate the excellence theme as its own in wake of *A Nation at Risk* and the other national reform reports. The union's many publications were replete with references to the theme. In a single edition (1984–85) of *Today's Education,* an annual publication, there were such articles as "America's Schools: A Panorama of Excellence," "Our NEA: At Work for Excellence," "Quality Education: On the Cutting Edge," "Planning for Excellence," and "Setting the Course for Excellence," the last a review of the NEA's educational policies. The union's public relations staff, meanwhile, inundated the press with releases asserting that "NEA members across the United States are making education reform come alive" and that "the NEA today stands in the forefront of the drive to bring excellence to the nation's schools." In 1989 alone the organization earmarked $1.7 million to "secure favorable media coverage of NEA as a leading advocate of education reform." The union also launched advertisements on network television and in national publications, proclaiming "Our Subject Is Excellence." In major cities billboards carried the message.

The NEA also quickly made its new president, Mary Futrell, an important part of its public relations offensive. A statuesque black woman, earnest and affable, she was an ideal leader for the NEA's image makers, the perfect symbol of an organization deeply committed to improving the education of all the nation's students. Unlike earlier NEA presidents, who frequently ceded the role to the union's executive director during Herndon's tenure, Futrell immediately became the NEA's leading spokesperson and primary public representative. Whenever possible, the union sought to filter the public's perceptions of the NEA through her. In sharp contast to Herndon, the hot-tempered Cameron was kept off the public stage almost altogether. Such was Futrell's value to the NEA that in 1987 the union amended its bylaws to permit her to serve an unprecedented third two-year term.

Futrell shifted the NEA's rhetoric dramatically during her three terms. She replaced Herndon's shrill pronouncements on national and international affairs with rhetoric on the importance of educational excellence. And she pledged the NEA to supporting the reform movement in public education. "The time has come to clear away the mold and mildew that still cling to the educational status quo," she declared in a 1989 speech. "In place of stale orthodoxies, we need fresh, risk-taking strategies." Referring to the NEA in a 1989 interview, she said, "We aren't going to change schools by being intransigent. We aren't going to change schools by being very narrow in our focus, by simply blaming people. . . . We have to come up with recommendations, we have to be willing to cooperate."[95]

To the union's delight, such statements have led commentators to suggest that the NEA is adopting a more moderate stance in the teaching-reform debate. But there have been virtually no shifts in the NEA's policies to reinforce Futrell's pious rhetoric. And Futrell herself, in her many calls for a complete "restructuring" of the teaching occupation, ignored performance pay, peer review, differentiated staffing, and other reforms that the excellence movement has argued are fundamental to the new vision of teaching that Futrell so passionately embraced. Frequently, Futrell discussed the NEA's commitment to reform without mentioning the troubles in teaching at all, discoursing instead on the union's dedication to improving the plight of disadvantaged students and other issues. In a 1989 interview she said the NEA was unfairly criticized for attacking *A Nation at Risk* because the union "supported 85 percent of the report's agenda"; it didn't matter that virtually all the national commission's proposals for reforming teaching were among the recommendations in the report that the NEA did reject.

When pressed in interviews on the NEA's continued opposition to the major teacher reforms, Futrell waffled, saying, "Yes, we are for reform, but we are for quality reform," and, "We've tried to move forward in a very thorough and careful way." Eventually, Futrell refrained from publicly attacking individual experiments in performance pay and other teacher reforms when they were supported by local NEA affiliates. But such a step was a far cry from Albert Shanker's aggressive advocacy of major reforms in teaching.[96]

A major vehicle for Futrell's reform rhetoric was a bimonthly column the NEA ran as an advertisement under her byline in the *Washington Post* and *Education Week*. Conceived primarily by Cameron and his staff, and written by the NEA's professional wordsmiths, it was a skillful assemblage of empty platitudes, cynical righteousness, and flagrant misrepresentations of fact designed to mask the NEA's opposition to reform. "To be sure, we realize that the NEA alone cannot meet the challenges that face our schools," Futrell said in the first of the columns, published in April 1984, on the first anniversary of *A Nation at Risk*. "Nevertheless, we in NEA are moving ahead, as best we can, to respond to the [excellence] commission's recommendations." "We have worked hard to implement real educational reform, and we will continue to do so," she wrote in 1988, in a column entitled "Remembering the Message of *A Nation at Risk*. "We're continuing to work at every level to realize the dreams inspired by *A Nation at Risk*." In the same column, Futrell asserted that "almost all" of the state education reforms of the 1980s "were introduced or endorsed by NEA state affiliates." "America's appetite for education reform is still robust, and I am delighted that it is," she wrote two months later. "I am even more delighted that reform efforts are at last focusing on profound systemic change, on the comprehensive restructuring of schools."[97]

The NEA has also waged its public relations campaign on many other fronts. In 1984 it published *An Open Letter to America on Schools, Students, and Tomorrow*, the report of the twenty-member Blue-Ribbon Task Force on Educational Excellence it established in 1983 to respond to *A Nation at Risk*. The glossy document contained reams of pious rhetoric. "The dream of what America can be, the high goals her people share, and the great strengths her people possess have always been closely interwoven with our system of public education. The National Education Association refuses to accept the destruction of that dream," its authors declared. "Our nation's public schools must be totally restructured." But the report's recommendations were little more than a reiteration of the union's long-standing policy objectives. They were a defense of the status quo in public school teaching, presented under the pretense of reform. In addition to rejecting differentiated staffing, the report called for increased federal funding in education, a minimum starting-teacher salary of $24,000, state licensing boards "controlled by the profession," the expansion of public education to all four-year-olds (creating a need for thousands of new teachers), and a federal law extending collective bargaining rights under the 1935 Wagner Act to public employees. "Through collective bargaining, school staff and administrators will work together to create working conditions that support quality education," the report said of public education in the twenty-first century. "A national collective bargaining law supported by state legislation will ensure that all communities have access to this tested and effective process for resolving conflicts and planning for the future."[98]

The following year the NEA proclaimed a major shift in its policies when its convention delegates passed a resolution calling on school systems to initiate dismissal proceedings against incompetent teachers. The move gained the union a great deal of positive publicity, but in reality it was another disingenuous ploy to improve the NEA's public image, for the resolution was draped with demands for the same sorts of elaborate due-process protections that have traditionally made it all but impossible to fire teachers for incompetence. In practical terms, the resolution changed nothing. Moreover, the NEA also approved a resolution at the same convention calling for lifetime teaching licenses, a step that would make it tougher to dismiss bad teachers.

The NEA also won applause by endorsing the Carnegie Forum's 1986 blueprint for professionalizing teaching. In reality, however, the union had virtually no choice but to back the forum and its report. In light of the forum's tremendous influence, the widespread enthusiasm for its recommendations, and the volume of press coverage it received, it would have been suicidal of the NEA to do otherwise. Nonetheless, in a little-mentioned addendum to the report entitled "Statement of Support with Reservations," Futrell, who was a member of the task force, rejected virtually all of the report's major teacher reform recommendations: lead teachers ("It suggests that some teachers are more equal than others," she wrote), career ladders, performance pay, greater teacher accountability, and a greater emphasis on the liberal arts in teacher training. In addition, after endorsing the forum's recommendation for a national standards board in teaching, the union passed a resolution at its 1987 convention directing its leadership to take "whatever steps are reasonable and necessary" to prevent the new national board from establishing a "linkage" between teacher salaries and national certification, though the forum had strongly recommended that teachers who attain board certification be rewarded with higher salaries. The NEA modified its stand only slightly the following year, suggesting that any linkage between teacher salaries and national certification be subject to local collective bargaining. Earlier, in a May 28, 1986, column, Futrell had misrepresented the Carnegie report's stance on performance pay in attempting to use the report's prestige to discredit the reform. She implied in the column, published just after the report was released, that the forum opposed performance pay, when in truth it was a cornerstone of the Carnegie plan for professionalizing teaching.[99]

Moreover, it's clear from NEA documents that the union would have fought creation of the national standards board if it hadn't been convinced that NEA members would eventually hold a majority of the board's seats. In 1986 Carnegie appointed a panel of educators and policymakers to organize the national certification agency. The panel's plan called for a permanent sixty-three-member board (forty-two teachers who were themselves nationally certified and twenty-one other educators and public representatives), and a transition board that would function until enough teachers received national certification to empanel the permanent body. Futrell, a member of the panel, sought to have NEA-designated teachers constitute a majority of the teachers on the transition board, which would have to make decisions on such crucial issues as who would be eligible for national certification. She wasn't successful. In 1987 the panel appointed a transition board with equal numbers of NEA and AFT appointees, curriculum specialists, and teachers nationally recognized for their work. Nonetheless, the NEA leadership reasoned in a memorandum to the panel that since two-thirds of the board membership would eventually be nationally certified teachers, and since the NEA represented the majority of the nation's teachers, the union would eventually exercise strong influence over the board. Thus, the NEA hierarchy wrote, the union was "able to indicate support overall for the [panel's] document." Nonetheless, the NEA in 1990 attacked a decision by the standards board not to require applicants to have earned education degrees.[100]

The emptiness of the NEA's reform rhetoric was further revealed in 1989, when Futrell, in a speech to the Fairfax County, Virginia, Chamber of Commerce, praised the county's performance-pay plan. The Fairfax initiative, Futrell said, was a potential national "model." The next day the *Washington Post* ran a front-page story under the headline "NEA Lauds Fairfax Merit Pay," quoting a number of national educational leaders to the effect that the speech marked a major shift in NEA policy. In reality, Futrell's remarks were designed to put pressure on the Fairfax school board to fund the program fully in an upcoming vote (substantial salary increases for hundreds of teachers in the local NEA affiliate were on the line), and as soon as they appeared in a prominent newspaper, Futrell quickly backtracked, telling reporters that the union was strongly opposed to performance pay and that headlines to the contrary were "extremely misleading."

The NEA also has sought to associate itself with the movement to restructure teachers' roles in schools by sponsoring a series of pilot programs in "site-based decisionmaking" among its local affiliates. These programs—known as Mastery in Learning, Team Approach to Better Schools (TABS), Operation Rescue, and Learning Laboratories—have been the cornerstone of the NEA's public relations campaign in recent years. The union, for example, organized virtually its entire 1988 convention around the announcement of the Learning Laboratories project. In a convention news conference, Futrell proclaimed it "a major step toward . . . needed restructuring in America's schools." NEA press releases echoed the theme. "NEA Delegates Endorse Learning Laboratories; Step Up Efforts to 'Restructure' Education," said one. The union also released the report of the Special Committee on Restructuring Schools at the 1988 convention. "The learning laboratories will be the instruments for systemic change to improve educational opportunities for every learner," it declared.[101]

The pilot projects were also the constant subject of Futrell's speeches and columns. "We in the NEA are doing our best to break down the bureaucratic obstacles [facing teachers] so rightly lamented by [the Carnegie Forum report and other recent] studies," Futrell intoned in a December 1987 column. "We're particularly proud of one of our efforts, the NEA Mastery in Learning Project. . . ." And in 1988 the NEA reorganized its communications division to increase the public relations value of the pilot projects. In wake of an internal memorandum from Cameron calling for the NEA to be "proactive" rather than "reactive" in its image making, the union created a new department within its communications division, designed specifically to promote the pilot projects. "We brought in a whole [department] that deals with nothing but how we package" the public perception of the pilot projects, said Futrell in a 1989 interview. In 1990, under new NEA president Keith Geiger, who had succeeded Futrell the previous summer, the union merged its pilot programs into a National Center for Innovation in Education, which it touts as "the nation's widest-reaching school restructuring network."[102]

But the NEA pilots are hardly the ambitious experiments in teacher restructuring that the union has declared them to be. First, the NEA established three of the four—Mastery in Learning, TABS, and Operation Rescue—in 1985 as "excellence" projects by NEA members. Union members in a small number of schools received funds and staff support from the NEA to undertake improvement projects that they selected themselves. The Mastery in Learning program involved "mini-research studies" into such topics as increasing parent involvement in their children's learning; TABS projects ranged from upgrading a school playground to drafting a new discipline code; and Operation Rescue focused on dropouts. Only after the restructuring of teachers' responsibilities became a priority within the teacher-reform movement following the Carnegie report in 1986 did the NEA begin touting the projects as experiments designed to grant teachers a greater say in the running of their schools. The union merely relabeled the projects once "restructuring" became popular, in the same way it seized on the "excellence" theme in wake of *A Nation at Risk*.

Second, although the NEA's press releases proclaim TABS, Mastery in Learning, and Operation Rescue to be "successfully restructuring schools all over the United States," the site-based decision making in them bears little resemblance to that urged by teacher reformers. In virtually none of the projects' schools have new teacher roles been institutionalized, as they have been in Miami and Rochester through the creation of "management teams" and "faculty committees." Nor do teachers in the projects participate in general school decision making, whereas in Miami and Rochester they have been granted a say in budget, staffing, and instructional matters. Though many teachers participating in the projects praise them as a way of exercising initiative within their schools, the vast majority of project participants receive only a one-time opportunity to organize a single activity.

Nor do many of the projects include differentiated staffing or other of the major innovations the reformers have put forward as necessary for the true restructuring of teachers' roles in schools. On the contrary, the NEA has designed the pilot projects to ensure that the union's traditional policies are not overturned. For instance, the Learning Laboratories initiative, launched in 1988–89, urges states to designate at least one school system in which educators would be "free to turn their school systems upside down or inside out" in the name of restructuring. In announcing the project, Futrell proclaimed that the NEA was "willing to experiment" with teacher reforms it opposed. "We may have to swallow some bitter pills," she said. But in reality, the union has taken steps to ensure that that doesn't happen. First, the NEA's state affiliates must agree to have a learning lab in their state. Then they handpick local affiliates to participate in the program. The selected locals work out a "restructuring" plan with school system officials, which the state affiliates either approve or reject. Finally, the national NEA leadership selects a winning plan in each of the participating states. Under such a system the chances of major teacher reforms being approved are small. And indeed, only four of the eight plans approved in 1989 grant teachers a significant role in school governance, and only one contemplates differentiated staffing.

Moreover, despite its claims that the pilot programs represent a major investment by the union in teacher reform, the NEA has committed only a fraction of its vast resources to the programs. The union spent the same amount of money on hotel rooms for its leadership and delegates at the Democratic National Convention in Atlanta in 1988 as it spent on its much-publicized Learning Laboratories program in 1988–89: $400,000. Many of its 200 TABS grants have been as small as $1,250.

In a 1989 interview Futrell acknowledged that the NEA's pilot projects have not seriously restructured teachers' roles in schools. She retreated from the union's sweeping rhetoric, saying that the NEA is merely addressing the restructuring of teaching "from a research point of view" and that the NEA's pilot projects represent "an evolutionary process."[103]

Yet the Mastery in Learning, TABS, Operation Rescue, and Learning Laboratories programs have been a public relations coup for the NEA. Through them, the union has created the appearance of backing new roles for teachers in schools while avoiding the consequences of full-fledged teacher participation in school management in places such as Miami, namely, that teachers in decision-making roles have greater status than their peers; that they assume a responsibility for the performance of their peers; and that their increased status and responsibilities are accompanied by higher salaries. The token pilot projects have permitted the NEA to seem to support serious "teacher restructuring" while holding fast to its hard-line policies.

Despite its public posturing, the NEA has relinquished neither its traditional policies nor its industrial-trade-union vision of teaching. Indeed, in a speech to the NEA's 1988 convention, Executive Director Cameron stated that collective bargaining "was the key that unlocked the doors to the sacred temples of power," and that the NEA "must never sacrifice unionism on the altar of professionalism." And gaining the NEA's presidency in 1989, Keith Geiger declared the enactment of new teacher-collective-bargaining laws to be his highest priority.[104]

The NEA's resistance notwithstanding, the ferment within teaching in recent years has been unprecedented, and much progress has been made toward professionalizing the occupation. Teacher salaries have risen dramatically. The average American public school teacher earned $29,600 in 1988–89, an increase of 43 percent from 1982–83, nearly double the national inflation rate. In the same period, average teacher salaries rose by 98 percent in Connecticut, 75 percent in Vermont, 55 percent in Virginia, 53 percent in South Carolina, and 50 percent in California (where one-tenth of the nation's teachers work). By 1988–89 teachers were earning an average of $34,000 in Michigan, $35,300 in California, $35,500 in New York, and $37,300 in Connecticut. Many school systems have hiked their pay scales even higher. Dade County's 23,000 teachers will earn an average of nearly $40,000 in 1990–91, and veterans will earn as much as $69,000. And Rochester teachers earned an average of $42,000 in 1989–90; lead teachers earned as much as $68,500. As government employees, teachers will never earn the salaries investment bankers do, but in many school systems teaching has become very lucrative work.

The most dramatic increases have been in starting salaries, as policy-makers have sought to attract better recruits into teaching. The national average increased by 72 percent between 1982–83 and 1988–89, to $19,700. And at least thirty states have established statewide minimum salaries in recent years. Texas lawmakers established a minimum salary of $15,200 in 1984–85, which represented a one-year increase of 37 percent in the state's average starting-teacher salary; New Jersey legislators raised that state's average starting-teacher salary by 24 percent when it established a minimum salary of $18,500 in 1985–86. New teachers in New York City, the nation's largest school system, were paid $25,000 in 1989–90, an increase of 84 percent from 1982–83. Starting-teacher salaries increased to $23,150 in 1988–89. In Rochester starting salaries were $29,000 in 1989–90, up 52 percent in three years. In Dade County, salaries will start at $26,500 in 1990–91. And by 1991–92, starting salaries will rise to $28,000 in Pittsburgh and $29,500 in Los Angeles. Such increases have made teaching competitive with such occupations as finance (in which average starting salaries were $23,100 in 1988), marketing ($22,800), business administration ($22,900), accounting ($24,300), and even top-paying fields such as engineering ($29,000), computer science

($27,400), and mathematics ($26,100). In all, national spending on teacher salaries rose from $46 billion in 1982–83 to $65 billion in 1988–89.[105]

Much progress also has been made in reorganizing the reward system in teaching. Virtually no teachers were paid or promoted on the basis of performance when *A Nation at Risk* was released in 1983, and there were few career opportunities that did not require teachers to abandon the classroom for administration. Today dozens of states and scores of school systems have established or are planning career ladders and other initiatives that offer increased status, higher salaries, and new professional opportunities to teachers based on the quality of work. Hundreds of millions of dollars have been invested in such reforms. The Southern Regional Education Board (SREB) observed in 1988 that "career ladders and other performance-based incentive programs are the largest educational experiment in the United States today."[106]

In addition to the statewide career ladders in Tennessee and Texas, Utah funds locally developed career ladders in all of its school systems (the state even sent a team to study career ladders in Great Britain, where they have been in place for several decades). Missouri also funds career ladders in school systems that elect to have them, and by 1988–89 they were in place in over a third of the state's 545 districts. Georgia is phasing in a five-step career ladder mandated under 1985 legislation with pilot projects in five school systems, in which teachers will receive state salary supplements beginning in 1991. The career ladder is expected to cost taxpayers $212 million annually when it is implemented throughout the state in 1998.

Tennessee's annual career-ladder budget reached $99 million in 1988–89. The same year the Texas State Board of Education recommended increasing career-ladder funding to $330 million annually by 1990–91. By 1989 several other states—including North Carolina, Arizona, and Indiana—were sponsoring large-scale career-ladder pilot projects with the intention of expanding them statewide.[107]

Other state-sponsored incentive programs also have burgeoned. Over 10,000 teachers participated in California's mentor-teacher program in 1988–89, at a cost of $64 million. And by 1988–89, nine other states— New York, Minnesota, Oregon, and Indiana among them—either had implemented or were pilot testing mentor initiatives similar to California's.

South Carolina lawmakers in 1984 created the Teacher Incentive Program, which rewards teachers with salary bonuses funded by the state on the basis of a formula that includes teacher attendance, student achievement, classroom evaluations, and professional improvement. After beginning as a pilot project, it was expanded statewide in 1988–89, at a cost of $22 million. Similarly, South Carolina, Florida, and several other states have established incentive programs that reward schools as a whole for such things as student and teacher attendance and student-achievement gains. A fourth of South Carolina's 1,016 schools received $3.9 million in such incentive rewards in 1987–88. A number of states have also created fellowship programs for outstanding teachers. A program established under the Massachusetts Public School Improvement Act of 1985, for example, in 1988–89 provided fellowships to sixteen teachers to develop, disseminate, or replicate successful education programs in the state. According to the SREB, which established a national clearinghouse on career ladders and other teacher incentives in 1984, a total of twenty-five states either sponsored statewide teacher incentives or funded locally developed programs in 1988–89, and another nine were planning such initiatives. Additionally, many school systems have launched teacher-incentive programs independently. Communities ranging from Huntington Beach, California, to Cincinnati, Ohio, have followed Charlotte-Mecklenburg in establishing career ladders. Over 20 percent of the teachers who participated in a large-scale federal survey in 1987–88 said that they had received funds that year for career ladder progress, individual merit pay, or group merit bonuses. In all, perhaps a third of the nation's public school teachers are now working in states or school systems that in one way or another reward teachers on the basis of classroom performance.[108]

The career ladders and other new teacher-incentive initiatives are not flawless. Because they represent the most drastic departure from the traditional reward system in teaching, career ladders have been a challenge to administer. Tracking teachers' movements on the Tennessee ladder, processing thousands of evaluations a year, and communicating with teachers and school systems about career-ladder matters, for example, necessitated a complex computer system and cost Tennessee $7 million in 1987, though costs have declined recently as officials have increased the program's efficiency. Administrative troubles contributed to the demise of the Florida Master Teacher Program. After a state-appointed advisory committee failed to produce a blueprint for the program, Governor Bob Graham ordered a crash implementation schedule that resulted in school systems' being instructed to nominate principals and other local administrators as evaluators of the teachers less than a week before the nominees were scheduled to be tested on their evaluation skills. Then the state's administration of the evaluator examinations was marred by poor planning. In one instance 500 administrators crowded into the auditorium of a Tampa high school, where, as part of their examination, they struggled to evaluate videotapes of classroom teaching displayed on four televisions placed on the auditorium's stage. Meanwhile, only four months before scheduled implementation of the Florida plan (in September 1984), the state was forced to abandon a legislative requirement that all teachers seeking master-teacher status pass a written test in their subjects because officials were able to identify reliable tests in only six of the forty-eight subjects in which Florida licenses teachers. The state board of education arbitrarily voted to waive the testing requirement for teachers in subjects where tests were not available, requiring teachers instead to have a master's degree in such subjects, a very different standard. Later hundreds of tests were invalidated when computers used to score them were misprogrammed, and then rejection notices were sent to as many as 10 percent of the teachers who completed their master-teacher applications after a computer declared them ineligible to participate in the program on the basis of mistakes on their electronically scanned application forms.[109]

Another flaw in the Florida program was that the number of master teachers was determined by the amount of money appropriated by the legislature for salary bonuses, rather than by the number of teachers who met the state's master-teacher standards. As a result, many more teachers qualified for master-teacher status than received it during the program's two-year existence, a fact that contributed to widespread resentment among teachers toward the master-teacher initiative. Similarly, the Texas legislature appropriated only enough funds to pay the salary increases of a little over one-third of the teachers who qualified for the second level of the state's career ladder during the program's first year.

In addition, many of the new teacher-incentive programs have failed to reward teachers strictly on the basis of performance. Many teachers are able to raise their salaries and their status merely by doing extra work, as the Iowa supplemental-pay plans and many of California's mentor-teacher projects illustrate. Another example is Utah's career ladder: school systems are permitted to spend up to half of their state career-ladder funding on work-related incentives rather than on performance-based promotions (though the actual percentage is somewhat lower). Teachers who are paid or promoted on the basis of classroom performance are also frequently required to do additional work in return, as Tennessee's teachers are. Only five of Utah's forty-five school systems do not require the teachers on their career ladders to do additional tasks. Teachers unions' bent on diluting the significance of performance-based pay are the main source of the more-pay-for-more-work requirements in many teacher-incentive plans; in a 1987 report the SREB wrote: "In locally negotiated career ladder plans, the emphasis is on extra pay for extra duties or different duties."[110]

Requirements in Texas and elsewhere that teachers take graduate courses in education for advancement on career ladders also undermine the rewarding of performance. They reinforce the traditional system of paying teachers on the basis of experience and academic credentials (and in so doing, they subsidize education schools and their shoddy programs).

Further, in teacher-incentive programs where evaluations of classroom performance do play an important part in determining promotions and pay increases, the evaluations often emphasize teachers' pedagogical skills and not their knowledge of the subjects they teach. The six "areas of competence" in a new statewide evaluation instrument created for use in the Tennessee career ladder, for example, are "planning for instruction, teaching strategy, evaluation of student progress, classroom management, professional leadership, and basic communications skills." The instrument contains dozens of sometimes superficial "indicators" based on research about "things teachers know and do that contribute to good teaching," ranging from "uses responses and questions from learners in teaching" to "handles minor interruptions without disruption to the current task" and "arranges classroom furniture and equipment to facilitate movement." Similarly, the new Texas Classroom Evaluation System measures teachers' strengths in a series of seventy-one "observable generic teaching competencies."

Moreover, the promotion standards of many incentive programs are low. Nearly 80 percent of the Tennessee teachers who have applied to the top two rungs of the state's career ladder have done so successfully. Nearly 60 percent of the 3,300 Fairfax County, Virginia, teachers who completed the county's new evaluation system in 1987–88 received the highest rating and qualified for a 10 percent salary increase. Similarly, a 1988 study of the Utah career-ladder program by the Far West Laboratory found that in nine of twelve school systems, an average of 70 percent of the teachers who applied for performance bonuses received them. In another 1988 report the SREB wrote of the sixteen career-ladder pilot projects in North Carolina: "The evidence to date is that performance ratings tend to be inflated."[111]

Nonetheless, many teacher-incentive initiatives, particularly career ladders, are successfully reshaping the reward system in teaching. The career ladder in North Carolina's Charlotte-Mecklenburg school system is a good example. One of the first large-scale incentive plans developed in the 1980s, it was conceived after Charlotte's superintendent, alarmed at the low quality of the school system's teacher recruits and seeking "to do something different" to attract better teachers, appointed a committee in 1981 to study the feasibility of a merit-pay plan. After discovering merit pay's poor record, the committee of educators and local business leaders instead urged the superintendent, Jay Robinson, to establish "a comprehensive system of incentives" for teachers tied to a rigorous new evaluation system. Robinson agreed. The committee outlined its proposal in a 1982 report entitled "Recommendations for Improving the Career Opportunities of Teachers in the Charlotte-Mecklenburg Schools: A Constructive Alternative to Merit Pay." Following two years of planning, the experiment was launched in 1984–85 and continued through 1988–89.

Charlotte-Mecklenburg created a six-step career ladder (later reduced to four steps) that was mandatory for new teachers and voluntary for veterans. In its basic shape it was similar to Tennessee's ladder. A new employee spent two years at the "provisional" level, where his or her work was closely scrutinized by a three-person "advisory and assessment team" consisting of the principal, an assistant principal, and a mentor teacher; he or she received as many as eight classroom visits by the mentor, four by the assistant principal, two by the principal, and two by the school system's specially trained "observer-evaluators." The new teacher also conferenced with the full team half a dozen times during the year. The school system assigned the advisory team the responsibility of recommending whether teachers be rehired at the end of the year. A dismissal recommendation had to be upheld by two levels of review committees, and by the superintendent. The process was then repeated during the second provisional year, following which the successful teacher was promoted to the rank of "career nominee."

Career nominees continued to work with their advisory teams (albeit they were evaluated in their classrooms less frequently) and also designed projects to improve their teaching that were known as "professional development plans." If they received two years of favorable evaluations, they earned promotion to the rank of "career candidate." There, they continued the specialized teacher training begun at the provisional level (the school system provided child care so teachers could take courses during the afternoon), continued their professional-development activities, and received another series of evaluations. Finally, the Charlotte-Mecklenburg plan called for career candidates, on the recommendation of their advisory teams, to be promoted to the top rung of the ladder, "career level one," within two years or be dismissed. The teacher who endured the fifty-four required evaluations over the six-year period (a "fast track" permitted those with the highest ratings to reach the top level within four years) received tenure and a $2,000-a-year pay increase that would rise to $4,000 after three years, and also the opportunity to become a mentor to new teachers and an observer-evaluator.

Veteran teachers were permitted to enter the ladder at the career-candidate level. Each worked with an advisory team (two mentors and an administrator), completed a professional-development project, and underwent a series of evaluations. If he or she was not recommended for promotion at the end of the year by the advisory team, a second try was permitted the following year. During the five years of the experiment, nearly three-fourths of the school system's 4,200 teachers participated in the program. In 1989–90, the Charlotte-Mecklenburg program was reorganized under new North Carolina career-ladder guidelines, resulting in lower standards and smaller bonuses distributed to greater numbers of teachers. Charlotte-Mecklenburg decided to conform to the state guidelines primarily because it received substantial state funding for doing so. The school system needed the funds ($12 million in 1989–90) to cover the cost of bonuses for career-ladder teachers.

According to teachers in the program, the original Charlotte-Mecklenburg career ladder succeeded in creating incentives for talented teachers. "You get a sense of achievement, and there is recognition," said a veteran history teacher of her promotion to career level one. "It's giving me recognition for twenty years of good teaching," an elementary teacher said of her promotion. "It has prestige," said another of the ladder's top rung.

Teachers also generally supported Charlotte-Mecklenburg's extensive evaluation system as a fair way of rewarding teachers on the basis of performance. To be sure, there was criticism of the evaluation system (teachers complained that evaluators were inconsistent in their scoring, that many evaluation criteria were trivial or not applicable to their students, that the process resulted in rigid teaching), and in poorly designed incentive plans such as Florida's, charges of unfairness and favoritism in evaluations were well founded (a guidance counselor in a rural Florida high school matter of factly mentioned that he awarded teachers bonus points on their master-teacher evaluations "because they needed the money" that they would receive if named master teachers by the state). But much of the criticism in Charlotte-Mecklenburg reflected teachers' apprehension over a new and more demanding evaluation system (early on a story went around that a teacher was marked down during an evaluation for not wearing a tie), and eventually the evaluation system there, with its emphasis on multiple evaluations by a number of different people over an extended period of time, achieved acceptance. "It's as fair as it can be," a veteran elementary teacher told me. "I'm taking it seriously." "It's fair, it's better than anything we've ever had," added the president of the Charlotte Federation of Teachers.[112]

The Charlotte-Mecklenburg career ladder boosted the morale of many teachers who participated in the program. It was, in the words of an English teacher, "a shot of adrenaline." Nor did the performance-based promotion system engender extensive divisiveness among teachers in schools, as many, particularly teacher unions, predicted it would. In many instances, the contrary was true. "It's brought us closer together, we're all rooting for them," said an elementary teacher of her colleagues seeking promotions under the career ladder. Said a high school principal of the career ladder: "We've got problems, but it's the best thing we've ever done. It has opened up lines of communication." The discontent that the career ladder did foster was generally confined to teachers not participating in the program. That has been true of other teacher-incentive programs as well. A 1987–88 survey of Missouri teachers, for example, revealed that morale and job satisfaction were significantly higher among veteran teachers involved in career ladders than among non-career-ladder teachers.[113]

The Charlotte-Mecklenburg program also created a more purposeful atmosphere within the school system. Teachers saw the career ladder as a signal that the school system was serious about their work, and they responded in kind. There was an unmistakable enthusiasm in the voices of many career-ladder teachers as they described the professional-development projects that they were pursuing under the career ladder (in one instance, a veteran mathematics teacher was investigating why students were dropping out of the school system's "gifted and talented" math classes; in another, a second-grade teacher was designing "extension" activities in math so parents could help students at home). Under the career ladder, teaching qua teaching became a priority within Charlotte-Mecklenburg schools. "It's made me self-conscious in a positive way," an elementary teacher told me. "Teachers are working very hard at being better teachers," a high school principal commented. Both teachers and administrators reported increased discussion of teaching issues among school faculties. In addition, teacher absenteeism declined.

There also has been an increase in attention to pedagogical issues in other school systems that have established career ladders. In a 1987 survey 72 percent of the teachers participating in Arizona's career-ladder pilot projects said the career ladders were engendering better instruction in their school systems. Teachers interviewed in an in-depth 1988 study of one of Arizona's pilot programs reported unanimously that their teaching had improved as a result of the career-ladder evaluation process. Similarly, nearly two-thirds of the teachers who participated in North Carolina's pilot career-ladder programs reported in 1988 that the increased "observation and evaluation" they received made them better teachers.[114]

The career ladder in Charlotte-Mecklenburg also succeeded in improving the quality of the school system's teacher applicants. "It tended to attract the right people," Joseph Flora, the school system's assistant superintendent for personnel, told me.

Career ladders frequently have been the source of another important element of the increasing professionalism in teaching: an improved "induction" system. Extensive supervision of new teachers such as that required under Charlotte-Mecklenburg's career ladder has become increasingly widespread. Virtually nonexistent in the past, laws establishing new-teacher supervisory programs have been enacted in over half the states since the beginning of the excellence movement. As in Charlotte-Mecklenburg, many of the laws have created three-person advisory teams (also known as "support teams" or "assistance committees") to work with teachers during their first year in the classroom. The teams typically include a principal, a curriculum specialist, and a veteran teacher, as in Charlotte-Mecklenburg, or, as in the statewide program established by the Texas legislature in 1987, an administrator, a peer teacher, and a college faculty member. Other states, following the lead of the widely publicized Toledo plan, have assigned new teachers individual mentors during their first year. In Tennessee teachers on the top rung of the state's career ladder serve as mentors. In addition to signaling to beginning teachers that their work is important, the new induction programs have reduced the sense of isolation that in the past has dispirited and driven from the classroom many beginning teachers left to "sink or swim" on their own. They have also strengthened the teaching skills of many new teachers.

In a small but growing number of school systems, new teachers serve "internships" in special schools of the sort recommended by the Holmes Group and other reformers, schools that have been designed to serve much the same role as teaching hospitals do in the training of doctors. Also known as "clinical schools" or "professional-development schools," they have regular students but are jointly operated by school systems and universities, and are staffed by master teachers. New teachers work in the schools before being reassigned to other locations within their school systems. In a variation of this concept, the Louisville, Kentucky, school system has been developing clinical programs in approximately a quarter of its schools, and all new teachers are expected to participate in them beginning within several years. In addition, since 1988–89 a portion of the education majors at the University of Louisville have done their student teaching at seven of the city's training sites.[115]

The spread of career ladders and other performance-based incentive programs has also led to the bolstering of teacher evaluation, a key step in raising standards in teaching. Nearly 70 percent of the school systems in Utah have revamped their evaluation methods in wake of the state's career-ladder program, and over half of them have begun to factor student achievement in their evaluations, a rare practice in the past. Texas, Tennessee, Connecticut, and Kentucky all have introduced new *statewide* teacher-evaluation systems. And since the inception of its career ladder in 1984–85, Tennessee has spent $5 million annually on training, salaries, and expenses to evaluate applicants for the top rungs of its career ladder.[116]

Traditionally, teacher evaluation in the nation's public school systems has been superficial and arbitrary. As one expert on the teaching profession said in the early 1980s, "The standard drill is a short classroom visit or two a year by an inadequately trained principal who is looking for neat desks and clean blackboards."[117] Passing ratings on teacher evaluations were virtually automatic. A 1983 survey of 20,000 teachers in Philadelphia, Montgomery County, Maryland, and Baltimore revealed that a mere .3 percent received less than a satisfactory rating during the previous year. The new evaluations are different. If the high promotion rates on a number of career ladders suggest that the new evaluations are not as demanding as they might be, they are nonetheless much more thoroughgoing and objective and more rigorous than traditional methods. "More frequent and effective teacher evaluations is the single greatest effect of the career ladder system," the Far West Laboratory concluded in its 1988 study of

Utah's career ladders.[118] Many of the new evaluation programs call for much greater written documentation of teachers' performance. "It has gotten the paper-shufflers out of their offices," said Charlotte-Mecklenburg's career-ladder director of the school system's new evaluation system. Further, the widespread use of evaluation teams has reduced dramatically the level of favoritism and arbitrariness that plagued past systems.

As a result of the more rigorous evaluations, more of the weakest teachers are being weeded out of the occupation. Under the new evaluation system in Fairfax County, Virginia, teachers who are rated "ineffective," the lowest of five possible rankings (based on evaluations by their principal, a peer, and a curriculum specialist), are dismissed, and those who are rated "marginal," the next-lowest ranking, are placed on probation for a year. And though a disproportionate number of teachers have received the highest ratings under the system, 124 teachers were fired for incompetence and 150 others were counseled out of teaching in 1987–88, the program's first year of full operation. In contrast, Fairfax, the nation's tenth-largest school system, dismissed fewer than half a dozen teachers for incompetence in the three years prior to 1986–87. Similarly, since introduction of the mentor-teacher program in Rochester, where mentors recommend whether first-year teachers should be reemployed, 10 percent of all new teachers have not been rehired, a far higher percentage than in the past.

In addition, peer review, a technique used frequently in other professions but rarely in school teaching, is a feature of many of the new evaluation programs. A study by the University of Utah found that peer review was incorporated in one-third of that state's career ladders, representing what the study described as "a substantial beginning in using peer perspective in judging teacher quality."[119] Peer review is also a key element of the career ladder in Tennessee, where veteran candidates are evaluated under the auspices of the state by master teachers from other school systems. In some instances, teachers serving as mentors also participate in hiring and firing decisions, as they do in Toledo and Rochester. Peer review gives veteran teachers a larger role in both the policing of their occupation and management of their schools. Moreover, peer evaluation within career ladders has fostered greater collegiality among veteran teachers. It has brought teachers from different disciplines together and encouraged a sharing of ideas among them. A veteran art teacher I spoke with in Charlotte-Mecklenburg described discussions of teaching over lunch and collaborating on journal articles with the math teacher and debate instructor who were his mentors under the school system's career ladder. "I wasn't personal friends with them, I hadn't talked to the debate teacher in fifteen years," he said in explaining his reasons for selecting the two as his mentors, "but I respected their teaching, and I've learned a tremendous amount from them."

Meanwhile, nearly two dozen states have followed New Jersey's lead in establishing alternative-certification programs for liberal arts graduates, though a 1990 survey by the National Center for Education Information revealed that the majority offer their programs only to secondary teachers or in subjects in which school systems lack regularly certified teachers. Such restrictions have limited the number of new teachers hired under the programs. Arizona, for instance, issued only three alternative teaching licenses in 1989.[120] But a 1986 study of alternative-certification programs conducted for the U.S. Department of Education concluded that, as a whole, they "attract well-educated individuals with a sincere interest in teaching." As in the evaluation of New Jersey's program, supervisors of alternative-certification candidates "universally judged them above average in subject-matter preparation," the study observed, adding that they "are also rated highly in instructional skills in comparison with traditionally prepared beginning teachers."[121]

The excellence movement also has spawned several other initiatives to recruit teachers from the campuses of the nation's best colleges and universities. In 1984 Kenyon College, a traditional liberal arts school in Ohio, sought to encourage its graduates to enter public school teaching by creating a five-year program, known as 5-STEP, that combines a bachelor's degree in an academic subject with a master's in education. Students in the program spend four years at Kenyon, where they student-teach in local public schools and complete a teaching-related project during their senior year. In the summer between their junior and senior years, and during the fifth year of the program, they attend one of three graduate education schools affiliated with 5-STEP: Teachers College and the Bank Street School of Education in New York City, and Tufts University outside Boston. The program enrolls fifteen to twenty students per year.

Harvard University returned to training undergraduate teachers after a long hiatus in 1985–86, when it created a twenty-student program that includes education seminars and supervised teaching. In addition, Dartmouth, Yale, Princeton, Swarthmore, and a few other prestigious liberal arts schools are training public school teachers in small-scale programs in which students major in an academic subject and also complete their pedagogical course requirements in academic departments. Prospective teachers at Princeton, for example, take such courses as "developmental psychology" and "cognitive psychology" through the university's Psychology Department, "history of American education in the nineteenth century" in its History Department, and "social and cultural aspects of education" in its Sociology Department. Ironically, although Princeton trains about twenty public school teachers a year in this way, three times as many of its graduates are employed by private schools annually.

To recruit the best and brightest at 100 of the nation's top colleges, an ambitious twenty-two-year-old Princeton graduate, Wendy Kopp, in 1989 created a Peace Corps-like program called Teach for America. Backed by

over $1 million in foundation and corporate funding, Kopp and her staff
of fellow recent college graduates have organized affiliates in the Ivy
League, leading liberal arts colleges, and top public universities to recruit
noneducation majors for two-year stints as teachers in urban and rural
schools. With 2,500 applicants and just 515 openings in its first year,
1990–91, the program is both highly popular and highly competitive.

Other developments are also creating a more professional climate in
teaching. One is the establishment of the National Board for Professional
Teaching Standards. Since its inception in 1987, the independent, nonprofit board has been developing rigorous teaching standards in a range
of subjects, and beginning in 1993 it will offer a system of voluntary
national certification to teachers who meet the standards. In so doing, it
has the potential to increase greatly the status of public school teaching.
As a major part of its work, the board is also developing a more sophisticated system of evaluating teachers that is expected to include a general
test of knowledge of the liberal arts, presentation of a portfolio of various
examples of the teacher's work, completion of a series of exercises in an
"assessment center" (such as teaching sample lessons), and a residency in
a regular school. Founded with a $5 million grant from the Carnegie
Corporation of New York, the board is expected to spend $50 million in
its first five years, primarily on research and development on its standards and assessments.[122]
An increasing number of school systems have joined Rochester and
Dade County in granting teachers a greater say in the running of schools
through shared decision making and school-based management. In Hammond, Indiana, decisions on such matters as instructional strategies, staffing, scheduling, and disciplinary procedures—in the past made solely by
principals in the city's twenty-five schools—are now decided by committees of teachers, administrators, and community representatives that
have been established in each school. A "core team" of the principal, one
or two teachers, and a parent establish the agenda of the fifteen-to-
twenty-member committees. An agreement with the Hammond Federation of Teachers permits schools to circumvent provisions in the city's
collective bargaining contract in order to implement the committees'
improvement plans. Under Pittsburgh's 1988 teacher contract, the city's
schools are to be managed by a "cabinet" of teachers and administrators
rather than by principals alone. The contract also established a cadre of
senior "instructional teacher leaders" who, in addition to teaching part
time, are responsible for observing and assisting their colleagues, developing curriculum, and making instructional decisions. Similarly, 1988
legislation in Illinois stripped Chicago's principals of lifetime tenure and
created "councils" of parents, teachers, and administrators to govern
each of the city's schools. Boston School officials approved the creation of
school councils in 1989. And in 1990 the Kentucky legislature required

that *all* Kentucky school systems develop such councils in at least one school by July 1991.

In some instances experiments in the restructuring of school management are under way in school systems where NEA affiliates are the local collective bargaining agents—even though teachers are involved in the hiring and firing of their peers and other activities that violate the union's traditional policies. In 1988–89, the school systems of Montgomery County, Maryland, Easton, Pennsylvania, Columbus, Ohio, East Baton Rouge, Louisiana, and San Diego, California, launched pilot programs in shared decision making and school-based management that grant teachers a major role in school decision making through participation on a variety of newly established councils and "cabinets" similar to those in Hammond and Pittsburgh. The NEA affiliates are participating in the experiments independently of TABS and the NEA's other pilot programs.

There are also state-sponsored restructuring experiments in progress. The Washington legislature, for example, in 1987 established the Schools for the 21st Century Project, designed to encourage locally initiated school improvements as an alternative to state mandates, as well as to involve teachers more fully in school decision making. Two dozen schools are receiving state funding and waivers from state regulations to implement reforms of their own design. North Carolina initiated the Lead Teachers/Restructuring Project in 1988–89 in six schools in three counties. It is designed to change the decision-making structure in local schools and create new roles for teachers. Similar projects are underway in Arkansas, Maine, California, and Massachusetts. In addition, a leading national education association—the Association for Supervision and Curriculum Development—is sponsoring a consortium of eighteen public schools that are restructuring their organization and governance.

There is also evidence that career ladders are increasing teachers' authority in schools. In its 1988 evaluation of the Utah career-ladder program, the Far West Laboratory concluded that the program is transforming school management by sharply increasing teachers' role in curriculum development, teacher evaluation, and in decision making about school and school-system goals. Further, the management experiments seem to be paying substantial dividends. Teachers praise them, and they appear to be making teaching more attractive. Since the inception of its pilot program in 1986–87, Dade County has received nine applications for every teacher vacancy it posts, versus an average of two applications per opening in earlier years.[123]

As part of their school-based management experiments, a number of school systems have reduced and in some instances even eliminated the use of seniority in teacher assignments, granting schools the opportunity to select their teachers themselves. Under the city's 1988 collective bargaining contract, for example, San Diego principals are now permitted to fill teacher vacancies by selecting from among the five most-senior applicants for a position. In the past, they were forced to take the applicant with the greatest seniority, regardless of other qualifications. Cincinnati's 1988 contract went further, permitting principals to hire the best available applicants without regard to seniority. The same authority has been extended to school-management teams in Rochester, Boston, and Chicago. Similarly, under an arrangement negotiated with the local teachers union, all teachers in the Buffalo, New York, school system are notified of an opening in one of the city's many "magnet" schools, and all may apply for the job. Applications are screened by the school principal or a committee of teachers and parents, who express their preferences to the superintendent's office, where assignments are made without regard to seniority.

There also have been attempts to create more meaningful opportunities for veteran teachers to expand their knowledge of their subjects and sharpen their pedagogy skills. Traditionally, what is known as "staff development" in teaching has been a disorganized patchwork of often irrelevant workshops, lectures, and colleges courses forced on teachers by school systems and state regulations. Such requirements, together with largely unpoliced school-system policies that permit teachers to earn higher salaries by accumulating college credits beyond their bachelor's degrees, have spawned a billion-dollar-a-year industry for education schools, a myriad of consulting firms, and others, who vie to give teachers the most credits for the least amount of work. In one extreme case, forty-three Los Angeles teachers were indicted several years ago on charges of misdemeanor grand theft for receiving up to $3,000 in salary increases over three years for college credits from extension courses they never attended.[124] Many teachers disdain the superficiality of the staff-development system but say the opportunities for salary increases make it impossible to shun. Indeed, the economic incentive of staff development is the primary reason that over half the nation's teachers have master's degrees; unfortunately, it's also the reason that many of the degrees aren't worth the paper they're printed on.

The Pittsburgh school system has taken a very different approach. In 1983–84, it transformed a stately turn-of-the-century granite high school building into a permanent teacher-training center. Plagued by violence, poor attendance, and low morale, 950-student Schenley High School, poised precariously between Pittsburgh's impoverished Hill District and the campus of the University of Pittsburgh, was closed at the end of the 1982–83 school year and reopened the following fall with a new mission: during the next four years, all of the city's 800 secondary teachers spent six weeks on staggered sabbaticals as "visiting teachers" at the school, where they participated in a wide range of activities designed to improve their teaching.

A member of Schenley's "resident" staff of eighty veteran teachers handpicked by the school system (80 percent of Schenley's 1982–83 staff was transferred after the school was closed) was paired with two visiting teachers as their mentor. The two visiting teachers observed classes taught by their mentor (Schenley continued to function as a regular high school, with regular students) and by each other. The three members of each team taught the same subject, so the visiting teachers simply delivered lessons to their mentor's students during the dozen classes they taught as part of their training at Schenley. The teams discussed their teaching techniques in regular conferences (the teaching responsibilities of the thirty or so resident teachers working as mentors each year were decreased, allowing them more time for their mentoring duties) and visiting teachers also participated in regularly scheduled "clinics," where they discussed their colleagues' teaching in larger groups. They also attended a range of seminars: on pedagogy; on subjects within their teaching fields (taught by faculty members from local universities); and on adolescent development (teenage suicide, drug use, and the like). In addition, teachers on sabbatical received two full weeks of instruction in teaching strategies before attending Schenley.

Teachers praised Pittsburgh's sabbatical program. They were gratified—if slightly incredulous—that the Pittsburgh school system had made such a significant commitment to their professional well-being. Not only was the program (described by one history teacher as "meaningful relaxation") a tremendous boost to the morale and self-esteem of the city's high school teachers, they said, it also gave them an opportunity to reflect seriously on their work. "It's a chance to discuss why we do what we do," commented an English teacher on Schenley's resident staff. Teachers also praised the professional collegiality that they said Schenley offered; the program, one participant pronounced enthusiastically, amounted to "legalized thievery."

In 1987–88, after all of the city's veteran high school teachers had been through the program once—at a cost of $7 million—the Schenley High School Teacher Center shifted its focus to new teachers, who now spend four weeks in the program early in their teaching careers. Pittsburgh opened a similar teacher center for veteran elementary teachers in 1985–86 and a center for veteran junior high school teachers in 1988–89.[125]

Another innovative experiment in staff development is the Yale-New Haven Teacher Institute, cosponsored by the New Haven, Connecticut, school system and Yale University. Designed to offer New Haven teachers the benefits of Yale's academic resources and create new curriculum materials for New Haven's schools, the institute brings together Yale faculty members and New Haven secondary teachers in a rigorous five-month program.

New Haven teachers play a major role in designing the seminars, unlike in traditional graduate courses. Each fall one teacher, called a representative, in each of New Haven's middle schools and high schools canvasses his or her colleagues in the humanities and sciences to identify topics that they would like to study under the guidance of a Yale faculty member the following summer. The representatives jointly sort the requests into as many as eight topics; then the institute approaches Yale faculty members to lead the seminars. The institute begins in March with a series of general talks and workshops conducted by the Yale faculty. Between mid-May and the end of July the New Haven teachers, known as fellows, and the Yale faculty members meet weekly in seminars—groups of ten to twelve teachers and one scholar—and individually; seminar topics have ranged from geology to twentieth-century American history. Teachers are required to complete individual curriculum projects by the end of July, and their material is then distributed by the institute throughout the New Haven school system.

Not only has the institute strengthened New Haven teachers' grasp of their subjects and improved the school system's curriculum (surveys have shown that the hundreds of curriculum "units" developed by teachers in the institute are in wide use in New Haven's schools), it has also treated the city's teachers as serious scholars—an opportunity they say they value greatly—and has granted them a measure of prestige in the process. Teachers in the institute are paid a $1,000 stipend, and they receive a number of perks, including a Yale identification card that permits them use of all the university's facilities.

By creating opportunities for their intellectual growth, the Yale-New Haven institute has boosted morale among New Haven's teachers and kept many of the city's best teachers in the classroom. It's not uncommon to hear teachers say of the institute, as a twelve-year history teacher did several years ago, "It is the main reason I've stayed in teaching and stayed in New Haven."[126] In all, a third of New Haven's eligible teachers have taken part in the program since its inception in the late 1970s, and three-fourths of the participants are still working in the New Haven school system, two-thirds of them as teachers.

Other programs also have enlisted arts and sciences professors to bolster staff development in academic subjects, an area that school systems traditionally have neglected. One is the Center for the Liberal Arts at the University of Virginia. Since its inception in 1984–85, the center has made faculty members from the University of Virginia available to school systems throughout the state to conduct programs in academic disciplines, ranging from one-day seminars to lecture series and summer courses for credit, depending on the school systems' needs. Originally focused on American literature, the center now sponsors projects in eleven subjects, ranging from physics to art, German, and the classics. It also has organized teacher summer study abroad and produced televised courses in chemistry and physics that are transmitted across the state. By 1990 over 5,000 Virginia teachers and 268 faculty members (including

100 from other colleges and universities in Virginia) had participated in the center's programs.

Similarly, the federal National Endowment for the Humanities (NEH) has sponsored summer seminars in the humanities for high school teachers since 1983. Teachers who are selected through a competitive application process attend seminars of four, five, or six weeks taught by "distinguished university scholars." Participants in the program receive stipends of $2,000 to $2,750 from NEH to cover travel costs (the institutes typically are held on the scholar's campus), living expenses, and books. The program has expanded from fifteen seminars a summer in 1983 to roughly sixty today. Recent offerings have included "William Faulkner's Major Fiction," "Alexis de Tocqueville's *Democracy in America:* Religion in a Democratic Society," and "Beethoven's Ninth Symphony." In all, over 5,000 public school teachers have taken part in the program, which is able to accommodate only a third of the applicants it receives annually.

Duquesne University in Pittsburgh has enlisted local industries to bolster science teachers' grasp of their subjects. Since 1983 the university has placed Pittsburgh science teachers in summer jobs in the city's many high-tech companies, where they participate in a wide range of scientific research. In recent years teachers in the Summer Jobs in Industry program, who receive college credit through Duquesne for their work, have done research on such topics as waste water in coal mining (at the research division of Conoco), robotics (at Carnegie-Mellon University's Robotics Institute), and glass (at PPG Industries).

Finally, there have been scores of individual initiatives throughout the nation since the onset of the reform movement designed to recognize teachers and teaching: President Reagan's announcement in 1984 that a public school teacher would be the first private citizen in space attracted nearly 11,000 applications; with a $100,000 gift from a wealthy alumnus, Broughton High School in Raleigh, North Carolina, in 1986 established two endowed chairs in teaching, in math and science; and the Talented Teacher Act of 1983 authorized Congress to fund yearlong sabbaticals for two teachers from each congressional district and overseas territory. In 1986 Harvard established a fellowship program that permits Boston and Cambridge public school teachers to spend a year at the university on sabbatical; the King Television Company of Seattle and a local Pepsi bottler established the To Teacher program in 1984, which annually awards $1,000 honoraria to five local teachers nominated by students and selected by their peers; and since 1983 the Council for Basic Education has sponsored the Fellowships for Independent Study in the Humanities program (FISH) that has made grants of $3,000 to over 900 veteran public school humanities teachers to pursue six weeks of independent summer study in their disciplines. FISH—which annually has ten times more applicants than its funding can support—has spawned similar local programs in Philadelphia and in four suburban Washington,

D.C., school systems. New York, Houston, and Portland, Oregon, have created competitive "minigrant" programs that supply teachers with funds to develop teaching materials; Connecticut, Arkansas, and South Carolina have established statewide programs. Indiana created the Endowment for Educational Excellence in 1985 that annually permits 600 of the state's teachers to study free at Indiana universities under summer and yearlong fellowships. And in New Canaan, Connecticut, even the local country club has sought to support the town's teachers—by permitting them to take out special limited memberships for a nominal fee.

There are signs that the reformers' progress in professionalizing teaching is making the occupation more attractive. In 1982 only one in twenty first-year college students across the nation told researchers at the University of California at Los Angeles that they were interested in becoming teachers, but by 1988 one in eleven expressed interest in the field. A 1988 survey of state teacher-licensing officials by the private National Center for Education Information revealed increases in the number of applications for teaching certificates in twenty-two states between 1983 and 1987. The number of applications remained constant during the same period in twenty-one states. And in only six states did the number of applications decline. California education officials in 1988 reported that enrollment in the state's education schools increased by 33 percent between 1982–83 and 1986–87.[127]

The 2,500 applications received by Teach for America in its first year represents a level of interest in teaching unimaginable on top college campuses a decade ago. Another nonprofit organization, Recruiting New Teachers, received nearly 300,000 inquiries within twenty-four months of launching public-service advertisements promoting teaching in 1988. Also, new initiatives ranging from alternative certification to loan-forgiveness plans and midcareer retraining programs have improved the supply of mathematics and science teachers. According to a 1988 survey by the Rand Corporation, there were over sixty specialized math and science projects under way nationally in 1986–87, enrolling 2,443 prospective teachers. That's slightly more than 10 percent of the new math and science teachers that Rand researchers say public education needs annually during the next decade.[128]

Though the demand for math and science teachers still outstrips the supply, in several states there are more teachers in those disciplines coming through the traditional teacher-preparation pipeline as well. The number of potential math teachers graduated from Florida colleges and universities rose 155 percent between 1981–82 and 1985–86, and the number of science teachers rose 109 percent. In California the number of graduates recommended by colleges and universities for certification in math jumped 191 percent between 1982–83 and 1986–87, while the number recommended in physical science (which includes chemistry and physics) increased 166 percent, and the number recommended in life science (which includes biology) increased 233 percent.

Reliable national figures are unavailable, but many education schools individually report turning down a greater percentage of their applicants in recent years, a trend that suggests that the academic ability of teacher trainees perhaps is improving. Indeed, test scores of prospective teachers are rising. According to the College Board, the average SAT score of high school students who graduated in 1988 and indicated that they intended to major in education was 849, compared with 813 in 1982.

Moreover, the profound discontent among teachers in the early 1980s may be easing. Of 2,000 teachers polled by Louis Harris and Associates for the Metropolitan Life Insurance Company in 1989, 48 percent said they were earning a satisfactory living, 53 percent said they were respected by society, and 67 percent said they would advise a young person to go into teaching. In a similar poll five years earlier, 37 percent said they were earning a decent living, 47 percent said teachers were respected, and only 45 percent endorsed teaching as a career.

Yet despite the avalanche of new initiatives in teaching, many of them reforms rarely discussed in public education even a decade ago, the union-backed impediments to teaching reform—seniority, the single salary schedule, traditional state licensing laws, rigid distinctions between "labor" and "management" in schools—remain in place in the vast majority of the nation's school systems. In much of public school teaching, it's business as usual.

The movement to professionalize teaching must spread far further if public education is to attract the tremendous numbers of talented teachers needed to fulfill its new academic mission. But it's clear that public school teaching cannot achieve white-collar status as long as traditional union policies remain pervasive within it. There is an inherent conflict between traditional industrial-style teacher unionism—with its predisposition to confrontation, its commitment to limiting the responsibilities of teachers in schools, and its opposition to meaningful standards—and the high standards and accountability inherent in the professionalism that the reformers seek for teaching. Shanker and the AFT have acknowledged this reality and have sought to redefine teacher unionism and the role of teacher unions to accommodate it. The NEA has not, and it is the NEA, with its vast membership and resources, that has the greatest ability to shape the future of public school teaching.

CHAPTER 6

The Coins of the Realm: The Paradox of Standardized Testing

When U.S. Secretary of Education William J. Bennett proclaimed in a 1987 back-to-school speech that "accountability is the linchpin, the keystone, the *sine qua non* of the reform movement," he was exaggerating only slightly. Corporate leaders have demanded new accountability measures in exchange for their support of tax hikes and budget increases for education. "Run Education Like a Business," read buttons on the lapels of corporate lobbyists during the 1983 legislative debates in Florida over a sales-tax hike for school reforms.

State lawmakers also have sought greater accountability in public education, primarily for political reasons. By supporting sweeping educational reforms and the bigger budgets needed to pay for them, lawmakers have put themselves in the position of having to be able to demonstrate to constituents that reforms are paying dividends, especially in the face of the public's deep frustration with the performance of the nation's schools. "We got one very, very strong message," said Governor Thomas H. Kean of New Jersey of polls he commissioned in his state in late 1983, as the excellence movement gathered momentum. "If policymakers ask for more money for education, they better accompany them with proposals for *measurable* change." Likewise, the National Governors' Association warned its members in a 1987 report that "it is imperative to demonstrate the payoffs of [the] increased attention and expenditure [for education]."

More recently, and especially since the 1989 educational summit between President Bush and the nation's governors in Charlottesville, Virginia, many policymakers have urged that state and federal regulations on local educators be eased in exchange for greater accountability of their performance. Above all, the leaders of the reform movement have argued that schools must be scrutinized much more closely and educators made more directly answerable for the consequences if the nation's public education system is to achieve higher standards. Schools, they've argued, must no longer be measured mainly on the basis of their resources, as many educators have urged, but on the basis of the results they achieve.[1]

But to date, the primary result of the clamor for greater accountability in public education has been a tremendous increase in standardized testing in the schools. Political pressures for ways of measuring school progress that are quickly implemented and easily comprehended, in particular, have led to a myriad of new state and local testing mandates since publication of *A Nation at Risk*. In 1983 and 1984 alone, new testing laws were passed in thirty states. A national commission on testing sponsored by the Ford Foundation estimated in a 1990 report that nearly 130,000,000 standardized achievement tests are now administered to elementary and secondary students annually, probably double the number administered since the outset of the excellence movement in the early 1980s. The commission estimated the cost of purchasing, administering, and scoring such tests to be over $500 million a year. The tests have become so pervasive, and the reform movement has invested so much importance in them, that increasingly it is in terms of standardized test scores alone that the nation judges its schools and educators judge themselves. In the words of a Pennsylvania high school English teacher, standardized multiple-choice tests have become "the coins of the realm" in public education. But the new tests are failing the excellence movement in two crucial ways. They are falling far short as reliable measures of public education's performance. And they are undercutting the reform movement's academic aims.[2]

Standardized tests are being used in a wide variety of new accountability measures. They are a prominent part of school "performance reports" that have been introduced in California, South Carolina, New York, New Jersey, and a host of other states since the beginning of the excellence movement. Indeed, the Arkansas legislature went so far as to pass a School Report Cards Act in 1989. To pressure states into enacting school reforms, U.S. Secretary of Education Terrel H. Bell in 1984 launched what has become an annual federal ranking of the states' educational performance, primarily on the basis of standardized college admissions test results. Bell's "wall-chart" rankings, continued by his successors, receive wide publicity—and help rivet attention on standardized test scores.

Teachers or their schools in such states as South Carolina, Indiana, and Kentucky are able to win state-funded bonuses by boosting their students' standardized test scores. Under the South Carolina School Incentive Reward Program, launched by legislative mandate in 1984, the top 25 percent of schools in each of five socioeconomic categories receive cash awards (averaging $10,000 to $15,000 in 1989–90, but ranging as high as $70,000) by improving their students' previous year's standardized test scores. Schools are able to receive slightly higher awards by achieving student and teacher attendance goals. In addition, lawmakers in twenty states have passed legislation adding standardized tests to their graduation requirement. Oklahoma is a recent example; in 1989 lawmakers there made the passing of a competency test a diploma requirement beginning with the class of 1993. Skeptical of the standards in local schools, states and school systems are increasingly requiring that students be promoted from grade to grade at least in part on the basis of standardized test scores. South Carolina, for instance, stipulates that scores on its standardized achievement tests be given a 25 percent weighting in promotion decisions at five grade levels.

And increasingly, states and school systems are factoring students' standardized test scores into their decisions to hire, fire, and promote teachers. In a sharp break with tradition in public education, the St. Louis school system in 1985–86 added "student performance"—defined by scores on a series of commercial standardized examinations—as a category on its teacher evaluations. Teachers receiving an unsatisfactory rating in the category have their salaries frozen and face dismissal if there is no improvement in the scores within 100 days.

Yet there is an immense paradox in the recent surge in standardized testing. Despite the key role standardized tests are playing in the reformers' accountability campaign, the bulk of the new tests are severely flawed as measures of the excellence movement's progress. One major reason is that the tests do not measure the sorts of advanced skills and knowledge that the reformers have argued all students should master. Despite the reformers' demands for higher academic standards, the majority of the new standardized tests mainly measure rudimentary reading, language, and math competencies—basic literacy skills. It is largely impossible to gauge from the results of such tests whether students are mastering the intellectual skills that have been the focus of the reform movement: the abilities to judge, analyze, infer, interpret, reason, and the like. Nor do the majority of the tests gauge students' more advanced knowledge of literature, history, science, and other disciplines. Indeed, the recent surge in standardized testing amounts to little more than an extension of the minimum-basic-skills testing movement of the 1970s. The new achievement tests tend to be slightly more difficult than the minimum-competency tests of that era, and in some instances they include sections on subjects such as science or social studies. But overall, the differences are minimal. Today's tests, like their predecessors, are primarily multiple-choice measures of lower-level abilities.[3]

Consider Tennessee's Basic Skills First Achievement Tests, established by the state's legislature as part of the Comprehensive Reform Act of 1984. There are two types of standardized examinations in wide use in the nation's schools: criterion-referenced tests, designed to measure how well students have learned specific skills or subject matter, and norm-referenced tests, which typically measure not what students know in absolute terms but how much more or less they know than other students. The use of both types of tests has skyrocketed since the emergence of the reform movement. Tennessee's tests were criterion-referenced measures of reading and math skills in grades three, six, and eight. The eighth-grade reading test illustrates the tests' simplicity: students did no more than recognize simple vocabulary words, identify words in a story, and understand a sequence of events in a passage. It also required students to "draw conclusions." But the level of inference needed to answer such questions was usually so low as to be meaningless. "Which of the following is based on reasonable evidence from the passage?" asked a typical question. The question was preceded by a poem about the death of "Uncle Joe" that includes the line "And boarding up the store was done." The correct multiple-choice answer to the question was "The grocery store was closed soon after Uncle Joe's death." In 1989–90, Tennessee expanded its testing program to include criterion-referenced tests *and* norm-referenced examinations in grades two through eight. "It's still basic skills," says Angelia Golden, Tennessee's testing director.[4]

The caliber of new tests in other states is much the same. An Arkansas testing official described the level of difficulty of new achievement tests mandated by the state legislature in the Competency-Based Education Act of 1983 by saying that the tests are "not very easy for the very slow learner." "My science department feels that the stuff on the standardized test we use in that subject should be taught in home economics," the principal of a Virginia high school said of that state's tests. Pennsylvania, Georgia, Massachusetts, Colorado, Mississippi, Louisiana, Illinois, and Maine are among the other states that have introduced criterion-referenced assessments of low-level skills since the outset of the excellence movement.

Still other states have expanded their existing minimum-competency testing programs. The Texas legislature in 1984 added grades one, seven, and eleven to the Texas Educational Assessment of Minimum Skills, which since 1980 had tested students in grades three, five, and nine in rudimentary math and reading skills, and in the mechanics of writing.

Many of the new standardized tests flooding into the public schools make explicit claims to measure students' grasp of the sorts of advanced thinking skills that the school reformers have argued all graduates must possess. But they don't do a very good job of it. The latest edition of the California Achievement Tests (CAT), published in 1986, is a good example.

The CAT tests are widely used norm-referenced examinations. There are scores of norm-referenced instruments, but the elementary and secondary school market is dominated by five tests manufactured by three commercial publishing companies: the CAT tests and the Comprehensive Tests of Basic Skills, both published by CTB Macmillan/McGraw-Hill, a subsidiary of the McGraw-Hill Book Company; the Metropolitan Achievement Tests and the Stanford Achievement Tests, published by the Psychological Corporation, a subsidiary of Harcourt Brace Jovanovich; and the Iowa Tests of Basic Skills and their high school equivalent, the Tests of Achievement and Proficiency, both of which are published by Riverside Publishing Company, a subsidiary of Houghton Mifflin Company. First published in 1923, the Stanford tests are the oldest.

In its promotional materials, CTB Macmillan/McGraw-Hill calls the latest CAT "*the* test for the new era of excellence in American education." It asserts that in the test "inferential and critical comprehension are given increased emphasis" and that in the math section there is "increased emphasis on problem solving." The test's handbook includes a long list of serious-sounding "objectives" that are supposedly measured by the tests, among them, interpreting "figurative or persuasive language or structural techniques of writing"; drawing conclusions; identifying cause-and-effect relationships; predicting outcomes; interpreting "the main idea, the author's purpose or viewpoint or the tone or mood" of a reading passage; and interpreting and differentiating "between various forms of writing." One would think from such descriptions that the new edition of the CAT is a graduate school admissions examination. In reality, it's nothing of the sort.

At all grade levels the latest edition of the CAT consists of fifty-five multiple-choice questions on vocabulary, fifty-five on reading comprehension, thirty-five on spelling, thirty-five on capitalization and punctuation, fifty-five on usage and sentence structure, fifty on arithmetic, fifty-five on math concepts and applications, and forty on "study skills." Optional forty-question science and social studies tests are also available. Vocabulary, spelling, punctuation, usage, arithmetic, and study-skills questions don't test a student's advanced thinking skills, but such questions make up over two-thirds of the basic examination.[5]

Reading-comprehension questions, most agree, can measure advanced skills. So can math-application questions. But CTB Macmillan/McGraw-Hill's rhetoric notwithstanding, very few such questions on the CAT tests are designed to gauge higher-level abilities. On the version administered to eighth-, ninth-, tenth-, and eleventh-graders, for example, the majority of the reading-comprehension items require only that students recall facts in a passage, identify simple descriptions of characters in passages (so-and-so is cruel, fun-loving, and so on), and recognize the (usually obvious) main idea of a passage. One question on the test, for example, follows a passage describing a California lighthouse keeper in the 1890s. "Many ships traveled up and down the foggy central California coast during the 1890's. Little did the captains and sailors of these vessels know that they owed their well-being, and in many cases their lives, to a slender, fashionably dressed woman who collected rare books and raised French poodles," it reads in part. The question that followed asked, "Who became dependent on Emily Fish for their well-being? A) military officers B) captains and sailors C) writers and painters D) her husband and her servant."[6]

When the test does attempt to measure more sophisticated skills, it tends to do so with simple-minded questions. One reading question on the grades-eight-to-eleven version of the test purports to measure a student's ability to make inferences. It follows a passage about a boy who slips into a small-town pool hall to avoid a rain shower. "A voice to his left startled him," the passage reads. " 'Hey, want to play pool?' Gulping uneasily, Walter said, 'Sure.' Mike, his challenger, said, 'Chalk up,' and tossed Walter a cube of blue chalk. Walter had no idea that he was supposed to chalk the end of the stick. His finger seemed to fit the hole in the cube, so he chalked his fingertips. A chorus of snickers arose from the room." The question that follows the passage is, "The people in the pool hall snickered because:" The correct answer: "Walter had used the chalk the wrong way."

Another "inference" question on the same test follows a passage describing the warranty on a "Sleepsafe Overhead Sprinkler System." The question is, "The name of the sprinkler system is designed to make the buyer feel: F) secure, G) drowsy, H) victorious, I) sophisticated."

The level of difficulty of the science and social studies subtests of the CAT also tends to be low. In fact, the tests often aren't even true measures of achievement in those subjects, for in many instances all the information students need to answer questions is provided in a passage or table of some sort that precedes each question. "Fossils are the remains or traces of an organism that lived long ago" is the introduction to a typical question on the CAT science test for eighth-, ninth-, tenth-, and eleventh-graders. "Which of them is the best example of a fossil? A) iron ore, B) petrified wood, C) black lava rock, D) broken tree limb." It's not so much knowledge of science or social studies (much less the ability to apply such knowledge) that the CAT measures, as it is simple reading comprehension.

Many state testing officials are themselves candid in describing the CAT's simplistic content. "It's not too tough at all, we're using it to identify kids who lack basic skills and who need remediation," Steven Ballou, formerly codirector of testing in Indiana, told me. (The 1986 CAT examinations have been administered in Indiana statewide in grades one, two, three, six, eight, nine, and eleven since 1988.) Nor, according to testing experts, are any of the other widely used commercial norm-referenced achievement tests appreciably more difficult than the CAT tests. "The most striking difference between them is that one uses one color of ink and another uses a different color," said Margaret Jorgenson, a testing expert with the Southern Regional Education Board until 1987. As a national commission on reading wrote in 1985, "The nationally normed tests used by school systems may not accommodate the expanding view of literacy this society requires." Oklahoma, Georgia, and Washington are among the other states that have launched new norm-referenced testing programs in recent years.[7]

Moreover, if the standards of many of the new achievement tests are low, so are the scores needed to pass them. In Pennsylvania, students in 1989–90 needed to answer correctly only between 49 percent and 64 percent of the questions on the state's Test of Essential Learning Skills in reading and math, an examination administered since 1984 to all students in grades three, five, and eight. The passing score on Maryland's ninth-grade reading test, required by the state for a high school diploma, is a mere 60 percent, despite the fact that the material on the test is taught in Maryland's schools by the eighth grade.

The reasons that the new standardized tests fail to reinforce the reformers' notions of educational excellence are many, including the limitations of existing large-scale measures of academic achievement. One major reason is that those with a personal stake in the performance of the schools frequently have rejected demanding measures of student performance—even as they endorse calls for greater educational accountability—out of fear of large numbers of students performing poorly on such tests and the embarrassment that that would bring.

The Missouri Mastery and Achievement Tests, for example, were written by the state's department of education, under a 1985 mandate from the Missouri legislature. According to Margaret Jorgenson, who helped Missouri officials write their examinations, they are designed merely "to weed out kids who don't know *anything*" (emphasis in original). The reason for the low level of the tests, she said, is that "Missouri didn't want to have any more kids failing than any one else." A similar motivation resulted in the revamping of a standardized science test in Michigan. According to state testing officials, the Michigan state board of education canceled the examination because of "political pressure" from school systems that were embarrassed when over 60 percent of the state's fourth-, seventh-, and tenth-graders failed the test when it was first administered in 1986. A simpler version of the test was instituted in 1988.[8]

Test makers themselves testify to the pressure to keep standardized tests easy. According to Roger Farr, a coauthor of the Metropolitan Achievement Tests (MAT), word-recognition items (which measure only the lowest level of literacy) were removed from the reading-comprehension section of the MAT when it was revised in 1977. But when the test was revised again, in 1986, those low-level items were reintroduced, Farr said, because in the interim many school systems, eager to keep their scores as high as possible, had dropped the elementary MAT in favor of the California Achievement Tests and other rival examinations that contain the easier word-recognition questions. "They've forced us to not have anything that's too difficult on the tests," said Farr. "For a superintendent, the criteria is often, 'Give me a test that makes me look good.' "[9]

Nonetheless, school administrators have been quick to tout even the slightest rise in scores on such tests as evidence of marked improvements in their schools. Education officials marching before press conferences to proclaim on the basis of a blip in standardized-test scores that "excellence" has been achieved in their schools have become a common sight since the outset of the reform movement. When scores on the Texas Educational Assessment of Minimum Skills increased marginally in 1987, the state's commissioner of education asserted in newspaper interviews that the scores "indicate our reforms are working."[10]

In the current heightened climate of accountability it is increasingly on the basis of improved scores on standardized tests that school administrators and other educators establish reputations as leaders in their profession. The savviest education officials skillfully play the test-score game to their personal public-relations advantage. No one has done so more aggressively in recent years than Herbert Sang, the superintendent of the 105,000-student Duval County, Florida, school system between 1976 and 1989. Sang achieved an extraordinary degree of national fame as a successful urban school administrator during his tenure in Jacksonville. He was the subject of flattering network news coverage, and was praised by commentators ranging from Paul Harvey to National Public Radio. He was a guest on the "Phil Donahue Show." Secretary of Education Bell traveled to Jacksonville in 1984 to proclaim Sang's school system "an education miracle." And the same year the American Association of School Administrators gave Sang its Top Educator Award. Jacksonville appointed him to a seat on its Chamber of Commerce.

Sang did take a number of significant steps to reform the struggling system he took over in 1976. He established a series of districtwide academic competitions, eliminated credit for remedial courses, created a teacher-advisory program for dropouts, won accreditation for many of the city's schools that had not had it, and sparked renewed community interest in public education. But Sang's reputation for building what he likes to call "the model urban school district in the nation" rests primarily on improved standardized-test scores.

The standardized tests that Duval students take measure only the most rudimentary skills and knowledge. In general, the tests are able to do no more than ensure that students are literate; they judge students by standards far below those set by the excellence movement. Elementary school students take a series of locally written Essential Skills Tests and junior high school and high school students take Minimum Level Skills Tests in math, English, science, and social studies. Duval students also take the Florida State Student Assessment Test, a literacy test that is a state graduation requirement. And they take the nationally normed Stanford Achievement Tests. "The county's curriculum and testing program is a basic-skills effort," Duval's director of curriculum told me.

Yet Sang, who is currently superintendent of the Jefferson County, Alabama, schools, orchestrated a school-system-wide campaign to boost scores on these tests. Among other things, he ordered all instructional materials cross-referenced to the tests so that teachers know exactly what skills the tests measure and what page in the textbooks they can turn to to teach those skills. As scores rose, Sang publicized them relentlessly through a sophisticated public-relations apparatus that included slick brochures, videotapes, and promotional appearances by Sang himself— all in an effort to convince people that students were really learning what they should be learning in the Duval school system. Sang would say of his efforts: "It's not PR, it's progress reporting."

The National Assessment of Educational Progress (NAEP), however, tells a very different story than do basic-skills achievement tests about the performance of the nation's students. It suggests that public education is far from achieving the goals of the excellence movement. Congressionally mandated, NAEP has conducted regular assessments of large samples of the nation's students in a range of subjects since 1969. A report on writing skills, based on a 1988 examination of 18,000 students and published in 1990, revealed that a majority of high school juniors are able to do only minimal writing tasks. Over 70 percent of the sample members, for example, were unable to write a persuasive letter urging a U.S. senator to increase funding for the space program. "They can spell, they can punctuate and organize a simple sentence. But the quality of their ideas and their expression is very poor," said NAEP's director, Archie Lapointe, in releasing the report. Recent NAEP assessments have produced equally bleak portraits of students' grasp of the more challenging aspects of other subjects. For example, less than 5 percent of the twelfth-graders in a 1988 NAEP reading test demonstrated a deep enough understanding of a passage on "factory production of pizza" to supply details or arguments to buttress their interpretations of what they were reading. A 1990 NAEP report on its 1988 history assessment concluded that "many students seemed to lack knowledge of the basic contents of documents that have influenced our country's political, economic, and social life," and only 49 percent of the twelfth-graders tested in a 1988 civics assessment demonstrated an understanding of basic concepts and terms, such as "separation of powers," "chief executive," "veto," and "lobbyist." Nor do the nation's students measure up to their international peers in high-level learning. In a mid-1980s study of science achievement, American 17-year-olds finished ninth out of thirteen industrialized nations in physics, eleventh in chemistry, and last in biology.[11]

To comprehend fully the failure of the new wave of standardized tests to measure the performance of the schools reliably, it's necessary to peer into the arcane world of test-score reporting. A small-town West Virginia doctor, John Jacob Cannell, attracted national publicity in 1987 when he released a survey revealing that the majority of the thirty-two states using standardized norm-referenced tests that year reported above-average scores at every grade level in every subject. But Cannell's revelation amounts to the tip of an iceberg. Score reporting on norm-referenced tests, the tests used most frequently to gauge the performance of schools and school systems in the name of accountability, is full of obscurities and rife with abuses that lead to a badly distorted picture of academic achievement in the nation's schools.

To begin with, because they report the performance of students strictly in terms of comparisons with other students, norm-referenced test scores provide what is at best imprecise evidence of whether students are learning what they are being taught.[12] On a norm-referenced test, a student's "raw score" (the number of correct answers) is frequently reported as a percentile ranking on a scale of 1 to 99. If a student answers more questions correctly than all but 20 percent of his or her peers, the student's score would be at the 80th percentile. Conversely, if 80 percent of those taking the test answered more questions correctly than the student did, his or her score would be at the 20th percentile. But in absolute terms, percentile rankings don't mean very much. A student could earn an 80th-percentile ranking on a norm-referenced test by answering fifteen of fifty questions correctly, or by answering forty of fifty questions, depending on how well the students taking the test do as a whole.[13] A high percentile ranking, therefore, doesn't necessarily signify that a student has a grasp of the subjects being tested, nor does a low percentile ranking necessarily reflect a poor understanding of those subjects. Such conclusions simply can't be made on the basis of a percentile ranking— no small problem in this era of higher academic expectations.

It's also the case that shifts in percentile scores reflect different degrees of change in student performance at different points along the percentile scale. When students take a norm-referenced test, a relatively small number score at either end of the scale and a lot score in the middle of it; the scores form the classic bell-shaped curve when plotted on a graph. Consequently, large changes in raw scores produce only small changes in percentile rank at the top and bottom of the scale, while small changes in raw scores in the middle of the curve produce large changes in percentile rank. If this were not the case, the scale would not be able to make identifiable distinctions in student performance in the crowded middle ranges. A committee of testing experts convened by a branch of the National Academy of Sciences cited the following example of this scoring phenomenon in a 1982 report. A group of 407 students took a twenty-five-item standardized test. A raw score of 15 put students at the 50th percentile, the test's so-called norm. A raw score of 14, however, put students in the 42d percentile. Yet a raw score of 5 puts students in the 1st percentile, and a score of 6 puts them in the 2d percentile.[14]

As a result of this psychometric peculiarity, the significance of small shifts in student performance in the middle of the scale tends to be considerably overstated, an important fact because achieving the so-called national norm (the 50th percentile) has become crucial to the public perception of a school's or a school system's performance. Those with scores at or above the national norm enjoy something akin to a Good Housekeeping Seal of Approval; it's widely assumed that their students are getting the sort of education that they should be when their average test scores reach that magic plateau. The fact that a very small number of correct answers can make the difference between a 40th- and a 50th-percentile ranking suggests, however, that the importance attached to "achieving the norm" on such tests is overblown.

Because of these characteristics of the percentile scoring scale, the presence in a norm-referenced test of even a few flawed questions can have a significant effect on students' percentile rankings. Yet poorly designed questions are not difficult to find among the myriad of new standardized tests working their way into the public schools. A version of Maine's new eighth-grade reading test, for example, includes a passage on the Revolutionary War drawn from a social studies textbook. It reads, in part, "At first, Americans fought a defensive war. They won few victories but avoided a crushing defeat." A question following the passage asks, "Which aspect of the Americans' early efforts in the Revolution was most important to the outcome of the war?" Unfortunately for the students taking the test, they are provided with two equally correct answers to choose from. The answer that Maine was looking for was "Americans avoided a crushing defeat," answer C. But answer A, "Americans fought a defensive war," seems no less reasonable. The passage implies, after all, that the American forces avoided a crushing defeat because they fought a defensive war.

The science section of a recent elementary school edition of the Metropolitan Achievement Tests, on the other hand, presents students with a legitimate answer to a question, but one they aren't permitted to select. A question asks, "Which two of these tools do the same kind of work?" It is followed by pictures of a shovel, a spoon, a hammer, and a hatchet with a hammerhead (such as the type used by shinglers). The "correct" answer is "shovel and spoon." Yet an equally plausible answer—the hammer and the hatchet with a hammerhead—was not included among the possible answers, perhaps leaving a perceptive student more than a little confused.

Ambiguity is also a common trait in standardized-test questions. In fact, after reviewing a number of widely used tests, one is left with the impression that publishers often make questions ambiguous in an effort to make them more difficult. A junior-high-school-level reading passage in a recent edition of the Stanford Achievement Tests, for example, describes "two young men" huddled close to a fireplace in a room, trying to read by the dim light of coals. They hear "the soft, almost imperceptive rustling of something on the floor beside them. A creature had emerged from beneath one of the benches and now, with snake-like movements, it crept closer to the two young men. Scarcely breathing, it glided along the floor in the inky blackness of the room." A question that follows asks, "The intruder was most likely a A) homeless person, B) snake, C) mouse, D) stray dog." The "correct" answer is B, snake. The word *glided* conjures up an image of a snake. But what student with half a mind is going to choose snake as the answer when the term *snake-like* is used in the passage? And if *glided* is a clue, then it's contradicted by the use of *crept*. It seems perfectly reasonable for a student to think that the creature described in the passage is a mouse. Mice creep; snakes don't. At the very least, the evidence provided in the passage is ambiguous, mis-leadingly so.

It's also the case that some questions on standardized tests bear no real relationship to the subject they supposedly test. A question in the social studies section of the junior high school edition of the Comprehensive Test of Basic Skills is preceded by a reproduction of six postage stamps about the United Nations. The question asks, "Which stamp represents the medical function of the United Nations?" To get the correct answer, a student has to be able to recognize the caduceus depicted on one of the stamps. But what can such a question possibly reveal about a student's knowledge of social studies? Similarly, one might reasonably ask what, if anything, the question in the science section of the Metropolitan Achieve-ment Tests involving hammers, shovels, and spoons has to do with science.

Nor is it uncommon to find standardized tests, especially commercial norm-referenced tests that are distributed nationally, that measure stu-dents' knowledge of material that is not in their school's curriculum. In one of a number of studies that produced similar results, the Educational Products Information Exchange, an independent educational consumer group, in 1987 compared the sixth-grade math objectives measured by the Stanford Achievement Tests with a California school system's curricu-lum goals for the same grade level. It found that of the ninety-eight topics covered in either the test or the curriculum, only twenty were covered in both.[15]

The relationship between standardized-test scores and the actual level of learning in the schools is further obscured when percentile rankings are reported as "grade equivalents," as they often are with norm-referenced tests. A grade equivalent is a numerical representation of a particular point in the school year. The grade equivalent 5.8, for instance, stands for fifth-grade, eighth month. Under the grade-equivalent scoring sys-tem, the average score of all the students taking a test, the test's norm, is reported in terms of when students take the test. And it's the norm that determines how grade equivalents are matched up with percentile rank-ings. If a test is administered to fifth-graders in October (the second month of the school year), its norm would be reported as 5.2, and that score would represent the average performance of fifth-graders who take the test at that stage in the school year. The 5.2 figure would be "equivalent" to a 50th-percentile ranking.

Students who score at the norm under the grade-equivalent system are said to be "on grade level." Others are spread out along a continuum of grade equivalents similar to that of the percentile scale. A high-scoring student might be given a grade equivalent on the fifth-grade test of 7.0 (which might be the equivalent to, say, an 80th-percentile ranking); while a low-scoring student might be given a grade equivalent of 4.0 or lower. This convoluted system of reporting scores is widely used because it offers the appearance of being a precise and readily understandable means of measuring student performance. In reality, it does a great deal to encourage erroneous conclusions about achievement levels in the schools.

It's widely believed, for example, that students can perform academically at the level of their grade equivalent. A fifth-grader, say, who receives a score of 7.0 in reading is commonly assumed to be able to read at a seventh-grade level. In fact, a grade equivalent does not represent the level of academic work that a student has mastered, for the simple reason that a test is designed to measure only the material that is taught at the grade level of the students taking the test. A fifth-grade test is incapable of measuring whether a student can read at a seventh-grade level because it's a test of fifth-grade material and not a test of what's taught in the seventh grade. In reality, a grade equivalent of 7.0 is the score that the average seventh-grader would get on the fifth-grade test.

"The notion that fifth-graders who score a 7.0 on a fifth-grade test can read at a seventh-grade level is a myth," says Michael Zieky, a senior test developer for the Educational Testing Service, the nation's largest testing company. The Psychological Corporation, the publisher of the Stanford Achievement Tests and the Metropolitan Achievement Tests (MAT), acknowledges as much in the manual for teachers that it provides with the MAT. "It is possible," the company writes, "for [a third-grader] to obtain a grade equivalent of 5.7 [in math] and have almost no ability to work with fractions or other material commonly covered in the curriculum at grades four and five."[16]

It is also commonly assumed outside the testing world that a grade equivalent in one subject reflects the same level of achievement as does the identical grade equivalent in another subject. Such is not the case. Because the norm is invariably different from test to test, the same grade equivalent often represents different levels of achievement on different tests. A 5.5 on a reading test may represent either a higher or a lower level of achievement than does a 5.5 on a math test. The Psychological Corporation points out in its MAT manual that there are situations in which, say, a third-grader with a grade equivalent of 5.8 in language and a 6.2 in math might actually be doing better in language than in math in relation to his or her third-grade peers.

The grade-equivalent scoring system is also plagued by the same problem that distorts the percentile-ranking scale: shifts in grade-equivalent
scores of the same size reflect different degrees of change in student
performance at different points along the grade-equivalent scale. The
increase in achievement that is measured by a shift from a 5.0 to a 5.4 on
a fifth-grade reading test, for example, is likely to be considerably smaller
than the increase in achievement that is measured by a shift from a 6.0 to
a 6.4 on the same test. Conversely, as the Psychological Corporation
warns in its MAT manual, an increase in the number of correct answers
on a test may produce only a small change in grade-equivalent scores in
one portion of the scale and a huge change in another. "An increase in
raw score of 10 points may amount to only three months of change in
one part of the scale and three years in another," said the test publisher
by way of example.[17] It is in the middle of the scale where small shifts in
the number of correct answers produce the greatest changes in grade-
equivalent scores, thus giving the appearance that significant changes in
student performance have taken place, when in fact they haven't.

Finally, the notion of scoring "at grade level" is itself misleading. It
suggests (as does "at the national norm"; the two terms are synonymous)
that students who score at that level are learning what they are supposed
to be learning. It also implies that students who don't score at that level
are performing poorly in school. Neither interpretation is legitimate,
however, because in reality, the term *at grade level* represents nothing
more than the score on a norm-referenced test that places a student at
the 50th percentile. It is the point on the score scale that half of the scores
fall above and half fall below, but, again, it reveals nothing about student
performance in absolute terms.

It's hard to find a testing expert who won't acknowledge that the
concept of grade equivalents is, in the words of one, "vastly over-invested
with significance." Even test publishers caution in their technical manuals against the misuse of grade equivalents. "Because misinterpretation
can easily result if thorough explanation does not accompany the score, it
is strongly recommended that grade equivalents *not* be used in reporting
a student's scores to parents or other persons with little or no training in
testing," warns CTB Macmillan/McGraw-Hill in its test coordinator's
handbook for the Comprehensive Tests of Basic Skills (emphasis in original).[18] But the widespread use of grade equivalents shows no sign of
abating in the current educational climate.

The national samples of students to whom test publishers administer
their norm-referenced tests in order to set standards on the tests also
contribute to the often poor correlation between test scores and student
achievement. Publishers use the performance of students in the samples,
who take the tests before they are made available publicly, to translate
raw test scores into percentile ranks or grade equivalents once the pub-

lishers put their products on the market. The score of a student in a school system that purchases a norm-referenced test reflects the student's performance relative to that of the students in the publisher's national sample.

In theory these so-called norm groups must accurately reflect the demographic characteristics (racial, economic, and geographic) of the nation's students if the percentile rankings and grade equivalents based on the norm groups' scores are to be dependable as a measure of national performance. In reality, norm groups are often less than representative of the national student population. "Some are good, some aren't," said Roger Farr, the coauthor of the Metropolitan Achievement Tests. CTB Macmillan/McGraw-Hill, publisher of the CAT and the CTBS, acknowledged in a testing newsletter that it publishes that "not all publishers are equally successful in obtaining truly representative samples of schools and students upon which to standardize their tests." The result is that percentile rankings and grade equivalents frequently are inaccurate measures of comparison of the performance of a group of students to that of their peers nationally.[19]

Moreover, because of the cost involved, publishers of the major commercial achievement tests typically renorm them only every seven years or more. The norms of the Comprehensive Tests of Basic Skills, for example, had been updated only three times since 1950 before they were recalculated in 1989. While lawmakers call for comparisons of their students to their contemporaries, many students are in fact being compared to students tested years ago.

Nor is there any guarantee that school systems will use new norms when they are issued by the publishing companies. A common practice among score-conscious school administrators is to continue to administer older versions of achievement tests even after they have been updated and renormed. As late as 1989–90, Maryland was administering a version of the CAT normed in 1977, permitting the state's teachers to teach to the same test for twelve years, as well as have their students' performance measured against that of students in norming groups that lacked such advantages. In 1987 the District of Columbia replaced a standardized test with thirteen-year-old norms, selecting a new test, the CTBS, with seven-year-old norms. Nonetheless, school officials launched a citywide campaign to boost scores on the new examination, complete with meetings to spur the district's teachers, a slide show titled "Maintaining the Mark Despite the Change," and directives to do extensive test-preparation work with students throughout the 1986–87 school year.

Cannell's study highlights the consequences of such practices. He reported that there were virtually no states in 1987 with average scores below the 50th percentile on any of six major commercial norm-referenced tests at any elementary grade level. This permitted all states to declare that the majority of their elementary students were performing "above the national average." A 1989 study commissioned by the U.S. Department of Education corroborated Cannell's findings. It concluded that "with respect to national averages, [school] districts and states are presenting inflated results and misleading the public."[20]

Stung by Cannell's criticism, many of the major test publishers now issue what they advertise as annually updated norms. In truth, these "annual norms" are based not on scientific national samples of students but on estimates extrapolated from the previous year's performance by students in states and school systems that purchase the publishers' tests. Because the pool of students taking a particular test may or may not be representative of the nation's students as a whole, the reliability of many of the new annual norms is questionable, say test developers. And again, there's no incentive for states and school systems to use annual norms. Indeed, while they tout their commitment to annual norms in their public pronouncements, test publishers have become adept at playing to educators' sensitivity to test norms. The Psychological Corporation alludes directly to the public-relations value of using old norms in its promotional material for a recent edition of the Stanford Achievement Tests. "There are many political and administrative reasons to continue using the 1982 norms," it writes to potential clients. Riverside, maker of the Iowa Test of Basic Skills, offers school systems the opportunity to have their tests scored against "low socioeconomic norms" and "large city norms," thus increasing their chances of producing high scores.[21]

For all these reasons, the nature of test reporting itself makes many of the standardized tests that the reform movement is depending on so heavily unreliable measures of what's taking place in the nation's classrooms. "Test publishers should do a hell of a lot more to inform the public of the fuzzy bands that test scores really are," says Zieky of the Educational Testing Service. "They are not the exact points [that] they are made out to be. A test score is a sloppy thing."

The nation's media, it should be said, have only made matters worse. One can open practically any newspaper or magazine in the country and find articles such as one the *New York Times* ran in 1987, in which increases of just three percentile points in the average reading scores of black students in two elementary grades were enough for the paper to praise a suburban Washington, D.C., school system for bringing about "significant gains" in the education of minority students.[22] The seeming objectivity of standardized tests, the press's eagerness for a convenient way to gauge the performance of the reform movement, and the immense significance that the school reformers themselves have invested in standardized testing apparently make the temptation to turn test scores into tea leaves too great for the nation's media to resist.

Nor are educators using standardized tests strictly for accountability. Increasingly, important instructional decisions are being made on the basis of basic-skills test scores. Despite the many flaws in the tests and in the system of scoring them, school systems are using cutoff scores on standardized tests more and more as the primary and sometimes sole criteria for placing students in a variety of educational programs that often strongly influence students' educational opportunities. In Texas I visited a school system in which students who score at or below the 30th percentile on standardized reading tests are arbitrarily placed in watered-down English courses. In New Jersey I visited an urban school system that admits students to its "gifted and talented" program—which entitles enrollees to higher expectations, better teachers, and more resources—if they score at or above the 90th percentile on the CAT in reading and math. In Florida I visited a school system that places students in grades *kindergarten to three* in different academic tracks *solely* on the basis of whether they are 1.5 years above grade level in reading and math, between 1.5 above and 1.5 below grade level, or more than 1.5 years below grade level, as measured by standardized tests. And in a Pennsylvania school system, students who score in the 25th percentile or below on the California Achievement Tests are automatically placed in a federally funded remedial program—and hence are likely to be labeled "remedial students" for the duration of their school careers. "The computer picks the scores up and places kids in the program—we don't even touch it," said a special-education teacher in the school system.

The second major failing of the reform-driven surge in standardized testing is its influence in the classroom. Far from reinforcing the push for educational excellence, the new tests are driving down the level of instruction in many schools.

Local educators are becoming obsessed to ever-greater degrees with standardized test scores. Politically the paramount measure of school performance, they have become the primary focus of attention in many classrooms. "You are darn right I'm going to worry about those scores," said a California principal of the standardized achievement tests in California's statewide assessment program. "If they are going to put my school in the newspaper and judge it against others in the state and I choose not to worry about test scores, I'm playing a losing game." The pressure to raise scores is such that "we have to prime principals and teachers for standardized tests," Willie Herenton, superintendent of the Memphis public schools, told a symposium on school reform in Washington, D.C., in 1989. "That's the reality, like it or not."

In many schools a tremendous amount of time is taken up with prepping students for standardized tests. In Florida an elementary school principal told me that his school spends six weeks at the beginning of each school year coaching students for the state's standardized examinations. "To compete, you've got to do more," he said. At a suburban California high school I visited, the principal requires all of his teachers to spend fifteen minutes a week throughout the school year doing review questions with their students as part of a "test-improvement project." As an aid to teachers, he puts mimeographed copies of sample questions in their school mailboxes each week. A Florida high school I visited has gone so far as to assign sample test questions to students during homeroom period and announce the answers over the public-address system.

Superintendent Sang coupled his cross-referencing of Duval county's teaching materials to local, state, and national standardized tests with directives to teachers that they make the skills measured by the tests a priority in their classrooms. "Keyed items should be covered prior to test administration to ensure students' success," teachers were told in the prefaces to course outlines. In Prince Georges County, Maryland, where Superintendent John A. Murphy has parlayed rising scores on the California Achievement Tests into a national reputation, students receive an additional hour of computer time daily for two months prior to CAT testing, permitting them to practice on multiple-choice questions that have been loaded into the district's computers; second-graders in the 106,000-student school system, one of the nation's largest, spend afternoons in a special class on test taking; and teachers are shown videotapes on creative ways to prepare students for the CAT. Leaving no doubts about where he wants his principals and teachers to place their classroom priorities, Murphy has hung charts of the CAT scores of each of the county's 172 schools on the walls of the conference room adjoining his office, where his predecessor had hung student art work. Not coincidentally, the same version of the CAT has been administered in the school system since 1980, and Murphy has been an outspoken critic of Maryland's plans to update *its* ancient test norms.[23]

Many school systems now supply students with textbooks on test taking. Many do more, taking advantage of the fact that several test publishers produce test-coaching workbooks and worksheets that contain sample tests that are virtually indistinguishable from their actual standardized tests. As the *Wall Street Journal* has reported, McGraw-Hill, in a joint venture with Maxwell Communication Corporation, sells a test-practice kit called "Learning Materials" that includes some questions *identical* to ones on CTB Macmillan/McGraw-Hill's CAT test. Some 20,000 of the kits have been sold since the mid-1980s, as well as over 10,000,000 of another test-practice product copublished by McGraw-Hill that is known as "Scoring High." There also have been widespread reports of test tampering by teachers eager to raise their students' scores. In a celebrated 1989 case, reported in the *Wall Street Journal* and *Newsweek,* and on "60 Minutes," a respected high school social studies teacher in Greenville, South Carolina, was fired for giving students answers to questions on the California Test of Basic Skills prior to their taking the test. The teacher, who had previously been named Teacher of the Year at Greenville High School, had earned bonuses totaling $5,000 in the two years prior to her dismissal under South Carolina's program to reward teachers who raise their students' standardized test scores; her regular salary was $23,000. Other schools have prodded students to better performances on the tests the old-fashioned way: schoolwide pep rallies, complete with bands and cheerleaders. "Catch that testing spirit. . . . Pass that test, pass that test, pass that test," urged the lyrics to a song sung at one such rally in Florida.[24]

As the amount of test preparation in the schools has burgeoned, students from kindergarten through twelfth grade are spending more and more time studying the rudimentary math, reading, and grammar skills that are the focus of the tests. They are doing so at the expense of the more rigorous skills and knowledge urged by the school reformers. "It's hard to get teachers to teach on level three of Bloom's Taxonomy if testing is on level one," said Duval County's director of curriculum. The taxonomy, named for the educator Benjamin Bloom, groups learning into seven categories of increasing complexity: recall, restatement, interpretation, application, analysis, synthesis, and evaluation. Category three is considered to be the first involving advanced skills. At one California high school I visited, an eleventh-grade English teacher midway through class abruptly stopped a discussion of *The Red Badge of Courage* to hand out multiple-choice "word-identification" problems for students to practice with. Word identification is a skill on a standardized test they take. One of the problems read: "Only lucky people are able to go to the *zip*. There's no oxygen on the *zip*. Craters are all over the *zip*. Werewolves get hairy when they see the *zip*. What is a *zip*?" No wonder the 1988 NAEP writing examination revealed that fewer than two-thirds of the nation's eighth and twelfth graders were asked to write one or two paragraphs at least weekly.

In high schools there is a particular emphasis on coaching students for the Scholastic Aptitude Test, the well-known college-admissions examination. Full-scale courses on SAT preparation are getting to be commonplace, with students frequently receiving academic credit for completing them. SAT coaching also has become part of the syllabus in many regular academic courses. The course outline for "English 11" at one California high school I visited recommends to teachers that "SAT test preparation" occupy 15 percent of class time in the spring semester. By comparison, it suggests that "reading" occupy 10 percent of class time. Typically, SAT preparation is no more academically productive than the preparation done for basic-skills tests. In many SAT courses, students do little more than learn the tricks of taking the test and work their way through reams of sample questions. A major activity is vocabulary memorization because the verbal section of the two-part multiple-choice test is to a significant degree a measure of the vocabulary that a student possesses.

The increasing influence of standardized tests in the nation's classrooms is also doing damage on a deeper level. The vast majority of standardized tests are multiple-choice because by being machine-scoreable, they offer a fast and relatively inexpensive means of testing large numbers of students. But the multiple-choice nature of so much of standardized testing falsely suggests to students, as educators such as Theodore Sizer have argued, that knowledge is nothing but a mass of tiny, disconnected pieces of information, and that learning is nothing more than the ability to consume such snippets of information and reproduce them on demand. By urging students to see their role in the classroom as merely pursuers of "right" answers supplied by others, multiple-choice tests encourage students to be passive learners; they suggest to students that their ideas and insights are unimportant. The tests fail to convey the complexity and interrelatedness of knowledge and the ambiguity that is so much a part of life; they trivialize truth. "It's not just unproductive to teach science as a string of definitions for a standardized test," said a New York City principal, "you are also giving kids a false notion of what science is." In classrooms where standardized tests are the focus of instruction, there is invariably less debate and fewer opportunities to synthesize differing types of information; students have fewer chances to develop original solutions to problems, to become creative, independent thinkers.

Ironically, the surge in multiple-choice testing is reinforcing the very sort of instruction that the school-reform reports of the 1980s decried. In *A Place Called School,* his exhaustive 1984 study of 1,000 public school classrooms, the educator John Goodlad charged that "mastering mechanics" dominated the English curricula of the nation's schools. There is, Goodlad wrote, "a repetitive reinforcement of the basic skills of language use throughout the twelve grades." Of instruction in mathematics, Goodlad said, "The impression I get from the topics, materials, and tests of the curriculum is of mathematics as a body of fixed facts and skills to be acquired, not as a tool for developing a particular kind of intellectual power in the student." What's the effect of such instruction? A Connecticut English teacher put it this way: "Kids can go from page to page in workbooks getting nothing but 100's, but if you talk to them about the ideas in a book, they just look at you."[25]

The pressure on teachers to tilt their instruction toward standardized testing has been increased further by a trend in public education known as "curriculum alignment." At the heart of the development are state curriculum frameworks. Invariably long and often detailed descriptions of the content that states expect their teachers to cover in each course, many of these curriculum documents are designed to buttress accountability and have been linked directly to standardized tests. With the notable exception of California—where education officials have drafted curriculum documents calling for greater use of biographies, speeches, and other primary source materials, thorough treatment of controversial topics, and other measures promoting rigorous instruction in academic subjects for all students—the majority of the frameworks are focused on basic skills. Missouri's "Key Skills," for example, are calibrated to the state's new Mastery and Achievement Tests, and Tennessee's 2,000-page "Basic Skills First Curriculum," first published in 1985, parallels the state's skills-level testing program. Florida has legislation—the torturously named Florida Accountability in Curriculum, Educational Instructional Materials, and Testing Act of 1984—linking the state's curriculum frameworks to a statewide standardized testing program. In many places educators have rewritten their syllabuses so the material they teach can be readily measured by multiple-choice tests; one Southern California school system that I visited had twenty curriculum subcommittees at work overhauling instructional manuals to emphasize the teaching of "measurable" skills. Similarly, in its explanation of the teaching "objectives" listed in its new curriculum frameworks, the Tennessee education department writes that they "break learning into manageable, measurable bits."

Textbooks are also being linked to standardized testing as part of the curriculum alignment campaign—with damaging results. Educators are requiring publishers to produce textbooks focused on long lists of particular basic skills measured by standardized tests. The result, as the researcher Harriet Tyson-Bernstein writes in *A Conspiracy of Good Intentions: America's Textbook Fiasco,* an insightful 1988 report on the nation's textbook industry, is that school textbooks are increasingly a "melange of test-oriented trivia."

The increasing influence of standardized testing only exacerbates a host of other problems with textbooks. Because of the high cost of developing textbooks, frequently running into tens of millions of dollars, publishers must sell a lot of books to make a profit. That requires meeting the curriculum requirements of the twenty-two states that select books centrally as well as the demands of the thousands of school systems that set their own textbook standards. The result is a phenomenon known as "mentioning," whereby publishers make references in their textbooks to as many ideas, issues, events, people, and places as possible in order to meet the curriculum requirements of as many potential purchasers as possible. As a result, textbooks frequently treat topics so superficially that students can't make sense of what they are reading. "The context necessary to make facts meaningful has been edited out to make room for still more facts," writes Tyson-Bernstein.[26]

Another bane to textbook quality are so-called readability formulas, used by publishers to match the difficulty of textbooks to students' reading ability—so that fifth-graders, for example, are reading "fifth-grade" books. The widely used formulas are typically based on a textbook's average word and sentence length; an average sentence length of, say, fourteen words and an average word length of 1.24 syllables might be used as the benchmark for fifth-graders. Readability formulas make sense in theory; there's no point in assigning students books that they can't comprehend. But in practice, they are frequently more harmful than helpful. The logical organization of information, the clarity of sentence structure, and the complexity of ideas—important ingredients in a student's ability to grasp a reading assignment—are ignored by readability formulas. More important, in relying excessively on the monosyllabic words and short sentences required by the formulas, many publishers produce textbooks with dull, mechanical writing that is frequently more rather than less difficult to grasp because cause-and-effect relationships and other key information have been removed. "Inevitably, overreliance on readability formulas by the schools and their misuse by the publishing industry [have] contributed to bad writing in schoolbooks," concluded the national commission on reading in its 1985 report. Making matters worse, the bulk of the nation's textbooks are not written by professional writers with a flair for language but by educators, particularly education professors. In many instances school textbooks are coauthored by teams of contributors, who have different prose styles and approaches to their subject.[27]

Together, these problems result in books that are shallow, vapid, vague, lacking in unifying tone, and frequently inaccurate. In Tyson-Bernstein's words, the majority of the nation's textbooks are "a thin stream of staccato prose winding through an excessive number of pictures, boxes, and charts."[28]

The quality of textbooks is crucially important because they are the cornerstone of instruction in the nation's public schools. It is estimated that 75 percent of teaching time is spent on textbooks. As a Texas English teacher put it, "What the publishers put in the textbooks determines the content of our courses." Yet attempts by the school reformers to upgrade textbooks have been largely unsuccessful. Terrel Bell railed against the "dumbing down" of textbooks during his tenure as U.S. Secretary of Education. And Florida political leaders in 1984 brought together representatives from the twenty-two states that adopt textbooks centrally in an attempt to establish "a cartel of excellence" to pressure publishers into producing better books. The project received substantial funding from Secretary Bell and was transferred to an organization representing top state education officials, the Council of Chief State School Officers. But it made no progress and collapsed, a victim of bureaucratic inertia and petty jealousies between states.

Apart from Florida's overturning of a statute requiring school textbooks to be kept in circulation until they were physically unusable, the greatest strides toward textbook reform have been made in California, where Superintendent of Public Instruction Honig has sought to use the state's size and its centralized system of textbook adoption to pressure publishers into supplying higher-caliber books. California schools purchase 11 percent of the $1.7 billion spent on school textbooks annually. Local educators must buy books for kindergarten through eighth grade that are approved by the state board of education, making the board the gatekeeper to the single largest textbook market in the nation. In 1985 the board, with Honig's backing, rejected twenty-four science textbooks submitted for state approval for failing to meet standards established in the state's science curriculum framework. Important but controversial topics such as genetics, evolution, human reproduction, sexually transmitted diseases, and nuclear energy were given short shrift in the books, the board charged. The following year it rejected all fourteen elementary math textbooks submitted for state adoption, admonishing publishers to place greater emphasis on problem solving and less on rote memorization.

But though such steps have received wide publicity, they haven't always produced dramatically higher quality textbooks. University scientists reviewed revised science texts submitted by publishers later in 1985 and charged that many still contained numerous errors of scientific fact; state officials said the new books were also badly written. Nonetheless, the California board of education approved the books.

Many publishers have resisted California's textbook campaign. In 1989 Honig and his allies in the California legislature successfully watered down a bill backed by the publishing industry that would have severely weakened Honig's textbook-reform drive by diminishing the state board's authority to reject textbooks that fail to follow California's curriculum frameworks. The original legislation seemed to be aimed in particular at an ambitious history/social studies framework drafted by the state in 1987 that demanded that topics be treated in greater depth and that books have a vivid narrative style, as well as more primary source material. But when the state held a competition in 1990 for history/social studies texts based on the new framework, only nine publishers submitted books for adoption, compared to twenty-two in 1983, when California last adopted new history/social studies books. Of the nine, moreover, the state's curriculum commission approved books from only two, a K-8 series by Houghton Mifflin, and an eighth-grade text by Holt, Rinehart and Winston. The commission praised the books for setting "a new standard" in the textbook industry. The lower number of submissions and high rejection rate were attributed to the unwillingness of publishers to customize their textbooks for the California market for fear of being unable to sell their books elsewhere. In another illustration of California's apparently limited influence over the nation's textbook market, a publisher that produced a much improved revised science book for California in 1986 marketed a 1987 edition in the rest of the nation that was identical to the original book that California rejected in 1985.[29]

In a growing number of states and school systems, standardized tests, textbooks, and new curriculum frameworks are forming the basis of elaborate computerized "instructional management systems" designed to track student performance. The seeming simplicity of the instructional systems has made them increasingly popular with education officials:

teachers are given checklists or handbooks of coded skills that students are to master. (Tennessee's curriculum framework in "language arts," for example, includes such ninth-grade objectives as 9E1A3, "To understand written directions"; 9E1C1, "To understand location of reference materials"; 9E2F1, "To understand the parts of speech"; 9E2H2, "To understand the elements of form and style"; and 9F2G2, "To understand the importance of correct spelling.") Students then take the standardized tests that are keyed to the skills being measured. The tests are machine scored and the results are fed into computers, which produce printouts that break down the results by student, by teacher, and by school—thereby providing school officials with an instant report card on student achievement, teaching ability, and school performance. "By using AIMS, teachers are able to record student test scores, update skill checklists, and monitor their classes' mastery of objectives and academic progress at the touch of a few buttons," the District of Columbia school system wrote of its "Automated Instructional Management System" (AIMS) in its 1983–84 annual report.

The problem is that the increasingly widespread computerized systems are focused overwhelmingly on individual basic skills—"bits" of learning, as the Tennessee officials put it—largely because such skills are what multiple-choice tests, the key element of the new instructional systems, can measure most easily. Thus teachers find themselves under still more pressure to focus their teaching time on low-level skills. Said the superintendent of schools in Pittsburgh of the "test-managed" instructional program he introduced in the mid-1980s: "We're not educating kids with it, we're getting them ready to be educated."[30]

"Measurement-driven instruction" and "competency-based education" are also turning many classrooms into rigid, bureaucratic places. In many school systems, curriculum frameworks and skill checklists now dictate teachers' every move. To deviate, they fear, would jeopardize test scores. More and more it is the need to "cover" curriculum outlines that is given the highest priority in the classroom. "They want you to hit X,Y, and Z, or A,B, and C. Coverage, not depth, not learning how to learn, is the goal," the director of instruction at a Florida high school told me. "We're just skimming," said a New Jersey history teacher. In a rural Texas community a seventh-grade science teacher expressed frustration at not being able to use the recent flooding of a shallow river running through town to teach her students about erosion because she was rushing to get through the state's new "Essential Skills" curriculum. To be sure, Texas's essential skills are a bureaucratic nightmare for teachers. In the second grade, for instance, there are 214 separate skills that students must master in eight subjects, ranging from mathematics to fine arts. A record must be kept of each student's progress on each skill. Thus, in a class of twenty-two students, a teacher must track over 4,700 different pieces of information.[31]

The new instructional-management systems are trivializing teaching. By forcing teachers into the pedagogical equivalent of painting-by-the-numbers, measurement-driven instruction is reducing a potentially exhilarating occupation to a rigid, uncreative task. Many school boards and state legislatures, of course, have introduced the new instructional systems with just that goal in mind. Measurement-driven instruction reflects a profound distrust of the ability of public school teachers; it represents, in effect, an attempt to "teacher-proof" instruction in the schools. But by undercutting the autonomy of teachers, measurement-driven instruction clashes with the reformers' campaign to draw greater numbers of able and ambitious people into the teaching profession by "empowering" teachers in schools. Indeed, such instruction is the antithesis of teacher professionalism; rather than afford teachers greater decision-making opportunities and a more engaging work environment, measurement-driven teaching does the opposite. In transferring decisions about instruction to central offices and state capitals, the new instructional systems are also at odds with the increasingly popular notion of school-based management. And because of its emphasis on often-lifeless basic skills, test-based instruction is frequently intensely boring, making the important task of enlivening academic instruction in the nation's schools that much tougher.

There have been attempts to upgrade standardized testing. Mississippi recently scrapped its kindergarten examination after discovering that its 5-year-olds were spending their days hunched over Ditto sheets. Georgia replaced its paper-and-pencil bubble test with one that measures listening, speaking and writing skills, and number understanding. North Carolina and Texas recently stopped testing students in several early elementary grades. And Illinois in 1989 enacted legislation limiting state-mandated standardized testing to five hours per student annually.

North Carolina and California, through its so-called Golden State Examinations, have introduced rigorous end-of-course tests in high school academic subjects. Students who pass the California tests receive a special notation on their diplomas. The tests have the strength of focusing directly on the specific course content that students are expected to learn, and if colleges and universities required students to submit scores on such examinations—which are similar to the achievement tests sponsored by the College Board—rather than SAT scores, they no doubt would create a powerful new incentive for academic achievement in the nation's high schools. North Carolina expects to have a dozen tests in subjects ranging from geometry to U.S. history prepared by 1993. Such states as Pennsylvania, Texas, New Jersey, and California, meanwhile, have toughened their basic-skills achievement tests. In 1990 Pennsylvania replaced its Test of Essential Learning Skills, an assessment of low-level math and reading competencies administered to the state's third-, fifth-, and eighth-graders since 1984. The new test places less emphasis on vocabulary and grammar and more on reading comprehension and problem solving.

More ambitiously, several states are developing alternatives to multiple-choice testing. Instead of having students select from among answers supplied by their test booklets and darken in bubbles on a machine-read page, educators are creating large-scale assessments involving such varied tasks as science experiments and oral presentations, tasks that require students to develop their own responses to questions, to analyze, integrate, and communicate what they've learned. The most common type of "performance testing," as it's called, is writing, and California, Maine, Maryland, Connecticut, Georgia and perhaps a dozen other states have added a rudimentary writing requirement to their standardized tests—in most instances, a brief response to a statement or question. States are also experimenting with open-ended questions on their standardized tests. The questions use a fill-in-the-answer format. On California's twelfth-grade mathematics test, for example, students are shown three geometric shapes in their test booklet: a triangle, a trapezoid, and a circle. Lengths and the size of angles are printed on each shape. To test their knowledge of the properties of the shapes, students are asked to identify any inaccuracies in the information that's supplied, as well as explain the inaccuracies. They have to notice, for instance, that the angles of the triangle—90 degrees, 25 degrees, and 55 degrees—are erroneous because they don't add up to 180 degrees. California added the open-ended questions to its twelfth-grade test in 1989–90; the state is scheduled to add similar questions to its eighth-grade math test in 1990–91 and to its science tests in 1991–92.

Connecticut is pioneering the use of student demonstrations, or "exhibitions," in statewide assessments. With a $1 million grant from the National Science Foundation, the state is pilot testing these hands-on examinations in eight high school mathematics and science subjects in sixty Connecticut classrooms and in sixty classrooms in other states. Working individually and in groups, students are assigned a series of projects ranging from forty-five minutes and two weeks in length that requires them to frame questions, collect and analyze data, and communicate their results in both written reports and oral presentations. A prototype project in geometry called "building a dog pen" asks students to calculate the size of the largest possible pen using eighty feet of fencing. Designed to measure students' knowledge of the concepts of perimeter and area, and the formulas for perimeter, circumference, and area, the first part of the project requires students to explain in writing which geometric shape would produce the largest pen and why. Then students break into groups of three or four, share their hypotheses, and work out a solution to the problem. Then they construct a visual display of their answer, using graph paper, string, and other materials. In a final step, they present their solutions orally to their class and answer queries from other students. The aim of the demonstrations, says Connecticut testing official Douglas Rindone, is "getting kids to integrate their understanding of math and science concepts by actually *doing* performances and experiments—in ways that are fun." Boldly, Connecticut is planning to eliminate multiple-choice testing in favor of such demonstrations in its statewide assessment of high school math and science achievement, beginning in 1991–92.[32]

Vermont has initiated another alternative to multiple-choice testing, a concept known as "portfolios." Early in the 1990–91 school year, fourth- and eighth-graders in forty of the state's schools received special folders. As the year progresses, they are to fill the portfolios with their best classroom work in writing and mathematics. At year's end, teams of state-trained teachers from other school systems are to evaluate the portfolios. Vermont is planning to expand the program statewide in 1991–92, when it will begin factoring the evaluator's scores into its fourth- and eighth-grade school and statewide assessments in the two subjects.

Though potentially promising, such experiments are in the very early stages of development and on the whole are being conducted on a very small scale. And the nascent performance-testing movement, in particular, is fraught with potential problems that its proponents are just beginning to grapple with. While performance tests are much more likely to promote good teaching than their multiple-choice counterparts, they are also much more costly to administer and score. It is especially expensive to train and pay teachers to score performance tests. Sampling techniques that produce school-level or statewide scores by administering test questions to a matrix of students help cut costs. There are only eight open-ended questions in California's twelfth-grade mathematics assessment, for example, and each student is assigned only one of them. But with the cost of scoring some performance measures as much as ten times that of multiple-choice questions, the price still adds up. In 1989–90 funding shortages permitted California to score only 10 percent of its open-ended mathematics questions—hardly enough to pressure anxious educators to stop drilling their students for low-level multiple-choice questions. In addition, demonstration questions such as Connecticut's pose serious test-security problems if they are reused from year to year; but if they are not, the cost of test development increases. The difficulty of training teachers to score performance tests to the same standards is a further challenge, as is the related task of equating the results on different demonstration projects from year to year, which is necessary to produce the sorts of performance trends sought by policymakers and the public. In short, the long-term feasibility of performance testing is far from clear; it is simply too early to tell whether the initiatives in such states as Connecticut and Vermont will be workable on a large scale. "Performance testing is no piece of cake," says Dale Carlson, California's director of assessment. In addition, students may score substantially lower on performance measures than they do on multiple-choice tests. If they do—and they have in several pilot tests to date—political opposition to performance testing may emerge.[33]

Greater accountability is a necessity in public education, and good tests can help spur improvements in schools and classrooms. But standardized multiple-choice achievement tests are preeminent in the nation's schools today, and they are doing little to promote educational excellence. On the contrary, they are contributing significantly to the ill-conceived teaching and learning that they were designed to counter. And because multiple-choice tests afford a means of measuring school performance that is administratively manageable, relatively inexpensive, and seemingly easy to interpret, it will take a tremendous commitment to diminish their presence in the nation's classrooms.

PART III

A FURTHER
AGENDA

CHAPTER 7

Conant Was Wrong:
The Human Side of Schools

"School? It's just a getting out of the house thing. Kids don't come to learn, they just come," a junior at a California high school told me. At a Virginia high school I asked a senior if his four years at the school had been meaningful. He laughed, saying, "I'm just doing my time." Unfortunately, such attitudes are widespread among the nation's students; they pervade affluent suburban schools as well as their urban and rural counterparts. By one estimate as many as two-thirds of the nation's public secondary students are "disengaged" from their studies.[1]

Educators are quick to blame the problem on outside influences, such as apathetic parents, drugs, and television, and to be sure, such problems make teaching and learning tougher. But there is little about public schools themselves that kindles an enthusiasm among students for being in school or encourages a commitment to the work they do while they are there. The vast majority of the nation's public schools simply fail to create a climate in which teachers want to teach and students want to learn. It is a problem at the heart of the poor performance of so many of the nation's public secondary schools. And it stands as a tremendous impediment to the nation's goal of broadening public education's academic reach. The many reforms that have been enacted in recent years to bolster academic instruction in the public schools will amount to little if students lack the motivation to learn. But to date, the widespread disinterestedness among students and the schools' contribution to the problem has received scant attention within the excellence movement. In its eagerness to strengthen the quality of academics, the movement has neglected this crucial *human* element of the crisis in public education.

The majority of the public junior and senior high schools in the United States are drab, uninviting institutions, almost prisonlike, with cinderblock walls and long, often ill-lit corridors that are commonly cordoned by heavy metal grates at the end of the day. The coldness and impersonality of such surroundings is heightened by the huge size of many schools. Only a quarter of the nation's 22,000 secondary schools (those with no grade below seventh) enroll 1,000 or more students, but they enroll over half of the nation's secondary students.[2] Nor is it unusual to find high schools of 2,000, 3,000 or even 4,000 students, and junior high schools of 1,500 or more, especially in urban school systems. In such schools, students are so many numbers in a computer, the principal a voice heard over a public-address system or a face glimpsed amongst the crush of bodies during "passing period" between classes. Guidance counselors, or "career technicians" as they are called in many schools, frequently must cope with case loads of 500 students or more.

In one instance I was interviewing a vice-principal of a suburban Texas high school of 2,700 students when an awkward sophomore who had forged a note excusing himself from school arrived with his father. A secretary ushered them into the cramped office and handed the vice-principal a three-by-five card on the student from the school's files. The vice-principal glanced at the card and then began to ask the student why he had forged the note. "Why did you do it, why did you do it," she demanded repeatedly. Confused and intimidated, the student never did manage a coherent answer. The vice-principal, it turned out, had never seen the student before; all she knew about him was written on the three-by-five card. But that was enough for her to suspend the student for a week and to conclude the meeting by saying to the student's father, in the presence of his son and me, "Your son has a very serious problem," implying that he was a veritable juvenile delinquent. Earlier in the day the vice-principal had been introduced to the school's student-president in my presence; the student had been president of the student body for nearly a year.

There is a preoccupation—one is tempted to say obsession—with order in many of the nation's secondary schools. Movement is controlled by elaborate pass systems. The location of students during the school day is tracked by computers, as is class attendance. In some schools students are automatically suspended when computers identify them as having excessive numbers of latenesses or absences from class. Administrators, many of them bulky former athletic coaches, keep up a continuous patrol of hallways and grounds, linked by networks of gasping and crackling walkie-talkies, like so many cops on the beat. Indeed, there is no more apt a symbol of the menacing atmosphere that pervades public secondary schools today than the echo in an empty corridor of the oddly disconnected sounds from a walkie-talkie.

Strangely, many administrators seem to relish their role as disciplinarians; they seem much more interested in controlling students than educating them. They speak proudly of "sweeps" to clear halls of students late to class and are quick to share their latest discipline statistics. A Florida principal sat in his office one afternoon and enthusiastically recounted to me shipping off a seventh-grader to the local juvenile detention center earlier in the day for trying to extort ten dollars from a classmate. In Texas I asked a high school principal his reaction to the reform bill passed by the Texas legislature in 1984. His first comment was that he was frustrated by the law's ban on student suspensions.

Indeed, to many educators, there seems to be no infraction too small to be punished by suspension. I visited a New Jersey high school that in a recent year suspended thirty-two students for refusing to take gym class and over 100 for swearing. A *junior high school* in the same city issued 4,200 suspensions, or nearly three per student, in the same year, including seven for "discourteousness," ninety-four for "rudeness," and sixty for latenesses to school. A favorite punishment of secondary-school educators is to "suspend" students in school. I visited a Florida high school where students under in-school suspension spend all day (except for lunch) in a cramped "timeout room," ostensibly working on homework assignments but as often as not staring into space, ignored by the teacher in the room.

To many, a get-tough environment is the sign of a good school. The principal of an obscure high school in Paterson, New Jersey, became a national folk hero in 1988 when the Paterson school board brought him up on charges of "unbecoming conduct" and "insubordination," and threatened to fire him for expelling sixty-six students without due process or the board's approval. Joe Clark had ruled troubled 3,200-student Eastside High School—called a "cauldron of terror and violence" by the local prosecutor in 1979—with a bullhorn and a baseball bat since becoming its principal in 1982. "I've got the most orderly high school in America," he boasted to one interviewer. And when the explusions—he called the sixty-six students "hoodlums, thugs, and pathological deviants"—got him into trouble, Paterson parents came to his defense, turning a school board meeting into a pep rally with chants of "We want Joe." Local television news reported the controversy and soon afterward the national media picked up the story. Clark landed on the cover of *Time* magazine, he was profiled on CBS's "60 Minutes," and Warner Brothers came calling with a six-figure contract for the movie rights to his life story. The movie, *Lean on Me,* released in 1989, elevated Clark to the status of near-saint. U.S. Secretary of Education William Bennett sang Clark's praises. And the Reagan White House offered him a job as a policy adviser (he declined).

Lost in the crush of publicity and in *Lean on Me*'s canonization of Clark as an urban savior, however, was the fact that during Clark's tenure academic achievement remained largely unchanged at Eastside (less than one-third of its students passed New Jersey's none-too-rigorous gradua-tion examination, one of the worst performances in the state) and the school's dropout rate nearly doubled.[3] Happy-ending Hollywood story lines notwithstanding, the repressiveness and anonymity of many public secondary schools have transformed them into joyless, uninspiring places. Rather than encourage the natural enthusiasm and intellectual curiosity of adolescents, many schools suppress it. Instead of suggesting to students that learning can be enjoyable and fulfilling, public schools often do just the opposite.

The rigid, impersonal climate of many public schools also creates a disaffecting environment for teachers to work in, a problem that other circumstances compound. Teacher unionism, for example, has made schools much more bureaucratic places, where roles and relationships are prescribed by the language of collective bargaining contracts. In so doing, it has reduced the authority of principals and the accountability of teachers, and thereby diminished their commitment to their work. Under the confinements of bargaining contracts, principals have less opportunity and teachers less incentive to promote the greater good of their schools. During a visit to a New Jersey junior high school I was invited to attend a faculty meeting called by the principal to nominate students for a series of new academic-achievement awards. Thirty minutes into the meeting, at three o'clock, the hour their collective bargaining contract allowed them to leave school, half of the teachers in the meeting abruptly stood up and walked out without saying a word to the principal, who in turn didn't acknowledge their departure.[4]

The union-negotiated seniority rules that govern teacher assignments have a particularly negative influence on the teaching climate in schools. In granting teachers with the greatest seniority the right of first refusal on job openings anywhere in their school systems, and in permitting them to take the jobs of less-senior colleagues in the event of layoffs, such rules result in the frequent and often involuntary movement of teachers from school to school, damaging the morale of teachers transferred against their will (the Carnegie Foundation for the Advancement of Teaching has written that such teachers tend not to give schools "much of their hearts and souls") and undermining the stability and cohesion of many school faculties. As a measure of the extent of the problem, a study of the Chicago school system found that no less than 20 percent of the city's 24,000 teachers were transferred from one school to another between the 1980–81 and 1982–83 school years.[5] The seniority-assignment system also gives principals little or no say in who teaches in their schools. As a result, they are rarely able to build a faculty that shares an educational philosophy, and they are reluctant to delegate authority to their teachers.

The collegiality of school faculties has been eroded further by the state and federal education programs established in the past two decades to expand the educational opportunities of special student groups, such as the handicapped and the non-English-speaking. In many instances, the programs are isolated by walls of complex legal requirements and the allegiance of teachers in them is to the state and federal bureaucracies that have been created to regulate the programs rather than to their schools. Frequently, bilingual-education teachers, special-education teachers, and Chapter I teachers have only minimal contact with their "mainstream" faculty colleagues. Further, by investing a great deal of educational authority in the distant state and federal agencies that finance and administer the specialized programs, the past two decades have further undermined the autonomy of local educators and increased the bureaucratic rigidity of schools.

Many schools have become paralyzed by the threat of lawsuits charging teachers and principals with violations of the "due-process" rights of students in special programs. As Gerald Grant has argued, the student-rights movement of the 1960s and 1970s "put many school officials on the defensive and established a whole new set of procedural guarantees that changed the climate in many schools." Schools became "rule-bound and legalistic" and "infected" by "an adversarial mind-set" that stripped teachers and principals of authority and discouraged them from setting standards "that went beyond the legal minimum." Similarly, the educator Edward A. Wynne has argued that the "spread of legalistic relationships between students and faculty . . . has aggravated the depersonalization of . . . schools." "When teachers and administrators feel comparatively powerless to shape or reshape the conduct of the students around them," Wynne has written, "their indifference towards their students begins to increase."[6]

Ironically, the myriad reform mandates issued by the states since the onset of the excellence movement in many instances have further constricted the authority and autonomy of local educators. The highly detailed state curriculum outlines that are being introduced in conjunction with new standardized tests in many states, in particular, have diminished the autonomy of teachers in their classrooms. Many complained to me of being transformed into "assembly-line workers" or "cogs in a machine" by the new curriculum and testing mandates. The reform movement thus has created a paradox: the poor performance of local educators has led state policymakers to tighten the external controls on schools, but in doing so they have intensified the climate of bureaucracy and repressiveness in schools that has eroded teachers' and principals' commitment to their work.

Finally, the huge size of many of the nation's junior and senior high schools also has contributed to their bureaucratic climate. As schools get larger, more and more layers of leadership are needed to administer them and more and more rules and procedures are required to maintain order.

Charles E. Silberman wrote in his trenchant 1970 critique of public education, *Crisis in the Classroom*, that "education is not only a preparation for later life; it is an aspect of life itself. The great bulk of the young now spend a minimum of twelve years in school. . . . The quality of that experience must be regarded as important in its own right." Yet the climate in many of the nation's public schools has alienated vast numbers of secondary students and teachers. Estranged by the hostility of the school environment, they are wholly indifferent to its mission. To many students and teachers, the repressiveness and anonymity of their schools have made the joy of learning and the rewards of teaching incomprehensible.[7]

The climate in public secondary schools and the alienation it engenders among students is an important element of the troubling dropout problem. Over 25 percent of the nation's students leave high school before graduation, and in many urban school systems the number is twice as high. Significantly, in a 1986 dropout study, the largest such study to date, four researchers at the Educational Testing Service reported that two-thirds of the nearly 2,000 dropouts they interviewed said their most recent job was more enjoyable than school was. Further, they received the same response from over half of the students in the study who stayed in school until they graduated. Nor are only poor academic performers dropping out, as is commonly assumed. A study in Worcester, Massachusetts, found that nearly 40 percent of the city's dropouts were enrolled in college-preparation courses and only 17 percent were failing a course; yet 80 percent of the dropouts interviewed in the study said their reasons for leaving school were school-related. Similarly, researchers in the Houston school system, the nation's seventh largest, discovered that 25 percent of the city's dropouts are in the top quarter of their classes in reading and mathematics scores.[8]

Policymakers have pushed to cut dropout rates recently by establishing a range of incentive programs aimed at persuading dropouts to return to school or encouraging potential dropouts to get their diplomas. The same Boston business leaders who promised high school graduates jobs under the Boston Compact in 1982, in 1986 created a $5 million endowment to guarantee to every high school graduate in the city the financial resources for college. Under a $5-million-a-year initiative launched in 1984–85, New York State sponsors after-school jobs and training opportunities to 2,800 dropout-prone students. North Carolina also uses part-time jobs as inducements to keep students in school, and several years ago it established job-placement centers in each of the state's high schools. Since 1986–87, as part of a dropout-prevention program costing $40 million annually, New York City has hired paraprofessionals to locate dropouts and social workers to counsel them at thirty-six high schools and ninety-eight junior high schools. Moreover, many schools have initiated night schools to entice students to return to the classroom. But such incentives, while well-intentioned and sometimes successful, in many instances appear to treat only the symptoms of the alienation that causes many students to drop out, rather than the disease itself. Despite the incentives offered under the Boston Compact, the city's dropout rate increased significantly between 1982 and 1989, from 33 percent to 40 percent.

Another measure of students' estrangement from their schools is their eagerness to hold jobs during the school year. According to a 1988 study by the National Assessment of Educational Progress, no less than half of the eleventh-graders and two-thirds of the twelfth-graders in the public schools work after school. One-sixth of the eleventh-graders work more than twenty hours a week.[9] In many instances, it is not economic necessity that compels students to work. A recent survey in Austin, Texas, for example, revealed that 80 percent of the city's high school students hold some sort of job after school, and that the highest rate of employment was among affluent students. Rather, it is indifference to their education that seems to motivate many students to join the job market. "Anything for $3.35 an hour," said a junior at a high school north of Seattle. "School is a bore." A guidance counselor in an urban Texas high school told of several bright ninth-graders who deliberately performed poorly on standardized tests so as to qualify for a vocational work-study program that allowed them to leave the classroom at midday.

The failure of schools to motivate students also is reflected in high rates of class cutting and truancy throughout the nation. A 1985 study by two University of Oregon researchers revealed that secondary school students skip an average of 100 classes a year, the equivalent of 10 per-cent of the instruction in a typical school year. Daily truancy rates of 20 percent or more are commonplace in many secondary schools, especially in urban systems. A top official in one of Texas's largest school systems acknowledged to me that a new, statewide tutoring program for students who fail courses under Texas's new "no-pass, no-play" law has been "a total failure." "Students will not come," the official said. "They are in an alien environment from 8 [A.M.] to 4 [P.M.]. Why should they stay in it another hour?"

In many school systems truancy is so bad that educators have resorted to what can only be described as bribing students to come to school. One New Jersey town uses federal job-training funds to pay seventy potential dropouts $100 a month to stay in school; to earn the money, the students simply have to attend school daily, arrive on time, do their homework, and behave decently. At a Louisville, Kentucky, elementary school, students who meet attendance and behavior requirements get special checks that can be redeemed at a K-Mart "mini-store" located on the school's second floor that is part of a consumer-education program. And since 1988 Cleveland has paid its 33,000 students in grades seven through twelve $40 for every "A" they earn in an academic subject, $20 dollars for every "B," and $10 for every "C." No less desperately, West Virginia lawmakers in 1988 passed legislation revoking the driver's licenses of dropouts under the age of eighteen, and in Atlanta, officials in 1989 resorted to assigning police patrolmen to full-time truant duty. At least eight other states have gone down the same road as West Virginia.[10]

Further, the pervasive apathy and alienation among students and teachers in many schools engender what Theodore Sizer has called a "conspiracy of the least" in the classroom, a sort of unwritten, unspoken pledge between students and teachers to put as little energy as possible into their work. The then-superintendent of schools in the District of Columbia, Floretta D. McKensie, described the phenomenon in a 1986 issue of *Harper's* magazine. "So many of these [secondary-school] kids are just marking time," she said, "just playing the game to get through the day. And a good deal of the time teachers are doing the same thing, doing just enough to get through the hour. The two sides are partners; neither side pushes the other."[11]

The "conspiracy" is carried out in a number of often-subtle ways. Teachers start classes late and finish them early. They lead discussions off the assigned topic, filling time with irrelevant digressions. In *The Shopping Mall High School*, Arthur Powell describes an English teacher he observed who used nearly a full class period in an honors course to talk about an old girlfriend. The teacher later told Powell that he lectured on his teenage love life as a way of introducing his students to a unit on love in literature.[12] Many teachers lighten their work load and that of their students by assigning little or no homework. "I don't give homework," a Florida history teacher explained to me. "There are seven periods in the day; if they had thirty minutes of homework a night with each class, that's too much. They have to have some social life. I try to gear it so they can do the work in class." And many teachers simply don't bother to hold students to academic standards. "Kids who show up and who turn something in are going to pass, whether they master the material or not," said the chairperson of the English department of a California high school. A Texas English teacher who supervises a "learning lab" for remedial students commented that "over 50 percent of my students are students whose basic problem is that no one has ever demanded that they learn."

Students themselves say as much. "No one really cares if you work or not" a Texas senior told me. At a California high school I visited, it was *school policy* to allow students with good disciplinary records to go home early one day a week. In many classrooms, nothing more is expected of students than that they aren't disruptive. Keeping their classrooms free of hassles, rather than educating students, seems to be the first priority of many teachers. "It doesn't bother me at all if you are reading something else," a California algebra teacher told two students seated toward the back of his classroom, "but it bothers me when you talk to someone else about it." "Walkman" radio/cassette players are a not-uncommon sight in public school classrooms; wearing headphones, students listen impassively to the radio or tapes, totally disconnected from the activities in the class. Nor is it difficult to find classrooms with students asleep at their desks. At a suburban Texas high school I visited, a student slept head-in-arms at his desk in the front row of a history class, as the teacher, who was seated atop a table a few feet away, propped his feet on an uno portion of the student's desk.

In many public school classrooms, moreover, the time teachers are spend on the subject at hand also frequently is used in a manner that reinforces teachers' attempts to keep the level of engagement in their classes to a minimum. Lectures, by far the most widely used teaching format in the nation's secondary schools, assign a passive classroom role to students; they simply sit and listen. In a "Great Books" course at a suburban California high school I visited, the teacher spent fifty minutes delivering a "lecture" on Dickens's *Great Expectations* that merely summarized the book's plot. Not once during the class were students granted an opportunity to comment on the book. Similarly, teachers have students watch an inordinate number of films and filmstrips. In a world history classroom in an urban California high school I visited, the lights went out immediately after attendance was taken, and as they did, a student shouted, "Another movie?" In a sophomore English class at a rural Texas high school, the teacher showed a forty-minute filmstrip on William Shakespeare's life. None of the fifteen students in the class took notes as she read the commentary that accompanied the frames, and several slept through the entire exercise. The strip ended just before the conclusion of the period. The teacher asked, "What can you remember about the filmstrip?" "The clothes they wore, they were really different," said a student. Then the bell rang and the class dispersed. Students also spend a tremendous amount of class time working silently at their desks, doing workbook exercises, reading textbooks, or copying information from blackboards. Students in a biology class at a Florida high school I visited sat copying definitions from their textbooks to notepaper in preparation for a vocabulary quiz. In many classrooms I found students working silently on the next "homework" assignment.

The classroom conspiracy between alienated students and equally disaffected teachers thus is a major source of the bad pedagogy that pervades so many of the nation's public schools, especially in bottom-track courses. Lacking commitment to their work, teachers embrace poor teaching techniques because they are less demanding on both themselves and their students. Moreover, the reluctance of many teachers to set high standards for themselves in the classroom is perhaps the primary reason that so many public educators maintain that the majority of students are incapable of doing demanding academic work, and thus it undoubtedly has contributed significantly to the pervasiveness of tracking in public schools. By believing that many students can't handle academic work, teachers absolve themselves of the responsibility of teaching it to them. Instead of making the effort needed to exact high academic standards from all students, teachers relegate those who are more difficult to educate to bottom-track classes, where it's acceptable not to challenge students academically.

❧   The teaching strategies engendered by the conspiracy of the least also help to make many public school classrooms extraordinarily lifeless places, devoid of energy and enthusiasm. Given the aridness of instruction in so many classrooms, it's no wonder that students complain of boredom, which John Goodlad has called "a disease of epidemic proportions" in the nation's public schools. Moreover, the lifelessness of the instruction in many public schools renders the subject matter of their courses all but meaningless to many students. At a suburban California high school, a student in an advanced-placement history course (no less) told me, "History only satisfies people's curiosity of where they came from—that's it. There's no *need* for history. Who needs to know when Columbus came in order to get a job?"[13] The instruction in the nation's public schools typically fails to communicate to students either the intrinsic or the practical value of the subjects they study. On the contrary, the insipidness and seeming irrelevance of much teaching only further alienates students from their schools.

The educational consequences of the widespread alienation among students and teachers in the public schools thus are devastating. Both by tangible measures such as dropout and truancy rates, and in the less visible classroom compromises between students and teachers, teacher and student apathy takes a tremendous toll on the public schools' productivity. Yet demographic trends suggest that the nation may pay an even greater educational price for the alienating climate in many public secondary schools in the future. There is mounting evidence that the level of stability and support in the lives of many students is diminishing. And if that's so, the schools increasingly will be forced to rely on their own capacity to persuade students to dedicate themselves to their education.

As has been widely reported, the number of single-parent families has risen dramatically in recent years. Between 1970 and 1984, the proportion of the nation's households with children under eighteen that were headed by one adult doubled, from 13 percent to 26 percent, and demographers estimate that no less than 59 percent of the children born in 1983 will live in a one-parent home before reaching their eighteenth birthday. In a sign of the times, the teacher of a Virginia high school history class that I sat in on asked her students, "What did women of the Progressive Era want?" The first answer was not "The right to vote" but, rather, "Separate bank accounts if they got divorced." As a result of the increase in single-parent families and a dramatic rise in the proportion of working women, there are now as many as 7,000,000 "latch-key" students under the age of thirteen left at home alone before and after school.[14]

Meanwhile, the increasing mobility of the nation's work force has turned many students into virtual nomads, forced to forfeit friends and familiar surroundings as their parents shift them from town to town or from state to state in pursuit of new job opportunities. I visited a suburban Florida high school where virtually none of the graduates in the class of 1985 had attended the school as first-year students. Invariably, the constant uprooting that many students experience makes more difficult the schools' efforts to win the allegiance and the commitment of their students.

Recent demographic developments among the nation's disadvantaged may be particularly troubling to the schools. There has been a marked increase in out-of-wedlock births. Nearly 50 percent of all black women, for example, now have a child before their twentieth birthday, and nearly 90 percent of those births are illegitimate.[15] In all, nearly 60 percent of the nation's black babies are now born to unwed mothers, up from 33 percent twenty years ago. Further, the proportion of black households in the nation with a child under age eighteen headed by a single parent reached 60 percent in 1984, more than double the national average. According to the U.S. Census Bureau, single-parent families are four times more likely to live in poverty than two-parent families.

These trends threaten to diminish further the already weak reinforcement that disadvantaged students receive in their lives—at a time when such students are the fastest-growing portion of the school population. Indeed, the surge in teen pregnancy is partly a consequence of the tremendously low self-esteem of many disadvantaged teenagers. As the director of a Los Angeles center for teen mothers told *Time* magazine in an article on teen pregnancy: "The girls tell me, 'Before I was pregnant, I was nothing. Now I am somebody. I'm a mother.' "[16] Not surprisingly, the 1986 Educational Testing Service dropout study revealed that students from disadvantaged families leave high school at nearly four times the rate their affluent peers do. Only 7 percent of the affluent students among the nearly 30,000 high school sophomores in the study dropped out before they were scheduled to graduate in 1982, compared to about 26 percent of the low-income students in the study. The researchers also found that compared to the students in the study who graduated from high school, the dropouts had fewer "study aids" in their homes, had less opportunity for "non-school learning," had mothers with lower levels of education and with lower educational expectations for their children, were less likely to have both natural parents living at home, and had mothers who were more likely to be working—all characteristics of disadvantaged students.[17]

As a result, if schools themselves do not offer disadvantaged students a reason for taking their education seriously, the likelihood that such students will invest much of themselves in the classroom is small. As an administrator of New York City's Community School District 4, which serves 14,000 mostly poor black and Hispanic students in East Harlem, put it: "We have a lot of kids that bring baggage with them to school, lots of baggage. It has to be dealt with. It's not enough to say that the function of a school is to be open from 8:30 to 3:00. It's not enough to say we give the kids the academics and we can't help it if the parents are screwed up and the streets are screwed up. We have to deal with those things. I'm not saying that you stop class and have a therapy session, but if we don't reach these kids, they won't learn anything." Frequently, however, public schools only exacerbate the sense of alienation and purposelessness that frequently plagues disadvantaged students in their lives outside school.

There are school systems, nonetheless, where students and teachers are drawn into school life rather than alienated from it. Though all too uncommon in public education, such systems have successfully created school environments in which learning flourishes. What distinguishes the schools, whether they are in the nation's best neighborhoods or its bleakest, as indeed many are, is a strong sense of community: students and teachers feel a part of their schools and share a commitment to their success.

There are two ways, in particular, that school systems have engendered a sense of community within schools swiftly and successfully. The first is by permitting students to select the public schools they attend. That notion has been at the heart of a major strand of the excellence movement: the use of market forces to improve the performance of public schools.

A chorus of influential reformers has called for measures that would put public schools in competition for students. Allow students to be consumers, they have argued, allow them to choose where they get their education rather than assign them to a school on the basis of where they live, the traditional practice in public education, and schools will be compelled by the marketplace, by the threat of dissatisfied "customers" taking their "business" elsewhere, to ensure that the education they offer is a good one. This free-enterprise approach to school improvement is nothing if not radical, for it takes direct aim at the nation's celebrated neighborhood schools.

Free-market economists and their conservative allies have championed the expansion of market forces in education for a long time. In *Capitalism and Freedom* (1962) and *Free to Choose* (1979), for example, Nobel Prize-winning economist Milton Friedman derided public education as an inherently inefficient governmental, or "nationalized," monopoly. These traditional proponents of "consumer sovereignty" in education have promoted policies designed to encourage competition for students between public schools and private schools. In particular, they have pressed for tuition tax credits and educational vouchers that permit parents to use public funds to pay tuition at private schools.[18] Prohibitions against public support of private schools "protect most the worst public schools, those public schools that would be most depopulated by families' freedom to choose," argued the prominent sociologist James Coleman in a 1982 issue of *The Public Interest*.

The Reagan administration, itself a vocal advocate of an expanded marketplace in education, pressed for tuition tax credits and vouchers on the same grounds. "My belief in the tuition tax credit is a belief in competition," the president told a group of high school valedictorians at the White House in 1983. In 1982, 1983, and again in 1984, his administration submitted legislation to Congress calling for federal tax credits of up to $300 for parents paying private school tuition. In 1984, 1985, 1986, and 1987, it proposed legislation to distribute $3.7 billion in federal aid to disadvantaged students through a system of vouchers redeemable at either public or private schools. Neither initiative gained congressional approval. In 1983 the Department of Justice filed an *amicus* brief at the U.S. Supreme Court on behalf of a Minnesota tuition-tax-credit law that the Court eventually upheld that year in *Mueller v. Allen*.

The Reagan administration's advocacy of an expanded marketplace in education stemmed from its deep commitment to free enterprise and limited government. Indeed, calls within the school reform movement for greater consumer choice in elementary and secondary education are part of a wide-ranging reevaluation of the performance of government services and the role of government launched in the Reagan era, a reevaluation that has greatly increased the popularity of market-oriented ideas in public policy. In many areas of national life the new appeal of the marketplace has led to the "privatization" of public services. Seeking to supply services more efficiently with less government involvement, dozens of communities in at least fifteen states, for instance, have hired private fire departments, and in Kentucky and Florida, private corporations now own and operate maximum-security prisons under state and local contracts.[19]

But the majority of contemporary school reformers who back a marketplace approach to school improvement have rejected the traditional idea of public school–private school competition. They aggressively opposed the Reagan administration's calls for vouchers and tuition tax credits as a way of fostering such competition. And they have taken even less seriously those who have recommended the privatization of public education, the dismantling of it as a government service, and the replacement of it with a system of private providers. Government must be made to work more efficiently, but it is not itself the problem, some of the school reformers have said. Others have opposed vouchers, tax credits, and privatization out of a commitment to public education as a unifying national institution.

Instead, most of the reformers who support the use of market forces to spur school improvement have insisted that public schools compete only with one another for students. Yet *that* idea—of competition *among* public schools—has won influential supporters from across the political spectrum and among many camps within the reform movement.

As early as 1984 Governor Lamar Alexander of Tennessee, a Republican, called for the creation of "public-school vouchers" that parents would be free to redeem at the public school of their choice. "If no one buys Fords one year, the guy building them is fired and someone else is brought in to do the job," Alexander said at a policy forum in Washington, D.C. "A voucher plan would produce the same sort of change in education. If the line is long outside one school, it must have something good to offer; if the line isn't long, it's going to have to make improvements if it wants to stay in business."[20] The following year, Governor Rudy Perpich of Minnesota, a Democrat, unveiled a package of school reforms that had as its centerpiece a voucher proposal to permit any Minnesota student to attend any of the state's public schools.

Then a series of influential reports endorsed marketplace reforms. "Certain market incentives and disincentives can and should be introduced into public schooling," wrote the Committee for Economic Development, the consortium of corporate leaders and university presidents, in its 1985 report *Investing in Our Children*. Granting students the freedom to choose their school, said the committee, "would reward schools that meet the educational objectives of the families that select them and send a message to those schools that are bypassed." The next year, the bipartisan National Governors' Association wrote in *Time for Results: The Governors' 1991 Report on Education* that "choice plans . . . unlock the values of competition in the educational marketplace." "We believe that we can remain dedicated to a system of public schools, and still increase consumer sovereignty," the association argued in urging states to pass laws permitting families to choose among public schools. The Carnegie Corporation's task force on teaching also threw its weight behind the marketplace notion in 1986 when it wrote in *A Nation Prepared: Teachers for the 21st Century:* "Markets have proven to be very efficient instruments to allocate resources and motivate people in many sectors of American life. . . . They can also make it possible for all public-school students to gain access to equal school resources."[21]

Several prominent educators also backed marketplace reforms, including Bill Honig, the California superintendent of public instruction, and Albert Shanker. In addition to promoting professionalism in teaching, Shanker saw a marketplace in public education as a means of short-circuiting the Reagan administration-led campaign for tuition tax credits and vouchers. "Expanding public school choice—within schools, among schools in a district, among districts—would go a long way toward . . . getting rid of the notion that people are captives [within public education]," he said in his Niagara Falls speech.[22]

By 1989 "choice" was a dominant theme of the school-reform debate. In January, in the waning days of the second Reagan administration, the president and the president-elect, George Bush, sponsored the Workshop on Choice in Education at the White House, a full-day series of speeches and seminars promoting the choice concept. In an address to the gathering of 200 educators and political leaders, Bush termed expansion of parents' right to choose public schools a "national imperative." Significantly, neither Bush nor Reagan, who also addressed the workshop, mentioned vouchers or tuition tax credits.[23] Later in 1989 Secretary of Education Lauro F. Cavazos, who succeeded William Bennett in 1988, sponsored a series of regional meetings designed to encourage the development of choice plans in the states.

As the popularity of the marketplace approach to school reform has grown in recent years, so has the degree of choice within public education. A small but expanding number of school systems have implemented open-enrollment policies, permitting students to attend any appropriate school within a school system's borders. The first to do so was New York City's Community School District 4. Acting on the principle that "a school should get students because of the results it achieves, not simply because people live near it," as Anthony J. Alvarado, the district's former superintendent, said several years ago, District 4 in 1982–83 abolished its junior high school attendance zones and established in their place a system that permits any of its 3,500 junior high school students to apply to any of the twenty-two junior high school programs in the school system (New York City's thirty-two community school systems educate students through the eighth grade; the city's high schools are administered centrally). Each spring District 4 sends information to parents of sixth-graders describing its junior high programs, and parent associations hold informational meetings in each elementary school for sixth-graders and their parents preparing to select a program for the following school year. All sixth-graders then receive "option sheets," on which they rank the District 4 junior high programs that they want to attend. Then the school system places students in available programs, managing to enroll nearly all of them in one of their first three choices. The school systems in Rochester, New York (1988–89), East Baton Rouge, Louisiana (1988–89), and New York City's Community School District 2 (1988–89) are among the others that recently have launched open-enrollment programs to stimulate school improvement.

The only apparent precedent for open enrollment in American public education was the use of "freedom-of-choice" plans in the late 1950s and 1960s by 2,000 or so southern school systems seeking to circumvent the spirit of the U.S. Supreme Court's prohibition in *Brown v. Board of Education* of dual educational systems for blacks and whites. By permitting all students of both races to attend the schools of their choice within their school systems, the plans technically ended dual systems. In reality they left the status quo largely unaltered (a small percentage of black students attended white schools, and virtually no white students attended black schools), and Congress and the courts soon demanded that southern school systems take more aggressive steps to desegregate their classrooms.[24]

A number of desegregating school systems have been in the vanguard of the present open-enrollment movement, however, seeking to enhance desegregation through voluntary student transfers. The Cambridge, Massachusetts, school system, for instance, adopted a "controlled" open-enrollment policy in 1982–83, permitting parents to send their children to any one of the school system's thirteen primary schools (which include grades kindergarten through eighth grade), as long as space is available in the schools they choose (parents choose three schools in order of preference), and as long as the selection process doesn't increase the segregation of black and white students in the school system. The Fall River, Massachusetts, school system introduced a controlled open-enrollment plan similar to that in Cambridge in 1986–87, one of several Massachusetts systems to do so. It divides the city into four quadrants, each containing a middle school and up to a dozen feeder elementary schools. Parents are permitted to apply for their children's admission to any of the feeder schools in their quadrant, as long as their choices don't impede desegregation efforts. Similarly, the Boston School Committee has implemented a controlled-choice plan that divides the city into three zones, with equal numbers of elementary, middle, and high schools in each. Beginning in 1990–91, Boston's 55,000 students will be permitted to attend any school within their particular zones, as long as racial guidelines are met. In addition, the plan requires the school system to assist undersubscribed schools, but it also grants officials the authority, in instances where there is no improvement in enrollment within three years, to remove such schools' principals, reorganize their curricula, consolidate them with other schools, or close them. The Seattle, Washington, school system implemented a similar open-enrollment plan in 1989–90, as the centerpiece of a revamped desegregation campaign. In Massachusetts, open-enrollment schools recruit new students through state-funded parent-information centers. The centers "sell" the schools by taking out advertisements in local newspapers, promoting them at local nursery schools (in instances where open enrollment is limited to elementary schools), and sponsoring "meet-the-principal nights," at which parents can assess the schools' leaders.

Meanwhile, several states have established open-enrollment systems permitting students to transfer *between* school districts. Minnesota is one. Governor Perpich's radical public school voucher proposal died in the 1985 Minnesota legislature after dominating the session, despite the fact that the governor had fought hard for his "Access to Excellence" legislation, recruiting respected and politically astute legislative sponsors, personally lobbying lawmakers on behalf of the bill, and making twenty trips across Minnesota over a two-and-a-half-month period to kindle grass-roots support for open enrollment. His efforts generated an intense statewide debate on an issue unknown to most Minnesotans previously, but the bill fell victim to a tremendous lobbying campaign by the state's powerful education associations, which couldn't bear the thought of competition sorting out "winners" and "losers" among the state's schools and school systems. The Minnesota Education Association, the National Education Association's state affiliate, led the attack against the legislation. "We see [open enrollment] as mass chaos," the MEA's executive director said in the midst of the legislative fight over the Perpich bill. "It won't motivate teachers to do better work. . . . It's an effort to cut costs. You ought to offer everything to everyone in every school district. They are attacking the public school system in America."[25] To counter Perpich's statewide barnstorming on behalf of open enrollment, the MEA produced a six-minute videotape excoriating the idea and distributed copies of it to forty television stations in Minnesota and surrounding states. The tape asserted—erroneously—that open enrollment "was for rich kids" and that it "would destroy programs for educating the handicapped." It also charged that school systems would "use pretty cheerleaders to sell students on coming to their schools." "Sometimes reasonable positions aren't listened to," said the MEA's executive director in defense of the tape. Open enrollment was amended out of the Perpich bill in the education committee of the Minnesota House of Representatives by one vote, fourteen to thirteen, on a motion proposed by Representative Leonard Price, a social studies teacher and a member of the MEA's board of directors.[26]

But in 1987, after Perpich had successfully turned public opinion against the state's education establishment (in 1985 Minnesotans opposed open enrollment two to one; in 1987 they supported it by the same margin), the Minnesota legislature created an optional open-enrollment program: students were allowed to enroll elsewhere in the state so long as their home school systems permitted them to do so. The following year, 1988, the legislature stripped school systems of the right to block transfers. As a result, beginning in 1990–91 Minnesota students will be able to attend any school system that declares itself open to students from beyond its borders, so long as the racial balance in desegregating school systems is not disrupted. Transferring students are required to supply their own transportation to the border of their new school systems, though state subsidies are granted to disadvantaged students. The key to the program's effectiveness as a marketplace incentive to school improvement is its provision that Minnesota's per-pupil education aid "follow" students to their new school systems. "We decided that since in education money talks, we would empower the parents," said Lani Kawamura, Perpich's chief policy adviser, in describing the legislation's intent. "Schools were playing to a captive audience. We wanted to give students the right to vote with their feet. We reasoned that once they had that right, their neighborhood school would pay a lot more attention to them and to their teachers."[27] Meanwhile, the one element of Perpich's 1985 open-enrollment package that did survive the legislative battle that year has further increased the degree of choice in the state's high schools. The so-called postsecondary option program permits eleventh- and twelfth-graders to take courses in colleges, universities, and postsecondary vocational schools in the state at no cost; tuition for "option" students is set at the level of per-pupil aid Minnesota pays to school systems, and the state merely transfers the students' aid from their school systems to the postsecondary institutions in which they are enrolled.[28]

As revolutionary as Minnesota's open-enrollment legislation was, lawmakers in five other states—Nebraska, Iowa, Ohio, Arkansas, and Colorado—enacted similar measures in 1989 and 1990. Yet the new open-enrollment programs have many of the weaknesses that have prohibited the Minnesota program from reaching its full potential as a marketplace reform; only 3,790 of Minnesota's 735,000 public school students applied to transfer school under open enrollment in 1990–91. Like Minnesota, Arkansas (where open enrollment begins in 1990–91) and Ohio (1993–94) permit school systems to refuse to accept transfers. All of the open-enrollment states have barred transfers that diminish the racial balance of desegregating school systems, which further diminishes the size of the marketplace for students. In Minnesota, for example, virtually no white students have been permitted to leave Minneapolis, St. Paul, or Duluth, the state's three largest school systems. Parents in Minnesota seeking to take advantage of open enrollment also have been hampered by a lack of such basic information about schools as course offerings, while many less-well-educated low-income Minnesota parents are unfamiliar with open enrollment itself. As a result, the state's program has been used least by inner-city minority students, who arguably have the greatest to gain from open enrollment. To remedy the problem, Minnesota launched an initiative in 1989 to publicize the program through churches, welfare offices, and even fast-food restaurants because many of them employ minority students.

Transportation is another problem for disadvantaged students. Arkansas requires transferring students to supply their own transportation, though the state reimburses both home and receiving school systems if they bus transferring students. Like Minnesota, Ohio requires students to provide their own transportation to the border of their new school system. But Minnesota's reimbursements to disadvantaged students for carfare aren't much help to poor parents lacking cars. Also, the long distances that many students would have to travel to attend another school system make open enrollment an impracticality for them. Not surprisingly, many parents have selected schools out of convenience—

such as a school's proximity to another child's day care center—rather than for academic reasons. Though such decisions are perfectly legitimate, they don't provide any incentive to schools losing students to make academic improvements. Finally, the effectiveness of the state-sponsored interdistrict open-enrollment programs is diminished by the fact that students participate in them voluntarily. They must "choose to choose" a new school system. In contrast, the marketplace pressures are much stronger under *intra*district open-enrollment schemes such as those in Community School District 4 and Cambridge, Massachusetts, where students *must* select the school they attend, even if that means choosing to attend their neighborhood school. Says Richard Elmore, a Michigan State University education professor: "The stakes are much higher when all students are put in motion." Ohio and Colorado are requiring intradistrict open enrollment statewide. But both programs are voluntary for students, and Colorado requires students to supply their own transportation.

Despite the spread of open enrollment, the primary impetus for the recent expansion of choice in public education has been an enormous increase in recent years in the number of "magnet" schools, specialized programs that draw students from beyond the boundaries of regular attendance zones. Ironically, they were not designed to create competition among schools, at least not originally.

A few academically elite public schools—such as the Bronx High School of Science, Boston Latin, and Lane Tech in Chicago—have had citywide and competitive admissions policies for a long time, but it was two developments in the 1960s that set the stage for the recent magnet-school boom. One was the decision by policymakers to enlist magnets in the campaign to desegregate the nation's schools. The first magnet school built to contribute to a desegregation plan was established by the Boston School Committee in 1967, in the predominantly black neighborhood of Roxbury. The school offered a special advanced academic curriculum, and its mission was to reduce "racial isolation" within the Boston school system by drawing talented white students voluntarily into Roxbury. Magnets gained popularity as a less coercive alternative to integrating school systems through the mandatory busing of students across attendance zones, a hugely controversial practice that became widespread after the U.S. Supreme Court in the landmark 1971 case *Swann v. Charlotte-Mecklenburg* upheld a busing plan imposed on North Carolina's Charlotte-Mecklenburg school system by a federal judge in 1970. As a result, the Boston model soon spread to other desegregating school systems. Thus today's open-enrollment plans in Cambridge, Boston, Seattle, and elsewhere extend the concept of voluntary transfers first embodied in magnet schools.

The Supreme Court gave the fledgling magnet movement a further boost when in the 1974 case *Milliken v. Bradley* it forbade busing plans that involved sending students from one school system into another—from a city school system to a suburban system, for example—except in cases where all school systems involved in the plan had been proven guilty of intentionally segregating students. The Court forbade such interdistrict busing even in cases where busing was the only apparent remedy for segregation in a school system. Magnets, as a result, became one of the only viable desegregation alternatives for many urban school systems.

The second source of magnet programs was the discontent of the neo-Progressives during the 1960s with the climate and pedagogy of public schools. That discontent led to the establishment of many "alternative" schools in public education. And they, too, frequently admitted students without regard to traditional attendance zones. Their specific approaches varied, but the alternative schools generally sought a more child-centered system of instruction than was found in regular public schools. They took their pedagogical bearings from *Summerhill* and the other influential neo-Progressive educational treatises of the period. As a result, the early alternative schools were distinguished by their nontraditional teaching methods, while the desegregation magnets typically used a specialized curriculum, such as the arts or math and science, to attract students. Yet both types of schools are "magnets" in a broad sense, for they both offer students something educationally special and they both draw students voluntarily from beyond regular attendance boundaries. In many school systems, alternative schools are now used as desegregation magnets.[29]

In addition to being an early catalyst of magnet programs, school desegregation has figured prominently in the recent spread of magnets. Courts increasingly have approved desegregation plans that rely heavily on magnets. Chicago's latest school-desegregation plan, approved in 1983, led to the creation of seventy magnet programs in the city's school system, for example, and in 1986 the Kansas City school system won approval from a federal appellate court to remedy a desegregation order by creating fifty-three magnet programs. Under the plan, all of the city's high schools and junior high schools, and over half of its elementary schools are scheduled to become magnets by 1991. Court-ordered desegregation agreements with magnet proponents have been signed in recent years in Cincinnati, Phoenix, and St. Paul, as well.

The revival and expansion of a federal desegregation-assistance program first established in 1976 also have fueled the magnet movement. Despite its professed support for voluntary school-desegregation techniques and its adamant opposition to mandatory busing, the Reagan administration sought and won elimination of the program (which provided funds to desegregating school systems for the establishment of magnets) in the Omnibus Budget Reconciliation Act of 1981. But Congress created a new program—over the administration's objections—under the Education for Economic Security Act of 1984. In fiscal 1989 it provided $113 million in federal magnet funds to desegregating school systems from San Diego, California, to Providence, Rhode Island. Congress also established another magnet program in 1988 specifically to help school systems increase parental choice, but it did not fund the program in fiscal 1989.[30]

The excellence movement itself has engendered new magnet schools, as policymakers have sought to respond to calls for advanced programs for high-achieving students. Further, school officials have viewed the creation of academic magnets as a way of stemming the defection of students to private schools that has slowly but steadily eroded public school enrollments over the past decade. In addition to the statewide public boarding schools established by North Carolina and half a dozen other states, scores of local school systems have launched new academic magnets in recent years.

Also, there has been a spate of new corporate-sponsored magnets, programs funded by and in some instances operated in tandem with businesses seeking ways to improve the vocational training of prospective employees, especially in the cities. General Motors, Xerox, and Control Data, for example, are among the corporations that fund magnets in the District of Columbia in communications, computer sciences, engineering, hotel and restaurant management, and finance.

The only systematic survey of magnets that has been conducted, a 1982 study sponsored by the U.S. Department of Education, identified 1,090 magnet programs (some magnets are schools unto themselves, others are "schools" within schools) in the nation's 84,000 public elementary and secondary schools. But anecdotal evidence alone suggests that the number of magnets is now far higher—as high as 10,000, according to some estimates—and growing. Not all magnets are educationally sound; the instruction in many vocationally oriented programs, in particular, is suspect. Moreover, perhaps a third of the nation's magnets have selective admissions policies, and thus represent alternatives only to high-achieving students.[31]

Nonetheless, students increasingly are able to select from a wide range of magnet programs in many school systems, especially in urban school systems. In Los Angeles alone, 24,000 students attend eighty-five magnet programs, ranging from the King-Drew Medical Center High School, a program for students interested in the medical and health professions that is housed in a postgraduate medical school next to a downtown hospital, to the Animal and Biological Sciences Center, a program located at the Los Angeles Zoo for tenth-, eleventh-, and twelfth-graders; nearly one-third of Buffalo's schools now house magnet programs as varied as Native American studies, visual arts, and bilingual education; among the magnets in St. Louis, where 8,000 students are enrolled in twenty-eight programs, are four visual-and-performing-arts programs, a military school, and a mass-media program; Pittsburgh's twenty-two magnet programs include a "classical academy," a program with a curriculum that emphasizes the cultures of ancient Greece and Rome; and in Milwaukee, where 20,000 of the school system's 89,000 students are enrolled in one of the city's forty magnets, students can select from programs with themes ranging from environmental studies to agri-business.

Where it is well established, the marketplace in public education seems to work. In school systems in which students are granted the opportunity to select their schools, there is competition among schools for students. And such competition, it appears, does act as an incentive for schools to improve themselves.

Turning students into consumers has had a dramatic effect in District 4 in New York City, for example. Since introduction of open enrollment in 1982–83, two of the school system's four comprehensive junior high schools have been closed for lack of students. Students abandoned them in favor of magnets created before open enrollment was introduced and a variety of new and often innovative programs that have been established in the buildings that once housed the two schools. The two remaining comprehensive junior highs have established new academic programs to attract students. As popular programs have grown, the school system has assigned them additional space. "No school is going to stand still in the face of competition," said Seymour Fliegel, a District 4 deputy superintendent for many years. "I recall when a principal would say you can't come to my junior high school because you don't live in this zone. Today, that same principal is running around the district with his Kodak carousel selling his school."[32]

Principals in District 4 who have failed to compete successfully for students have been stripped of much of their authority. Lifelong tenure makes it virtually impossible to fire a principal in New York City ("I don't care what happens, they've got to give me a job somewhere," the principal of Junior High School 14 told me just before District 4 closed the school in 1985). As an alternative, District 4 has transferred control of educational programs to a cadre of "directors" (the majority of whom are senior teachers) and made unsuccessful principals "building managers" with responsibility for safety, transportation, food services, room assignments, and other schoolwide activities.

District 4's administrators readily acknowledge that there are students who don't exercise their choice of junior high programs judiciously. "Sure, we have children who make choices on the basis of, 'Well, my friend Tommy is going there, so I'm going there, too,'" said Fliegel. A ninth-grader explained to me that she decided to attend the district's Maritime Academy because the school provides students the opportunity to swim three times a week. Fliegel also acknowledged that open enrollment hasn't produced uniformly strong programs in the school system.

Yet, although District 4 had hundreds of empty classrooms in 1980, it now attracts over 1,000 students from other parts of New York City. That many students probably wouldn't venture into East Harlem's often-dangerous neighborhoods if they and their parents didn't think it was educationally worth their while to do so. And even though District 4 is in one of New York's most blighted sections and has one of the city's densest concentrations of impoverished students, it outperforms half of the city's other community school systems on citywide exams.

The impact of open enrollment has been much the same in District 4's central Harlem neighbor, Community School District 5, where students have had to select their junior high school for a number of years. Unpopular schools have closed and new magnet programs have proliferated. In Cambridge, Massachusetts, school system officials replaced the principal and revised the curriculum of the elementary school that attracted the fewest students under the open-enrollment program launched in Cambridge in 1982–83. The school now ranks first among the city's thirteen elementary schools on citywide tests of basic skills. "The choice process acts as a referendum in which parents judge the relative effectiveness of each school," concluded Michael Alves, then an official in the Massachusetts Bureau of Equal Education Opportunity, in a 1986 evaluation of the Cambridge plan. Nearly two-thirds of Cambridge's elementary school students are now enrolled in schools outside their attendance area. And the proportion of Cambridge students attending public rather than private or parochial schools has increased from 70 percent to 90 percent since the inception of open enrollment.[33] Another measure of the marketplace power of choice in public education is the huge number of applications received by magnet programs. In Prince Georges County, Maryland, 4,300 students apply for the 1,500 spaces in forty-two magnets established by the school system since 1985. And in Buffalo, no fewer than 10,000 students have sought one of the 2,200 openings in the city's magnets in recent years.[34]

Meanwhile, Minnesota education authorities report that since the introduction of the state's postsecondary-options program in 1985–86, many school systems have taken steps to make themselves more attractive to their eleventh- and twelfth-grade students. Many have increased their Advanced Placement offerings; according to state figures, the number of AP courses taught in Minnesota high schools quadrupled between 1985–86 and 1988–89. Many have established cooperative programs with local colleges, so that students may earn college credits without leaving their school systems. And there has been a sharp increase in the number of arrangements between small school systems to "pair" their high schools, enabling them to offer a wider range of courses. By 1990 nearly 10,000 students were participating in the Minnesota postsecondary-options program, and nine other states had established similar programs.[35] Similarly, school administrators report that the creation of magnet schools—be they for advanced students or not—has compelled their nonmagnet counterparts to upgrade programs. "The non-magnet schools feel a need to compete for students, and, as a result, many non-magnets do as well, if not better, than the magnets," the superintendent of the Buffalo school system told a newspaper interviewer in 1987.[36]

The spread of a marketplace in public education has the potential to help resolve the conflict within the excellence movement between regulatory reforms and the push for school-based management and other initiatives that grant greater authority to educators in schools. As researchers John E. Chubb and Terry M. Moe have argued in work sponsored by the Brookings Institution, the introduction of a marketplace into public education through student choice creates the accountability that the reformers have sought while diminishing the need for prescriptive mandates. A marketplace, they have reasoned, makes it possible to free schools from many external rules and regulations, and thus to grant teachers and principals a greater degree of autonomy because the power of students to abandon bad schools spurs educators to do their best work. Such a strategy of "deregulating" schools is by itself insufficient. Local educators do not merely need to be freed of their bureaucratic shackles. They also need to be trained in new management methods and teaching techniques, or, once granted a greater say in the running of their schools, they are likely to perpetuate the failed educational strategies of the past because those are typically the only strategies that they know. Clearly, however, the marketplace is a far superior source of accountability in public education than standardized testing.[37]

Yet, if permitting students to select the schools they attend represents a powerful force for reform in public education, the reason has as much to do with the capacity of choice to engender a sense of community in schools as it does with the market forces choice creates. Where students have a say in where they attend school, they frequently develop strong ties to the schools they select; having invested in their schools, they typically share in the schools' identities. That sense of ownership, in turn, seems to be a powerful source of motivation among students; it seems to strengthen greatly their dedication to their studies. "The key is ownership, and ownership comes from choice," said Seymour Fliegel during a discussion I had in 1985 with District 4 administrators about their "open-zoning" policy. "The more children you have that really want to be in a certain place because that place gives them something that they want, the more they are going to put themselves into it. With open zoning, you have a much greater chance of having the child in a place where the child really wants to be. You are able to get kids in schools where there is perhaps more commitment on their part to performing."[38]

Students' identification with their schools is further enhanced when they are permitted to select from among schools that are educationally special. Students in magnet schools, for example, are keenly aware of the distinctiveness of their programs—be it a curriculum emphasizing math and science or a commitment to interdisciplinary instruction—and they identify with it strongly. Among many magnet students, the specialness of their schools is a tremendous source of pride. The educator Arthur G. Powell has written about schools that "a common purpose makes the institution itself an active factor in the educational process, rather than merely a neutral physical setting in which education goes on," and his observation seems to be particularly apt in regard to magnet schools and the connection students make to their various themes.[39] Indeed, Fliegel noted that District 4 has established a wide range of magnet programs in recent years—the school system currently offers fifty-two programs in twenty school buildings—largely to tap the ability of such programs to motivate students. "The concepts [of the magnets] are vehicles," he said. "At the performing-arts schools, we aren't trying to train actors, we're using the arts to draw kids into the learning process, we're using them as vehicles to teach academic subjects. . . . If the concept schools don't raise academic achievement, they've failed."

There is strong evidence suggesting that the strategy works, that permitting students to select from among distinctive programs (a far cry from Joe Clark's bat-and-bullhorn tactics) does "draw kids into the learning process." A comprehensive 1985 study of magnet schools in eight New York cities, for example, revealed higher attendance rates and lower dropout and suspension rates in magnets than in nonmagnets in the school systems studied—Buffalo, Syracuse, Mount Vernon, Newburgh, New Rochelle, New York, Poughkeepsie, and Rochester. And importantly, the magnets were primarily inner-city schools with large minority enrollments and nonselective admissions policies. A total of 29 percent of the first-year students in the magnets failed to graduate from high school, versus 41 percent of nonmagnet students in the eight cities. The New York State Department of Education sponsored study also revealed that in Rochester, the only city that collected such statistics, there were lower student-suspension rates in magnets than in the school system generally in the majority of the junior high school and high school grades.[40]

The New York magnet study also surveyed teachers and principals, who reported a high level of "school spirit and pride" in their schools. Likewise, a 1988 study by the Montgomery County, Maryland, school system of its fourteen elementary magnet programs reported that "in spite of their travel to a school outside of their immediate neighborhoods and the adjustments to new surroundings and friends, magnet transfer pupils report higher liking for school [than] their classmates," for whom the magnets are their neighborhood schools.[41] At several urban magnets I visited, students voluntarily attended school on Saturdays and routinely remained after school to work informally with their teachers.

The positive attitude toward learning among students permitted to select their schools typically translates into greater academic achievement. In the New York study, students in magnet schools outperformed their peers in a control group of nonmagnets over a ten-year period on New York's reading and math tests. The study also reported "substantial increases" in academic achievement in the magnets compared to their performance prior to becoming specialized schools; the largest gains were registered in "minority schools," those with over 90 percent minority enrollment, where scores rose nearly 30 percent following reorganization of the schools into magnets. Similarly, 80 percent of the schools in the 1983 U.S. Department of Education-sponsored evaluation of magnets reported average achievement-test scores that were higher than their school system averages—despite the fact that only 31 percent of the magnets studied had competitive admissions policies. In New York's District 4, the proportion of students reading at national norms reached 64 percent in 1986, compared to 15 percent in the early 1970s, before the school system began creating magnet programs. In addition, the number of District 4 students admitted annually to New York City's four specialized high schools with admissions examinations increased from 10 to 250 during the same period.[42]

In some instances schools reinforce the sense of ownership that choice and special themes engender by requiring students to fulfill school-related responsibilities outside the classroom. District 4's Central Park East Secondary School, for example, requires all its students to contribute two hours of work a week to the school or the surrounding community, doing such things as readying science experiments, manning the circulation desk in the library, serving food in the cafeteria, delivering food to shut-ins, or working as tour guides at the nearby Museum of the City of New York. Similarly, at the Louisiana School for Math, Science, and the Arts, a 600-student public boarding school established by Louisiana in 1983, students serve meals and do other on-campus tasks, and are required to do community-service work in Natchitoches, where the school is located. By way of contrast, Stanford education professor Henry M. Levin has pointed out that virtually all students in Japanese public schools spend a part of the school day cleaning and maintaining their schools, "a collective activity that gives them a sense of ownership and pride."[43]

Another motivating technique is peer tutoring. A 1986 report prepared for the Carnegie Forum on Education and the Economy entitled "Students as Teachers" noted that peer teaching and tutoring programs frequently "claim dramatic changes in self-confidence and self-image as well as higher motivation to learn and to achieve" among students who teach or tutor other students. "The literature is replete with anecdotes of alienated, troublesome youths conducting themselves in a serious and dignified manner while teaching younger students," the report concluded. Further, it said, there's substantial evidence that the academic achievement of both tutors and tutees improves markedly.[44]

Many teachers also identify strongly with educationally special schools such as magnets. Teachers are frequently attracted to magnets out of a particular interest in the subject matter emphasized by the schools, or because they are sympathetic to the schools' educational philosophy. In St. Petersburg, Florida, teachers at the successful International Baccalaureate magnet at St. Petersburg High School are hired on the basis of their commitment to the program's use of interdisciplinary instruction. Similarly, a teacher recruited from South Carolina to teach at Louisiana's new public math and science boarding school said he was drawn to the school by its "cohesion, its sense of shared goals." In many magnet schools teachers play a direct role in designing their schools' distinctive curriculum or teaching style. And in a few instances teachers actually have been placed in charge of specialized schools. District 4 has appointed senior teachers as "directors" of its many magnets largely to increase teachers' sense of ownership of their schools, and thereby strengthen their dedication to their work, according to the school system's administrators. Far from being functionaries in a bureaucratically controlled instructional system, District 4 directors are granted the authority to hire staff teachers and to shape their schools' curricula.[45] Said one District 4 administrator of the school system's policy: "When teachers have a piece of the action, they care more." Similarly, Minneapolis has appointed "head teachers" to lead several of its magnet programs. In addition to doing their own teaching, they coordinate the work of the other teachers in their specialized programs and coordinate administrative duties with the principals in the schools where the magnets are housed.

Further, the distinctive curricula or instructional strategies of magnet schools require teachers to work together closely, thereby reducing the sense of isolation that many teachers complain of and creating a healthy measure of accountability through peer pressure; in an environment where teachers are working as a specialized team, there's a greater incentive for teachers to motivate colleagues who aren't pulling their weight. Two-thirds of the teachers and principals surveyed in the 1985 New York magnet study said that teachers were actively involved in school decision making; three-fourths said that there were "positive staff relations" in the magnets; and four-fifths responded that there was a good working environment in the schools.[46] Again, the majority of the schools in the study were located in beleaguered urban neighborhoods. Moreover, since students are present voluntarily, pride is also a motivating factor among teachers in magnet schools and where open-enrollment plans are operating; as a Minneapolis magnet teacher told me, "It makes a difference when they are selecting *your* program rather than *a* program."

The heightened sense of identification of many magnet teachers with their schools seems to be as significant a source of motivation among teachers as it is among students. The teacher attrition rate among the schools in the 1985 New York magnet study, for instance, dropped from an average of 25 percent annually in the schools' premagnet eras to nearly half that level in 1985. In Buffalo and Poughkeepsie, the decrease was even more pronounced, from 31 percent to 13 percent and from 29 percent to 12 percent, respectively.[47] Magnets and open-enrollment schools also report lower rates of teacher absenteeism. And the enthusiasm one finds in many magnet classrooms contrasts sharply, particularly in city schools, with the uninspiring instruction that pervades much of public education. The teachers in District 4, as an example, are tough urban educators; they have no illusions about the often-difficult students they work with, but many care, and they make a difference.

The leadership roles played by teachers in many magnet programs complement the recent "restructuring" experiments in site-based management and shared decision making that are a key element of the teacher-professionalization campaign. The authority granted to magnet teachers in Minneapolis and East Harlem closely parallels that envisioned in the Carnegie "lead-teacher" idea as a way of "empowering" teachers and thereby making teaching a more attractive occupation to the best and brightest in the nation's work force. Conversely, by granting teachers a greater say in the running of their schools, the "restructuring" experiments in Miami, Rochester, and elsewhere have increased teachers' sense of ownership. And in doing so, in increasing teachers' stake in their schools' success, they have created a powerful incentive for teachers to work harder. Thus, the recent experiments in shared decision making and site-based management represent a potentially potent antidote to the alienation and apathy that pervade so many public school faculties. Indeed, one Miami school has reported that teacher absenteeism is down 50 percent since the introduction of site-based decision making in the Dade County school system in 1987.

Significantly, the notion of employee "ownership" has figured prominently in recent efforts by business and industry to bolster the productivity of the American workplace. In their best-selling 1982 study of the nation's "best-run companies," *In Search of Excellence,* Thomas J. Peters and Robert H. Waterman, Jr., identified a shared sense of ownership as a key ingredient of successful organizations. "Culture," a common set of values and goals within an organization, was an "essential quality" of excellent companies, they concluded; employees were "invested" in the companies' goals and they "subscribed" to their values.[48] By 1989, *Business Week* reported in a cover story titled "The Payoff from Teamwork," an increasing number of major corporations, including Digital Equipment, General Electric, Boeing, and LTV Steel, had adopted employee "ownership" as an organizational priority, replacing traditional assembly-line work with "self-managing" teams responsible for large blocks of the production process or, in some instances, completed products. The five-to-fifteen-member teams typically were granted wide latitude in organizing themselves, and they frequently assumed managerial responsibilities, such as ordering materials or setting schedules. Granting employees greater authority in the workplace increased productivity by 30 percent or more, *Business Week* reported, and raised product quality substantially. The magazine concluded that in companies where self-managing teams have been introduced, they have "permanently altered the old industrial relations system, based on the idea that efficient mass-production inevitably breeds alienated workers who must be bought off with high pay. [Employee participation in workplace management] puts the lie to that assumption. When jobs are challenging, workers are committed and perform superbly."[49] The experiments in restructuring teachers' roles in Rochester, Miami, and several other cities represent the potential beginnings of a comparable revolution in public education, where teachers have played assembly-line roles in a factory model of organization since the turn of the century.

A second way that school systems have achieved a sense of community in their schools effectively and relatively easily is by reducing educational settings to a more human scale.

In an extraordinarily influential 1959 report titled *The American High School Today*, former Harvard University President James B. Conant convinced the nation that secondary schools should be large and "comprehensive." Such schools, he argued, were able to offer students a sufficiently broad curriculum through economies of scale, and, in tending to the educational needs of all students "under one roof," were an important source of the "democratic spirit" in public education. "I can sum up my conclusions in a few sentences. The number of small high schools must be drastically reduced through district reorganization," Conant wrote in a section entitled "A Unique Feature: The Comprehensive High School." "Aside from this important change," he added, "I believe no radical alteration in the basic pattern of American education is necessary in order to improve our public high schools."[50] Conant's charge that small schools represented "one of the serious obstacles to good secondary education throughout most of the United States" quickened a nascent movement to consolidate school systems, and within a decade of the release of his report, the number of public school systems shrank from over 40,000 to under 18,000. And though "small" to Conant meant schools with a senior class of less than 100 students, his pronouncements on comprehensiveness led educators to think in terms of vastly larger secondary schools. In New York City that meant designing high schools of 4,000 students.

Conant's defense of large schools has continued to resonate within public education. Illinois, Arkansas, South Carolina, Georgia, and Nebraska all have acted to increase the size of their schools and school systems in recent years. The Georgia State Board of Education, for instance, in 1986 began earmarking state funds to pay 75 percent of the cost of constructing new high schools with at least 970 students, as an incentive for school systems to consolidate their secondary schools.[51]

But by the measure of the alienation and apathy that so pervade the nation's large, comprehensive secondary schools today, Conant was wrong. In their failure to create an environment conducive to teaching and learning, such schools are educationally inefficient, and in their imposition of an extraordinary burden on disadvantaged students, they are profoundly undemocratic.

A small number of school systems, however, have rejected Conant's doctrine. They have abandoned their commitment to comprehensive secondary schools in favor of organizational arrangements that encourage closer ties between the students, teachers, and administrators within them. Some have sought to subdivide comprehensive schools. The Columbus, Ohio, school system, for instance, has created a "house" system in several of its seventeen high schools. The schools have been reorganized into largely autonomous units, each with an administrator, a team of teachers, a guidance counselor, and approximately 250 students who remain together throughout their high school careers. Students complete the bulk of their core academic studies in courses taught by their house teachers. Columbus plans to eventually expand the program citywide.

On a much larger scale the New York City school board several years ago mandated creation of ninth-grade "houses" in each of New York's 110 high schools. Progress toward that goal has been slow and imperfect, studies suggest. But there have been notable developments in several schools, including 3,000-student Theodore Roosevelt High School in the Bronx, where the ninth and tenth grades have been divided into "interest clusters" of 175 to 250 students. Each cluster has an academic theme, and each has its own "coordinating teacher," guidance counselor, and paraprofessionals.

Other school systems have created small, autonomous educational programs within their comprehensive secondary schools. The spread of magnets, in particular, has increased the number of such "schools-within-schools" in recent years, since at the high school level many magnets are organized as small, independent programs rather than as whole-school initiatives. Many secondary magnets thus furnish both educational choice and smaller school settings.

The 400-student International Baccalaureate magnet in St. Petersburg, Florida, is one such school-within-a-school. Established in 1984, the four-year program operates largely independently within St. Petersburg High School, with its own administrator and teachers, a specialized liberal arts curriculum, and separate admissions procedures. Similarly, the Minneapolis school system houses an "open-education" magnet in a wing of the city's comprehensive South High School. The program enrolls 410 students in grades nine through twelve. Its staff includes a "head teacher" and a faculty of eight that designs the program's interdisciplinary curriculum. Unlike South High students, students in the open-education program live throughout Minneapolis. Both groups of students participate in nonacademic and extracurricular activities together.

As in St. Petersburg, the Minneapolis program is for high-achieving students. In Philadelphia, in contrast, school officials, in cooperation with a consortium of local businesses known as the Committee to Support Philadelphia Public Schools, have established a network of eleven self-contained "academies" within the city's most troubled high schools that combines academic and vocational training with on-the-job experience. The academies are small and offer training in such areas as health and electronics. The 160 students in the Business Academy at Strawberry Mansion High School, for example, study data processing, bookkeeping, and computer use in addition to the academic instruction they receive from a teaching team that remains with students for the three-year duration of the program. Similar school-within-a-school academies have been launched under joint school-business auspices in Portland, Oregon, Pittsburgh, and twenty-one California cities, where local businesses provide equipment, mentors, and summer jobs for students.[52]

In a few instances, school systems seeking a more human scale have shut down their large secondary schools and use the buildings to house a number of independent programs. No school system has taken more ambitious steps in that direction than Community School District 4 in New York City. It has dismantled both of the comprehensive junior high schools that failed to attract sufficient students following introduction of open zoning. First it closed J.H.S. 117 at the end of the 1982–83 school year and reopened it the following fall as an "alternative education complex." The building now contains five separate schools: an elementary program for gifted and talented students in grades kindergarten through three; a 210-student junior high school performing-arts program that sponsors a weekly soap opera written and produced by students; a program for 75 academically troubled seventh- and eight-graders; the East Harlem Career Academy, a 175-student program for underachieving junior high students that incorporates frequent field trips to the "working world" into its instruction; and a special-education program for 70 emotionally and mentally handicapped students. The schools share the building's gym, art studio, and science labs, and the school's older students tutor its younger ones twice a week.

After the 1984–85 school year, District 4 closed J.H.S. 13. When the building reopened the following fall—as the Jackie Robinson Educational Complex—it had five new schools under its roof: an elementary-grades program for 225 students that uses an open-classroom instructional approach; a remedial program for 80 seventh-graders; a junior high school that offers enriched instruction in music; a special-education program; and the Central Park East Secondary School, an experimental school that is part of the Coalition of Essential Schools, a consortium of fifty-two public and private schools organized in 1984 by former Harvard education dean Theodore Sizer to implement the reforms he proposed in *Horace's Compromise.* The school is scheduled to include 500 students in grades seven through twelve by 1990–91.

District 4 also reorganized Benjamin Franklin High School, a crime-ridden, one-building school overlooking the East River that it took over from New York City's high school division in 1982. District 4 closed the school, which had recently graduated only 6 percent of its students, and reopened it as the Manhattan Center for Science and Mathematics. It now houses three separate schools: River East Elementary School, a "progressive" elementary program with 220 students; Isaac Newton School for Math and Science, a junior high school program for 250 advanced seventh- and eighth-graders; and Manhattan Center High School, a high school of 1,300 students with average and above-average academic backgrounds.

Invariably there is more personal contact between students and teachers in small school settings. "It's impossible in a school of 1,700 to know all the students," said the director of the junior high performing-arts program at District 4's alternative education complex, referring to J.H.S. 117 before its reorganization. "Here, in a school of only 210, I know every new face within two weeks. In a school where there's only one floor, kids don't get lost as easily." "You have a feeling of belonging, it's a very tight place," said a student in the program.

The closer ties between students and teachers in small schools result in a level of genuine caring and mutual obligation that is found far less frequently in comprehensive schools. Those are largely intangible qualities, but they are crucial ingredients of successful schooling, for when students and teachers feel mutually responsible to one another, they tend to work harder on one another's behalf. Such mutual responsibility is a powerful source of motivation among both students and teachers, one that is negated by the anonymity of many public secondary schools. As the educator David S. Seeley has written, "Loyalty provides a different kind of accountability from the political/bureaucratic accountability upon which we mostly now rely in public education. It is the direct, face-to-face accountability of people working together on shared goals."[53]

A number of magnet schools have taken steps to reinforce further the student-teacher ties that their smallness promotes. At the International Baccalaureate magnet in St. Petersburg, Florida, for instance, each teacher serves as an advisor and mentor to a group of students for the four years that the students are in the program. At Central Park East Secondary School, one hour is devoted each day to an advisory group session, where fifteen students meet informally with a teacher and discuss subjects ranging from current events to personal problems. The "advisory" is kept together from grades seven through twelve, and each advisory takes a trip together once a year. As part of its reform blueprint, the Rochester, New York, school system has implemented a student-advisory system on a far broader scale. Under its so-called home-based guidance program, every Rochester high school teacher guides twenty freshmen through to graduation, meeting with them regularly, acting as cheerleaders, confidants, and cajolers, communicating with parents, and visiting their homes.

In many magnets I visited, students and teachers are particularly well known to one another because the programs have extended the notion of a long-term relationship between students and teachers into the classroom. Teachers work with the same group of students for several years.

Encouraging close student-teacher relationships, of course, has long been a high priority of the nation's most prestigious private schools. Advisory systems for students that involve not just guidance counselors but all faculty members, regular written reports from those involved in all aspects of students' school life, small classes, and regularly scheduled schoolwide activities are commonplace at the Lawrencevilles, Choates, and Andovers of the nation.

There are many other beneficial consequences of "smallness" in schools. Small schools are less dependent upon bureaucratic governance. For teachers, there are fewer rules and regulations defining their roles and relationships, and a greater degree of collegiality. There is also a greater degree of shared responsibility among teachers in small schools. "It's hard to be a poor teacher on a small team of teachers," as one Seattle-area teacher told me. For students, there is less preoccupation with maintaining order in small schools. Able to use more personal and informal methods of communication and organization, small schools are often free of the rigidity and oppressiveness that characterize so many comprehensive secondary schools. In general, teachers and students alike have a larger stake in small schools.

Small schools frequently are able to pay greater individual attention to students in the classroom. Many comprehensive high schools and junior high schools, preoccupied as they are with the logistical challenge of moving large numbers of students through their classrooms, are forced to subscribe to what Neil Postman and Charles Weingartner once termed "the vaccination theory of education." It holds that a subject is something students "take," and when they have taken it, they have "had" it, and when they have had it, they are "immune and need not take it again"; whether students learn the subject matter of a course is largely irrelevant.[54] In smaller school settings, on the other hand, teachers are apt to share insights on students that they have in common and to coordinate their teaching of such students. "Teachers here don't just deal with a student one-sixth of the day," a teacher in St. Petersburg's International Baccalaureate magnet told me. Similarly, the director of District 4's performing-arts program noted that "we have ten teachers teaching the same students through seventh, eighth, and ninth grade, so we can build on students' strengths and work with their weaknesses."

District 4's Central Park East Secondary School has used its small size to reorganize the bulk of its instruction into just two broad subject areas, humanities and mathematics/science, to integrate the material in various subjects better, a goal that is virtually impossible to achieve in comprehensive high schools, where students study five or six separate subjects a day with as many teachers. At Central Park East, many teachers are hired on the basis of their ability to teach two subjects, and many classes are team taught. The school's teachers also write its interdisciplinary curriculum, which emphasizes "coaching" by teachers rather than lecturing. Creating a more personalized academic learning environment and actively engaging students in their own learning through independent projects and class presentations are guiding principles of Sizer's Coalition of Essential Schools, of which Central Park East has emerged as the flagship. It is also easier to introduce alternatives to standardized testing, such as essay examinations and "demonstrations," in small-school settings, and that, too, is a goal of Sizer's coalition.

In addition to the obvious fact that students who receive greater personal attention in small-scale schools stand to get a better education than they would in the factory-like atmosphere of many comprehensive schools, the increased measure of attention also signals to students that learning is important and that *they* are important. Moreover, small-scale schools are less intimidating to parents (walking into a 4,000-student school can indeed be an unnerving experience), and they therefore encourage parental participation in their children's education. And in many instances small schools are able to do things to promote a sense of community that would be more difficult if not impossible to do in large schools. I visited a very successful elementary school in the impoverished Anacostia section of Washington, D.C. (75 percent of the schools' students live in public housing), for instance, that takes advantage of its small size (300 students) by holding mother-daughter teas and father-son banquets each year. The school also schedules several days a year when parents can come to school and have lunch with their children and their teachers. It has "color days," when all students come to school dressed in a particular color, and "grandparent days," when grandparents are invited to watch student performances. It sponsors an annual "day-at-the-park picnic" with parents. And each year the school takes all of its students on at least one outing to the John F. Kennedy Center for the Performing Arts.[55]

Nor has the value of small schools been lost on the contemporary school reformers who have investigated life in public schools firsthand. John Goodlad, in *A Place Called School* and Ernest Boyer in *High School*, as well as Sizer in *Horace's Compromise*, urged schools to reorganize themselves into "houses" and "schools-within-schools" to gain the advantages of "smallness." Stanford's Henry Levin, a perceptive observer of public schools, has argued that "as a rule of thumb, any school is probably too large if the principal and teachers do not know most of the students by name."[56] But such recommendations have not received the attention they deserve.

There is strong evidence suggesting that the attributes of smaller schools combine to create a healthier academic environment. A 1987 study of 744 comprehensive high schools nationwide found that the dropout rate at schools with over 2,000 students is twice that of schools with 667 or fewer students.[57] A 1988 study of 4,450 students in 160 high schools by two University of Chicago researchers reported that discipline problems, student absenteeism, and dropout rates are greater in large schools. "The effects of school size . . . are substantial," concluded Anthony S. Bryk and Yeow Meng Thum, "acting to either facilitate (in small schools) or inhibit (in large schools) the development and maintenance of a social environment conducive to student and faculty engagement with the school."[58]

Another 1988 study, of 357 high schools, by Bryk and a second collaborator, Mary Erina Driscoll, revealed higher rates of class cutting, absenteeism, and classroom disorders in large schools. And it reported that gains in mathematics achievement over the course of students' high school careers were smaller in large schools. "Increasing size acts to diminish a sense of community within schools and the positive consequences attendant to this," they concluded.[59] Similarly, a study of students barred from interscholastic sports under Texas's 1984 "no-pass, no-play" law revealed that the percentage of ineligible students in a school increased with school size: from 13 percent in schools with fewer than 134 students, to 17 percent in schools with between 715 and 1,439 students, and 23 percent in schools with over 1,440 students.[60]

Researchers also have found teacher morale to be higher in small schools. "Although [large] schools have greater faculty resources in terms of teachers with more experience, more advanced degrees, and higher starting salaries," wrote Bryk and Thum, "principals [in such schools] are also more likely to report a greater incidence of staff absenteeism and lack of interest."[61] Bryk and Driscoll used a variety of indicators (ranging from the presence of school rituals to a common curriculum) to measure the sense of community within schools and found that school size was a key factor in determining the level of communality within schools. "Substantial psychic rewards appear to accrue to teachers who work in a communal environment," they concluded, resulting in a "heightened sense of efficacy and commitment among staff."[62] In another study involving 538 high schools published in a 1988 issue of *Teachers College Record*, teachers in small schools, those enrolling fewer than 750 students, reported higher levels of teacher morale, staff cooperation, and good student behavior than did teachers in schools with over 1,850 students. "Teachers in high schools with low total enrollments report significantly more control over classroom and school practices, and greater consensus on the school's goals. . . . They also claim better morale," the study's authors concluded.[63] Similarly, a 1989 evaluation of New York City's new house plan, conducted by researchers at the Bank Street College of Education, reported that in the schools where well-organized houses had been established there was "an immediate, positive impact on student and teacher esprit de corps."[64]

Smaller schools are particularly beneficial to disadvantaged students. In their study, Bryk and Thum reported a strong correlation between tracking and school size; the larger the school, the greater the degree of tracking. Similarly, in magnet schools with students of all levels of ability, teachers report fewer students being assigned to bottom-track classes, and fewer being referred to special-education programs, compared to comprehensive high schools. Indeed, in smaller schools far fewer teachers express the skepticism about the ability of disadvantaged and minority students to learn that is so pervasive in traditional comprehensive schools. Bryk and Driscoll reported that "teacher consensus that students can learn decreases sharply as school size increases."[65] And the study of the Montgomery County, Maryland, magnet program concluded that "at any given level of pupil academic performance, teachers in the magnet schools predict about the same level of future academic success for blacks, whites and Hispanics."[66] "A smaller school size contributes to engaging the disadvantaged student," Bryk and Thum concluded. "The greater opportunity to sustain informal face-to-face adult-student interactions in such contexts would seem to provide a compelling explanation for these results."[67]

A number of small urban schools have achieved extraordinary results with disadvantaged, inner-city students. By 1988 Manhattan Center High School graduated 87 percent of the students who entered the school in 1982 following its reorganization by District 4, compared to a citywide average of 54 percent.[68] At Central Park East Secondary School, a school that enrolls students with a wide range of ability, daily attendance is 90 percent and the dropout rate is nearly zero. Both are astonishing statistics for a school situated in the middle of a drug-torn slum. The dropout rate is also negligible within the business academy at Philadelphia's Strawberry Mansion High School, while in the school as a whole the rate is 40 percent. Indeed, despite being near-dropouts for much of their school careers, the 160 students in the academy voluntarily attend school an extra hour each day.[69] Among the first group of students to complete three years in one of the thirty-one similar academies in California, the dropout rate was 7 percent, versus nearly 15 percent for a control group of nonacademy students.[70]

Ironically, many school systems are attempting to combat their dropout problems by assigning truants and other "borderline" students to "alternative schools" with enrollments of 200 to 300 students that provide intensive remedial instruction and extensive student-teacher contact. If similarly supportive environments were more generally available for students before they reached the point of dropping out, perhaps the need for such schools, which are widely viewed as academic dumping grounds, would not be as great.[71]

As the school reformers have argued, excellence in public education requires a tougher academic curriculum that's taught to all students, far stronger teachers than are now found in many classrooms, a revamping of teaching and testing methods, improved textbooks, and greater public accountability. Indeed, what makes improving the public schools so difficult is that such reforms are interdependent: virtually all of them must be achieved if any of them are to make a difference. Little is achieved by requiring additional academic courses of students in the absence of qualified people to teach the courses, and so on. If the regulatory aspects of the excellence agenda have had negative consequences—such as creating a more bureaucratic environment for many teachers and engendering a veritable cult of standardized testing in the public schools—many of the regulatory reforms have been necessary. If state laws and regulations increasing graduation requirements, expanding kindergarten, raising teacher salaries, establishing career ladders, banning extracurricular activities during the school day, and the like had not been enacted, it is doubtful that local educators would have taken such steps voluntarily. On the contrary, despite the dismal condition of public education in the early 1980s, few educators were advocating reform, and as the battle over H.B. 72 in Texas so vividly illustrates, the public education establishment fought tooth and nail against much of the reform agenda.

Significant strides have been made on some reform fronts, especially in the campaign to professionalize teaching and in strengthening the academic training of the nation's top students. But unless dramatic changes are made in the climate in the nation's public schools, unless schools become places where teachers want to teach and students want to learn, the progress to date will have little lasting effect. The billions of dollars and enormous amount of national energy that have been expended since the early 1980s on improving the performance of the public schools will be largely for naught.

In particular, the education of disadvantaged students is unlikely to improve without dissolving the alienation and apathy that pervade so many of the nation's public secondary schools. Unless schools "reach" disadvantaged students, instilling in them a sense of belonging and a measure of enthusiasm for learning, other reforms are unlikely to help them, and the central goal of the excellence movement, the broadening of public education's academic mission, is likely to fail. Indeed, unless a human element is added to the reform movement, the gulf between the educational haves and have-nots in public education and in the nation is likely to increase, for the excellence movement has strengthened the quality of academic instruction received by high-achieving students.

The notion of public secondary schools as educational factories—with students moving from class to class and grade to grade under an impersonal, highly standardized system, like so many sewing machines or farm implements on an assembly line—suited public education's turn-of-the-century enthusiasm for the principles of industrial production and its increasing need to provide secondary education on a mass scale.[72] And despite turning out few well-educated students, the factorylike organization of public schools sufficed in subsequent decades, when the majority of the nation's work force was employed in low-skilled industrial jobs. Economically, it didn't really matter that only a fraction of the nation's students received a rigorous academic education because the success of business and industry didn't require a better performance of public education. But today it does. And as a result of the nation's new mandate to public education that it educate many more students academically rather than vocationally, and as a result of the rapidly changing composition of the public school population, schools as factories are no longer adequate. Public schools must become far more humane places. Rather than factories, they must become communities, operating on the basis of commitment among the students and teachers within them rather than on the basis of compliance with rules and regulations alone.

The recent experiments in "restructuring" schools, in increasing "school-based management," have begun to address the alienation that is so pervasive among the nation's teachers. But apart from several modest initiatives such as Sizer's Coalition of Essential Schools, few reformers, and even fewer educators, have addressed directly the alienation and resulting apathy among so many of the nation's students.

What is needed, it seems, is a synthesis on a broad scale within public education of the 1960s reformers' desire to humanize schools and the 1980s reformers' commitment to rigorous academic standards. Though the excellence movement was in part spawned by the excesses of the 1960s educational philosophy, the observations of the public schools that led the reformers of two decades ago to their radical prescriptions are still valid and remain largely unaddressed. If the reforms they engendered led eventually (through an overemphasis on child-centeredness and a diminution of traditional academic disciplines) to a decline in academic standards, their criticisms that the public schools were repressive, impersonal places that promoted conformity at the expense of personal expression and rendered learning boring and lifeless were and remain essentially accurate. And their attempts to reshape the curriculum and classroom teaching to tap students' natural curiosity, to make them active participants in the educational process rather than passive receptacles of facts and figures, to make school more personal and more fun, were important and necessary steps, even if their particular methods of achieving those goals were flawed.

The increasing degree of student and parent choice within public education and the spread of schools-within-schools and other smaller educational settings are trends that present a new opportunity to address the human dimension of the public education crisis on a large scale. They represent the possibility of infusing into public schools the sense of community necessary to make book learning meaningful to a wide range of the nation's students.

Despite the magnitude of the problems in public education, despite the many impediments to reform, and despite the slow pace and numerous missteps of the excellence movement, that goal surely is attainable, as I learned from an eighth-grader in District 4's performing-arts program. I happened to sit next to him during a performance by a local dance troupe in the school's auditorium. He told me that to get to school from his home in the Bronx each day, he had to take two subways into East Harlem, a trip that took an hour each way. When he began traveling to District 4 a year earlier, his friends in the Bronx couldn't believe that he would go to so much trouble to attend school. They also ridiculed him for enrolling in a program with an emphasis on the performing arts. "At first, they thought I was a faggot because I danced," he said with a streetwise matter-of-factness. But his friends' disdain didn't last. "They all got into break dancing and they started to appreciate what I do," he told me. "I showed them how to warm up; I made them better dancers." His dancing had taught him another lesson, he said. "To get better in dance, you have to push yourself. It's the same in the classroom, you've got to take on tougher things. If you don't get your math and your science, you won't advance yourself."

As we talked, I asked the student what he thought of the performance that we were watching. He paused. And then, in the unemotional tones of inner-city adolescents who have endured much more than their years would warrant, he spoke with extraordinary eloquence about the relationship of the dancers to their music, about the emotions the dancers conveyed, and more. He spoke without interruption for nearly five minutes.

Before we left the auditorium, I asked him his goal in school. "To go to La Guardia [the Fiorello H. La Guardia School for the Performing Arts, one of New York's elite high schools]," he said. "It's the best in the city." There was no pride in his voice, just a quiet resolve.

Epilogue

The public schools are at a pivotal point in their history. On the one hand, they are poised to take the American experiment in free universal education to a new level, one where all students have not only an equal right to walk through the schoolhouse door but also equal intellectual opportunities. The reform movement has challenged public education to become a much more truly democratic institution than it has ever been.

But the reform movement also has raised tremendous expectations for improvement among political leaders and the public. And if, after the multi-billion-dollar national investment in reforms in recent years, public education's performance does not improve significantly, its future may be very bleak. If substantial progress is not made, if the nation's lofty expectations are ultimately frustrated, public education stands to suffer a loss of political and financial support far greater than it did in the late 1970s. And as a result of the increasing commitment to parental choice in education in recent years, a loss of confidence in the public schools is likely to spark an exodus to private education much larger than that of a decade ago. There would undoubtedly be tremendous pressure for legislative passage of vouchers and tax credits to help parents pay private school tuitions, and the number of private schools would likely increase dramatically. Families with the wherewithal to do so would abandon public schooling.

Public education, of course, would not disappear; it is too deeply ingrained in the political and economic life of the nation's communities. But it would likely degenerate into an educational backwater, supplying a second-rate education to primarily disadvantaged students unable to pay for a privately provided alternative. It would, in other words, become less of a cultural common ground and more of a dumping ground in an increasingly two-tiered society. And that, in an era of rising economic expectations and an increasingly minority work force, is an unnerving possibility.

Notes

INTRODUCTION

1. Carnegie Foundation for the Advancement of Teaching, *The Condition of Teaching* (Princeton, 1983), 10.

2. Proposition 13, enacted in June 1978, limited property taxes to 1 percent of market value and scaled assessments back to 1975–76 levels. As a measure of the educational consequences of such initiatives, nearly 8,000 Massachusetts teachers were laid off within twelve months of enactment of Proposition 2 1/2.

3. Frederick M. Wirt and Michael W. Kirst, *Schools in Conflict* (Berkeley: McCutchan, 1982), 17.

4. See Paul E. Peterson and Barry G. Rabe, "The Role of Interest Groups in the Formation of Educational Policy: Past Practice and Future Trends," *Teachers College Record*, Spring 1983, 708–19.

5. U.S. Department of Education figures, cited in *Education Daily*, 15 November 1985, 4.

6. As a member of the U.S. Court of Appeals for the Ninth Circuit, Hufstedler had argued a position in the *Lau* case that was rejected by the majority of the appellate court but eventually upheld by the Supreme Court.

7. Quoted in Charles E. Silberman, *Crisis in the Classroom* (New York: Vintage Books, 1971), 71.

8. Christopher Jencks, *Inequality* (New York: Basic Books, 1972), 256.

9. National Center for Education Statistics, *College Level Remediation* (Washington, D.C., 1986), 8.

CHAPTER 1

1. Southern Regional Education Board, *The Need for Quality: A Report to the SREB by Its Task Force on Higher Education and the Schools* (Atlanta, 1981), 1.

2. National Commission on Excellence in Education, *A Nation at Risk: The Imperative for Educational Reform* (Washington, D.C.: Government Printing Office, 1983), 5.

3. The description of the evolution of the commission's work is based primarily on interviews with Bell and Milton Goldberg, its executive director, and on an account of the commission's work by Holton in the fall 1984 issue of *Daedalus*.

4. These figures are cited in Tommy M. Tomlinson, "A Nation at Risk: Background for a Working Paper," an essay in *Academic Work and Educational Excellence*, edited by Tomlinson and Herbert J. Walberg (Berkeley: McCutchan, 1986);

A Nation at Risk subsequently was translated into Korean, Japanese, and Chinese, among other foreign languages.

5. In a 3 May 1987 article in the *New York Times Magazine* entitled "The Idea Merchant," Randall Rothenberg suggests that the nation's economic health and the plight of the public schools were first linked by the term *competitiveness* in an early 1983 report by the Business-Higher Education Forum, an organization of some 100 university presidents and Fortune 500 CEOs that called for a comprehensive national strategy to keep the nation competitive in the global economy, focusing on education, training, and research and development.

6. In Tennessee, Alexander established a twelve-person task force of officials "on loan" from various state agencies to promote his reform program. It ran a speakers bureau, set up toll-free telephone hot lines, and distributed thousands of brochures touting Alexander's reforms. Alexander himself made an unprecedented appearance before a joint meeting of the state's House and Senate education committees on behalf of his education package. He used receptions at his executive residence to encourage lobbyists from Tennessee's powerful beer, liquor, insurance, grocery, and real estate industries to work the state legislature on behalf of his education agenda. And between 1984 and 1986 he visited every one of Tennessee's 141 school systems to promote reform.

7. Cited in Leonard Lund and E. Patrick McGuire, *The Role of Business in Precollege Education* (New York: Conference Board, 1984), 4.

8. Madeleine B. Hemmings, *American Education: An Economic Issue,* Human Resources Report (Washington, D.C.: Chamber of Commerce of the United States, 1982), 3–4. Eugene Epstein and Ira Gels, *People and Productivity: A Challenge to Corporate America* (New York: New York Stock Exchange, 1982), 2.

9. Cited in Sheppard Ranbom, "Business, Education Group Urges Presidential Leadership," *Education Week,* 25 May 1983.

10. The number of business and school partnerships increased from 40,000 to 140,000 between 1984 and 1988.

11. The prayer proposal and most of the rest of the Reagan legislative agenda in education were blocked by Congress. The administration's only notable success was in gaining elimination of a number of mostly modest federal programs.

12. Personal interview with Bell on 1 April 1985 in Salt Lake City and phone interview on 16 February 1988. Phone interview on 7 May 1986 with Martin Anderson, head of domestic policy in the Reagan White House at the time. Bell says he broached the subject of a presidential education commission with Reagan at a cabinet council meeting early in 1981, and that on the basis of the president's negative response, he declined to make a formal written proposal to Reagan for such a commission.

13. See Chester E. Finn, Jr., "Teacher Politics," *Commentary,* February 1983, 33, and Chester E. Finn, Jr., "The Drive for Educational Excellence: Moving Toward a Public Consensus," *Change,* April 1983, 20.

14. Bell's key allies on the White House staff were Chief of Staff James Baker and Cabinet Secretary Craig Fuller.

15. Holton's remark is quoted in Edward B. Fiske, "Top Objectives Elude Reagan as Education Policy Evolves," *New York Times,* 27 December 1983.

16. Telephone interview, 6 May 1986.

17. Personal interview, 30 April 1986.

18. Ibid.

19. Wirthlin measured the popularity of each cabinet secretary as part of his regular polling duties, and the secretary of education was doing especially well after release of the commission's report. As a result, Bell, who previously had had little clout in the administration, suddenly found himself flying to these events with the president aboard Air Force One.

20. Personal interview with Deaver, 30 April 1986.

21. By 1984 Reagan was declaring that the education reform battle had been won, and that he was responsible for the victory: "In community after community, principals have turned schools around," he said in remarks to the National Association of Secondary School Principals annual convention. "It's been one of those great American stories, a little like how neighbors used to band together to raise a house out of the wilderness," he said in a radio address to the nation on 8 September 1984.

22. So great was the press coverage that the Department of Education logged over 400 telephone requests for the report within one hour on April 27.

23. See, for example, "Saving Our Schools," *Newsweek,* 9 May 1983; "Business Awakes to the Crisis in Education," *Business Week,* 9 July 1983; "Education Under Siege," *National Journal,* 19 September 1983; and "What to Do About America's Schools," *Fortune, 19 September 1983.*

24. Thomas A. Shannon, "Let's Heed This 'Excellence' Advice," *American School Board Journal,* July 1983, 43. Editorial, *NASSP Newsleader,* May 1983, 2.

25. These figures are from the U.S. Department of Education's National Center for Education Statistics. In early 1990, however, a controversial but compelling study released by the Economic Policy Institute, a liberal Washington, D.C., think tank, argued that the United States ranks much lower in education spending when expenditures for higher education are subtracted. According to the study, the nation spent only 4.1 percent of its gross national product in 1985 on K–12 education, third lowest among sixteen industrialized nations investigated in the study. Japan spent 4.8 percent of its GNP on k–12 schooling, ranking sixth. See M. Edith Rasell and Lawrence Mishel, "Shortchanging Education" (Washington, D.C.: Economic Policy Institute, 1990), 11.

26. The National School Boards Association; the American Vocational Association; the National Association of Elementary School Principals: the Association for Supervision and Curriculum Development; the National Association of State Boards of Education; and the American Federation of Teachers.

27. Quoted in Cindy Currence, "Education Lobbies Shift Focus to States," *Education Week,* 2 October 1985.

28. Given generally to sentimentality, sophomoric inspiration, self-congratulation, and defensive posturing, the National School Boards Association journal and many other public education association publications like it are symptomatic of the narrow intellectual life that many of the nation's school leaders live.

29. Rayma C. Page, "NSBA's Convention: A Place to Learn," *American School Board Journal,* December 1982, 50.

30. Thomas Shannon, "Adopt a Public Relations Action Plan," *American School Board Journal,* July 1984, 38.

31. Iowa Task Force on Excellence in Education, "First in the Nation," October 1984, 19.

32. The department mailed 2,000 invitations, expecting 1,200 acceptances. It received double that number responses.

33. *Los Angeles Times,* 8 June 1983.

34. Nonetheless, many legislators openly questioned the ability of public educators to produce the sort of schools the nation needed.

35. The state figures are from Steve D. Gold, "The Cost of Fixing up the Schools," *State Legislatures,* May/June 1988, 19–21. The national figures are from William Bennett, *American Education: Making It Work* (Washington, D.C.: Government Printing Office, 1988), 42.

CHAPTER 2

1. On the nation's transformation from an industrial society to an information society, and the implications for the public schools, see Roy Forbes and Lynn Grover Gisi, "Information Society: Will Our High School Graduates Be Ready?" (Denver: Education Commission of the States, 1982); Committee for Economic Development, Research and Policy Committee, *Investing in Our Children* (Washington, D.C.: Committee for Economic Development, 1985); Harlan Cleveland, "Educating for the Information Society," *Change,* July/August 1985. The quotation by Sizer is from *Horace's Compromise* (Boston: Houghton Mifflin, 1984), 135. The citation for the NAS task force is "The Changing Workplace: The Employers' View" (Washington, D.C.: National Academy Press, 1984), xi. See National Commission on Excellence in Education, *A Nation at Risk* (Washington, D.C.: Government Printing Office, 1983), 7.

2. Twentieth Century Fund, *Making the Grade* (New York, 1983), 4; National Commission on Excellence in Education, *A Nation at Risk,* 6; See also Richard C. Anderson et al., *Becoming a Nation of Readers: The Report of the Commission on Reading* (Washington, D.C.: National Academy of Education, 1985), 3. The report warns that "the world is moving into a technological-information age in which full participation in education, science, business, industry, and the professions requires increasing levels of literacy. What was a satisfactory level of literacy in 1950 probably will be marginal by the year 2000."

3. One measure of the troubles in urban school systems today is that public school teachers in Nashville, Atlanta, Chicago, and elsewhere send their children to private schools at nearly twice the rate nonteacher parents do.

4. National Education Association, *Journal of Proceedings and Addresses, Session of the Year 1892* (New York, 1893), 226.

5. Ernest L. Boyer, *High School* (New York: Harper & Row, 1983), 46.

6. The document's official title was *Report of the Committee on Secondary School Studies Appointed at the Meeting of the National Education Association, July 9, 1892* (Washington, D.C.: National Education Association, 1893); on the Committee of Ten's goals, see Richard Hofstadter, *Anti-intellectualism in American Life* (New York: Knopf, 1970), 329–32.

7. Quoted in Hofstadter, *Anti-intellectualism,* 331.

8. Lawrence A. Cremin, *The Transformation of the School* (New York: Vintage Books, 1964), 186.

9. David Owen, *None of the Above* (Boston: Houghton Mifflin, 1985), 180; see also Cremin, *Transformation,* 185–90.

10. Hofstadter, *Anti-intellectualism,* 339.

11. Lewis Terman, *Intelligence Tests and School Reorganization* (New York: World, 1923), 27–28, as cited in Jeannie Oakes, *Keeping Track: How Schools Structure Inequality* (New Haven: Yale University Press, 1985), 36–37. Terman became known as the "father" of the IQ.

12. Cremin, *Transformation,* 193.

13. Ibid., viii, 88.

14. Ibid., 58–75.

15. Quoted in Cremin, *Transformation,* 48; Cremin's account of the origins of the Progressive movement in education in the century's early decades is indeed lucid.

16. Ibid., 100–105.

17. Cremin, *Transformation,* 103–4; to Hofstadter, "the central idea of the new educational thought" was that "the school should base its studies not on the demands of society, nor on any conception of what an educated person should be, but on the developing needs and interests of the child." Hofstadter, *Anti-intellectualism,* 369.

18. Cremin, *Transformation,* 220.

19. Ibid., 126; the words here are Cremin's.

20. Ibid., 124.

21. All the quotations here are Cremin's, except for Dewey's phrase "intellectual results"; see Cremin, *Transformation,* viii–ix, 124–26.

22. Arthur G. Powell et al., *The Shopping Mall High School* (Boston: Houghton Mifflin, 1985), 260.

23. Ibid., 242.

24. Commission on the Reorganization of Secondary Education, *The Cardinal Principles of Secondary Education: A Report of the Commission on the Reorganization of Secondary Education, 1918* (Washington, D.C.: U.S. Department of the Interior, 1962), 8, 10–11, 14. At the National Education Association's annual meeting in 1921, the commission stated in a report that the *Cardinal Principles* "throws into the discard the last vestige of the idea that abstract standards are more important than the needs of actual boys and girls." See National Education Association, "Addresses and Proceedings of the 59th Annual Meeting" (Washington, D.C., 1921), 165.

25. Commission on the Reorganization of Secondary Education, *Cardinal Principles,* 10–11.

26. Diane Ravitch, *The Troubled Crusade: American Education, 1945–1980* (New York: Basic Books, 1983), 48.

27. Commission on the Reorganization of Secondary Education, *Cardinal Principles,* 22.

28. Hofstadter, *Anti-intellectualism,* 341–42.

29. George Van Dyke, "Trends in the Development of the High School Offering," *School Review,* November 1931, 737–47. Cited in Powell et al., *Shopping Mall,* 252.

30. Ibid.

31. Ibid.

32. Powell et al., *Shopping Mall,* 252.

33. Van Dyke, "Trends," 662, cited in Powell et al., *Shopping Mall.*

34. Powell et al., *Shopping Mall.*

35. I owe this characterization of teachers and administrators to David T. Kearns and Denis P. Doyle in *Winning the Brain Race: A Bold Plan to Make Our Schools Competitive* (San Francisco: ICS Press, 1988), 35–36.

36. Educational Policies Commission, *The Purposes of Education in a Democracy* (Washington, D.C.: NEA, 1938); B. L. Dodds, *That All May Learn* (Washington, D.C.: NEA, 1939); Educational Priorities Commission, *Education for ALL American Youth* (Washington, D.C.: NEA, 1944). Quotations are found in Ravitch, *Troubled Crusade*, 61–63.

37. Quoted in Cremin, *Transformation*, 234–35.

38. Quoted in Ravitch, *Troubled Crusade*, 58–59.

39. Cremin, *Transformation*, 220.

40. John Dewey, *Democracy and Education* (New York: Macmillan, 1916), 231. Quoted in Cremin, *Transformation*, 124–25.

41. U.S. Office of Education, *Life Adjustment for Every Youth* (Washington, D.C., n.d.), 17. Quoted in Cremin, *Transformation*, 335.

42. Hofstadter, *Anti-intellectualism*, 344.

43. Ibid., 350.

44. Ibid., 344.

45. Cremin, *Transformation*, 336–37.

46. U.S. Office of Education, *Life Adjustment for Every Youth*. Quoted in Hofstadter, *Anti-intellectualism*, 345.

47. Charles A. Prosser, *Secondary Education and Life* (Cambridge: Harvard University, 1939). Quoted in Hofstadter, *Anti-intellectualism*, 345–46. It was during the ascendency of the life-adjustment movement, in the late 1940s and the early 1950s, that courses in driver education and consumer education, among others, became commonplace in the curricula of the nation's secondary schools.

48. Hofstadter, *Anti-intellectualism*, 350.

49. Quoted in Ravitch, *Troubled Crusade*, 72.

50. U.S. Census Bureau, "School Enrollment—Social and Economic Characteristics of Students," October 1984.

51. Quoted in Powell et al., *Shopping Mall*, 295.

52. Ibid.

53. Lawrence A. Cremin, *Popular Education and Its Discontents* (New York: Harper & Row, 1990), 17.

54. Frank Riessman, *The Culturally Deprived Child* (New York: Harper & Row, 1962), 80. Quoted in Ravitch, *Troubled Crusade*, 155.

55. Ravitch, *Troubled Crusade*, 251.

56. Joseph Adelson, "What Happened to the Schools?" *Commentary*, March 1981, 39.

57. For a discussion of the ideology of the New Right and "movement conservatives," who sought a return to a "stable conventional culture," see Sidney Blumenthal, "Verities of the Right Have Young Roots," *Washington Post*, 25 September 1985. A second indication of the importance of education to the broader conservative movement was the Reagan administration's rapid transformation of *American Education*, the department's monthly journal, from a publication of primarily light features on federal education programs into a vehicle for strongly conservative educational thought.

58. In addition to a steady flow of articles and essays in professional and

general-circulation publications and in several conservative anthologies on education, Finn published *Scholars, Dollars and Bureaucrats* (Washington, D.C.: Brookings, 1978), a critique of federal education policy, in 1978 and he coedited an anthology on the humanities in 1984 entitled *Against Mediocrity* (New York: Holmes & Meier, 1984), in which he and Ravitch argued in a concluding essay for a core academic curriculum. Finn also collaborated with Ravitch on the establishment in 1981 of the Educational Excellence Network, which they used primarily as a vehicle for publicizing the conservative educational agenda through monthly duplicated compilations of their own and other writings that were distributed with foundation funding to education writers around the nation and to several hundred individual subscribers. As secretary of education, Bennett funneled a $375,000 federal grant through the Excellence Network to Finn and Ravitch to conduct research in support of their campaign on behalf of the humanities in the nation's schools.

Finn was a driving force behind a number of conservative education manifestos published during the 1980s over the signatures of many prominent lawmakers and educators. He also drafted *Making the Grade,* the report of the Twentieth Century Fund's education reform task force. He was a consultant to the Carnegie Foundation's study of American high schools. And he was a leading architect of the sweeping education reform legislation proposed by Tennessee Governor Lamar Alexander in early 1983. Between 1985 and 1988, Finn was a top adviser to Bennett in the U.S. Department of Education.

59. Chester E. Finn, Jr., "The Future of Education's Liberal Consensus," *Change,* September 1980, 26.

60. Chester E. Finn, Jr., "The Excellence Backlash: Sources of Resistance to Educational Reform," *American Spectator,* September 1984, 13.

61. Prior to release of *A Nation at Risk,* some of Bell's most significant speeches were made before groups like the Bannock County Republican Party in Pocatello, Idaho, and the Council for the Development of French in Louisiana in Lafayette, Louisiana.

62. Twentieth Century Fund, *Making the Grade,* 6; National Commission on Excellence in Education, *A Nation at Risk,* 13; Boyer, *High School,* xii.

63. Joseph Adelson, "Why the Schools May Not Improve," *Commentary,* October 1984, 43.

64. Chester E. Finn, Jr., "The Futile Quest for No-Fault Excellence in Education," *Education Week,* 23 November 1983, 24.

65. Quoted in George Neill, "President Reagan Values Education, Meese Proclaims," *Education Week,* 21 December 1981, 1.

66. Chester E. Finn, Jr., et al., eds., *Against Mediocrity* (New York: Holmes & Meier, 1984), 240–41.

67. Christopher Lasch, *The Culture of Narcissism* (New York: Norton, 1978), 145.

68. Patricia A. Graham, "Schools: Cacophony about Practice, Silence about Purpose," *Daedalus,* Fall 1984, 29–57; Bill Honig, *Last Chance for Our Children* (Reading, Mass.: Addison-Wesley, 1985), 82; Bill Honig, testimony before the California Senate Education Committee, 23 January 1985, 2.

69. William J. Bennett, *American Education: Making It Work* (Washington, D.C.: Government Printing Office, 1988), 31.

70. Finn "The Futile Quest," 24; Chester E. Finn, Jr., "The Excellence Backlash: Sources of Resistance to Educational Reform," *American Spectator*, September 1984, 13; Neill, "President Reagan Values Education, Meese Proclaims," 18.

71. Ravitch, *Troubled Crusade*, 51.

72. Andrew Oldenquist, "The Decline of American Education in the 60's and 70's," *American Education*, May 1983, 14; Adelson, "Why the Schools May Not Improve," 45; A. S. Neill, *Summerhill: A Radical Approach to Child Rearing* (New York: Hart, 1960), 4, 25, 29, quoted in Ravitch, *Troubled Crusade*, 235.

73. Graham, "Schools," 29–57.

74. E. D. Hirsch, Jr., "Cultural Literacy," *American Scholar*, Spring 1983, 167; Bill Honig, speech to the American Association of School Administrators, 8 March 1985, 3; Honig, *Last Chance for Our Children*, 33.

75. Mortimer J. Adler, *The Paideia Proposal* (New York: Macmillan, 1982), 30; Boyer, *High School*, 95; National Commission on Excellence in Education, *A Nation at Risk*, 7. The anxiety over the schools' failure to transmit cultural knowledge and values became such that in 1987 over 150 leading educators and prominent citizens—including former Presidents Jimmy Carter and Gerald Ford—issued a manifesto calling for a "decisive improvement" in the teaching of the nation's democratic ideas and institutions through a strengthened curriculum of history, geography, and civics, and through a broader exposure of all students to the humanities in general. See American Federation of Teachers, *Education for Democracy* (Washington, D.C., 1987).

76. E. D. Hirsch, Jr., "Keynote Address to the Annual Statewide Staff Development Conference," California State Department of Education, Asilomar, January 22–24, 1985; E. D. Hirsch, Jr., *Cultural Literacy* (Boston: Houghton Mifflin, 1987), 3, 126. Hirsch's argument was endorsed by numerous reading experts. In its 1985 report, *Becoming a Nation of Readers*, the Commission on Reading, empaneled by the U.S. Department of Education, noted, "Reading, comprehension, and things with language and the printed word are cultural phenomena. . . . Meaning is constructed as a reader links what he reads to what he knows. . . . The ability to comprehend readings is directly linked to knowledge of the subject of the reading." See Richard Anderson et al., *Becoming a Nation of Readers: The Report of the Commission on Reading* (Washington, D.C.: National Institute of Education, 1985), vi.

77. Honig, *Last Chance*, 6–7.

78. Remarks of Secretary of Education William J. Bennett to the Columbia College Club of Washington, D.C., 6 May 1987; "The Nation's Top Teacher Is Already Handing out Demerits," *New York Times*, 17 February 1985; William J. Bennett, *To Reclaim a Legacy* (Washington, D.C.: National Endowment for the Humanities, 1984), 7.

79. William J. Bennett, speech to the Ethics and Public Policy Center, 19 April 1985. Reprinted in *Education Week*, 1 May 1985, 11.

80. Honig, *Last Chance*, 100.

81. Sizer, *Horace's Compromise*, 127; Honig, *Last Chance*, 93.

82. Not that there was a bygone golden era of cultural literacy in the nation. A 1951 survey of 30,000 Los Angeles students revealed that nearly one of seven eighth-graders was unable to locate the Atlantic Ocean on a map. Cited in Hofstadter, *Anti-intellectualism*, 304.

83. Oldenquist, "The Decline of American Education in the 60's and 70's," 14.

84. Allan C. Carlson, "Moral Communities and Education," *Education Week*, 4 April 1984, 24. Indeed, the NEA even recognizes the "differences" of left-handed students in its official policies.

85. Quoted in Lynn Olson, "Opinions Clash at Conference to Define History Curriculum," *Education Week*, 5 September 1984, 1. Ironically, Bennett's view was not shared by many of his allies on the far right. In language nearly identical to Huggins's, Paul C. Vitz, a professor of psychology at New York University, argued in a 1985 op-ed essay in the *Wall Street Journal* that "a fair presentation of all of the ethnic, racial, political and religious traditions important in American life is possible only at a level so shallow as to be meaningless or offensive." Vitz and other right-wing conservatives argued that parents should thus be given "the chance to sustain their [individual] values and heritage" through enactment of educational vouchers or tuition tax credits that would permit them greater freedom to send their children to nonpublic schools. Bennett's allies on the far right did not accept the reformers' premise that public education was a force for social cohesion. See Paul C. Vitz, "Textbook Bias Isn't of a Fundamentalist Nature," *Wall Street Journal*, 26 December 1985, 5.

86. Hirsch, *Cultural Literacy*, 21–22; Honig, *Last Chance*, 66, 77, 102.

87. Bennett, remarks to the Columbia College Club of Washington, and speech to the Ethics and Public Policy Center.

88. Gerald Grant, "The Character of Education and the Education of Character," *Daedalus*, Summer 1981. He expanded his argument into a 1988 book entitled *The World We Created at Hamilton High* (Cambridge: Harvard University Press, 1988).

89. Sidney Simon, quoted in Honig, *Last Chance*, 95; "Education and the Humanities: A Conversation with William J. Bennett," reprinted in *American Education*, November 1982, 29; Honig, *Last Chance*, 97.

90. Lynn V. Cheney, *American Memory* (Washington, D.C.: National Endowment for the Humanities, 1987), 8.

91. "Secretary of Education Calls for Improved School Curricula," U.S. Department of Education, 11 March 1985.

92. Hirsch, "Cultural Literacy and the Curriculum," Keynote Address to the Annual Statewide Staff Development Conference (Asilomar, CA: California State Department of Education, 1985), 5.

93. Hirsch, *Cultural Literacy*, 12.

94. Allan Bloom, *The Closing of the American Mind: How Higher Education Has Failed Democracy and Impoverished the Souls of Today's Students* (New York: Simon & Schuster, 1987), 41, 239.

95. Arthur Bestor, *Educational Wastelands: The Retreat from Learning in Our Public Schools* (Urbana: University of Illinois Press, 1953). Quoted in Cremin, *Transformation*, 344.

96. See, for example, Hyman G. Rickover, *Education and Freedom* (New York: Dutton, 1959). Admiral Rickover frankly called for separate schools for talented students, with admissions based on special examination and "teachers of above-average intelligence and training." "When a society becomes more complex technologically, it needs proportionately more, and qualitatively better, trained professionals. . . . We must keep their ranks replenished by a continuous inflow of properly trained youth of superior mental ability."

CHAPTER 3

1. Quoted in Richard Dunham, "Perot Holds Key to Teacher Pay Raises," *Dallas Times-Herald*, 11 July 1983.

2. The recommendations of the Select Committee on Public Education, 19 April 1984, 3.

3. Correspondence with H. Ross Perot (through his secretary), 17 April 1986; telephone interview with Mark W. White, Jr., 12 September 1985.

4. These details of "Operation Hotfoot" are drawn primarily from an account by Ken Follett in *On Wings of Eagles* (New York: Signet, 1983).

5. Ibid., 51–54.

6. Richard Fish, "Computer Highlights Education Meeting," *Dallas Morning News*, 14 July 1983, 28A.

7. Personal interview, 4 April 1986.

8. "Perot Blasts Texas Schools as 'Places Dedicated to Play,' " *Houston Chronicle*, 30 July 1983.

9. Tom Luce recalled that "patterns of issues" emerged soon after SCOPE began its work, and that he was "amazed" at the extent to which different sources echoed similar concerns. Personal interview, 17 June 1985.

10. Richard S. Dunham, "Perot Produces Sharp 'Readin', Ritin'' Rhetoric," *Dallas Times-Herald*, 3 October 1983.

11. Quoted in Paul Taylor, "Perot Electrifies State of Education," *Washington Post*, 31 May 1984.

12. Personal interview, 17 June 1985.

13. Texas Research League, "Texas Public Education: A Matter of Priorities" (Austin, 1984).

14. In a telephone interview on September 12, 1985, White said he endorsed the SCOPE agenda because it included reforms he felt were needed in Texas.

15. Personal interview with Carl Parker on 18 March 1985. It should also be noted that Parker himself was by the end of the special session speaking during Senate debates of a need to reform Texas's schools.

16. When I spoke with Haley in his office on 19 March 1985, he denied that Lewis had threatened him. He said he rewrote H.B. 72 because "it was clear" that Lewis had the votes in the House to pass a floor substitute to the committee's bill and that by agreeing to cooperate he won concession on the composition of the state board and in the state funding formula that he wouldn't have gotten if he refused to cooperate. People privy to Lewis's conversation with Haley, however, interpreted Lewis's remarks as a threat to Haley's chairmanship.

17. Texas Research League, "Texas Public Education," 3–4.

18. *Texas House Journal*, 5 June 1984, 18–19.

19. Personal interview, 18 March 1985.

20. The widely publicized story also was rhetorical fodder for allies of the SCOPE agenda.

21. Arnold Hamilton, "Group Praying, Fighting Against School Reform," *Dallas Times-Herald*, 27 June 1983.

22. Personal interview, 20 March 1985.

23. Quoted in David Barron, "Official Blasts System After TSTI Tour," *Waco Tribune-Herald*, 12 June 1984.

24. Personal interview, 17 June 1985.

CHAPTER 4

1. National Commission on Excellence in Education, *A Nation at Risk* (Washington, D.C.: Government Printing Office, 1983), 18, 24.

2. No fewer than thirty-six states raised their graduation requirements in 1983 and 1984 alone. Typical was Indiana, which required the class of 1989 to complete nineteen courses to graduate, including four years of English and two years each of history, math, and science. Previously, Hoosier students needed only sixteen credits to earn a high school diploma, including three in English, one in math, and one in science. In some instances, the increase in state academic requirements was even greater. Beginning in 1989 Louisiana graduates had to complete four years of English and three years each of history, math, and science—one year more of each subject than had been required of their predecessors. In raising course requirements for admission to public colleges, the states have responded to charges that the easing of admissions requirements during the 1960s and 1970s contributed to the decline of the academic disciplines in the nation's high schools.

3. Likewise, Arkansas established the Governor's Scholars Program in 1983, the Virginia legislature created the Virginia Scholars Program in 1984, and Tennessee established the Academic Scholars Program in 1985. All three programs offer scholarships to in-state institutions on the basis of academic achievement.

4. The huge number of athletes and other students who failed to meet the Texas standard—including half of the high school students in Dallas in the spring of 1985—made front-page headlines throughout Texas and around the nation. Such was the opposition to "no-pass, no-play" that in late 1985 both the Texas Association of Secondary School Principals and the Texas High School Coaches Association established political action committees to win the law's repeal, though they were ultimately unsuccessful.

5. Virtually all of California's 1,029 districts met both goals within a year.

6. Westat, Inc., "*Nation at Risk* Update Study" (Washington, D.C.: U.S. Department of Education, 1988), preliminary tables, table 12.

7. The comparative figures are geometry (61 percent in 1987, 46 percent in 1983); second-year algebra (46 percent, 35 percent); trigonometry (20 percent, 12 percent), biology (90 percent, 75 percent); chemistry (45 percent, 31 percent); and physics (20 percent, 14 percent). Despite the rise in AP enrollments, only 2 percent of the nation's public high school students participated in the program in 1989.

8. Westat, "*Nation at Risk* Update Study," 25. Significantly, an expert who worked on the survey points out that the number of students in remedial courses would likely be higher if all students, not just high school graduates, were surveyed. Another study, of California course-enrollment trends between 1981–82 and 1986–87 by an independent research organization known as Policy Analysis for California Education (PACE), reported declines in statewide enrollment in low-level courses such as "consumer math" and "developmental reading." See *Conditions of Education in California 1988* (Sacramento: Policy Analysis for California Education, 1988), 62–63.

9. Telephone interview with Robert Lumsden.

10. Telephone interview with Robert Lumsden.

11. A few states have restricted the number of low-level academic courses for

which students may receive graduation credits. Such a limitation was included in Florida's original reform legislation, but it was lifted by the state's lawmakers in 1985 amendments, permitting students to earn all of their elective credits in "remedial or compensatory" courses if they choose.

12. William H. Clune, "The Implementation and Effects of High School Graduation Requirements: First Steps Toward Curricular Reform," draft, September 1988, ii, 25.

13. Between 1982–83 and 1987–88 chemistry enrollment in the state increased by 60 percent, physics by 86 percent, trigonometry by 103 percent, and honors geometry by 176 percent. Yet the enrollment in such courses still represents a fraction of Florida's total high school enrollment: chemistry, 6 percent; physics, 3 percent; trigonometry, 3 percent.

14. Thomas Hanson, "Curricular Change in Dade County; 1982–83 to 1986–87: a Replication of the PACE Study," draft, September 1988, 10.

15. Ronald H. Field, *State Legislative Perceptions of Vocational Education* (Columbus, Ohio: National Center for Research in Vocational Education, 1984), 3.

16. National Commission on Secondary Vocational Education, *The Unfinished Agenda: The Role of Vocational Education in the High School* (Columbus, Ohio: National Center for Research in Vocational Education, 1984), 1,2,8. An important ally of the AVA is the National Education Association. Like the AVA, the NEA sees a robust vocational-education program as a source of jobs for its members, many of whom are vocational educators. The Arlington (Virginia) Education Association, an NEA affiliate, captured the sentiment of the organization when it wrote in response to Virginia's new graduation requirements: "No classes should be canceled simply because of low enrollment. Offering more courses will require more teachers if instruction is to remain of the highest level. This will require an increased financial commitment from the community." See Arlington County School Board, "*A Nation at Risk:* Response and Recommendations," 23 January 1985, 17.

17. Marvin Feldman, "In the Name of Excellence: The Ambush of Vocational Education," remarks to AVA Technical Educational Division, New Orleans, 1 December 1984. Michael J. Dyrenfurth, "State Trends in Graduation Requirements, *VocEd,* January/February 1985, 43.

18. Basic data from "1987–88 Schools and Staffing Survey: Public School Teachers Profile" (Washington, D.C.: National Center for Educational Statistics, 1990). The specific statistic was drawn from the basic data by Dr. Sharon A. Bobbitt of the U.S. Department of Education. In many parts of the country the rate of teacher misassignment is even greater than that recorded in the federal survey. The Utah State Office of Education reported that in 1987–88 one-third of the state's social studies and math teachers, one-fifth of its English and biological science teachers, and no less than half of its physical science teachers did not have a college major or minor in their primary field of assignment.

19. Council of Chief State School Officers, *Teacher Supply and Demand Survey: 1987–88,* telephone conversation with Martha J. Miller, 20 October 1988; telephone conversation with Michael Neuschatz, American Institute of Physics, 17 October 1988; Joanne Capper, *A Study of Certified Teacher Availability in the States* (Washington, D.C.: Council of Chief State School Officers, 1987).

20. Lorraine M. McDonnell, "Coursework Policy in Five States and Its Implica-

tions for Indicator Development," working paper (Santa Monica: Rand, 1988), 16–17.

21. See Richard K. Mastan, ed., *1988 Manual on Certification and Preparation of Educational Personnel in the United States* (Sacramento: National Association of State Directors of Teacher Education and Certification, 1988).

22. Council for Basic Education, *Making Do in the Classroom: A Report on the Misassignment of Teachers* (Washington, D.C., 1985), 8.

23. McDonnell, *Coursework Policy in Five States,* 17; telephone conversation with William Aldridge, 18 October 1988.

24. Spillane quoted in Jonathan Friendly, "States Are Urged to Compete in Filling Teacher Vacancies," *New York Times,* 15 December 1985. To be qualified to teach, one doesn't necessarily have to be certified as a teacher. And a certified teacher is not necessarily a qualified teacher. But as Spillane suggests, teachers on emergency certificates are typically neither certified nor qualified.

25. The Chicago figure was cited in "Chicago Schools: 'Worst in America' " (Chicago: Chicago Tribune Company, 1988), 61.

26. National statistics on teacher absenteeism do not exist, but at high schools that I visited in New Jersey, California, Florida, Pennsylvania, Texas, and Virginia, teacher-absenteeism rates of 15 percent were typical.

27. New Jersey State Department of Education, "Revisions of Seniority Regulations," June 1983, 3.

28. McDonnell, *Coursework Policy in Five States,* 17.

29. Mastan, *1988 Manual on Certification and Preparation,* b-36, b-69; Council for Basic Education, *Making Do in the Classroom,* 6–7.

30. Personal interview, 1 November 1988.

31. Personal interview, 28 October 1988. In addition to experts in curriculum and instruction, several of the reform reports of the early 1980s also urged a revamping of pedagogy in public education. The major voices were Theodore Sizer in *Horace's Compromise* (Boston: Houghton Mifflin, 1984), and John Goodlad in *A Place Called School* (New York: McGraw-Hill, 1984). But there were others as well; "We must take care to develop teaching materials aimed at attracting, motivating, and establishing competency in every ability group," wrote the authors of *Action for Excellence* (Denver: Education Commission for Excellence, 1983). Among the more recent reports urging new teaching techniques in the nation's public schools are *Science for All Americans,* published in 1989 by the American Association for the Advancement of Science, and *Everybody Counts,* a 1989 study of mathematics education issued by the National Research Council, the research arm of the National Academy of Sciences and the National Academy of Engineering, private organizations that advise the federal government on public policy issues.

32. Marvin Lazerson et al., *An Education of Value* (Cambridge: Cambridge University Press, 1985), 23.

33. Diane Ravitch, *The Troubled Crusade: American Education, 1954–1985* (New York: Basic Books, 1983), 232. For a general discussion of the curricular reforms of the 1950s and early 1960s, see ibid., 228–32, and Lazerson et al., *An Education of Value,* 23–46.

34. Ravitch, personal interview, 31 October 1988.

35. At a New Jersey junior high school I visited the degree of tracking was

overwhelming. The school places students in each grade in one of nine tracks on the basis of their scores on a standardized test of basic skills. The students in each track take *all* of their courses together.

36. Jeannie Oakes, *Keeping Track: How Schools Structure Inequality* (New Haven: Yale University Press, 1985), 76–77. Oakes's data was collected as part of educator John I. Goodlad's Study of Schooling, a project that culminated in his 1984 book, *A Place Called School.*

37. Ibid., 67–72, 85–89.

38. Ibid., 98–99.

39. "California High School Curriculum Study: Paths Through High School," Stanford University Graduate School of Education, 5 January 1984, 3.

40. Edward McDill et al., "A Population at Risk: Potential Consequences of Tougher School Standards for Student Dropouts," *American Journal of Education,* February 1986, 148, 169.

41. In *A Place Called School,* John Goodlad writes that "an extraordinary degree of student passivity stands out. . . . In most classes at all levels . . . we didn't see much opportunity for students to become engaged with knowledge. . . . It is but a short inferential leap to suggest that we are implicitly teaching dependence upon authority, linear thinking, social apathy, passive involvement." This "hidden curriculum" is "disturbingly apparent," he concludes. See pp. 230–31.

42. Michael Rutter et al., *Fifteen Thousand Hours* (Cambridge: Harvard University Press, 1979), 187.

43. Roughly 20 percent of the nation's high school teachers teach vocational courses.

44. Committee for Economic Development, Research and Policy Committee, *Investing in Our Children: Business and the Public Schools* (Washington, D.C.: Committee for Economic Development, 1985), executive summary, 4.

45. See chapter on the "Vocational Aspects of Education" in John Dewey, Democracy and Education (New York: Macmillan, 1961 edition), 306–320.

46. "New Special-ed Official Seeking To 'Identify the Gaps,' " *Education Week,* 9 November 1983.

47. Letter to the editor, *Education Week,* 11 December 1985.

48. *Tenth Annual Report to Congress on the Implementation of the Handicapped Act.* Cited in Debra Viadero, "Study Documents Jump in Spec-ed Enrollments, *Education Week,* 2 March 1988.

49. U.S. Department of Education, National Center for Education Statistics, *High School And Beyond,* August 1982. Cited in *Equality and Excellence: The Educational Status of Black Americans* (New York: College Board, 1985), 34–35.

50. Minneapolis Public Schools, *Superintendent's Blue Ribbon Committee on Educational Standards: 1984–85 Final Report* (Minneapolis, 1985), v. American Association of School Administrators, *Raising Standards in School: Problems and Solutions* (Arlington, Va., 1985), 15. Ironically, the Pennsylvania guidance counselor I spoke with works at a school in the Monongahela Valley, where a lack of basic literacy skills has left thousands of the area's steelworkers unretrainable and unemployed in wake of widespread plant closings.

51. Floretta McKensie et al., "Paideia Proposal: A Symposium," *Harvard Educational Review,* Nov. 1983, 389–92. NASSP Board of Directors, *Statement on National Reports* (Reston, Va.: National Association of Secondary School Principals,

1983), 4. Arlington County School Board, "*A Nation at Risk:* Response and Recommendations," 17.

52. Mary Conroy, "Are the Curriculum Reforms Elitist?" *New York Times Education Review,* 6 Jan. 1985. As a measure of the widespread allegations within public education that the curriculum reforms were elitist, the Virginia affiliate of the National Education Association lobbied against honors diplomas on grounds that they would foster elitist attitudes among those who earned them. "The changes they are making in the English program are not aimed at keeping kids in school, if they are not academic kids. They can't have it both ways," said the chairperson of the English department of a California high school in response to her school system's decision to raise graduation requirements in English.

53. However, in the second half of the 1989–90 school year, some 120 of the state's 1,086 school systems received exemptions from the requirement from the State Department of Education.

54. Further, the evaluation found that low income, low parental education, and the absence of a parent from a family—common circumstances for "at-risk" children—were found to have little or no relationship to the performance of the children whose parents did participate in the pilot program. Cited in Edward Fiske, "Early Schooling is Now all the Rage," *New York Times Education Life,* 13 April 1986, 29.

55. John R. Berrueta-Clement et al., *Changed Lives: The Effects of the Perry Preschool Program on Youths Through Age 19* (Ypsilanti, Mich.: High/Scope Press, 1984). Sixty-seven percent of the children who took part in the program graduated from high school, compared with 49 percent of the equally disadvantaged children in a "control" group who did not participate in the preschool program. The study also found that 50 percent of those who received preschool instruction were employed (compared with 32 percent of the control group), 31 percent had been arrested (compared with 51 percent of the control group), and 19 percent were on welfare (compared with 32 percent of the control group). The findings of the Perry Preschool Project were reinforced in 1985 by a study conducted by three researchers at the New York University School of Education of 750 black children from Harlem who took part in early-education programs in the New York City public schools from 1961 to 1970. The study revealed that 50 percent of those who had participated in a preschool program earned a high school diploma (double the rate of 500 students from the same area and the same background who didn't get preschool instruction) and that 40 percent had gone on to college or vocational training (compared with 28 percent of the control group).

56. In all, at least fifteen states had taken similar steps by late 1985, according to an *Education Week* survey published 16 October 1985. Not all of the states' actions can be taken at face value, though. In 1985–86, some 310 school systems educating over 50 percent of Texas's students sought and received temporary exemptions from the State Board of Education from the 1984 law that called for a limit of twenty-two students in first- and second-grade classes by 1985–86.

CHAPTER 5

1. Gene I. Maeroff, "Shanker Urges Teachers Move Past Bargaining," *New York Times,* 28 April 1985. Albert Shanker, "The Making of a Profession," edited

transcript of the Niagara Falls speech (Washington, D.C.: American Federation of Teachers, 1985), 6, 12. See also "Futrell and Shanker Face Off," *Instructor*, October 1985.

2. Carnegie Forum on Education and the Economy, *A Nation Prepared: Teachers for the 21st Century* (New York: Carnegie Corporation, 1986), 12.

3. See C. Emily Feistritzer, *The Condition of Teaching* (Princeton: Carnegie Foundation for the Advancement of Teaching. 1983), 50.

4. Victor S. Vance and Phillip C. Schlechty, "The Distribution of Academic Ability in the Teaching Force: Policy Implications," *Phi Delta Kappan*, September 1982, 22–28. Thomas Toch, "Teachers Today are Older, Poorer, and Much Less Happy with Careers," *Education Week*, 10 March 1982.

5. Willard Waller, *The Sociology of Teaching* (New York: Wiley, 1976; originally published 1932), 58, 61. Richard Hofstadter, *Anti-intellectualism in American Life* (New York: Knopf, 1970; originally published 1962), 313.

6. On the percentage of teachers possessing college degrees see Hofstadter, *Anti-intellectualism*, 318. Both studies of education majors are cited in James D. Koerner, *The Miseducation of American Teachers* (Boston: Houghton Mifflin, 1963), the first on pp. 39–40, the second on pp. 42–43. Koerner's quotation is from *Miseducation*, 46. Hofstadter, *Anti-intellectualism*, 311. Indeed, even today many teachers are the first in their families to attend college.

7. A 1987 Census Bureau report revealed sharp increases between 1979 and 1986 in the percentage of females in such traditionally male-dominated fields as accounting and auditing (34 percent to 45 percent), computer programming (28 percent to 40 percent), law (10 percent to 15 percent), and various managerial and administrative categories (22 percent to 29 percent). See U.S. Census Bureau, "Women Making Headway in Share of Male-dominated Occupations," 4 September 1987.

8. Cited in Thomas Toch, "How to Attract Better Teachers," *Journal of Contemporary Studies*, Summer 1984, 59.

9. David W. Grissmer et al., *Teacher Attrition: The Uphill Climb to Staff the Nation's Schools* (Santa Monica: Rand, 1987).

10. See Carnegie Forum on Education and the Economy, *A Nation Prepared*, 31, and National Commission for Excellence in Teacher Education, *A Call for Change in Teacher Education* (Washington, D.C., February 1985), 6.

11. Holmes Group, *Tomorrow's Teachers: A Report of the Holmes Group* (East Lansing, 1986).

12. Carnegie Forum on Education and the Economy, *A Nation Prepared*.

13. National Governors' Association, *Time for Results: The Governors' 1991 Report on Education* (Washington, D.C., 1986).

14. California Commission on the Teaching Profession, *Who Will Teach Our Children? A Strategy for Improving California's Schools* (Sacramento, 1985).

15. Carnegie Forum on Education and the Economy, *A Nation Prepared*, 39.

16. Shanker, "The Making of a Profession," 12.

17. Ibid., 2.

18. AFL-CIO Committee on the Evolution of Work, *The Changing Situation of Workers and Their Unions* (Washington, D.C.: American Federation of Labor-Congress of Industrial Organizations, 1985), 12, 18. See also AFL-CIO Committee on the Evolution of Work, *The Future of Work* (Washington, D.C.: American Federation of Labor-Congress of Industrial Organizations, 1983).

19. See also Albert Shanker, "The Revolution That Is Overdue," transcript of speech to the AFT leadership at the union's 1985 Quest conference, 11 July 1985, 23.

20. American Federation of Teachers, 1983 annual report, 76. In a speech to the AFT's New York affiliate on 30 April 1983, just days before release of *A Nation at Risk,* Shanker spoke of the possibility of a "massive infusion" of political and financial support for public education if teachers unions remained open to reforms.

21. Shanker, "The Meaning of a Profession," 18.

22. Personal interview, 6 January 1989. It can frequently take up to several years and $200,000 to remove a teacher under a traditional union contract.

23. Koerner, *Miseducation,* 262.

24. Shanker, "The Making of a Profession," 15. Shanker also endorsed "choice" as a way of heading off support for tuition tax credits and vouchers. See chapter 7.

25. Shanker, "The Revolution That Is Overdue, 30–31.

26. Personal interview, 6 January 1989.

27. Ibid.

28. Ibid.

29. George A. Kaplan, "Shining Lights in High Places: Education's Top Four Leaders and Their Heirs," *Phi Delta Kappan,* September 1985, 12. Timothy Noah, "Albert Shanker, Statesman," *New Republic,* 24 June 1985, 17.

30. "Statement of the American Federation of Teachers, AFL-CIO, on Teacher Education and Retention," Subcommittee on Postsecondary Education, U.S. House of Representatives, 10 September 1981. Thomas Toch, "Teachers Evaluate Teachers in Unusual Project in Toledo," *Education Week,* 27 October 1982. "AFT President Shanker Comments on Variety of Educational Issues," press release, 23 February 1983.

31. Maurice Carroll, "Shanker Opposing 'Career Ladders,'" *New York Times,* 16 January 1985. Ironically, the AFT failed to attract significant support in Tennessee, and the union closed its Nashville office in 1984. For Shanker's remarks in Los Angeles, see the AFT's 1983 annual report, 75.

32. Gayle Fallon, quoted in William J. Warren, "Alternative Certificates: New Path to Teaching," *New York Times,* 28 September 1988.

33. Personal interview, 6 January 1989.

34. National Education Association, *Employee Participation Programs: Considerations for the School Site* (Washington, D.C., 1988), 24, 27.

35. Albert Shanker, "School Change Is Union Made," *Education Week,* 5 October 1988. American Federation of Teachers, "1988 Convention Revolutions," 9. Albert Shanker, column in the *New York Times,* 13 May 1987.

36. Administrators' organizations, for example, might want to test the limits of teacher authority.

37. Susan Moore Johnson, "Can Schools Be Reformed at the Bargaining Table?" *Teachers College Record,* Winter 1987, 297.

38. In 1984 the NEA eclipsed the Teamsters as the nation's largest union.

39. Stanley Elam, "National Education Association: Political Powerhouse or Paper Tiger?" *Phi Delta Kappan,* November 1981, 171.

40. "Every major contemporary education issue is—in its origin, its development, or its disposition—a political issue," Herndon told the Washington Press Club on 10 September 1981.

41. Lynn Olson and Blake Rodman, "Seeking Profession's 'Soul,' " *Education Week,* 4 November 1987.

42. Ken Bresin, executive director of the Minnesota Education Association, personal interview, 10 May 1985.

43. Quoted in Alan Ehrenhalt, "In Alabama Politics, the Teachers Are Sitting at the Head of the Class," *Governing,* December 1988, 27.

44. Donald Cameron, address to the 1983 NEA convention in Philadelphia, 10. National Education Association, *Studying the Studies* (Washington, D.C., 1983), 8.

45. It is the NEA's official policy that the federal government should pay one-third of the cost of public education; in 1983 the federal share of education funding was 6.2 percent.

46. Bill Haley, personal interview, 19 March 1985. One reason for the NEA's preoccupation with salaries is self-interest. NEA dues are tied to the average national teacher salary. As salaries have gone up dramatically in recent years, NEA's budget has burgeoned, rising from $74 million in 1982–83 to $124 million in 1988–89.

47. Quoted in Koerner, *Miseducation,* 4, 21. Koerner was writing as the post-World War II Baby Boom generation was crowding into the schools, and his recommendations were largely ignored by policymakers hard pressed to find sufficient teachers to staff classrooms.

48. Eva C. Galambos, *Teacher Preparation: The Anatomy of a College Degree* (Atlanta: Southern Regional Education Board, 1985), 13–14, 21. Further evidence of the weak academic preparation of teachers was furnished in a 1985 study of 101 graduates of the elementary-education program at Central Washington University, which found that of 3,479 courses taken by the students during their teacher training, only forty-nine were in history, and forty-four of those were in Northwest history. Only one student took a course in Western civilization.

49. Ibid., 23, 29.

50. Fredric Mitchell and Michael Schwinden, "Profiles of the Education of Teachers," Arizona State University, 1984, 4.

51. Southern Regional Education Board, *Access to Quality Undergraduate Education* (Atlanta, 1985), 5.

52. Galambos, *Teacher Preparation,* 27, 30; see also American Council on Education, *Recent Changes in Teacher Education Programs* (Washington, D.C., 1985), 7. Thomas Eliot, director of teacher education in Virginia, personal interview, 17 October 1988.

53. American Council on Education, *Recent Changes in Teacher Education Programs,* 2–4.

54. New Jersey State Department of Education, *The Provisional Teacher Program, Fourth Year Report* (Trenton, 1988), 11.

55. Ibid.

56. Dennis Gray and David H. Lynn, *New Teachers, Better Teachers* (Washington, D.C.: Council for Basic Education, 1988), 9.

57. New Jersey State Department of Education, *Provisional Teacher Program, Fourth Year Report,* 11. Gray and Lynn, *New Teachers, Better Teachers,* 17. Gray and Lynn noted that "a solid majority of the principals and administrators with whom we spoke believe that, all other things being equal, they would rather hire a certified teacher than a provisional candidate and escape the expense of extensive supervisory time and financial cost." A New Jersey principal with whom I

spoke commented that "the word is going around to go 'traditional' to avoid the extra work" involved in hiring teachers through alternative certification.

58. Fulton's remarks cited in Peter Marks, "N.J. Legislators Plan Education Bills to Counter Kean's Proposal," *Education Week*, 12 October 1983. The battle against alternative certification was led in the New Jersey General Assembly by Assemblyman John A. Rocco, a professor of education at Rider College.

59. National Education Association 1985 resolutions C-1, C-8.

60. For these same reasons the NEA has demanded that any national system of "board certification" for teachers be separate from the licensing of teachers by the states. If teachers were permitted into classrooms on the basis of meeting the requirements of a national certification board rather than state licensing laws, the criteria for entrance into teaching would shift from the traditional requirement that teachers earn a degree from an education school to the simple demand that they pass the national board examinations—a shift in emphasis from where a teacher candidate went to school, to what he or she knows. This would make entrance into teaching more flexible, thus allowing a broader range of people into teaching, which the NEA opposes.

61. National Education Association, *Teacher Education: An Action Plan* (Washington, D.C., 1982), 36.

62. National Education Association 1988 resolutions, D-1, F-23. Shanker of the AFT, it should be noted, has also been less than completely candid on this issue. He has said, "There should be a law that puts into prison any public official who allows people to practice without a proper certificate" and that misassigning teachers is "a cynical practice." But he has often failed fully to acknowledge that union-negotiated seniority provisions promote teacher misassignment. See Shanker "The Revolution That's Overdue," 34 and Shanker's column on teacher misassignment in *Education Week*, 6 November 1985.

63. Council of Chief State School Officers, *State Education Indicators, 1988* (Washington, D.C., 1988), 35.

64. In 1988 the Educational Testing Service, which writes the NTE, announced that by 1992 it will retire the fifty-year-old multiple-choice examination, currently used by some thirty states, and replace it with a more complex examination that includes such technology as interactive video, computer simulations, and portfolios documenting a teacher's accomplishments. Whether the new examination will be any more demanding is an open question.

65. James Popham, quoted in *Education Week*, 26 February 1986. A practice question on the examination asked: "Where could an educator find the page on which the foreword in a book begins? A) a table of contents, B) a library card catalogue, C) a bibliography, D) an encyclopedia."

66. "Arizona Board Lowers Standard for Teacher-Training Admission," *Education Week*, 14 June 1989.

67. About 7,500 of the 8,500 applicants who fail the California examination retake and subsequently pass the test.

68. George F. Madaus, "Legal and Professional Issues in Teacher Certification Testing: A Psychometric Snark Hunt" (Paper prepared for the fifth annual Buros-Nebraska Symposium on Measurement and Testing, October 1987), 70.

69. Many civil rights advocates and test critics have charged that the state teacher tests are culturally biased against minorities. Perhaps some are, but it's difficult to see how such bias can be built into multiple-choice arithmetic questions.

70. Futrell expressed the NEA's official opposition to teacher testing in a 1983 interview. See Thomas Toch, "Putting Teachers to the Test," *Washington Post Education Review*, 30 November 1983. Shanker, on the other hand, attacked the tests because they were too easy.

71. Personal interview, 18 March 1985.

72. "Baltimore Schools Hire Teachers with Poor Skills," *Education Week*, 2 October 1985.

73. Committee report, White House Conference on Education, 1955, 6. Rockefeller Brothers Fund, *The Pursuit of Excellence: Education and the Future of America* (Garden City, N.Y.: Doubleday, 1958), 24. Nor was linking pay to performance a new idea. In 1963 Koerner urged in *The Miseducation of American Teachers* (pp. 248–49) that "the individual's talent and performance on the job must become the primary criteria in the determination of his salary. . . . Until school boards face up to this whole matter . . . teaching will continue to be a field that fails to attract high-quality people."

74. Susan Moore Johnson, "Merit Pay for Teachers: A Poor Prescription for Reform," *Harvard Educational Review*, May 1984, 179–80.

75. Sizer, Goodlad, and Boyer were among the other reformers who called for career ladders in teaching. Sizer called for "hierarchies" of teachers and Goodlad backed the notion of "head teachers." The reformers' aim, Ernest Boyer wrote in *High School*, was to create a "career path" that attracts talented people to teaching and keeps them there.

76. Public Relations Newswire, 15 July 1983.

77. Don Cameron, personal interview, 2 June 1983. Willard McGuire, "Merit Pay Good for Teachers?" *U.S. News and World Report*, 22 May 1983.

78. National Education Association, "The Teacher and His Staff: Differentiating Teaching Roles" (Washington, D.C., 1969), v. The following year the union went so far as to publish guidelines for school systems seeking to experiment with the concept. See *The Washington Memo* (National Education Association Division of Field Services), April 1970, 17.

79. In addition to three elected executive officers (a president, a vice-president, and a secretary-treasurer), the NEA has an executive committee (comprised of the three executive officers and six teachers elected at large by the union's 8,000-member delegate assembly), and a 151-member board of directors appointed by state affiliates.

80. National Education Association, *An Open Letter to America on Schools, Students, and Tomorrow* (Washington, D.C., 1984), 8, 28.

81. "Even Meritorious Imperiled by Rickety Ladders, Geiger Declares," *TEA News* 15 August 1985. Donald Cameron, address to the NEA Representative Assembly, Washington, D.C., 4 July 1985.

82. For example, 87 percent of a national poll of teachers by Harris in early 1984 said they favored career ladders that provide teachers with greater opportunities to take on more responsibility at higher pay.

83. The Tennessee career-ladder plan was drafted by a six-member committee organized by the state's commissioner of education, who had been instructed by Alexander as early as 1981 to develop an "incentive-pay" system for Tennessee's teachers. Chester Finn is generally recognized as the plan's author.

84. Headlines such as "Even Meritorious Imperiled by Rickety Ladders" filled the union's newspaper. See also 15 August 1985 and 17 March 1986 issues of *TEA News*.

85. Letter to the editor, *Education Week*, 6 April 1988.

86. The Texas career ladder "seriously diminishes the traditional value attached to master's and doctorate degrees," the organization charged in its newspaper, the *TSTA Advocate*, June/July 1984.

87. *North Carolina Association of Educators News Bulletin*, December 1984.

88. Jade Moore, personal interview, 12 April 1985.

89. Southern Regional Education Board, *Is 'Paying for Performance' Changing Schools?* (Atlanta, 1988), 18–19.

90. T. Bird, *The Mentor's Dilemma* (San Francisco: Far West Laboratory for Educational Research and Development, 1986). Cited in Lorraine M. McDonnell and Anthony Pascal, *Teacher Unions and Educational Reform* (Santa Monica: Rand, 1988), 42.

91. National Education Association 1988 resolution D-14. See Minnesota Education Association, *Agenda for Educational Excellence*, 30 November 1984, 3. For a discussion of the NEA's opposition to peer review in California, see McDonnell and Pascal, *Teacher Unions and Educational Reform*, 30–31.

92. Thomas Toch, "Miami Union Cooperates on Tough Evaluations," *Education Week*, 8 December 1982. Similarly, a 1988 bill sponsored by the Ohio Education Association would have granted new teachers immediate tenure.

93. Lynn Olson, "Performance Pay: New Round for an Old Debate," *Education Week*, 12 March 1987. See also McDonnell and Pascal, *Teacher Unions and Educational Reform*, 29. In Dade County, Rochester, Pittsburgh, and elsewhere the AFT also has won significant salary increases in return for supporting teacher reforms.

94. Futrell acknowledged, in a personal interview early in January 1989, the union's campaign to "repackage" its image "so that it comes across more positively."

95. Mary Hatwood Futrell, "Education Reform and America's Workforce," speech to the Fairfax County Chamber of Commerce, 27 January 1989. Futrell, personal interview, 5 January 1989.

96. Personal interview, 5 January 1989.

97. Mary Hatwood Futrell, column in *Education Week*, 25 April 1984. Futrell, column in the *Washington Post*, 23 April 1988. Futrell, column in *Education Week*, 6 June 1988.

98. National Education Association, *An Open Letter to America on Schools, Students, and Tomorrow*, 8–9, 32.

99. Carnegie Forum on Education and the Economy, *A Nation Prepared*, 117–18. Futrell, column in *Education Week*, 28 May 1986.

100. See Albert Shanker column in the *New York Times*, 9 August 1987. Also see National Education Association 1989 Annual Meeting, New Business Item E.

101. National Education Association, *Report of the Special Committee on Restructuring Schools* (Washington, D.C., 1988), 4.

102. Futrell, column in *Education Week*, 9 December 1987. Personal interview, 5 January 1989.

103. Personal interview, 5 January 1989.

104. Don Cameron, "Representative Assembly Address," National Education Association, 5 July 1988, 3, 6–7. Julie Johnson, "Michigan Teacher to Head Education Union," *New York Times*, 4 July 1989.

105. F. Howard Nelson, *American Federation of Teachers Survey and Analysis of Salary Trends, 1988* (Washington, D.C.: American Federation of Teachers, 1988), 46.

106. Southern Regional Education Board, *Teacher Incentives: The Outsiders' View* (Atlanta, 1988), 1.

107. North Carolina's Career Development Plan was piloted in sixteen school systems, beginning in 1985–86; the project was discontinued at the end of the 1988–89 school year. Arizona launched its career-ladder pilot program in 1985–86; in 1990 the state legislature voted to add 14–15 districts to the program over four years.

108. Lynn Cornett, *Is 'Paying for Performance' Changing Schools?* (Atlanta: Southern Regional Education Board, 1988), 2. Erving E. Boe, "Teacher Incentive Research with SASS," unpublished paper (University of Pennsylvania, 1990), 8.

109. Thomas Toch, "Teaching: The Pressure for Change Is Mounting," *Education Week,* 21 March 1984. The attempts by the state affiliate of the NEA to "overload" the Florida program only exacerbated the troubles of the system.

110. Southern Regional Education Board, *1987 Career Ladder Report* (Atlanta, 1987), 2, 9.

111. M. Amsler et al., *An Evaluation of the Utah Career Ladder System: Summary and Analysis of Policy Implications* (San Francisco: Far West Laboratory for Educational Research and Development, 1988), cited in Southern Regional Education Board, *1988 Career Ladder Report* (Atlanta, 1988), 8. Ibid., 4. One reason for the high promotion rates is that in many communities, school teachers are lifelong community residents. In many instances teachers work at schools they once attended. As a result, it's tough for administrators not to promote them, much less dismiss them. A guidance counselor in a rural Florida high school told me he gave teachers extra points on their career-ladder evaluations, "because they needed the money" that the promotions on the ladder would produce.

112. Charlotte-Mecklenburg went to great lengths to win teacher support for the evaluation system (and the career ladder generally): establishing career-ladder liaison committees in each of its 100 schools, setting up a systemwide training program for evaluators, and amending the evaluation system in response to teacher recommendations (numerical evaluation scores were replaced with prose descriptions of teachers' performance; for example, postevaluation conferences between teachers and evaluators were added, and teachers were permitted to throw out one evaluation a year). Even a telephone "hot line" was made available to teachers with questions about the career ladder.

113. Southern Regional Education Board, *1988 Career Ladder Report,* 9–10. See also, Southern Regional Education Board, *1987 Career Ladder Report,* 7.

114. Southern Regional Education Board, *1987 Career Ladder Report,* 7. McDonnell and Pascal, *Teacher Unions and Educational Reform,* 47. Southern Regional Education Board, *1988 Career Ladder Report,* 7.

115. Lynn Olson, " 'Clinical Schools': Theory Meets Practice on the Training Ground," *Education Week,* 12 April 1989.

116. Southern Regional Education Board, *1988 Career Ladder Report.*

117. Gary Sykes, quoted in Thomas Toch, "Teacher Reforms Linked to Evaluation Systems," *Education Week,* 21 March 1984.

118. Amsler et al., *An Evaluation of the Utah Career Ladder System,* 4.

119. Michael J. Murphy et al., *Analysis of Utah Career Ladder Plans: A Report Prepared for the Utah State Office of Education by the Career Ladder Research Group* (Salt Lake City: University of Utah, 1987), 4.

120. C. Emily Feistritzer, *Alternative Teacher Certification: A State-By-State Analy-*

sis 1990 (Washington, D.C.: National Center for Education Information, 1990), 6–7.

121. Nancy E. Adelman, *An Exploratory Study of Teacher Alternative Certification and Retraining Programs* (Washington, D.C.: Policy Studies Associates, 1986), iv. Alternative certification should not be confused with emergency certificates or retraining programs, which frequently do not require applicants to have a degree in the subject that they are applying to teach.

122. Support for the board is by no means unanimous, however. In 1987 the president of the American Association of School Administrators, June Gabler, described the board as "an attempted takeover of American schools by teacher unions." See Lynn Olson, "With Board in Place, Broader Agenda Looms," *Education Week*, 27 May 1987.

123. Southern Regional Education Board, *1987 Career Ladder Report*, 6–7.

124. Thomas Toch, "Inservice Efforts Fail a System in Need, Critics Say," *Education Week*, 29 September 1982.

125. The director of Schenley says the cost of maintaining a permanent system of sabbaticals for Pittsburgh teachers at the school would be prohibitive.

126. Thomas Toch, "Yale Program Aids New Haven School System," *Education Week*, 14 September 1981.

127. C. Emily Feistritzer, *Teacher Supply and Demand Surveys 1988* (Washington, D.C.: National Center for Education Information, 1988), 14–15. California Commission on Teacher Credentialing, *Enrollment in Professional Preparation Programs During the 1986–87 Academic Year and Fall Semester 1987* (Sacramento, 1988), 1.

128. Neil B. Carey, Brian S. Mittman, and Linda Darling-Hammond, *Recruiting Mathematics and Science Teachers Through Nontraditional Programs: A Survey* (Santa Monica: Rand 1988), viii. Many incentive programs, however, have had limited success. For example, a 1987 study by the Florida Department of Education of the state's Teacher Scholarship Loan Program, which permits college students to cancel up to $8,000 in special loans if they teach math, science, and other shortage subjects in public schools after graduation, revealed that two-thirds of the students who had graduated in the program's first three years (1983–84 to 1986–87) had chosen not to teach but to repay their loans. Similarly, many school system programs to retrain teachers in other fields to teach math and science have been less than successful. An evaluation of the New York City Mathematics and Science Relicensing Program found that one-third of those in math and one-half of those in science dropped out before completing their first retraining course, and only 32 percent of those who completed their college course work in the program passed a required citywide subject matter examination. See Bruce S. Cooper, "Retooling Teachers: The New York Experience," *Phi Delta Kappan*, May 1987, 606–9. See also Adelman, *An Exploratory Study of Teacher Alternative Certification and Retraining Programs*, iv.

CHAPTER 6

1. Bennett, quoted in Julie A. Miller, "Combative Bennett Charges Into Final Year," *Education Week*, 16 September 1987. A mid-1983 Business Poll of 1,300 corporate executives reported that 85 percent of those surveyed "strongly" approved of standardized basic-skills tests for all students. Kean, quoted in Thomas

Toch, "Forum Said Successful in Rallying Support for Change," *Education Week,* 14 December 1983.

2. See *Education Week,* 6 February 1985. National Commission on Testing and Public Policy, *From Gatekeeper to Gateway: Transforming Testing in America* (Chestnut Hill, Mass., 1990), 15–17.

3. The standardized-testing movement gained momentum in 1983 when a federal appellate court upheld Florida's practice of withholding diplomas from students who failed the state's standardized functional literacy test. In 1978 Florida became the first state to enact a law that linked a high school diploma to such a test. That year black students filed suit against the Florida law on the grounds that it discriminated against them. In its decision in the case, *Debra P. v. Turlington,* the federal court held that as long as minority students were given an adequate opportunity to learn the material included on the Flordia examination, the examination was constitutional. The decision validated similar laws enacted in other states between 1978 and 1983, and it cleared the way for the introduction of new ones in still other states.

4. Basic Skills First Achievement Test, Grade 8, Reading, Objectives and Sample Items (Tennessee State Department of Education, 1987). Telephone interview with Angelia Golden, 2 July 1990.

5. Such tests also frequently misrepresent who is learning what in a classroom. Students in classes that do a lot of reading of real literature in elementary grades were found in a study in Ohio, for example, to do no better on standardized achievement tests than students who spent their school day drilling on basic skills—simply because the tests examined the individual basic skills that the control group in the study spent their time learning. But the teachers of the students who spent more time reading and writing in class were much more likely to describe their students as "superior writers" and "independent thinkers." See Sheppard Ranbom, "Using 'Real Books' to Teach Reading Said to Heighten Skill, Interest," *Education Week,* 14 December 1983.

6. CAT Form E and F, level 19 (Monterey, Calif.: CTB Macmillan/McGraw-Hill, 1986).

7. Telephone interview with Steven Ballou, 14 October 1986. Telephone interview with Margaret Jorgenson, 14 October 1986. Jorgenson notes that tests manufactured by the same publishers—the CAT and the CTBS, and the MAT and the SAT—have but one significant difference: they are updated on different cycles. Nor are the commercial norm-referenced tests appreciably different from the state and local criterion-referenced tests. They tend to cover a slightly broader range of skills than the state and local tests do, and they typically include some questions that are tougher than those usually found on the criterion-referenced tests. But like the many new criterion-referenced tests, they are multiple-choice tests of primarily basic skills. Richard C. Anderson et al., *Becoming a Nation of Readers* (Washington, D.C.: National Academy of Education, 1985), vii.

8. Telephone interview with Margaret Jorgenson, 14 October 1986. Telephone interview with Lynne Estell, Michigan Department of Education, July 1990.

9. Telephone interview with Roger Farr, 15 October 1986.

10. Karen Holloway, "Grading Education Reform," *Dallas Morning News,* 31 May 1987.

11. Arthur N. Applebee et al., *The Writing Report Card, 1984–88* (Princeton:

National Assessment of Educational Progress, 1990), 28. Lapointe is quoted in Kenneth J. Cooper, "Tests of U.S. Students Show Little Progress," *Washington Post*, 10 January 1990. Judith A. Langer et al., *Learning to Read in Our Nation's Schools: Instruction and Achievement in 1988 at Grades 4, 8, and 12* (Princeton: National Assessment of Educational Progress, 1990), 93–95. David C. Jammack et al., *The U.S. History Report Card* (Princeton: National Assessment of Educational Progress, 1990), 9. Lee Anderson et al., *The Civics Report Card* (Princeton: National Assessment of Educational Progress, 1990), 28. *Science Achievement in Seventeen Countries: A Preliminary Report* (Oxford: Pergamon Press, 1988), 3.

12. Some publishers have begun to break down scores on normed tests by proficiency, but doing so is a statistically unreliable procedure in the opinion of many testing experts.

13. In practice, norm-referenced tests are typically rewritten until the 50th percentile is equivalent to getting half the questions on the test correct; it is this procedure that produces the classic bell-shaped curve distribution of scores.

14. Alexandra K. Wigdor and Wendell R. Garner, eds., *Ability Testing: Uses, Consequences, and Controversies* (Washington, D.C.: National Academy Press, 1982), 42.

15. Lynn Olson, "Districts Turn to Nonprofit Group for Help in 'Realigning' Curricula to Parallel Tests," *Education Week*, 28 October 1987.

16. Psychological Corporation, *Teacher's Manual for Administering and Interpreting Metropolitan Achievement Tests, Elementary Forms JS and KS* (San Antonio, 1978), 31.

17. Ibid.

18. CTB Macmillan/McGraw-Hill, *Test Coordinator's Handbook, Forms U and V, Comprehensive Tests of Basic Skills* (Monterey, Calif., 1982), 59.

19. Telephone interviews with Roger Farr, 15 October 1986 and 4 February 1988. "It's getting very difficult for publishers to get good, representative samples," Farr told me. "School systems don't want to participate. Or they want to be paid." The CTB Macmillan/McGraw-Hill quotation is from *Criteria* (CTB Macmillan/McGraw-Hill), no. 18, 2.

20. John Jacob Cannell, *How All Fifty States Are Above the National Average: National Normed Elementary Achievement Testing in America's Public Schools* (Beckley, W. Va.: Friends for Education, 1987), 1–6. U.S. Department of Education study cited in Robert Rothman, "Physician's Test Study was 'Clearly Right,' " *Education Week*, 5 April 1989.

21. Psychological Corporation, "Stanford 7 Plus" (promotional brochure) (San Antonio, 1986), 3. See Riverside Publishing Co., *Test Resource Catalog* (Chicago, 1987), cited in John Jacob Cannell, *How Public Educators Cheat on Standardized Achievement Tests* (Albuquerque: Friends for Education, 1989), 28.

22. "School Test Scores Rise for Blacks in Maryland," *New York Times*, 1 February 1987.

23. See Robert Rothman, "A District Ties Goals to Scores," *Education Week*, 22 March 1989, and Amy Goldstein, "The Secret Behind the Scores," *Washington Post*, 20 May 1990.

24. See Garty Putka, "Tests Often Match Materials in Kits and Study Booklets," *Wall Street Journal*, 2 November 1989.

25. John I. Goodlad, *A Place Called School* (New York: McGraw-Hill, 1984), 207, 209.

26. Harriet Tyson-Bernstein, *A Conspiracy of Good Intentions: America's Textbook Fiasco* (Washington, D.C.: Council for Basic Education, 1988), 9.

27. Anderson et al., *Becoming a Nation of Readers,* 65.

28. Tyson-Bernstein, *A Conspiracy of Good Intentions,* 9.

29. Ibid., 49–51.

30. Personal interview with Richard Wallace, 1 May 1985.

31. Cited in Thomas B. Timar and David L. Kirp, *Managing Education Excellence* (New York: Falmer Press, 1988), 79.

32. Telephone interview with Douglas Rindone, 2 July 1990.

33. Telephone interview with Dale Carlson, 6 July 1990.

CHAPTER 7

1. See Michael W. Sedlak et al., *Selling Students Short: Classroom Bargains and Academic Reform in the American High School* (New York: Teachers College Press, 1986).

2. National Center for Education Statistics, *Digest of Education Statistics, 1988* (Washington, D.C.: U.S. Department of Education, 1988), 94.

3. See David L. Kirp, "Education: The Movie," *Mother Jones,* January 1989, 37.

4. A 1988 report by the National Governors' Association charged that "evidence on the impact of collective bargaining suggests that unions have served to increase the extent of bureaucratic control by making teaching work more rationalized, more highly specified and inspected, and by increasing the number and specificity of rules determining work roles and conditions." Michael Cohen, *Restructuring the Education System: Agenda for the 1990's* (Washington, D.C.: National Governors' Association, 1988), 18.

5. *Education Week,* 16 May 1984.

6. Gerald Grant, "Children's Rights and Adult Confusions," *Public Interest,* Fall 1982, 88. Also Gerald Grant, *The World We Created at Hamilton High* (Cambridge: Harvard University Press, 1988), 192–95. Edward A. Wynne, "What Are the Courts Doing to Our Children?" *Public Interest,* Summer 1981, 14,16.

7. Charles E. Silberman, *Crisis in the Classroom* (New York: Vintage Books, 1970), 115.

8. Ruth B. Ekstrom et al., "Who Drops out of High School and Why? Findings from a National Study," *Teachers College Record,* Spring 1986, 362. Bruce E. Wells, "Dropouts Are Not Always Failures," *Education Week,* 6 April 1983. "Study Finds Many School Dropouts Are Talented," *New York Times,* 16 February 1987.

9. Paul E. Barton, "Earning and Learning" (Princeton: National Assessment of Educational Progress, 1989), 5,7.

10. " 'Typical' Student Cuts 100 Classes Annually," *Education Week,* 2 October 1985. Ellen Flax, "Cashing in on School," *Education Week,* 2 March 1988. The Cleveland initiative is known as a scholarship-in-escrow program, funded by local businesses; after graduation, students have eight years to use the funds either for college or job training.

11. "How Not To Fix The Schools," *Harper's,* February 1986, 39.

12. Arthur G. Powell et al., *The Shopping Mall High School* (Boston: Houghton Mifflin, 1985), 85. In many schools, Powell writes, "subjects are regarded not as

vehicles for the development of thinking but as materials to be absorbed with as little passion and commitment as possible. . . . There is near total randomness in what is said. The mood is one of desperate chaos. Anything goes. Nothing matters, except keeping things going until the end [of the period]."

13. Many educators and sociologists have argued that students, particularly students in impoverished areas, reject school because they see no economic payoff from their studies. But that explanation assumes—erroneously—that adolescents are forward-looking. The truth is, most kids live largely in the present. The real problem is the failure of schools to "turn on" students to learning.

14. Glenn Collins, "Latchkey Children: A New Profile Emerges," *New York Times*, 14 October 1987.

15. *Time*, 9 December 1986. Many of the high schools that I visited had "mother-and-infant-care" or "teenage-parent" programs that taught school-age mothers parenting skills in the school nursery, where their children were looked after while they attended classes. Nor is the problem limited to high school students. I spoke with a nurse at a junior high school in a New Jersey city who said she was aware of six students who were pregnant at the time. "That doesn't count the kids who've had abortions," she added.

16. Ibid., 90.

17. Ekstrom et al., "Who Drops out of High School and Why?" 356–73. See also R. W. Rumberger, "Dropping out of High School: The Influence of Race, Sex, and Family Background," *American Educational Research Journal*, 20 (1983): 199–220.

18. They've also argued that a greater degree of educational choice would free parents from governmental control of how their children are educated. And they have argued that social justice demands the extension of choice to all parents. "When we talk about enhancing choice, we're mainly talking about giving working-class and poor people the opportunity to choose schools and programs that the more affluent already have," Chester Finn, an assistant secretary in the U.S. Department of Education, argued in congressional testimony in 1985.

19. Martin Tolchin, "Localities Shift to Private Fire Fighters," *New York Times*, 28 July 1985. See also John J. DiIulio, Jr., *Private Prisons, Crime File Study Guide* (Washington, D.C.: National Institute of Justice, 1988), 1.

20. Thomas Toch, "Governor Says He'd Try Public-School Vouchers," *Education Week*, 12 December 1984.

21. Committee for Economic Development, Research and Policy Committee, *Investing in Our Children* (New York: Committee for Economic Development, 1985), 28–29. National Governors' Association, *Time for Results: The Governors' 1991 Report on Education* (Washington, D.C., 1986), 12. Carnegie Forum on Education and the Economy, *A Nation Prepared: Teachers for the 21st Century* (New York: Carnegie Corporation, 1986), 92.

22. Albert Shanker, "The Making of a Profession," speech before the representative assembly of the New York State United Teachers, 27 April 1985, transcript, 14–16. Shanker was responding to polls showing popular support for greater parental choice in education, particularly for the use of public monies to help parents pay for tuition in private schools. In asking a question on the topic for the first time, the annual Gallup poll of the public's attitudes toward the public schools in 1986 found that 68 percent of the public with children in school favored giving parents greater freedom to choose among public schools. A year

earlier a similar Gallup poll revealed that 48 percent of the public supported vouchers for private school tuition, compared with 38 percent 14 years earlier. See "17th Annual Gallup Poll," *Phi Delta Kappan*, September 1985, 30.

23. William Snider, "Parley on 'Choice,' Final Budget Mark Transition," *Education Week*, 18 January 1989.

24. Cited in Massachusetts Department of Education, *Family Choice and Public Schools* (Boston, 1986), 41. In practice, the open-enrollment plans in the South did little to desegregate schools. A study of thirty-seven school districts in Louisiana, for example, revealed that between 1963 and 1967 only 5.4 percent of the districts' black students elected to attend formerly all-white schools, and virtually no white students chose to attend formerly all-black schools. The U.S. Supreme Court outlawed freedom-of-choice plans in *Green v. County School Board* (1968).

25. Personal interview with Kenneth Bresin, 10 May 1985.

26. The NEA is adamantly opposed to statewide choice plans. In 1989 the organization's 8,000 convention delegates passed a resolution opposing any state or federal choice plan in public education, and another that makes it virtually impossible for local choice plans to pass NEA muster.

27. Personal interview, 9 May 1985.

28. In 1986 the legislature diluted the program by prohibiting students from earning college credit for the college courses they take, unless they pay for the credits, or unless they enter the institution after graduation from high school. Maine passed a similar law in 1987.

29. Ironically, the effort to integrate the nation's schools, long a liberal goal, is now helping to create choice and a marketplace for students in elementary and secondary education, long a conservative goal.

30. In fiscal 1990 and 1991 the Bush administration proposed $100 million for desegregation magnets and $100 million for magnet schools designed to increase parental choice and competition among schools. Congress has declined to fund the latter program, however.

31. Rolf K. Blank et al., *Survey of Magnet Schools* (Washington, D.C.: James H. Lowry and Associates, 1983), executive summary. The exact proportion of magnets with admission standards isn't known. The U.S. Department of Education-sponsored survey of magnets, however, included an in-depth study of the characteristics of forty-five magnet programs. Fourteen of them were found to use achievement test scores, grade point average, or other methods to admit students selectively.

32. Personal interview, 28 April 1985.

33. Massachusetts Department of Education, *Family Choice and Public Schools*, 49.

34. A more personal sort of evidence of parents' inclination to make choices among public schools was reported in 1985, when three poor Hartford, Connecticut, families were arrested and charged with larceny for "stealing" an education valued at $4,100 because they sent their inner-city children to school in the nearby and more affluent community of Bloomfield without permission.

35. D. Anderson, "Small School Pairings Increasing Across State," *Minneapolis Star and Tribune*, 18 May 1986.

36. William Snider, "The Call for Choice: Competition in the Educational Marketplace," *Education Week*, 24 June 1987.

37. See John E. Chubb, "Why the Current Wave of School Reform Will Fail,"

Public Interest, Winter 1988. John E. Chubb and Terry M. Moe, *Politics, Markets and America's Schools* (Washington, D.C.: Brookings, 1990). Says Chubb: "The best way to increase autonomy [of local educators] without sacrificing accountability or getting excessive regulation is to rely less on relationships of authority and more on the signals of the market."

38. Interview with Seymor Fliegel and other District 4 administrators, 24 April 1985. The need for a positive school climate, in which individual members of a school form a more cohesive identity, is emphasized in a body of research on so-called effective schools conducted in the 1970s and early 1980s. Though that research focused on elementary schools, its lessons hold true for secondary schools as well. See, for example, Michael Cohen, *Instructional Management in Effective Schools* (Washington, D.C.: National Institute of Education, 1983).

39. Powell et al., *Shopping Mall,* 201.

40. Magi Educational Services, *New York State Magnet School Research Study* (Albany: New York State Department of Education, 1985), x, 30, 44. Teachers and administrators in urban school systems with magnets and open enrollment that I visited reported similar results.

41. Montgomery County Public Schools, *A Microscope on Magnet Schools 1983 to 1986* (Rockville, Md., 1988), 2: 2-1, 2-3.

42. Magi Educational Services, *New York State Magnet School Research Study,* 20–22. Blank et al., *Survey of Magnet Schools,* executive summary, 29. Seymour Fliegel, "Parental Choice in East Harlem Schools," in *Public Schools by Choice,* edited by Joe Nathan (St. Paul: Institute for Learning and Teaching, 1989), 105.

43. Henry M. Levin, *Educational Reform for Disadvantaged Students: An Emerging Crisis* (Washington, D.C.: National Education Association, 1986), 34.

44. Diane Hedin, *Students as Teachers: A Tool for Improving School Climate and Productivity* (Washington, D.C.: Carnegie Forum on Education and the Economy, 1986), 3, 8.

45. But they have been able to do so only through the good graces of the United Federation of Teachers, the city's powerful teachers union. The UFT has not protested the granting of hiring authority to District 4 directors, even though it violates provisions of the city's collective bargaining contract. The reason, says Shanker, is that the policy is successful in District 4, and there has not been pressure to expand it citywide.

46. Magi Educational Services, *New York State Magnet School Research Study,* 43, 45.

47. Ibid., 47–49.

48. Thomas J. Peters and Robert H. Waterman, Jr., *In Search of Excellence* (New York: Harper & Row, 1982).

49. John Hoerr, "The Payoff from Teamwork," *Business Week,* 10 July 1989.

50. James B. Conant, *The American High School Today* (New York: McGraw-Hill, 1959), 40.

51. Conant's large-school philosophy also has helped fuel the spread of "middle schools," those with grades six through eight. The trend has shifted scores of ninth-graders who traditionally had been in junior high schools into high schools, where enrollments are traditionally larger, and it has moved many sixth-graders out of elementary school environments. There were 2,000 public middle schools two decades ago; today there are 8,000.

52. Nancy J. Perry, "The Improved Vocational School," *Fortune,* 19 June 1989.

See also Academy for Educational Development, *Partnerships for Learning: School Completion and Employment Preparation in the High School Academies* (New York, 1989).

53. David S. Seeley, "The Choice-Equity Dilemma: A Partial Solution," *Equity and Choice,* Winter 1987, 59.

54. Neil Postman and Charles Weingartner, *Teaching as a Subversive Activity* (New York: Delacort Press, 1969), quoted in Charles E. Silberman, *Crisis in the Classroom* (New York: Vintage Books, 1971), 344–45. The director of New York City's high school division, Frank L. Smith, acknowledged that students' movement through secondary schools often bears little relationship to their mastery of the subjects that they study when he proposed in 1986 that the city scrap its use of grade levels to identify students' status in high school.

55. "The minds are there," said the school's principal of his ghetto-dwelling students. "The job is to motivate them."

56. In 1989 a report on junior high schools by a task force created by the Carnegie Corporation of New York made "small communities for learning" a centerpiece of its recommendations for reforming such schools. Peters and Waterman (*In Search of Excellence*) found that good companies, instead of compensating for the weakness of employees (an education parallel would be the creation of "teacher-proof" curricula), tended to decentralize decision making, creating small units of operation.

57. Robert B. Pittman and Perri Haughwout, "Influence of High School Size on Dropout Rate," *Educational Evaluation and Policy Analysis,* Winter 1987, 337–43.

58. Anthony S. Bryk and Yeow Meng Thum, "The Effects of High School Organization on Dropping Out: An Exploratory Investigation" (unpublished paper, University of Chicago, 1988), 26.

59. Anthony S. Bryk and Mary Erina Driscoll, "An Empirical Investigation of the School as Community" (unpublished paper, University of Chicago, 1988), 54–63.

60. Theodore L. Goudge and Byron D. Augustin, "An Analysis of Suspension Rates for Texas Athletes," *Texas Coach,* March 1987. Cited in Richard E. Lapchick, *Student Athletes and Academics* (Washington, D.C.: National Education Association, 1989), 26.

61. Bryk and Thum, "Effects of High School Organization on Dropping Out," 26.

62. Bryk and Driscoll, "Empirical Investigation of the School as Community," 55–56.

63. Aaron M. Pallas, "School Climate in American High Schools," *Teachers College Record,* Summer 1988, 549, 551.

64. Judith Baum, ed., *Making Big Schools Smaller: A Review of the Implementation of the House Plan in New York City's Most Troubled High Schools* (New York: Public Education Association and Bank Street College of Education, 1989), 11.

65. Bryk and Driscoll, "Empirical Investigation of the School as Community," 44.

66. Montgomery County Public Schools, *Microscope on Magnet Schools 1983 to 1986,* 2–3.

67. Bryk and Thum, "Effects of High School Organization on Dropping Out," 26.

68. Center for Educational Innovation, *Model for Choice: A Report on Manhattan's District 4* (New York: Manhattan Institute for Policy Research, 1989), 18–19.

69. Julie Amparano Lopez, "System Failures," *Wall Street Journal Reports: Education,* 31 March 1989.

70. *Fortune,* 19 June 1989.

71. Such "alternative" schools should not be confused with the progressive alternative schools that students attended by choice beginning in the 1960s.

72. "Our schools are, in a sense, factories in which the raw products (children) are to be shaped and fashioned into products to meet the various demands of life," wrote Ellwood P. Cubberley, an educator and educational historian, in 1916. Cited in Evans Clinchy, "Quiet Revolution Begins," *Equity and Choice,* Fall 1984, 16.

Bibliography

Adler, Mortimer J. *The Paideia Proposal.* New York: Macmillan, 1982.
———. *Paideia Problems and Possibilities.* New York: Macmillan, 1983.
AFL-CIO Committee on the Evolution of Work. *The Future of Work.* Washington, D.C.: American Federation of Labor-Congress of Industrial Organizations, 1983.
American Association for the Advancement of Science. *A Report on the Crisis in Mathematics and Science Education: What Can Be Done Now?* New York: J. C. Crimmins, 1984.
Anderson, Richard C., et al. *Becoming a Nation of Readers: The Report of the Commission on Reading.* Washington, D.C.: National Academy of Education, 1985.
Bennett, William J. *To Reclaim a Legacy: A Report on the Humanities in Higher Education.* Washington, D.C.: National Endowment for the Humanities, 1984.
———. *James Madison High School: A Curriculum for American Students.* Washington, D.C.: Government Printing Office, 1987.
Berrueta-Clement, John R., et al. *Changed Lives: The Effects of the Perry Preschool Program on Youths Through Age 19.* Ypsilanti, Mich.: High/Scope Press, 1984.
Bloom, Allan. *The Closing of the American Mind: How Higher Education Has Failed Democracy and Impoverished the Souls of Today's Students.* New York: Simon & Schuster, 1987.
Boyer, Ernest L. *High School: A Report on Secondary Education in America.* New York: Harper & Row, 1983.
Bunzel, John H., ed. *Challenge to American Schools: The Case for Standards and Values.* New York: Oxford University Press, 1985.
Business-Higher Education Forum. *America's Competitive Challenge.* Washington, D.C., 1983.
Carnegie Forum on Education and the Economy. Task Force on Teaching as a Profession. *A Nation Prepared: Teachers for the 21st Century: The Report of the Task Force on Teaching as a Profession.* New York: Carnegie Corporation of New York, 1986.
Center for Public Resources. *Basic Skills in the U.S. Workforce.* New York, 1983.
Cheney, Lynn V. *American Memory.* Washington, D.C.: National Endowment for the Humanities, 1987.
Coleman, James B., Thomas Hoffer, and Sally Kilgore. *High School Achievement: Public, Private and Catholic Schools Compared.* New York: Basic Books, 1982.
College Entrance Examination Board. *On Further Examination: A Report of the Advisory Panel on the Scholastic Aptitude Test Score Decline.* New York, 1977.
———. *Academic Preparation for College.* New York, 1983.

Committee for Economic Development. Research and Policy Committee. *Investing in Our Children: Business and the Public Schools.* New York: Committee for Economic Development, 1985.

―――. *Children in Need: Investment Strategies for the Educationally Disadvantaged.* New York: Committee for Economic Development, 1987.

Conant, James B. *The American High School Today.* New York: McGraw-Hill, 1959.

Cooperman, Paul. *The Literacy Hoax.* New York: Morrow Quill, 1980.

Cremin, Lawrence A. *The Transformation of the School: Progressivism in American Education, 1876–1957.* New York: Vintage Books, 1964.

―――. *Public Education.* New York: Basic Books, 1976.

―――. *Popular Education and Its Discontents.* New York: Harper & Row, 1990.

Drucker, Peter F. *The Age of Discontinuity: Guidelines to Our Changing Society.* New York: Harper & Row, 1978.

Education Commission of the States. Task Force on Education for Economic Growth. *Action for Excellence.* Denver: Education Commission of the States, 1983.

―――. *Action in the States.* Denver: Education Commission of the States, 1984.

Etzioni, Amitai. *An Immodest Agenda: Rebuilding America before the 21st Century.* New York: McGraw-Hill, 1984.

Finn, Chester E., Jr., Diane Ravitch, and Robert T. Francher, eds. *Against Mediocrity: The Humanities in America's High Schools.* New York: Holmes & Meier, 1984.

Finn, Chester E., Jr., Diane Ravitch, and P. Holley Roberts, eds. *Challenges to the Humanities.* New York: Holmes & Meier, 1985.

Ford Foundation. *Hispanics: Challenges and Opportunities: A Working Paper.* New York, 1984.

Gardner, John W. *Excellence.* Rev. ed. New York: Norton, 1984.

Goodlad, John I. *A Place Called School: Prospects for the Future.* New York: McGraw-Hill, 1984.

Grant, Gerald. *The World We Created at Hamilton High.* Cambridge: Harvard University Press, 1988.

Gross, Beatrice and Ronald, eds. *The Great School Debate: Which Way for American Education?* New York: Simon & Schuster, 1985.

Hirsch, E. D., Jr. *Cultural Literacy: What Every American Needs to Know.* Boston: Houghton Mifflin, 1987.

Hodgkinson, Harold L. *All One System: The Demographics of Education.* Washington, D.C.: Institute for Educational Leadership, 1985.

Hofstadter, Richard. *Anti-intellectualism in American Life.* New York: Knopf, 1970.

Holmes Group. *Tomorrow's Teachers.* East Lansing: Michigan State University, 1986.

Honig, Bill. *Last Chance for Our Children: How You Can Help Save Our Schools.* Reading: Addison-Wesley, 1985.

Kearns, David T., and Denis P. Doyle. *Winning the Brain Race: A Bold Plan to Make Our Schools Competitive.* San Francisco: ICS Press, 1988.

Kirst, Michael W. *Who Controls Our Schools?* New York: W. H. Freeman, 1984.

Kirst, Michael W., and Frederick M. Wirt. *Schools in Conflict.* Berkeley: McCutchan, 1982.

Koerner, James D. *The Miseducation of American Teachers.* Cambridge: Riverside Press, 1963.

Kozol, Jonathan. *Illiterate America.* Garden City, N.Y.: Anchor Press/Doubleday, 1985.

Lasch, Christopher. *The Culture of Narcissism: American Life in an Age of Diminishing Expectations.* New York: Norton, 1979.

Lazerson, Marvin, Judith Black McLaughlin, Bruce McPherson, and Stephen K. Bailey. *An Education of Value: The Purpose and Practices of Schools.* Cambridge: Cambridge University Press, 1985.

Lund, Leonard, and Patrick E. McGuire. *The Role of Business in Precollege Education.* Research bulletin 160. New York: Conference Board, 1984.

Maeroff, Gene I. *Don't Blame the Kids: The Trouble with America's Schools.* New York: McGraw-Hill, 1982.

Mayer, Martin. *The Schools.* New York: Harper & Brothers, 1961.

National Academy of Science. Panel on Secondary Education for the Changing Workplace. *High Schools and the Changing Workplace: The Employers' View.* Washington, D.C.: National Academy Press, 1984.

National Coalition of Advocates for Students. *Barriers to Excellence: Our Children at Risk.* Boston, 1985.

National Commission for Excellence in Teacher Education. *A Call for Change in Teacher Education.* Washington, D.C., 1985.

National Commission on Excellence in Education. *A Nation at Risk: The Imperative for Educational Reform.* Washington, D.C.: Government Printing Office, 1983.

National Governors' Association. *Time for Results: The Governors' 1991 Report on Education.* Washington, D.C., 1986.

National Research Council. *Ability Testing: Uses, Consequences, and Controversies.* 2 vols. Washington, D.C.: National Academy Press, 1982.

National Science Board. Commission on Precollege Education in Mathematics, Science and Technology. *Educating Americans for the 21st Century.* Washington, D.C.: National Science Foundation, 1983.

Oakes, Jeannie. *Keeping Track: How Schools Structure Inequality.* New Haven: Yale University Press, 1985.

Owen, David. *None of the Above: Behind the Myth of Scholastic Aptitude.* Boston: Houghton Mifflin, 1985.

Peters, Thomas J., and Robert H. Waterman, Jr. *In Search of Excellence: Lessons from America's Best Run Companies.* New York: Harper & Row, 1982.

Powell, Arthur G., Eleanor Farrar, and David K. Cohen. *The Shopping Mall High School: Winners and Losers in the Educational Marketplace.* Boston: Houghton Mifflin, 1985.

Rand Corporation. *The New Federalism in Education.* Santa Monica, 1983.

Ravitch, Diane. *The Troubled Crusade: American Education, 1954–1985.* New York: Basic Books, 1983.

———. *The Schools We Deserve: Reflections on the Educational Crisis of Our Time.* New York: Basic Books, 1985.

Rutter, Michael, Barbara Maughan, Peter Mortimore, and Janey Ouston. *Fifteen Thousand Hours: Secondary Schools and Their Effects on Children.* Cambridge: Harvard University Press, 1979.

Sarason, Seymour B. *Schooling in America: Scapegoat and Salvation.* New York: Collier Macmillan, 1983.

Shanker, Albert. *The Making of a Profession.* Washington, D.C.: American Federation of Teachers, 1985.

Silberman, Charles E. *Crisis in the Classroom: The Remaking of American Education.* New York: Vintage Books, 1971.

Sizer, Theodore R. *Horace's Compromise: The Dilemma of the American High School.* Boston: Houghton Mifflin, 1984.

Southern Regional Education Board. Task Force on Higher Education and the Schools. *The Need for Quality: A Report to the SREB by Its Task Force on Higher Education and the Schools.* Atlanta: Southern Regional Education Board, 1981.

Twentieth Century Fund. Task Force on Federal Elementary and Secondary Education Policy. *Making the Grade: Report of the Twentieth Century Fund Task Force on Federal Elementary and Secondary Education Policy.* New York: Twentieth Century Fund, 1983.

Tyson-Bernstein, Harriet. *A Conspiracy of Good Intentions: America's Textbook Fiasco.* Washington, D.C.: Council for Basic Education, 1988.

U.S. Chamber of Commerce. *Business and Education: Partners for the Future.* Washington, D.C., 1985.

U.S. Congress. House of Representatives. Republican Research Committee. *Ideas for Tomorrow, Choices for Today.* Washington, D.C., 1985.

U.S. Department of Education. *The Nation Responds.* Washington, D.C.: Government Printing Office, 1984.

Wesley, Edgar B. *NEA: The First Hundred Years.* New York: Harper & Brothers, 1957.

Wolters, Raymond. *The Burden of Brown: Thirty Years of School Desegregation.* Knoxville: University of Tennessee Press, 1984.

Index

ABC News, 28, 81
Academic Preparation for College, 16
Academic Scholars Program, Florida, 100
Academic track, 127
Accountability, 205–6, 232
Action for Excellence, 15–16, 17, 21, 138
Adelson, Joseph, 55, 56, 58, 62
Adler, Mortimer, 77
Administrators, as disciplinarians, 236–38
Adolescence (Hall), 45
Adopt-a-school programs, 22, 25
Advanced Placement tests, College Board, 100, 102
Advanced studies diploma, Virginia, 100
Advisory teams, for teachers, 191, 193
AFL-CIO, 135
   Committee on the Evolution of Work, 142
Against Mediocrity, 59
Alabama, 36, 121
Alabama Education Association, 154, 166
Aldridge, William, 113
Alexander, Lamar, 18, 19, 35, 142, 148, 168–69, 172, 248
Alienation, 239–40
   educational consequences, 244–46
Alternative certification, 159–61, 196
Alvarado, Anthony J., 249
Alves, Michael, 257
American Association for the Advancement of Science (AAAS), 118
American Association of Colleges for Teacher Education, 52
American Association of School Administrators, 29, 57, 63, 129, 212
American Chemical Society, 118
American Education: An Economic Issue, 20, 62, 66
American Federation of Teachers (AFT), 25, 72, 92, 109, 134–35, 142, 148
The American High School Today (Conant), 263
American Institute of Physics, 111
American Mathematical Society, 119
American Math Project, 118, 120
American Psychological Association, 43

American Scholar, 55, 63
American School Board Journal, 31–33
American Spectator, 55, 61
American Vocational Association, 109
Amherst College, 160
And Madly Teach (Smith), 52–53
Anti-intellectualism in American Life (Hofstadter), 43, 136
A+ Program for Education Excellence, Indiana, 37
Appleby, Arthur, 116
Arizona, 106
   Board of Regents, 164
Arizona State University, teacher education at, 157
Arkansas, 18, 35, 36
Arkansas Education Association (AEA), 166
Army Mental Tests, 43
Ashland Oil, 22
Association for Supervision and Curriculum Development, 198
Association of Texas Professional Educators (ATPE), 91
Atlanta, truancy policy, 241
Augenblinck, John, 77
Austin American Statesman, 81
"Automated Instructional Management System" (AIMS), 228

"The Ballad of the Second Called Session" (Hobby), 87
Ballou, Steven, 210
Baltimore, 22
   teacher certification, 167
   teacher evaluation, 194
BankAmerica Foundation, 22
Bank Street College of Education, NYC, 196, 270
Barr, Mary A., 117
Basic Skills First Achievement Tests, Tennessee, 207–8
Basic-skills movement, 64
Bauman, Robert, 56
Baylor University, 73

v